Acupuncture, Meridian Theory, and Acupuncture Points

Written by
Professor Li Ding

English Translation by
You Benlin and Wang Zhaorong

China Books & Periodicals, Inc., San Francisco
Foreign Languages Press, Beijing

Jacket design by Linda Revel

Copyright © 1992 by China Books & Periodicals, Inc.

Original edition published by Foreign Languages Press of Beijing, China in 1990.
This edition is printed with the permission of Foreign Languages Press.

ISBN 0-8351-2143-7

Published in the United States of America by CHINA
BOOKS
& Periodicals, Inc.
Printed in the United States of America

Author's Acknowledgement

I wish to express my sincere thanks to all who have contributed to the work involved in preparing this text for publication. I would especially like to mention: Wang Dechen, researcher of the Institute of Acupuncture and Moxibustion, Chinese Academy of TCM; Cheng Xinlong, professor of Beijing International Training Centre on Acupuncture and Moxibustion; Yang Jiasan, professor of Beijing College of TCM; Geng Enguan, associate professor of Beijing College of TCM: Shi Huaitang, doctor-in-chief of Shanxi Institute of TCM.

I also wish to thank the publishers for the courtesy of using some of the figures from "Chinese Acupuncture and Moxibustion," the national standard teaching material for TCM colleges.

Prof. Li Ding
Shanxi Medical College

Add: 12 Fuxing Ave., Beijing, China
Tel: 3063316
Telex: 222213 GEN, CN
Fax: 3061971

Translators' Acknowledgements

The translators wish to express their gratitude for assistance in checking the text, which was given by

M. E.A. Treharne, Lic. Ac., C.Herb (Nanjing), of Middlesex, England, and Mr. B.W. Du Vé, B. Ac., Maiac, C.Herb (Nanjing), of Galway, Ireland.

Both of these gentlemen are experienced practitioners of Traditional Chinese Medicine and past students of Nanjing College of TCM, Jiangsu, the People's Republic of China.

Mr. Treharne made an initial check of Part I of this book.

Mr. Du Vé gained considerable experience in the preparation and editing of various documents and technical works, during eleven years of association with the Irish semi-state bodies, Gaelarra Eireann and Unaras Na Gaelatachta.

Although pressed for time and at very short notice, he undertook a complete review of the pre-editorial draft of this book. His experience and knowledge have been invaluable assistance in the presentation in English of many of the difficult concepts associated with China's ancient medical system.

We also wish to thank Dr. Meng Xiankun, director of the acupuncture department, Dongzhimen Teaching Hospital of Beijing College of TCM, for his kind help and advice during our translation.

You Benlin
Wang Zhaoyong
Nanjing International Training Centre
on Acupuncture and Moxibustion

Translators' Bibliography

Essentials of Chinese Acupuncture, People's Health Publishing House, 1979.

A Concise TCM Dictionary in Chinese, Xu Yuanzhen et al, Henan Press of Science and Technology, 1983.

Leijing Tuyi (*Classics of Categories*), Zhang Shibin, A.D. 1624.

Common Medical Terms in English, People's Health Publishing House, 1979.

Common Terms of TCM in English, Beijing Medical College, 1980.

An English-Chinese Medical Dictionary, People's Health Publishing House, 1978.

Selected Classics of TCM, Shanghai Press of Science and Technology, 1984.

Huangdi Neijing Suwen Baihua Jie (*Contemporary Explanations of the "Canon of Medicine": Plain Questions*), People's Health Publishing House, 1958.

A New English-Chinese Dictionary, Shanghai Press of Science and Technology, 1979.

CONTENTS

Yaoyi
Xiazhishi
Yaotongxue
Luozhen
Lanwei
Dannang

Preface

Professor Li Ding deserves congratulations for a clear and evocative text that conveys the subtleties of Chinese Medical thought in a way that bridges the gap between Eastern and Western modalities. Professor Li Ding's achievement lies in his ability to move the student from a general pictorial image of a particular point or meridian to an increasingly abstract understanding of its indication or function. The result is a text vastly superior to others at the introductory level—one that more nearly approaches the spirit of the ancient masters. The essential fundamental background of Chinese Medicine is discussed in a systematic yet compelling fashion that practitioners and students alike will turn to as a reference.

The first chapters give an exceptionally good overview of the Meridian System, including Luo-collaterals, Divergent, and Tendino-muscular Meridians. Particularly thorough is the description of the pathways of the Eight Extraordinary vessels and their respective functions. Sections explaining the nomenclature of points as relative to their functional, anatomical, or cosmological significance demystify the often daunting task of learning the names of several hundred points.

English translations of the pinyin transliteration provided for each acupuncture point are an important addition to the standard means of point identification generally included in introductory texts. The standard numbering system is a convenient means of point identification for students who are unfamiliar with Chinese characters, yet it bears no relationship to the indication for various points. Pinyin transliterations go one step further to create a more distinctive understanding by associating a sound with each point, but similarly convey no meaning to those unfamiliar with the Chinese language. Professor Li Ding's expanded definitions at last give English-speaking students an enriched intellectual understanding and a pictorial image, more in keeping with Eastern sensibilities, which convey the thought process from which the name was created. For example, S.I.12 Bingfeng or Wind Receiver (Bing meaning to accept or receive, and Feng, meaning wind), is a point attacked by pathogenic wind and one that also treats that condition. The image of Wind Receiver is much more meaningful to a student in learning the indications for this point than understanding it only as S.I.12. Though all translations are subjective, either leaning towards a literal rigidity or loosely figurative interpretation, Dr. Li Ding has achieved a functional and insightful balance between the two extremes.

Professor Li Ding's coverage of Extra Points is a thoughtful and manageable selection of those noted for their clinical efficacy from the thousands of non-meridian points that have been identified. Approximately 60 points were chosen and grouped according to their common location within the body because there is no Meridian thread to provide a context within which to understand the relationship of these points. The listing represents a potent nucleus for students and practitioners to utilize in treatment; it is more complete than most introductory texts, and not intimidating.

The illustrations included, using male and female models, are an important improvement over existing texts, especially in citing the differences in muscle structure in men and women and showing how locating acupuncture points is affected by these differences. The diagram on proportional measurement is a useful gauge for measurement of people of varying ages, sizes, and development.

One of the most difficult aspects of the Meridian system is the complexity of secondary branches. How these branches make internal connections to Zangfu organs, and the understanding of coalescent points or points of intersection with other Meridians is the least tangible aspect of the Meridian system. Consequently, existing sources disagree, and conflicting information on this topic is abundant. Dr. Li Ding systematically describes the course of each meridian and follows up with what he calls an "analytical display of the course of the Meridian" or a flow chart for each Meridian. Again, this two-fold instructional method helps to create a context for seemingly abstract information. Related Zangfu organs and Coalescent points are then listed specifically to avoid any confusion.

Professor Li Ding's achievement with this text goes beyond a simply comprehensive overview of the basics; he has correctly identified the inadequacy of existing modern English texts as more than an insufficiency of material, and has brought this missing element to bear on this work. His graceful style and tone, and the context he creates for the theoretical and practical information he describes, transform a purely intellectual understanding into an experience of the art of healing based on Chinese thought as it has developed through the ages.

Susan Arima, L.Ac., Dipl. Ac.
David Chan, OMD
Faculty, Emperor's College of Traditional Oriental Medicine

PART ONE
Generalization of Meridians and Points

Chapter I

GENERALIZATION OF THE MERIDIANS

Section 1 THE THEORY OF THE MERIDIANS

I. The Concept of the Meridian Theory

The meridian theory is an important component of Traditional Chinese Medicine (TCM). It is the study of the physiological function and pathological change on the meridians, and their related zangfu organs. The essential functions of the meridian system are to "transport qi and blood," "to maintain conductivity" and "to resist invasion of exogenous pathogenic factors." The meridian system distributes to all parts of the body. The endless circulation of qi and blood in the meridians is responsible for the maintenance of life and the variety of functions which support it. Over the last two thousand years, the meridian theory has been the guiding principle for the clinical practice in the realms of TCM, particularly in those of acupuncture, massage and qigong. By combining the meridian theory with the theories of the zangfu organs and the etiology of TCM, one can thoroughly explain both the physiological activities and pathological change which take place in the body. In this manner, a theoretical basis for the principle of treatment in accordance with the.differentiation of symptoms and signs was established. Physicians throughout Chinese history have all paid great attention to the study of meridians, which has now become an independent branch of learning in acupuncture and moxibustion.

II. The Origin and Formation of the Meridian Theory

Many physicians have tried to explain the development of the meridian theory, but two of them predominate:

A. Origin from "Bian" Stones

A knowledge of points preceded the discovery of meridians. The "bian" stone, a kind of sharp instrument, is considered to be the most primitive healing facility adopted by human beings before the invention of iron tools. Chinese ancestors in the early Stone Age knew little about medicine. Survival in the harsh environment and recovery from trauma and exposure to the elements was largely a matter of chance. They would press, rub or hit the affected part of the body so as to alleviate pain when they became ill. Occasionally, after part of the body was scorched, hit by a piece of rolling stone or cut by some brambles, then would follow marked alleviation or disappearance of pain from some

previously diseased part. Countless repetition and observation of such random phenomena over millennia led to the establishment of a basis for rational investigation.
Unexpected stimuli which reduced pain were then intentionally applied for healing
purposes, e.g. scorching or hitting. Finally the concept of therapeutic point began to
emerge. In those days there was no recognized name nor location for a point except
"where there is pain, there is a point". This was the earliest concept of an acupuncture
point and referred to such tender spots on the body surface, as might make a person cry
"Ah" if they were pressed. Thus the term: Ahshi (Ah-yes) Point came into being. In the
process of using "bian" stones to heal diseases, more and more locations for puncturing
or for moxa heating were gradually discovered. Moreover, the common experience of
sensation radiating along the specific lines, when these points were being punctured, led
to the discovery of the inner relations between specific groups of points. Knowledge about
the therapeutic effect of points increased along with the accumulation of clinical
experience. Points bearing similar indications were recognized to be arranged in lines
along the surface of the body, particularly those points below the elbow and knee.

Puncturing some of these points was seen to produce certain therapeutic effect or
influence on particular zangfu organs, body tissues and even superficial parts of the body,
locally or at a considerable distance from the point used. Observation of such phenomena
led to the conclusion that these points must be internally linked with the zangfu organs
and externally connected with the specific areas of the body surface. And these observations led to the formation of the meridian theory.

B. Origin from Qigong

As well as acupuncture, moxibustion and massage, qigong was also extensively
practised for healing purposes in ancient China.

Qigong, popular since the early 4th century, traces back to the exercises developed
by the early Taoists. During the practice of qigong exercises, a feverish sensation can be
felt, as though energy were circulating around the body along specific pathways. So, it is
also possible that the meridian theory may have originated from the observation of
qigong practitioners.

Qigong was called "guiding the qi" (daoqi) or "activating the qi" (xinqi) in the
Chinese classics. Its practice required unwavering concentration of the mind on a specific
body part for a period of time, after which the attention would be transferred, in sequence
to a series of locations. While exercising, a sensation of qi circulating in certain parts of
the body can be felt, particularly in the Dantian [1-3 cun inferior to the umbilicus,
between Qihai (Ren 6) and Guanyuan (Ren 4)]. Sometimes, this feverish sensation
radiates to the perineum, winds up posteriorly to the vertex along the spinal column and
then descends along the anterior midline again to the Dantian. This phenomenon is
known as "communication from the Ren Meridian to Du Meridian." The Ren Meridian
dominates the Yin of the body on the anterior aspect and Du Meridian dominates the
Yang of the body on the posterior aspect. Consequently, "communication between Ren
Meridian and Du Meridian" was also called "the communication between Yin and
Yang." For a long time, the phenomenon of qi communication remained unacceptable to
many who had not experienced it subjectively. However, modern research into the
mechanism of qigong has demonstrated the existance of meridians, and mapped their
courses by measuring the difference of electrical skin resistance. Also, some meridian

phenomena have been observed visually. And individuals who are strongly sensitive to qi flow in the meridians concurred as to the nature of their experiences.

In conclusion, it would seem likely that the concept of meridian grew out of the use of "bian" stones. In addition, the findings of the later researchers, working in the field of qigong, offered further support to the theory.

The meridian theory was not based on empty assumptions, but rather on the accumulated observations of many generations of ancient Chinese medical practitioners. This theory is the quintessence of TCM. Much detailed study has been devoted to the meridians since ancient times as the concepts associated with them facilitated an understanding of the physiological functions and pathological change that take place within the human body. To this day, the meridian theory is the fundamental guiding principle for acupuncture therapy. The chapter Jingmaipian of the book *Lingshu* states, "A thorough understanding of the meridians is an important prerequisite to correct diagnosis and pregnosis. Puncturing points along the courses of the meridians assists in the treatment of various diseases by regulating either excess or deficiency." Only by gaining a knowledge of the meridians, can one establish a reliable basis for diagnosis and treatment. Yu Jia-yan, a noted physician of the Ming Dynasty, further added, "Malpractice will result if one starts to treat patients without a thorough understanding of the theories of the zangfu organs and the meridians."

Research into acupuncture anaesthesia in New China was started in the early 1950's. When, almost two decades later, the successful conclusions were announced to the world, scholars in many countries were motivated to carry out studies of the mechanism of acupuncture and the nature of the meridians. Subsequently, a variety of different views concerning the nature of the meridians have been put forward.

First, the application of the existing knowledge about the human organic structures and their functions in an attempt to explain the nature of the meridians. This school of thought believes that the meridians are related to the peripheral nerves and blood vessels, or to nerve ganglia; or that both meridians and nerves are related to the regulating functions of the body fluid.

Second, the application of the existing knowledge of organic structures to explore unknown organic functions. This school of thought basically believes that meridians are related to the central nerve system. Others have been focusing their attention on cybernatics and bioelectric current and their relationships with meridians.

And the third group is trying to establish whether or not the meridians might be a kind of organic structure, a unique system which as yet awaits an explanation.

It is to be hoped that with the advance of science and technology, modern researches will be able to clarify the nature of the meridians and thereby contribute to an expansion of the horizon of both practical and theoretical medicine.

Section 2 THE MERIDIAN SYSTEM

I. The Concept of the Meridians

The meridian system was discovered by medical practitioners in ancient China. They considered the meridians to be a series of passages through which qi and blood circulated in the body. These passages or meridians were called "MAI," written (脈) in the characters of the Qin Dynasty. In its original meaning, this character implies that the meridians distributed in the body are like the networks of streams and rivers on the surface of earth. Using the analogy of woven cloth, the major ones, i.e. the channels, could be likened to the warps, while the minor ones, i.e. the collaterals, could be likened to the woofs. The term meridian actually covers both the channels and collaterals, which form the passages for circulation of qi and blood in the body.

Internally, meridians link the zangfu organs together, and externally, they connect with the extremities to unite the body into an integral whole. They transport qi and blood, distribute essence, help the zangfu organs to perform their various functions and maintain the normal physiological activities of the body.

"Jing" (經) means a passage or pathway, referring to the channels that are likened to the warps of cloth. Most of them penetrate deeply into the body to connect with the zangfu organs, distribute qi and blood to the muscles and connect with the sense organs, openings, pores, tendons, bones and muscles. Different muscle groups are controlled by the different meridians which pass through them. "Luo" (絡) describes the meridians as being arranged in networks. There are also branches or subbranches which run between the channels like the woofs of cloth. These tiny collaterals arranged in a network which covers every part of the body are conventionally called the superficial branches of the meridians, though some of the larger ones have acquired their own names. Collaterals are distributed in the superficial tissues of the body. They have special relationship with the skin, connecting it to the meridian network.

In short, the zangfu organs and all the organic structures of the body are welded into an integral by the network of channels and collaterals.

II. Formation of the Meridians

The meridian system consists of both channels and collaterals. Meridians are divided into Regular Meridians and Extra Meridians. Collaterals are further divided into three groups: a) the fifteen major collaterals; b) the superficial collaterals; and c) the tertiary collaterals. In addition, there are the inner portions of the 12 regular meridians, the tendinomusculatures of the 12 regular meridians and the cutaneous zones of the 12 regular meridians.

The 12 pairs of regular meridians constitute the major part of the meridian system. They are the 3 Yin meridians of the hand, the 3 Yang meridians of the hand, the 3 Yang meridians of the foot and the 3 Yin meridians of the foot, 12 in all pertaining specifically to the 12 zang and fu organs.

The 8 extra meridians include Du Meridian, Ren Meridian, Chong Meridian, Dai Meridian, Yinqiao Meridian, Yangqiao Meridian, Yinwei Meridian and Yangwei Meridian.

Each of the 12 regular meridians, Du Meridian and Ren Meridian has one collateral, in addition to which there is the major collateral of the spleen. They are jointly called "the 15 major collaterals" or "the 15 collaterals". Each of them diverges from its pertaining meridian to connect with its related meridian, forming the internal-external relationship of meridians.

Superficial collaterals are the tiny branches of the divergent collaterals.

Tertiary collaterals are the very superficial branches of the superficial ones.

The inner portion of the 12 regular meridians refers to the parts of the main courses of the regular meridians which penetrate deeply into the body to nourish the zangfu organs and the deeper tissues.

Tendinomusculatures of the 12 regular meridians are the segments through which meridians pass in their distribution over the superficial areas of the body. Its main function is to link the four limbs and joints, and control the joint movement.

The cutaneous zones of the 12 regular meridians are divisions of the body surface along the courses of the 12 regular meridians and the specific collaterals. They are included in the areas supplied by the 12 regular meridians. They manifest the pathological changes of those meridians.

	Regular meridians	3 Yin meridians of the hand 3 Yang meridians of the hand 3 Yin meridians of the foot 3 Yang meridians of the foot
Meridians	Extra meridians	Du, Ren, Chong, Dai, Yinqiao, Yangqiao, Yinwei and Yangwei meridians
Meridian system	Collaterals	Fifteen major collaterals Superficial collaterals Tertiary collaterals
	Others	Inner portions of the 12 regular meridians Tendinomusculature of the 12 regular meridians Cutaneous zones of the 12 regular meridians

In the meridian system described above, the most important components are the channels. Diseases affecting the body can be treated through the points lying along the courses of the meridians.

This book is an elaboration of the 14 meridians, i.e. the 12 regular meridians, the Du Meridian and Ren Meridian, each of which has its own specific points. These points are generally known as the regular points of the 14 meridians.

Section 3 THE PHYSIOLOGICAL FUNCTIONS AND PATHOLOGICAL CHANGES OF THE MERIDIANS

I. The Physiological Functions

The zang and fu organs play an essential role in maintaining the normal functional activities of the human body. The meridians and zangfu organs coordinate to perform the manifold variety of physiological functions, these activities of the meridians being manifested in different ways.

A. Communication Between the Exterior and the Interior and Unification of the Body Parts and Functions into an Integral Whole

The 12 regular meridians originate in the internal zangfu organs. They are arranged in pairs according to their external-internal relationships and various roles of connecting, pertaining, infusing and transporting. The 12 regular meridians communicate with all the zang and fu organs, maintaining harmony between them in their performance of the normal physiological functions which support life.

The 12 regular meridians are distributed over the trunk, limbs, head and facial area. They connect to the eyes, lips, teeth, tongue, throat, external genitalia, anus, etc. They also nourish the tendons, muscles and joints of the body, through the tendinomuscular pathways of the meridians. Furthermore, they dominate the skin via the collaterals. Thus the whole body is organized into an integrated unit by the network of the meridians and collaterals.

The physiological functions and the pathological changes of the internal zang and fu organs are manifested at their corresponding sense organs through the meridians and collaterals. Normal functions of the sense organs on the body surface indicate normal physiological functions of their corresponding internal zangfu organs. Conversely, the pathological changes of sense organs may reflect the derangement or dysfunction of internal zangfu organs.

B. Transportation of Qi and Blood to Nourish the Whole Body

Qi and blood are the products of the functional activities of the zangfu organs, being manifested from essential materials obtained from food or air. Whereas the production of qi and blood is dependent on the good condition of the zangfu organs, their transportation relies on the proper function of the meridians and collaterals. The meridians and collaterals carry qi and blood to all parts of the body, to promote Yin and Yang, nourish the organs, muscles, tissues and bones, and moisten the joints, thus maintaining the normal body functions.

When a disease affects the meridians and collaterals, their function of transportation of qi and blood is disturbed. Subsequently, symptoms may appear, such as stagnation of qi, retardation of blood, obstruction of meridians and collaterals, pain, swelling and ecchymosis. When the deficiency of qi and blood results in failure to nourish the meridians properly, Xu symptoms will appear. For example, numbness due to poor nourishment of the meridians and collaterals may develop, certain zangfu organs may exhibit deficiency. Blood deficiency may lead to the formation of interior heat, or consumption of Yin may result in the stirring up of the interior wind with spasm and convulsion. Prolonged Xu or Shi conditions lead to deficiency of qi and blood, resulting in malnutrition of the meridians, thus emaciation or atrophy may develop in serious cases.

C. Adjustment of Yin and Yang to Maintain Balance

The 12 regular meridians adjust the physiological functions of the zangfu organs, maintaining harmony and preventing the occurrence of either hyper or hypoactivity. This function of the meridians is especially accentuated during the acupuncture treatment, e.g. needling Neiguan (P.6) can either hasten or slow down the heart rate and can either stop or induce vomiting, according to the xu and shi nature of the disease being treated. Needling Zusanli (St.36) can either relieve gastrointestinal spasm or promote peristalsis, lower the blood pressure in case of hypertension, or raise the blood pressure in hypotension. An understanding of the function is essential to the clinical practice of acupuncture.

The meridians have a self-regulating function. The eight extra meridians store or supply the qi and blood of the 12 regular meridians, according to conditions of abundance or deficiency. Similarly, each of the 12 regular meridians also adjusts the conditions of excess or deficiency maintained on either side of the body. Consequently, disease affecting the left side of the body can be treated by selecting points from the right side of the body, and vice versa.

D. Maintenance of Conductivity and Prevention of Exogenous Invasion

Transportation of qi and blood is a vital function of the meridians and collaterals. The conduction of qi inside of the meridians and collaterals is not subjectively perceptible under normal physical conditions. However, when a point is stimulated by needling, application of moxa, or electric stimulation, a person may feel radiating sensation (soreness, numbness, heaviness, or distention) travelling along the meridians in specific directions. This is the conduction of qi, the motivating force which maintains the normal physiological functions of the meridians and collaterals. All other special functions of the meridians and collaterals are dependent on the normal condition of qi.

The defensive qi travelling inside the meridians is the material foundation for the prevention of the exogenous pathogenic factors. It is transported together with qi, blood and nutrients by the meridians and distributed to the superficial layers of the body and to the pores.

The invasion of exogenous pathogenic factors always starts from the exterior of the body and moves to the interior. That is to say, it enters through the skin and pores before invading deeper to attack the internal organs. When the defensive qi of the collaterals in the superficial layers of the body is adequate, the opening and closing function of the pores will be normal. The internal zangfu organs will be warm and comfortable, the skin delicate and smooth and the resistance against the exogenous pathogenic factors will be strong. Conversely, when the defensive qi is deficient, it fails to warm and nourish the subcutaneous tissues and also to control the opening and closing of the pores. Resistance against the exogenous pathogenic factors will be low and invasion of the exogenous pathogenic factors may easily occur.

II. The Pathological Changes

Once the normal function of the meridians and collaterals is impaired, the body may easily be invaded by exogenous pathogenic factors and diseases may occur. The pathological changes of the meridians and collaterals are mainly manifested in the following ways.

A. Transmission of Diseases as a Passage of Exogenous Pathogenic Factors

Meridians and collaterals are the pathways for the transportation of qi and blood, but they may also act as passages through which exogenous pathogenic factors can invade the body. The qi of the meridians is strong, the circulation of qi and blood is regular, zangfu functions are normal, and the body is well protected from the invasion of diseases. Dysfunction of the meridians and collaterals leads to irregular circulation of qi and blood, the antipathogenic factors are weakened and exogenous pathogenic factors may easily invade the body. Under such circumstances, the meridians and collaterals may act as the passages for the transportation of disease. The book *Suwen on Cutaneous Zones* says, "When pathogenic factors attack the body, they firstly force the pores to open and lodge in the superficial collaterals. Once established in the superficial collaterals, they may move deeper into the meridians, and when they have developed sufficient strength at this level, they may invade deeply to attack the corresponding zangfu organs."

B. Reflection of Disorders as Images of Internal Diseases

Meridians and collaterals also reflect the pathological changes within the system, as they connect to all the tissues and organs of the body.

1. Reflection of disorders of the zangfu organs at the five sense organs.

Internally, the meridians and collaterals are associated with zangfu organs and externally, they connect with the body surface and the five sense organs. Consequently, internal diseases may be reflected at the corresponding sense organs, e.g. excessive liver fire may be manifested by redness of the eyes. Redness, pain or ulceration at the tip of the tongue indicates heart fire. Toothache indicates stomach fire. And sudden tinnitus or sudden deafness can be due to hyperactive fire of the gall bladder.

2. Reflection of zangfu organs on the superficial parts of the body.

When the internal organs become diseased, some symptoms may appear at certain superficial areas or points of the body, along the courses of the meridians of the involved zangfu organs, e.g., stagnation of liver qi may cause hypochondriac pain on both sides, because the course of the Liver Meridian of Foot-Jueyin is distributed along the lateral aspect of the lower abdomen and the hypochondriac region. Angina pectoris may not only cause pain in the heart area, but the pain may also radiate down along the posterior border of the medial aspect of the upper arm, the course of the Heart Meridian of Hand-Shaoyin. In the case of cholecystitis, a patient may have tenderness at Yang-lingquan (G.B.34) from the Gall Bladder Meridian of Foot-Shaoyang. In appendicitis, tenderness may be felt at Lanwei (Extra) in the area inferior to Zusanli (St.36) on the Stomach Meridian of Foot-Yangming.

C. As Passages Through Which Diseases of Individual Zangfu May Influence Other Organs

Zangfu organs are connected by meridians and collaterals. When a particular zangfu organ becomes diseased, that disorder may also disturb other related organs, e.g. the Liver Meridian of Foot-Jueyin pertains to the liver and curves around the stomach, so liver disorders may affect the stomach. The liver meridian also passes the lung, so liver fire may burn up the Yin of the lung, causing lung disorders. The Kidney Meridian of Foot-Shaoyin enters the lung and links with the heart. When kidney Yang is deficient, it may fail to raise water to nourish the heart and lung, giving rise to disorders of these organs. The Spleen Meridian of Foot-Taiyin pertains to the spleen, connects with the stomach, then passes through the diaphragm and enters the heart. A branch of the stomach meridian also ascends to enter the heart, so hyperactivity of stomach fire may disturb the heart, interfering with its function of housing the mind. Typical symptoms of heart problems associated with the Yangming meridian will be profuse sweating, night fever and dryness.

Externally-internally related meridians are closely connected to each other, and can often influence each other pathologically. For example, heart fire may disturb the small intestine. Excessive heat of the large intestine may cause derangement of lung qi, with associated symptoms and signs such as cough, fullness and heaviness sensation in the chest.

Section 4 THE CLINICAL APPLICATION OF THE MERIDIANS

I. The Diagnostic Aspect

When applying the four diagnostic methods in the differentiation of syndromes, doctors often make use of information obtained by carefully studying the locations and characteristics of symptoms and signs, reflected along the courses of the meridians.

A. Differentiation of Syndromes According to the Theory of Meridians

This is the study of pathological manifestations with reference to the courses of the meridians as well as the known physiological and pathological manifestation of their related zangfu organs. It is possible to determine which meridians are affected, by analyzing the characteristics of the pathological manifestations exhibited by the patient. For example, the lung dominates qi circulation, controls respiration and regulates water passages. Common symptoms of the dysfunction of the lung may be of cough, derangement of qi, heavy chest, scanty but frequent micturition, etc. Symptoms related to the distribution of the meridian may include pain in the supraclavicular fossa, mental restlessness, feverish sensation in the palm, pain along the radial aspect of the forearm or in the anterior aspect of the shoulder. The book *Shang Han Lun* (*On Febrile Diseases*), written by Zhang Zhongjing more than 1,700 years ago, describes, "differentiation according to the six major meridians". The author considered that accurate diagnosis depended on the combined application of the meridian theory, the theory of zangfu organs, etiology, pathology and the theory of Yinyang.

B. Differentiation of Syndromes According to the Location of the Diseases

In this case, the location of the symptoms and signs are analyzed in order to determine which of the meridians are mainly affected during the occurrence of disease. For example, headache may occur at different areas of the head, indicating disorders of different meridians:

Yangming meridian: pain in the forehead;

Shaoyang meridian: pain at the lateral side of the head;

Jueyin meridian: pain at the vertex;

Stomach meridian: pain of the upper teeth; and

Large intestine meridian: pain of the lower teeth.

C. Differentiation of Syndromes by Studying the Points

This is the study of pathological changes at acupuncture points along the courses of the meridians, such as tenderness, tuberculosis, or changes of electric potential. Analysis is made in order to determine which meridian is mainly affected, or which disease is in either shi or xu condition, e.g.

In case of lung disease, doctors often find a tenderness around Zhongfu (Lu.1), the Front-mu point of the lung.

In appendicitis, there may appear a tenderness at Lanweixue (Extra) below Zusanli (St.36).

In cholecystitis, tenderness may be felt at Dannangxue (Extra), inferior to Yanglingquan (G.B.34) of the gall bladder meridian. The book *Lingshu* (*On Functional Activities*) says, "By studying the symptoms and signs manifested at particular points, following the theory of meridians, one may assess the general condition of a disease and determine which meridian is mainly affected."

II. The Therapeutic Aspect

The most common application of the theory of meridians is as a guide to the prescription of suitable herbs which may be induced into the meridians in the treatment of a disease, or in the case of acupuncture treatment, the selection of points according to appropriate differentiation.

A. Making the Prescription of Herbs According to the Meridians

Clinically, having made a careful analysis of a disease, doctors often prescribe herbs which have an especially marked tendency to enter the particular meridians or zangfu organs affected. This is the practical application of the theory of classification of drugs according to their therapeutic actions on diseases of specific meridians. For example, Taiyang headache can be treated by using Rhizoma et Radix Ligustici (Gaoben 藁本) or Rhizoma sen Radis Notopherygii (Qianghuo 羌活) because the two herbs enter the Taiyang meridian and are consequently indicated for Taiyang disorders.

Yangming headache is usually treated with Radix Angelicase Dahuricue (Bai-zhi 白芷) which mainly deals with the disorders of Yangming meridians.

Shaoyang headache can be treated by using Radix bupleuri (Chaihu 柴胡) as this herb especially acts on the Shaoyang meridian.

Jueyin headache is sometimes treated by using Fructus Evodiae (Wuyi 吴萸) which enters the Jueyin meridian.

There are some herbs used to induce effect of the ingredients in a decoction to enter a certain meridian, in order to guide the therapeutic effect of the whole prescription into the diseased area.

B. Selecting Points According to the Course of the Meridian

Points are always distributed along the main courses of the meridians, so a prescription can be made by following the principle "that the indications of the points are associated with the courses of the meridians." This kind of application of points is widely used in the clinic. Also, the application of plum blossom needling, massage, manipulation, the folk methods treating children's digestive disorders by kneading and lifting the skin along the spine, etc. are all guided by the meridian theory.

Bleeding the collaterals by pricking with the three-edged needle can stimulate the skin zones to release retardation. This method can be applied to ease pain due to stagnation of qi and blood in the meridians and collaterals, and to expel exogenous pathogenic factors, e.g. bleeding Taiyang (Extra) and Shaoshang (Lu.11) for treating redness or pain of the eye; bleeding Shaoshang (Lu.11) for sore throat; bleeding Weizhong (U.B.40) for the lower back pain. "Where there is pain, there is a point", i.e. the application of Ahshi points actually stimulates the tendinomuscular structures of the meridians, as the pain and stagnation is sometimes caused by stiffness, spasm or convulsion of the muscles.

Acupuncture anesthesia has recently been developed on the basis of the meridian theory.

Thus, a study of the meridians can be seen to be of great value in developing an understanding of physiological function and pathological change, as well as playing an important role in the guidance of clinical differentiation, treatment and research.

Section 5 THE TWELVE REGULAR MERIDIANS

I. The Nomenclature of the Twelve Regular Meridians

Everything in the universe can be generalized in terms of Yin and Yang, and channels in the meridian system are categorized accordingly. Yin and Yang are neither absolute nor independent, but are terms used to describe the relativity to another of parts and functions within a given system. Being parts of the same system, they necessarily interrelate. Being diametrically opposite, they are antagonistic, and being inseperable, they are mutually dependent. The meridians are named in accordance with their internal-external relationship, and are classified with regard to the relative levels of activity of Yin, Yang, qi and blood within them. Yinqi is the most abundant in the Taiyin (Greater Yin) meridian, less so in the Shaoyin (Lesser Yin) meridian and least in the Jueyin (Least Yin) meridian. Yangqi is the most abundant in the Yangming (Bright Yang) meridian, less so in the Taiyang (Greater Yang) meridian and further less in the Shaoyang (Lesser Yang) meridian (Fig. I-1, Fig. I-2).

$$
\text{YIN} \left\{ \begin{array}{l} \text{Taiyin} (\text{-\,-\,-}) \text{----} (+++) \text{Yangming} \\ \text{Shaoyin} (\text{-\,-}) \text{-----} (++) \text{Taiyang} \\ \text{Jueyin} (\text{-}) \text{--------} (+) \text{Shaoyang} \end{array} \right\} \quad \text{YANG}
$$

The above terms describing the three Yin and three Yang meridians are widely used. The three Yin meridians on the medial side of the arm are arranged in the order of: Hand-Taiyin (Lu.), Hand-Shaoyin (H.) and Hand-Jueyin (P.), while the three Yang meridians on the lateral aspect of the arm follow the order of: Hand-Yangming (L.I.), Hand-Taiyang (S.I.) and Hand-Shaoyang (S.J.). The three Yin meridians on the medial side of the leg are in the order of: Foot-Taiyin (Sp.), Foot-Shaoyin (K.) and Foot-Jueyin (Liv.), while the three Yang meridians on the lateral side of the leg are in the order of: Foot-Yangming (St.), Foot-Taiyang (U.B.) and Foot-Shaoyang (G.B.). From the nomenclature of the meridians, it is clear that their distribution to the hands and feet was thought to be of considerable importance.

The theory of zangfu holds that zang organs, pertaining to Yin, store vital energy but have no function of excretion; fu organs, pertaining to Yang, transform food into essence but have no function of storage. The internal-external relationship exists between Yin and Yang, zang and fu. Yin meridians pertain primarily to zang organs, but also connect with fu organs, and Yang meridians pertain mainly to fu organs, but also connect with zang organs.

The theory of the zangfu was based on the study of the zang organs. The zang organs in the chest area (lung, heart and pericardium) are associated with the three Yin meridians of the hand, whilst the zang organs in the abdominal area (spleen, liver and kidney) are associated with the three Yin meridians of the foot. The six fu organs are respectively associated with the Yang meridians of the foot and hand in accordance with their specific internal-external relation to the zang organs. The Yang meridians of both foot and hand in general have their distributions over the head. Thus, a special relationship is formed by the distribution of the meridians to the head, chest and abdomen:

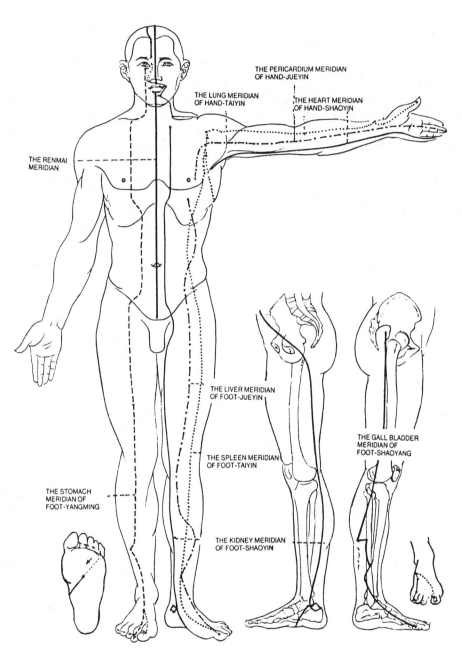

Fig. I-1

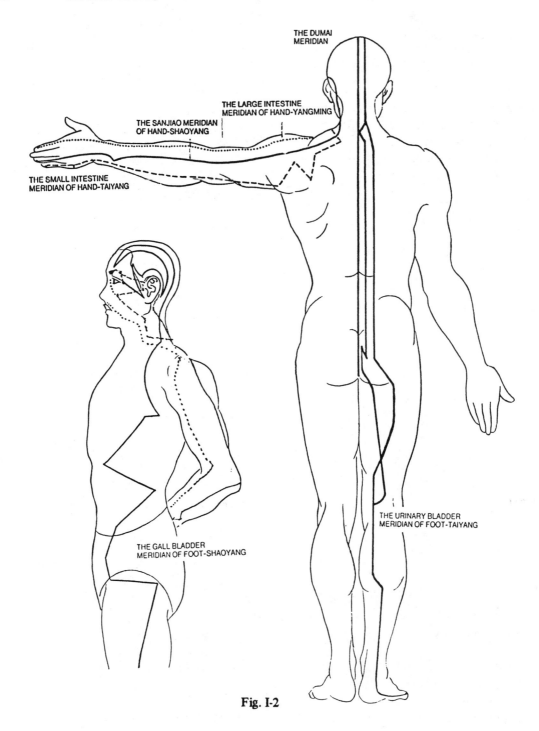

Fig. I-2

Yin meridians of hand—chest
Yin meridians of foot—abdomen
Yang meridians of both foot and hand—head

Thus, the three Yin meridians of the hand distribute from hand to chest, the three Yang meridians of the hand distribute from hand to head, the three Yang meridians of the foot distribute from head down to foot, and the three Yin meridians of the foot distribute from foot up to abdomen. Qi and blood travel along the courses of meridians, connecting Yin and Yang in an endless cycle. The 12 regular meridians were named with reference both to their courses and to their relations with the zangfu organs, viz:

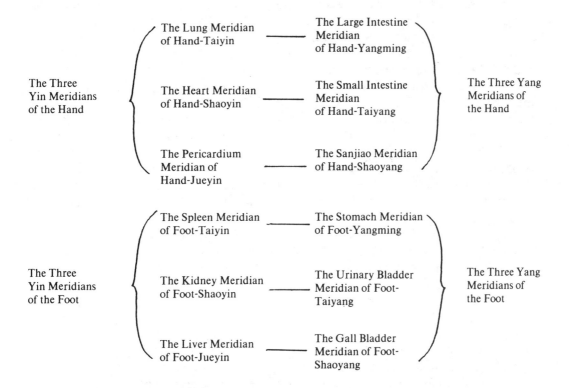

II. The Courses and Distributions of the Twelve Regular Meridians

A detailed description of the distribution of each meridian will be covered in Part II of this book. For the sake of maintaining continuity with the books *Meridian-Oriented Qigong* and *A Study on the Heritage of the Fourteen Meridians* by the same author (the author of this book), the courses of the 12 regular meridians will be described here in the same manner. However, the descriptions in Part II of this book vary slightly, being a study of the courses of the 12 regular meridians, and then the relationship with the sense organs and body openings.

From the previous description, it can be seen that the 12 regular meridians are divided into four groups, according to their varied Yin and Yang characteristics and in relation to their distribution on the foot and hand.

Group I consists of the three Yin meridians of the hand, i.e. the Lung Meridian of Hand-Taiyin (Fig. II-1), the Heart Meridian of Hand-Shaoyin (Fig. II-11) and the Pericardium Meridian of Hand-Jueyin (Fig. II-20).

A. The Lung Meridian of Hand-Taiyin originates from the middle jiao, running downward to connect with the large intestine. Winding back, it goes along the upper orifice of the stomach, passes through the diaphragm and enters the lung, its pertaining organ. Ascending along the throat, it enters the ear, connects with the tongue and communicates with the nose. From the division of the lung communicating with the throat, it comes out transversely, descends along the medial aspect of the upper arm, and terminates at the radial side of the tip of the thumb. The starting point is Zhongfu (Lu.1) and the terminating point is Shaoshang (Lu.11). The branch arising from the styloid process of the radius runs directly to the radial side of the tip of the index finger linking with the Large Intestine Meridian of Hand-Yangming.

B. The Heart Meridian of Hand-Shaoyin originates from the heart and descends to connect with the small intestine. Winding back to the "heart system" (i.e. the vessels connecting the heart with other zangfu organs), it passes through the throat, links with the eye system, communicates with the brain, connects with the tongue and enters into the ear. From the heart system, it emerges transversely at the axilla, descends along the posterior border of the medial aspect of the upper arm and terminates at the radial aspect of the tip of the small finger. The starting point is Jiquan (H.1) and the terminating point is Shaochong (H.9). The qi of this meridian flows from Shaochong (H.9) along the posterior aspect of the nail of the small finger, to Shaoze (S.I.1) at the ulnar side of the small finger, thus linking with the Small Intestine Meridian of Hand-Taiyang.

C. The Pericardium Meridian of Hand-Jueyin originates in the chest. It enters into its pertaining organ, the pericardium, descends through the diaphragm to the abdomen, and connects successively with the upper, middle and lower jiao (triple heater). Winding back, it ascends along the esophagus to the throat, communicates with the ear, disperses into the tongue, connects with the eye and enters into the brain. The superficial branch emerges 1 cun lateral to the nipple, travels down along the midline of the medial aspect of the arm and terminates at the tip of the middle finger. The starting point is Tianchi (P.1) and the terminating point is Zhongchong (P.9). Another branch arising at Laogong (P.8), travels to Guanchong (S.J.1) at the tip of the ring finger and links with the Sanjiao Meridian of Hand-Shaoyang.

The common factor in the distribution of the three Yin meridians of the hand, is that all of them start from the chest, descend along the medial aspect of the arm and end at the tips of the fingers, linking successively with the three Yang meridians of the hand. In short, the three Yin meridians of the hand travel from the chest and the hand.

Medial aspect of the arm
{
Anterior—The Lung Meridian of Hand-Taiyin
Middle—The Pericardium Meridian of Hand-Jueyin
Posterior—The Heart Meridian of Hand-Shaoyin

Group II consists of the three Yang meridians of the hand, i.e. the Large Intestine Meridian of Hand-Yangming (Fig. II-40), the Small Intestine Meridian of Hand-Taiyang (Fig. II-56) and the Sanjiao Meridian of Hand-Shaoyang (Fig. II-68).

A. The Large Intestine Meridian of Hand-Yangming starts at the radial end of the index finger. Running upward along the radial side of the finger and the lateral anterior aspect of the forearm, it goes to the shoulder region and crosses Dazhui (Du 14). It then goes to the supraclavicular fossa, where the meridian bifurcates. The internal division enters the chest to connect with the lung, passes through the diaphragm and enters its pertaining organ, the large intestine. From the large intestine, its qi communicates with its Lower He-sea point, Shangjuxu (St.37). The upper division ascends to enter the gums of the lower jaw, curves around the upper lip and crosses the opposite meridian at the philtrum. The left meridian then goes to the right and the right one to the left, terminating at either side of the nose and connecting with the Stomach Meridian of Foot-Yangming. The Qi of the meridian communicates with the ear through the nose. The starting point is Shangyang (L.I.1) and the terminating point is Yingxiang (L.I.20).

B. The Small Intestine Meridian of Hand-Taiyang starts from the ulnar side of the tip of the little finger. Ascending along the lateral posterior aspect of the upper limb, it reaches the scapular region and crosses Dazhui (Du 14). It then runs anteriorly, travelling to the supraclavicular fossa where it bifurcates. The internal division goes to the chest to connect with the heart and enters its pertaining organ, the small intestine. From the small intestine, the qi of the meridian communicates with Xiajuxu (St.39), its Lower He-sea point. The superficial division ascends along the lateral side of the neck, passes through Quanliao (S.I.18), reaches the outer canthus of the eye, then enters the ear at Tinggong (S.I.19). The starting point is Shaoze (S.I.1) and the terminating point is Tinggong (S.I.19). Another branch of the meridian ascends laterally from Quanliao (S.I.18) to the inner canthus of the eye at Jingming (U.B.1), linking with the Urinary Bladder Meridian of Foot-Taiyang.

C. The Sanjiao Meridian of Hand-Shaoyang starts from the tip of the ring finger. Ascending along the midline of the lateral aspect of the upper limb and through Jianliao (S.J.14), it crosses Dazhui (Du 14). It then runs anteriorly to the supraclavicular region where it enters the chest to connect with the pericardium and sanjiao. From the sanjiao, the qi of the meridian communicates with Weiyang, its lower He-sea point. A second branch starts from Shangzhong (Ren 17) and merges at the supraclavicular region. It runs at the neck and enters the ear at its posterior aspect. Then it passes in front of the ear to terminate at the outer canthus of the eye, where it links with the Gall Bladder Meridian of Foot-Shaoyang. The starting point is Guanchong (S.J.1) and the terminating point is Sizukong (S.J.23).

A common factor in the distribution of the three Yang meridians of the hand is that all of them start from the tips of the fingers, ascend along the lateral aspect of the upper arm and end in the head or facial region, linking successively with the three Yang meridians of the foot. In short, the three Yang meridians of the hand all start from the hand to end at the head.

Lateral aspect of the arm
{
Anterior—The Large Intestine Meridian of Hand-Yangming
Middle—The Sanjiao Meridian of Hand-Shaoyang
Posterior—The Small Intestine Meridian of Hand-Taiyang
}

Group III consists of the three Yang meridians of the foot, i.e. the Stomach Meridian of Foot-Yangming (Fig. II-98), the Urinary Bladder Meridian of Foot-Taiyang (Fig. II-116) and the Gall Bladder Meridian of Foot-Shaoyang (Fig. II-135).

A. The Stomach Meridian of Foot-Yangming starts from the lateral side of the ala nasi. Ascending to the bridge of the nose, it runs laterally to the infraorbital region. Descending from the facial region, it then travels to the throat and communicates with the ear. From Qishe (St.11) in the anterior lateral region of the shoulder, it runs posteriorly to meet Dazhui (Du 14) and then anteriorly to the supraclavicular fossa where it bifurcates. The internal division passes through the diaphragm, reaches the stomach, its pertaining organ, and connects with the spleen. From the spleen, the qi of the meridian communicates with Qichong (St.30). The superficial division emerges from the supraclavicular fossa, descends to the abdomen and joins the previously mentioned portion of the meridian at Qichong (St.30). Descending along the lateral posterior aspect of the leg, it ends at the lateral side of the tip of the 2nd toe. The starting point is Chengqi (St.1) and the terminating point is Lidui (St.45). One branch, arising from Zusanli (St.36), enters the lateral side of the middle toe. Another branch arises from Guanchong (St.42) to link with the Spleen Meridian of Foot-Taiyin at the medial side of the tip of the big toe.

B. The Urinary Bladder Meridian of Foot-Taiyang starts from the inner canthus. Ascending along the forehead, it reaches Baihui (Du 20) and enters into both the brain and the ear. It then descends along the neck to meet Dazhui (Du 14) on the posterior aspect. The meridian now bifurcates into two sections, respectively 1.5 cun and 3 cun lateral to the posterior midline, both of which descend to the lumbosacral region. From Shenshu (U.B.23), one division enters into the body, connects with the kidney and enters into the urinary bladder, its pertaining organ. The superficial division continues to descend from Shenshu (U.B.23), travels along the lateral posterior aspect of the leg, ends at the lateral side of the tip of the small toe, and links with the Kidney Meridian of Foot-Shaoyin. The starting point is Jingming (U.B.1) and the terminating point is Zhiyin (U.B.67).

C. The Gall Bladder Meridian of Foot-Shaoyang starts from the outer canthus. Running to the temporal region and the ear, it descends through the facial region and enters the chest. Passing through the diaphragm, it connects with the liver and enters into the gall bladder, its pertaining organ. From the gall bladder, the qi of the meridian reaches Huantiao (G.B.30). One division of the meridian goes anteriorly and laterally from Fengchi (G.B.20) to meet Tianrong (S.I.17), then crosses Dazhui (Du 14). Passing through Jianjing (G.B.21), it descends along the lateral aspect of the chest and abdomen to join the internal division of the meridian at Huantiao (G.B.30). Then, it descends along the midline of the lateral aspect of the leg and reaches the lateral side of the tip of the 4th toe. The starting point is Tongziliao (G.B.1) and the terminating point is Foot-Qiaoyin (G.B.44). A branch arises from Foot-Linqi (G.B.41) and travels the hairy region of the big toe, to link with the Liver Meridian of Foot-Jueyin.

The common factor in the distribution of the three Yang meridians of the foot is that all of them start from the head and facial region, descend along the body trunk and the lateral aspect of the leg, end at the tips of the toes and link with successively the three Yin meridians of the foot. In short, the three Yang meridians of the foot start from the head and terminate at the foot.

Lateral aspect of the
leg
{ Anterior—The Stomach Meridian of Foot-Yangming
Middle—The Gall Bladder Meridian of Foot-Shaoyang
Posterior—The Urinary Bladder Meridian of
Foot-Taiyang

Group IV consists of the three Yin meridians of the foot, i.e. the Spleen Meridian of Foot-Taiyin (Fig. II-166), the Kidney Meridian of Foot-Shaoyin (Fig. II-177) and the Liver Meridian of Foot-Jueyin (Fig. II-188).

A. The Spleen Meridian of Foot-Taiyin starts from the medial side of the tip of the big toe. Ascending along the midline on the medial aspect of the tibia, it crosses the Liver Meridian of Foot-Jueyin, 8 cun above the medial malleolus, and ascends to Yinglingquan (Sp.9). Running upward along the anterior medial aspect of the thigh, it goes to Chongmen (Sp.12) on the abdomen, where the meridian bifurcates. The superficial division ascends along a line four cun lateral to the anterior midline of the body to Fuai (Sp.16), then runs vertically up the chest on a line 6 cun lateral to anterior midline to Zhourong (Sp.20). From here, it descends laterally along the axillary line to Dabao (Sp.21). The internal division enters into the spleen, its pertaining organ and connects with the stomach. Running upward along the hypochondriac region and the side of the esophagus, it passes through the throat and communicates with the ear and mouth. Here the qi of the meridian disperses under the middle and posterior portion of the tongue. The starting point is Yinbai (Sp.1) and the terminating point is Dabao (Sp.21). A branch, arising from the stomach, passes through the diaphragm and enters the heart to connect with the Heart Meridian of Hand-Shaoyin.

B. The Kidney Meridian of Foot-Shaoyin starts from the inferior aspect of the small toe and runs obliquely towards the sole. Ascending along the posterio-medial aspect of the leg, it runs to the pubic region where it bifurcates. The superficial division goes to the anterior, passes the external genitalia and runs upward on a line 0.5 cun lateral to anterior midline until it reaches Youmen (K.21). From there, it ascends along the front of the chest on a line two cun lateral to the anterior midline and terminates at Shufu (K.27). The internal division arising from the pubic region runs around the anus, passes through Changqiang (Du 1), runs into the spinal column, enters the kidney, its pertaining organ, and connects with the urinary bladder. Running upward along the lateral abdomen, it passes through the lung and throat to the root of the tongue and communicates with the ear. The starting point is Yongquan (K.1) and the terminating point is Shufu (K.27). A branch arising from the lung runs into the heart system to link with the Pericardium Meridian of Hand-Jueyin.

C. The Liver Meridian of Foot-Jueyin starts from the dorsal hairy region of the great toe. Running upward between the great and second toes on the dorsum of the foot, it passes 1 cun in front of the malleolus. It ascends to a point 8 cun above the medial malleolus [i.e. 1 cun below Diji (Sp.8)], where it crosses and runs behind the Spleen Meridian of Foot-Taiyin. It then runs upward to the medial side of the knee, along the medial aspect of the thigh to the pubic region, where it curves around the external genitalia and ascends to the lower abdomen. Passing through Zhangmen (Liv.13), it reaches its terminating point Qimen (Liv.14). A branch arising from Zhangmen (Liv.13) passes the stomach to the liver, its pertaining organ, and connects with the gall bladder. Passing through the diaphragm and the hypochondriac region, it runs to the nasopharynx to communicate with the ear and brain. Descending along the cheek and winding around the lips, it disperses in the tongue and finally emerges from the forehead to connect with

Baihui (Du 20). The starting point is Dadun (Liv.1) and the terminating point is Qimen (Liv.14).

A branch arising from the liver ascends through the diaphragm to the lung, winds down to the middle jiao and links with the initial portion of the Lung Meridian of Hand-Taiyin.

The common factor in the distribution of the three Yin meridians of the foot, is that all of them start from the tips of the toes, ascend along the medial aspect of the leg and end in the abdomen, linking successivley with the three Yin meridians of the hand. In short, the three Yin meridians of the foot start from the foot and run to the abdomen and chest.

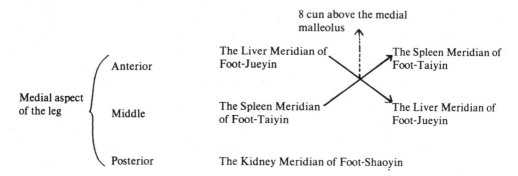

III. Summary of the Distributing Rules of the Twelve Regular Meridians

A. Courses and Linking Rules

The three Yin meridians of the hand travel from the chest to the hand, where they link with the three Yang meridians of the hand.

The three Yang meridians of the hand travel from hand to head, where they link with the three Yang meridians of the foot.

The three Yang meridians of the foot travel from the head down to the foot, where they link with the three Yin meridians of the foot.

The three Yin meridians of the foot travel from the foot up to the abdomen and chest, where they link with the three Yin meridians of the hand.

Thus, the twelve regular meridians form an endless cycle, linking both Yin and Yang and maintaining the circulation of qi and blood in the body.

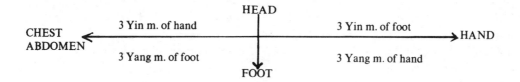

Diagram Showing the Courses and Linkages of the 12 Meridians

B. The Distributing Rules of the Twelve Regular Meridians

1. Head and Facial Region

Yangming meridians—facial region, forehead
Taiyang meridians—cheek, facial region, vertex and posterior aspect of the head
Shaoyang meridians—temporal region and ear

2. Body Trunk

Taiyang meridian of the foot—dorsal aspect
Shaoyang meridian of the foot—hypochondriac region
Yangming meridian of the foot—chest and abdomen
3 Yin meridians of the foot—abdomen and chest

3. Four limbs

Medial aspect	anterior/Taiyin meridian
	middle/Jueyin meridian
	posterior/Shaoyin meridian
Lateral aspect	anterior/Yangming meridian
	middle/Shaoyang meridian
	posterior/Taiyang meridian

C. The Internal-External Relationship of the Twelve Regular Meridians

The 12 regular meridians respectively pertain to and connect with the pairs of internally-externally related zangfu organs. Yin meridians pertain to zang organs and connect with fu organs whilst the Yang meridians pertain to fu organs and connect with zang organs. Although each of the 12 regular meridians pertains to a different zang or fu organ, these meridians are linked together in a system by the internal-external relationship that exists between them:

EXTERNAL	INTERNAL
Yangming meridians	—— Taiyin meridians
Shaoyang meridians	—— Jueyin meridians
Taiyang meridians	—— Shaoyin meridians

That is to say, the Large Intestine Meridian of Hand-Yangming communicates with the Lung Meridian of Hand-Taiyin;

The Sanjiao Meridian of Hand-Shaoyang communicates with the Pericardium Meridian of Hand-Jueyin;

The Small Intestine Meridian of Hand-Taiyang communicates with the Heart Meridian of Hand-Shaoyin;

The Stomach Meridian of Foot-Yangming communicates with the Spleen Meridian of Foot-Taiyin;

The Gall Bladder Meridian of Foot-Shaoyang communicates with the Liver Meridian of Foot-Jueyin; and

The Urinary Bladder Meridian of Foot-Taiyang communicates with the Kidney Meridian of Foot-Shaoyin.

Due to this internal-external relationship, the 12 regular meridians are closely related to each other physiologically while pathologically one influences the other. For example, the kidney dominates the water metabolism. The formation of urine depends on the function of the kidney in receiving qi, but the storage and excretion of urine is performed by the urinary bladder. That is to say that the formation and excretion of urine is jointly carried out by the kidney and the urinary bladder. Pathologically, changes in one organ may well affect the other, e.g. excessive heart fire can be transmitted into the small intestine, etc.

Also, the courses of the internally-externally related meridians distributed in the four limbs, are arranged in a lateral-medial symmetry:

Taiyin meridians and Yangming meridians—on the anterior border of both the medial and lateral aspect of the four limbs;

Jueyin meridians and Shaoyang meridians—on the midline of both the lateral and medial aspects of the four limbs; and

Shaoyin meridians and Taiyang meridians—on the posterior border of both the medial and lateral aspects of the four limbs.

D. The Order of the Twelve Regular Meridians

Lung meridian—Large Intestine meridian—Stomach meridian ———— Spleen meridian—Heart meridian—Small Intestine meridian—Urinary Bladder meridian—Kidney meridian—Pericardium meridian—Sanjiao meridian—Gall Bladder meridian—Liver meridian—and Lung meridian....

Section 6 **THE EIGHT EXTRA MERIDIANS**

The 8 extra meridians are the Du, Ren, Chong, Dai, Yinwei, Yangwei, Yinqiao and Yangqiao meridians, each of which has its own separate pathway. They differ from the 12 regular meridians, in that internally they do not pertain to any zangfu organs, and externally they are not necessarily arranged in pairs. Due to the degree to which they vary from the regular meridians, the term "extra" (奇) has been applied to describe them.

I. A Brief Comparison Between the Extra and Regular Meridians

Eight Extra Meridians	Twelve Regular Meridians
1. No direct association with any particular zangfu organs, except for the Du meridian, which curves around the kidney and passes through the heart system;	1. All are associated with their respective zangfu organs;
2. Not externally-internally related;	2. Externally-internally related;
3. No points other than some regular points being along the courses of some extra meridians, except for the Du and Ren meridians;	3. Each meridian has its own points along its course;
4. The distribution of the meridians runs from the lower part of the body to the upper part, except for Chong and Dai meridians;	4. The distribution of the meridians runs both upwards and downwards;
5. No distribution to the upper limb;	5. With distributions to both the upper and lower limbs;

6. The Du, Ren, Chong and Dai meridians are single meridians, the Yinqiao, Yinwei, Yangqiao and Yangwei meridians are distributed in pairs.

6. All the meridians are in pairs, one on either side of the body.

The courses of the 8 extra meridians are distributed among those of the 12 regular meridians. They have the function to regulate the circulation of the qi and blood of the 12 regular meridians. "When the 12 regular meridians have sufficient qi and blood, any excess infuses into the 8 extra meridians to be stored. When the qi and blood of the 12 regular meridians become decreased, the stored qi and blood of the 12 regular meridians are returned to supply them." The ancient physicians who made this statement were aware of the auto-controlling system which regulates the human body.

II. The Eight Extra Meridians

A. The Du Meridian

Du (督) means governor, controller or commander. The three Yang meridians of both the foot and the hand converge into the Du meridian at Dazhui (Du 14), like the streams merging into a lake, or rivers into the sea. Consequently, the Du Meridian is also referred to as "the sea of the Yang meridians." It regulates the circulation of qi and blood in them and thus is regarded as having the function of governing all the Yang meridians.

1. The Course of the Du Meridian

The Du Meridian originates in the uterus and descends to merge at the perineum. It then ascends along the posterior middle line, following the spinal column from Changqiang (Du 1), the first point of the meridian, to Fengfu (Du 16) at the nape of the neck where it enters the brain, its pertaining organ. It further ascends to the vertex and winds along the forehead to the columella of the nose, where it descends to Yingjiao (Du 28) at the end of the gingiva. It meets the Ren Meridian at Chengjiang (Ren 24).

The posterior branch emerges from the perineum, winds around the anus, ascends along the internal aspect of the spinal column and enters the kidney.

The anterior branch starts from the perineum, winds around the external genitalia, ascends to the middle of the umbilicus, passes through the heart and goes up to the throat and mouth. It winds around the lips and ascends to link with the eye.

Another branch emerges from Jingming (U.B. 1), travels upward to the forehead and the vertex, before descending to Fengfu (Du 16) where it enters the brain. Emerging once more, it descends from the lower part of the nape of the neck to Dashu (U.B. 11) and Fengmen (U.B. 12), continuing to the lower back where it links with the kidney.

2. General Functions

a. Regulation of the circulation of qi and blood in the Yang meridians. Hence, it is called "the sea of the Yang meridians";

b. Regulation of the functional activities of the brain and the spinal marrow; and

c. Regulation of the function of the urinary and reproductive systems.

3. General Indications

The book *Nanjing on Difficulty No. Twenty-nine* says, "When the Du Meridian becomes diseased, symptoms such as opisthotonos and syncope may occur."

a. Disorders along the course of the meridian, e.g. stiffness at the nape of the neck, back, and spinal column, pain in these areas or lumbar sprain;

b. Disorders associated with the brain function, marrow, urinary or reproductive system, e.g. opisthotonos, stiffness and pain of the vertebrae, mental illness, shock, syncope, infantile convulsion, headache and infertility.

B. The Ren Meridian

Ren (任) has two meanings, one of which is responsibility (任), the other being conception (妊) in the sense to become pregnant. This meridian dominates the Yin of the whole body. The three Yin meridians of the hand connect with the three Yin meridians of the foot, and the three Yin meridians of foot converge at Zhongji (Ren 3) and Guanyuan (Ren 4) on the Ren Meridian. Because the Ren Meridian links all the Yin meridians of the body, it is also known as "the sea of the Yin meridians". Furthermore, this meridian originates in the uterus and dominates that organ, being especially involved in the function of conception.

1. The Course of the Ren Meridian

The Ren Meridian originates in the uterus in females, or arises from the lower abdomen in males. It emerges at perineum, runs through the pubic region and ascends along the anterior line of the abdomen and chest to the throat. Running further upward, it curves around the lips where it divides into two branches which pass through the cheek and enter the infraorbital region of the eyes.

2. General Functions

a. Regulation of the circulation of both qi and blood of the Yin meridians. Hence the term: "the sea of the Yin meridians";

b. Regulation of menstrual flow, domination of the reproductive system, domination of the fetus and of the function of the uterus; and

c. Regulation of the qi circulation in the chest, promotion of the functional activities of the spleen and stomach, and general strengthening of the body constitution.

3. General Indications

The book *Nanjing on Difficulty No. Twenty-nine* says, "When the Ren Meridian is diseased, abdominal masses often result, herniae in males and splenomegaly in females." The book *Shuwen on Bone Diseases* says, "When a disease affects the Ren Meridian, abdominal masses or various kinds of herniae may occur in males, excessive leukorrhea or splenomegaly in females."

a. Diseases along the course of the meridian, e.g. herniae or any kind of mass in abdomen; and

b. Dysfunction of the meridian, e.g. leukorrhea, irregular menstruation, miscarriage, infertility and decreased sexual drive.

C. The Chong Meridian

Chong (冲) means vital. This meridian dominates the circulation of qi and blood of the other meridians. Consequently, it is also known as "the sea of the 12 regular meridians".

1. The Course of the Chong Meridian

Like the Du and Ren Meridians, the Chong Meridian also originates from the lower part of the abdomen or the uterus, descends and emerges from the perineum where it divides into three branches.

The first branch emerges from the perineum, curves around the anus and then enters the vertebral column.

The second branch emerges from the perineum, curves around the external genitalia, bifurcates and coincides with the Kidney Meridian of Foot-Shaoyin, running bilaterally up the abdomen and chest to the throat. It then winds around the lips of the mouth and ascends to the infraorbital region.

And, the third branch emerges from the perineum and also divides into two, descending along the medial aspects of the lower limbs to the heel and through the medial malleolus. A divergent branch passes through the dorsum of the foot and terminates between the great and second toes.

2. General Functions

a. Regulation of the circulation of the qi and blood of the 12 regular meridians. Hence the name: "sea of the 12 regular meridians";

b. Regulation of the menstrual flow. It regulates the volume of the menstrual blood, especially during the initial onset of the menstruation and at the menopause. The book *Shuwen on the Nature of the Ancients* says, "When a girl reaches the age of fourteen, her sex-stimulating kidney essence is formed, the Ren Meridian becomes strong, the qi and blood of the Chong Meridian become abundant and menstrual flow appears." "When a woman reaches the age of forty-nine, her sex-stimulating kidney essence is exhausted, because the qi and blood of the Chong Meridian is consumed. Consequently, the menstrual flow stops." As Chong Meridian is closely related to menstruation, as well as storing the qi and blood of the 12 regular meridians, it is also called "the sea of the blood;" and

c. Regulation of the ascending and descending of the qi of the body.

3. General Indications

The book *Nanjing on Difficulty No. Twenty-nine* says, "When the Chong Meridian is diseased, stagnation or derangement of the qi will occur."

a. Derangement of qi, e.g. bloody vomiting, hiccup and belching; and

b. Disorders of the reproductive system in females, e.g. uterine bleeding, irregular menstruation, amenorrhea and lactation deficiency. As the three meridians, Du, Ren and Chong all originate in the lower part of the abdomen or the uterus, they are also known as the three meridians of the same source or three branches of the same source. Clinically, disorders of the reproductive and urinary systems, especially gynecological diseases are all associated with the functions of these three extra meridians.

D. The Dai Meridian

The Dai Meridian originates below the hypochondriac region and circles around the waist like a belt. Hence the name Daimai "belt meridian" (帶脈). It has the function of binding up all the other meridians. It is the only meridian which runs transversely over the body surface, all the others, both extra and regular travelling vertically.

1. The Course of the Meridian

Starting below the hypochondriac region, proximal to the tip of the 12th rib, it circles around the waist, goes down obliquely to the lateral side of the abdomen and finally returns to its starting point at the lower portion of the hypochondriac region.

2. General Functions

a. The binding-up of all the meridians of the whole body; and

b. The control of leukorrhea in females.

3. General Indications

The book *Nanjing on Difficulty No. Twenty-nine* says, "When the Dai Meridian is diseased, the patient will complain weakness of the lower back with a sensation as sitting in water. The other symptoms that may appear are excessive leukorrhea, prolapse of the uterus, distention of the abdomen, weakness of the waist, etc."

E. The Yangqiao and Yinqiao Meridians

Qiao (跷) means heel, denoting motility or capacity of raising the foot. Yangqiao and Yinqiao Meridians both start from the heel, wind around the malleolus and ascend vertically. These meridians promote agile motility, hence the names Yangqiao and Yinqiao Meridians, meaning motility meridians of Yang and Yin.

1. The Courses of the Meridians

The Yangqiao Meridian, one of the branches of the Urinary Bladder Meridian of Foot-Taiyang, starts from the centre of the heel, and emerges at Shenmai (U.B.62), below the lateral malleolus. Passing Pushen (U.B.61), it ascends to Fuyang (U.B.59), its Xi-cleft point which is 3 cun above the lateral malleolus. Ascending along the posterior aspect of the thigh, it passes Femur-Juliao (G.B.29) before reaching the posterior aspect of the hypochondriac region. It then proceeds to the shoulder, passes through Naohu (S.I.10), Jianyu (L.I.15) and Jigu (L.I.16) and ascends along the neck to the corner of the mouth. It runs further upward to connect with Chengqi (St.1) and Jingming (U.B.1), finally entering the brain from Fengchi (G.B. 20).

The Yinqiao Meridian, one of the branches of the Kidney Meridian of Foot-Shaoyin, starts from Rangu (K. 2) in the centre of the heel, ascends along the medial aspect of the foot and ankle, passes Zhaohai (K.6) and meets Jiaoxin (K.8), its Xi-cleft point, 2 cun above the medial malleolus. It then runs vertically along the posterior border of the medial aspect of the thigh to the external genitalia, continuing to ascend along the abdomen and chest to the supraclavicular fossa. It further runs upward, lateral to the laryngeal prominence in front of Renyin (St.9), proceeds along the zygoma, reaches the inner canthus of the eye and connects with Jingming (U.B.1). From this point, it also communicates with the Small Intestine Meridian of Hand-Taiyang, The Urinary Bladder Meridian of Foot-Taiyang, the Stomach Meridian of Foot-Yangming and the Yangqiao Meridian.

2. General Indications

a. Domination of the closing and opening of the eye lids. Both Yangqiao and Yinqiao meridians circle the eye and enter the brain. They have a close relation with sleep. The Yangqiao Meridian represents Yang qi. Hyperactivity of Yang qi leads to restlessness, open eyes and poor sleep. The Yinqiao Meridian represents Yin qi. When the Yin qi becomes hyperactive, lassitude, closed eyes and somnolence result. The normal functional activities of both Yangqiao and Yinqiao meridians maintain agile motility, good sleep and high spirits;

b. The Yangqiao Meridian dominates Yang of the body on both sides and the Yinqiao Meridian dominates the Yin of the body on both sides. The two harmonize to maintain the balance of Yin and Yang of the whole body; and

c. Coordination of the muscular movement of the lower limbs.

3. General Indications

The book *Nanjing on Difficulty No. Twenty-nine* says, "When the Yinqiao Meridian becomes diseased, muscular spasm occurs at the medial aspect (Yin) of the limbs, while the lateral (Yang) side is flaccid, and vice versa."

a. Impairment of the eye in closing or opening, e.g. insomnia or somnolence, the former being associated with Yangqiao diseases and the latter with Yinqiao problems;

b. Lack of coordination of the movements of the lower limbs, e.g. inversion or eversion of the foot, the former being associated with Yinqiao problems and the latter with Yangqiao disorders.

F. The Yinwei and Yangwei Meridians

Wei (维) means connection. It indicates that the Yin meridians connect to the Yinwei Meridian and the Yang meridians connect to the Yangwei Meridian.

1. The Course of the Meridians

The Yinwei Meridian connects to all the Yin meridians of both hand and foot, as well as to the Ren Meridian. It starts from the medial side of the leg at Zhubin (K.9), its Xi-cleft point, and ascends along the medial aspect of the thigh to the abdomen, communicates with the Spleen Meridian of Foot-Taiyin. Passing through Chongmen (Sp.12), Fushe (Sp.13), Daheng (Sp.14) and Fuai (Sp.16), it meets the Liver Meridian of Foot-Jueyin at Qimen (Liv.14), ascends along the chest and communicates with the Ren Meridian at Tiantu (Ren 22) and Lianquan (Ren 23).

The Yangwei Meridian connects to all the Yang meridians as well as the Du Meridian. It starts from Jinmen (U.B.63) at the heel, ascends to pass the external malleolus to Yangjiao (G.B.35), its Xi-cleft point. It proceeds upwards along the Gall Bladder Meridian of Foot-Shaoyang on the lateral aspect of the lower limbs. Passing through the hip region, it ascends along the posterior aspect of the hypochondriac and costal regions and along the posterior aspect of the axilla to the shoulder. It continues to ascend to the forehead, passing Naoshu (S.I.10), Tianliao (S.J.15) and Jianjing (G.B.21), and runs up to the lateral side of the neck to the posterior aspect of the ear. At this stage, it turns back, descending to Fengchi (G.B.20) and along the back of the neck to meet the Du Meridian at Fengfu (Du 16) and Yamen (Du 15).

2. General Functions

Generally speaking, the functional activities of Yinwei and Yangwei meridians are to connect all the Yin and Yang meridians of the body. The function of Yinwei Meridian is to connect the Yin and dominate the internal aspect of the body. It connects the three Yin meridians of both hand and foot as well as the Ren Meridian. The function of Yangwei Meridian is to connect the Yang meridians and dominate the external aspect of the body. The three Yang meridians of the hand and foot as well as the Du Meridian are connected by Yangwei Meridian.

When Yinwei and Yangwei meridians are functioning normally, both Yin and Yang of the body will be in harmony and the circulation of qi and blood in the Yin and Yang meridians will be properly regulated. When these two meridians become diseased, disharmony of the Yin and Yang, as well as the disturbance of qi and blood circulation will be likely to occur.

3. General Indications

The book *Nanjing on Difficulty No. Twenty-nine* says, "When the Yangwei Meridian becomes diseased, the patient will be prone to invasion of exogenous cold or heat. When the Yinwei Meridian becomes diseased, heart pain will result."

a. Diseases associated with the Yangwei Meridian, e.g. aversion to cold, fever, acute febrile diseases due to exogenous invasion, etc. The Yangwei Meridian dominates the external aspect of the body and is closely connected with the Shaoyang and Yangming meridians. When it becomes ill, the patient becomes susceptible to exterior syndrome of either cold or heat.

b. Diseases associated with the Yinwei Meridian, e.g. heart pain, gastric pain, pain of the chest and abdomen. The Yinwei Meridian dominates the internal aspect of these meridians.

The above covers the general characteristics of the courses, functions and indications of the 8 extra meridians. In ancient times, the 8 extra meridians were described as lakes or seas in order to indicate their considerable influence on the normal functioning of the 12 regular meridians, which were represented as rivers or streams. Thus the 8 extra meridians are considered to play a very important role in the meridian system.

III. The Three Major Functions of the Eight Extra Meridians

1. Function of Governing

The Du Meridian enters the brain from the spinal column at the posterior aspect of the head and governs the Yang of the whole body. The Ren Meridian runs along the anterior midline, connects with the Du Meridian and is responsible for the Yin of the whole body. These two meridians govern the functions of all the Yin and Yang meridians of the body. The meridians and collaterals are anteriorly, posteriorly and laterally controlled to maintain the coordination of the vital activities, e.g. the functions of the Yinqiao and Yangqiao meridians in dominating Yin and Yang on either side of the body.

2. Function of Connecting

The Yangwei Meridian connects all the Yang meridians and the Yinwei Meridian connects with all the Yin meridians of the body. The two meridians are externally and internally associated to form a network in the meridian system. The Dai Meridian binds all the meridians together as well as communicates with the meridians and collaterals of the abdominal and lower back regions. The Chong Meridian flows up and down the body and is associated with the three Yin and three Yang meridians. Thus, all the meridians of the body are connected internally, externally, inferiorly to form an integrated network.

3. Function of Regulating

The ancient physicians conceived this function of the 8 extra meridians as "storing and supplying the qi and blood" of the regular meridians and represented them as lakes, seas or reservoirs. When the 12 regular meridians become deficient in qi and blood, the qi and blood of the extra meridians may be called upon to supply the shortage. On the other hand, when qi and blood are abundant in the 12 regular meridians, the excess may be stored in the 8 extra meridians. In this manner, the flow to the qi and blood is regulated and adapted to variations in physical conditions. Furthermore, the Yangqiao Meridian dominates motility and the Yinqiao Meridian dominates quietness. Under normal conditions, they regulate each other, controlling the changes of binding within the system, as it suits the varying requirements of how to balance rest and activating.

Section 7 OTHERS

I. The Fifteen Major Collaterals of the Meridians

These are the main collaterals of the 12 regular meridians, those of the Ren and Du meridians as well as the major collateral of the spleen, 15 in all. They communicate between the externally-internally related meridians of the four limbs, transmitting the circulation of qi and blood from one meridian to another, from a certain Yang meridian to its related Yin meridian, and vice versa.

The 15 major collaterals are named after the specific points from which they emerge.

Meridians	Point Names	Meridians	Point Names
Lung Meridian	Lieque (Lu.7)	Liver Meridian	Ligou (Liv.5)
Heart Meridian	Tongli (H.5)	Stomach Meridian	Fenglong (St.40)
Pericardium Meridian	Neiguan (p.6)	Urinary Bladder Meridian	Feiyang (U.B.58)
Large Intestine Meridian	Pianli (L.I.6)	Gall Bladder Meridian	Guangming (G.B.37)
Sanjiao Meridian	Waiguan (S.J.5)	Ren Meridian	Jiuwei (Ren 15)
Small Intestine Meridian	Zhizheng (S.I.7)	Du Meridian	Changqiang (Du 1)
Spleen Meridian	Gongsun (Sp.4)	Major collateral of the spleen	Daobao (Sp.21)
Kidney Meridian	Dazhong (k.4)		

II. The Inner Conduits of the Twelve Regular Meridians

Being extensions of the 12 regular meridians, the inner conduits also transport qi and blood, and are quite extensive in their distribution. They are known as the "secondary courses of the meridians."

The superficial divisions of the 12 regular meridians run from the four limbs to the chest or abdomen. The inner conduits then go from the superficial areas to the deeper parts of the body, to communicate with the internal zangfu organs according to their external-internal relationships. They merge at the vertex, the inner conduits of the Yang meridians rejoining their own meridians, and the inner conduits of the Yin meridians communicating with their related Yang meridians. The major function of the inner conduits of the 12 regular meridians is to establish communication with the internally and externally related zangfu organs. They do not have their own points or indications, the actions of the points lying along the accessible, superficial channels being manifested through them. For instance, the main course of the Urinary Bladder Meridian of Foot-Taiyang does not extend to the anus, but an inner branch does. Consequently, Chengshan (U.N.57) and Feiyang (U.B.58) can be applied to treat disorders associated with the anus.

III. The Tendinomuscular Structures of the Twelve Regular Meridians

The 12 regular meridians go between the muscles and tendons, the qi and blood of each meridian nourishing a specific area. The muscles and tendons are divided into 12 regions, corresponding to the distribution of the 12 regular meridians to which they are attached.

The distribution of the tendinomuscular structures of the 12 regular meridians is similar to that of the meridians themselves. They run from the end of the four limbs, upwards to the head region, along the surface of the body without meeting the inside zangfu organs. They are characterized by their actions of connecting, converging, associating and dispersing. They connect at the joints and the bony prominences, interlinking all the bones and muscles and maintaining normal movement.

IV. The Cutaneous Zones of the Twelve Regular Meridians

The skin is nourished by the qi and blood of the superficial collaterals of the meridians. The body surface is divided into 12 cutaneous zones, correspondingly reflecting the function and pathology of the 12 regular meridians.

		The 12 Regular Meridians	Collaterals
Hand	Three Yin:	The Lung Meridian of Hand-Taiyin,	Lieque (Lu.7)
		The Heart Meridian of Hand-Shaoyin,	Tongli (H.5)
		The Peridcardium Meridian of Hand-Jueyin	Neiguan (P.6)
	Three Yang:	The Large Intestine Meridian of Hand-Yangming,	Pianli (L.I.6)
		The Small Intestine Meridian of Hand-Taiyang,	Zhizheng (S.I.7)
		The Sanjiao Meridian of Hand-Shaoyang.	Waiguan (S.J.5)
Foot	Three Yin:	The Major Collateral of the Spleen	Dabao (Sp.21)
		The Spleen Meridian of Foot-Taiyin,	Gongsun (Sp.4)
		The Kidney Meridian of Foot-Shaoyin,	Dazhong (K.4)
		The Liver Meridian of Foot-Jueyin.	Ligou (Liv. 5)
	Three Yang:	The Stomach Meridian of Foot-Yangmiong,	Fenglong (St. 40)
		The Urinary Bladder Meridian of Foot-Taiyang,	Feiyang (U.B.58)
		The Gall Bladder Meridian of Foot-Shaoyang.	Guangming (G.B.37)

THE MERIDIAN SYSTEM
The Eight Extra Meridians

Du Meridian   Changqiang (Du 1)
Ren Meridian   Jiuwei (Ren 15)
Chong Meridian
Dai Meridian
Yinqiao Meridian
Yangqiao Meridian
Yinwei Meridian
Yangwei Meridian

The Inner Conduits of the Twelve Regular   The 15 Major
Meridians   Collaterals

The Tendinomuscular structures of the 12 Regular   Superficial Collaterals
Meridians   Tertiary Collaterals

The Cutaneous Zones of the 12 Regular Meridians

The above three are subdivided into three Yin and
three Yang of either hand or foot, corresponding to
the main related meridians.

Chapter II

GENERALIZATION OF THE POINTS

Section 1 **THE CONCEPT OF ACUPUNCTURE POINTS AND REGULAR POINTS**

I. The Concept of Acupuncture Points

Acupuncture points (腧穴), commonly known as points (穴位), are the stimulating spots from which both the qi and blood of zangfu organs infuse into the body surface, along the courses of the meridians. They are places over the body surface for acupuncture and moxibustion, being gradually discovered and accumulated by Chinese practitioners through centuries of struggle against various diseases.

The study of acupuncture points has now become an independent branch of learning, along with the development of acupuncture and moxibustion. Acupuncture point serves as a cover term including regular points, extra points as well as Ahshi points.

Regular points are virtually those from the 14 meridians. Extra points refer to those which have not been so far listed among those from the 14 meridians, yet widely used in practice. Ahshi points, i.e. where there is pain, there is a point, are basically those tender or reactive spots, being manifested by pressing over the affected parts of the body in a number of disorders or diseases.

Paradoxically, readers whose native tongue is not Chinese often fail to distinguish acupuncture points (腧穴) from either Shu-stream point (输穴) or Back-shu point (俞穴). Misunderstanding of such concepts will sometimes give rise to malpractice in the clinical setting.

Shu-stream point (输穴) comes 3rd among the Five-Shu points, i.e. Jing-well (井), Ying-spring (荥), Shu-stream (输), Jing-river (经) and He-sea (合).

Shu points (俞) refer to the Back-shu points on the back, being against the Front-mu points on the frontal aspect of the body.

Ahshi points are believed to be the earliest form of acupuncture points. In the prolonged medical practice, some of them got fixed locations and recognized names before they were accepted as extra points in history. The discovery of the meridians contributed greatly to the formation of regular points of the 14 meridians.

Over the last few decades, some new points were discovered. These newly-discovered points belong to extra points, e.g. Danlanxue (Extra), Lanweixue (Extra), etc.

Ahshi points are those tender or reactive spots at the moment when they are being pressed. Ironically, some of these tender spots may even appear on either regular or extra points. In this case, they are by no means Ahshi points. This is how the Ahshi points differ from the other types of points.

II. The Concept of Regular Points

The points of the 12 Regular Meridians, Du Meridian and Ren Meridian are referred to as "meridian points", or "points of the 14 meridians".

The points of the 14 meridians, the principal part of the Shuxue (acupuncture points), are the stimulating spots for acupuncture, being the places where both qi and blood are infused into the body surface, along the courses of the 14 meridians. The regular points are all located along the courses of the 14 meridians, and the points of the same meridian have some common actions in dealing with those diseases which affect the given meridian. Nevertheless, points of the same meridian may also reflect disorders of the particular zang or fu organ to which the meridian pertains. The development of regular points was first recorded in *Huangdi Neijing* (*Canon of Medicine*) which included some 160 points. Later, *Zhenjiu Jiayijing* (*A Classic of Acupuncture & Moxibustion*), *Mintang Kongxue* (*An Intensive Study of Acupuncture Points*) and *Qianjin Yifang* (*A Supplement to the Ducat Prescriptions*) thoroughly described acupuncture and moxibustion. The points, their locations, locating methods and needling techniques were dealt with in detail. A total number of 349 points was recorded. Then, in acupuncture classics as *Tongren Zhenjiu Shuxue Tu Jing* (*An Illustrated Classic of Acupuncture Points on the Bronze Model*) and *Shisi Jing Fahui* (*An Elucidation of the Fourteen Channels*), the total number of acupuncture points was increased to 354. The number of points in *Zhenjiu Dacheng* (*Compendium of Acupuncture & Moxibustion*) reached 359. The recognized number of regular points, i.e. 52 unilateral points and 309 bilateral ones was finally recorded in *Zhenjiu Fengyuan* (*Meeting the Source of Acupuncture & Moxibustion*) compiled by Li Xuechuan in the year of 1817. In terms of their names, the points number a total of 361. However, there are 670 points in all, when the bilateral ones are taken into consideration. 361 is the recognized number of regular points at the present time. But the number of points in the 14 meridians will further increase along with the continuous development of acupuncture and moxibustion in practice.

Major Works on Acupuncture in History & Their Record of Number of the Regular Points

Year (Century)	Author	Name of the Book	Number of Points		
			unilateral points	bilateral points	total
476-221 BC		*Huangdi Neijing*	about 25	about 135	160
256-260 AD	Huangfu Mi	*Zhenjiu Jiayi Jing*	49	300	349
682 AD	Sun Simiao	*Qianjin Yifang*			
1026 AD	Wang Weiyi	*Tongren Zhenjiu Shu-xue Tu Jing*	51	303	354
1341 AD	Hua Bairen	*Shisi Jing Fahui*			
1601 AD	Yang Jizhou	*Zhenjiu Dacheng*	51	308	359
1817 AD	Li Xuechuan	*Zhenjiu Fengyuan*	52	309	361

Section 2 THE NOMENCLATURE OF POINTS

The task of memorizing the names of several hundred points in a short period of time is formidable for beginners, especially for those who are unfamiliar with the language. However, a knowledge of how the names of the points were originally chosen may help both in comprehending their actions and memorizing their names. In general, points were named on the basis of the following aspects:

I. Nomenclature Based on TCM Anatomy and Its General Theories

A. Nomenclature According to Anatomical Terminologies of TCM:

Points in this category were named after the anatomical landmarks used to locate them.
Samples:

Hand-Wangu (S.I.4) (wrist bone), meaning pisiform bone, was thus named because the point is proximal to the pisiform bone.

Head-Wangu (G.B.12) (intact bone), referring to the mastoid process, is located on the mastoid process, posterior to the ear.

Qugu (Ren 12) (curved bone) is above the symphysis pubis, which was called "qugu" in ancient Chinese language.

Huiyin (Ren 1) (perineum) means the perineum, located between the anus and the external genitalia.

Daying (St.5) (great meeting) means mandible, because the point lies near this bone.

Jiache (St.6) (jaw vehicle) refers to the angle of the mandible, which was called "jiache" bone in ancient times.

Yuzhen (U.B.9) (jade pillow) refers to the occipital bone on which the point lies.

Quepen (St.12) (superclavicular fossa) is the old term for clavicular fossa in which the point is located.

In addition, the names of some of the points are associated with anatomical features of the places at which they are located. Samples:

Xinhui (Du 22) (fontanel) is located on the fontanel.

Rugen (St.18) (the root of the breast) is located at breast root.

Jianyu (L.I.15) means the lateroanterior part of the shoulder.

Jianliao (S.J.14) means the shoulder crevice, etc.

B. Nomenclature Based on the Physiological Functions and Pathological Changes Associated with the Points:

There are quite a few points which were named in this way, e.g.

Qimen (Liv.14) means the cyclic gate. The qi and blood of the human body start from Yunmen (Lu.2) of the Lung Meridian of Hand-Taiyin, flowing in turn through the large intestine, stomach, spleen, heart, small intestine, urinary bladder, kidney, pericardium, Sanjiao and gall bladder meridians, to Qimen (Liv.14) of the Liver Meridian of Foot-Jueyin, and back to the lung meridian again. Hence the name Qimen (Liv.14) (cyclic gate) refers to the endless circulation of qi and blood in the body. Again, the small intestine has the function to separate clean substances from turbid ones. One point from the Ren Meridian was named Shuifen (Ren 9) (to separate clean from turbid), being located directly below the lower orifice of the small intestine, 1 cun below Xiawan (Ren 10).

Points were also named according to pathological changes with which they were associated, e.g.

Fengmen (U.B.12) (wind gate) is a point through which exogenous pathogenic wind may invade into or be expelled from the body. Discomfort is often felt in this area in the early stage of common cold due to the invasion of exogenous pathogenic wind.

Fengfu (Du 16) (wind palace) and Fengchi (G.B.20) (wind pond) were so named for similar reasons. Other points thus named in this category include: Burong (St. 19) (container's limit), Chengman (St.20) (full receiving), Liangmen (St.21) (gate of Liang), Guanmen (St.22) (closed door) and Shimen (stone gate) (Ren 15).

C. Nomenclature Based on Special Indications of Points

Shenmen (H.7) (spirit gate) and Hunmen (U.B.47) (soul gate) were so named because of their indication in mental disorders.

Shuidao (St.28) (water passage) was so named because the point is indicated in the disorder due to retention of water.

Jingming (U.B.1) (eye brightness), Guangming (G.B.37) (bright light), Chengguang (U.B.6) (taking light) and Sibai (St.2) (all brightening) were so named because they are all indicated for eye disorders.

Yingxiang (L.I.20) (welcome fragrance) and Tongtian (U.B.7) (connecting heavens) were so named because they are indicated for nasal disorders.

Tinggong (S.I.19) (hearing palace), Tinghui (G.B.2) (hearing confluence) and Ermen (S.J.21) (ear gate) were so named because they can be applied to deal with ear problems.

Fengchi (G.B.20) (wind pond) and Fengfu (Du 16) (wind palace) are for wind problems, etc.

D. Nomenclature Based on Yin-Yang Properties

Points in this category were named according to the classification of Yin and Yang, because "interior is Yin whilst exterior is Yang, anterior is Yin whilst posterior is Yang, and foot is Yin whilst hand is Yang," e.g.

Yangchi (S.J.4), Yangxi (L.I.5), Yanggu (S.I.5), Yaoyangguan (Du 3), Yanglingquan (G.B.34), Zhiyin (U.B.67), Yinxi (H.6), Yingu (K.10), Abdominal-Yinjiao (Ren 7), Yinlingquan (Sp.9), Yinbao (Liv.9), Yindu (K.19), etc.

E. Nomenclature Based on Theories of Zangfu and Meridians

The Back-shu Points, for instance, were named on the basis of the fact that they are the sites at which qi of the zangfu organs is infused into the back, e.g.

Shufu (K.27) (point residence) was so named because it is the place where qi of the Kidney Meridian of Foot-Shaoyin, which rises from the sole of the foot, reaches its apex to merge into the chest.

Names such as Sanyinjiao (Sp.6) (crossroad of three Yin) and Baihui (Du 20) (hundred meetings) were based on the crossing of meridians at these points. Some names were given on the basis of the relationship between the five zang organs and the five emotional activities, in terms of zangfu theory. For example, Shenting (U.B.44) (soul house), Pohu (U.B.42) (spiritual house), Zhishi (U.B.52) (will residence) and Yishe (U.B.49) (emotion's residence). Other points were named with regard to their influence on qi and blood, such as Qihu (St.13), Qixue (K.13), Qihai (Ren 6), Qishe (St.11) and Xuehai (Sp.10), etc.

II. Nomenclature Based on the View of "Harmony Between Men and Nature (Heaven, Earth, Sun and Moon)"

People in the ancient times associated the circulation of qi and blood with natural phenomena, such as the flow of water in rivers; the movements of the sun and moon, etc. Points were named according to analogy, pictograph, association and realistic description, etc.

A. Nomenclature Based on Analogy

Concepts borrowed from astronomy, geography, water flow and topography were widely applied in the nomenclature of the 361 bilateral points. The flow of qi in the meridians is like that of water, so some points were named in accordance with this image. Hence, the appearance in the names of points of such words as: "quan" (spring), "chi" (pond), "ze" (marsh) or "hai" (sea), e.g. Shuiquan (K.5) (water spring), Yangchi (S.J.4) (Yang pond), Chize (Lu.5) (one-foot marsh) and Xiaohai (S.I.8) (little sea), etc.

The names of some points are related to anatomical topography, e.g. "shan" (mountain), "qiu" (hills) or "ling" (mound) because these points are located on the processes. Chengshan (U.B.57) (supporting hill), Qiuxu (G.B.40) (hillock), Shangqiu (Sp.5) (metal hill), Yanglingquan (G.B.34) (Outer Mound Spring), etc. Deep depressions formed by bony clefts or muscles were analogized as deep wells (jing) or shallow ponds (chi). So, the terms valley (gu), stream (xi), ditch (gou) and river (du) were also used in the nomenclature of points, e.g. Quchi (L.I.11) (curved pond), Yangchi (S.J.5) (Yang pond), Tianjing (S.J.10) (celestial well), Hegu (L.I.4) (converging valley) Taixi (K.3) (big stream), Houxi (S.I.3) (back stream), Zhigou (S.J.6) (limb ditch), Sidu (S.J.9) (four rivers), etc.

On the basis of the theory that points at the places where the qi of the meridians has converged near the body surface, terms such as dwelling places (fu), house (she), storehouse (ku) and gate (men) were used to describe the merging or emerging of qi, e.g. Zhongfu (Lu. 1) (central palace), Qihu (St.13) (qi residence), Kufang (St.14) (store house), Yumen (Lu.2) (door of cloud) and Shenmen (H.7) (spirit gate). Passage (dao) and unit of distance (li) were used in naming some points describing the places through which qi passes, e.g. Hand-Wuli (L.I.13), (five units from the lateral epicondyle of the humerus), Zusanli (St.36) (three li of foot) and Shendao (Du 11) (spirit passage). Room (shi), palace (gong) and hall (ting or tang) all describe the places where qi is stored, e.g. Qishe (St.11), Zhishi (U.B.52), Yutang (Ren 18), Tinggong (S.J.19) and Neiting (St. 44). Terms in astronomy and meteorology were also used, e.g. Riyue (G.B.24) (sun and moon), Shangxing (Du 23) (super star), etc.

B. Nomenclature Based on Pictography

Names of animals or utensils were borrowed to name points, according to outer features of sites at which points are located, e.g. Jiuwei (Ren 15) (turtledove tail), Yuji (Lu.10) (fish belly, or thenar eminence), Dubi (St.35) (ox nose), Femur-Futu (St.32) (hidden rabbit), Heding (Ex. LE7) (crane head), etc.

C. Nomenclature Based on Associations

Another method was to name points according to the physiological functions of parts of the body near which they were located, e.g. Tinggong (S.I.19) (hearing palace), Tinghui (G.B.2) (hearing confluence), Laogong (P.8) (labouring palace), Chengjiang (Ren 24) (receiving saliva) and Guanyuan (Ren 4) (closed head), etc.

D. Nomenclature Based on Realistic Descriptions

The names of some points were based on their locations as well as their indications, e.g. Xuehai (Sp.10), meaning the sea of blood, likens the behavior of blood to that of water merging into a sea. This point has the effect to activate blood circulation by resolving stasis of blood and guiding in orderly circulation. It is indicated in irregular menstruation, amenorrhea and uterine bleeding. Yamen (Du 15), meaning the key gate for mutes, is indicated for aphasia with tongue rigidity, and is a key point in the treatment of the mute.

For a detailed explanation of each of the points mentioned above, please refer to Part II of this book.

Tracing the methods used in the nomenclature of acupuncture points, it becomes clear that all points were named for some specific reason at least. Sun Simiao, a noted physician of the Tang Dynasty, pointed out in his book *A Supplement to Prescriptions Worth a Thousand in Gold* that "No point was named without any reason." No single method was adequate to provide names for the entire 361 points, so sometimes several approaches were combined. Yinlingquan (Sp.9) serves as a good example. This point is on the medial side of the knee which is a Yin side, the patella is like a mound (ling), and the point is from the Spleen Meridian of Foot-Taiyin. Further the spleen is the Yin part of Yin and the point is a water point which is located in a depression, hence the name Yinlingquan (Sp.9). Similar associations were used for naming other points, such as Yanglingquan (G.B.34), Ququan (Liv.8) and Fuai (Sp.16), etc.

Section 3 METHODS FOR LOCATING POINTS

Each point has its own location. Precise location of a given point will significantly affect the therapeutic result. The four commonly used methods for locating points are as follows:

I. Proportional Measurement

In order to locate points which are situated in places where there are abundant muscles without palpable landmarks, a special system of measurement has been developed. Prominent anatomical landmarks are used as references for the location of standardized body segments. "Cun", the unit of measurement used, varies from person to person, and from one part of the body to another in individuals. It is established for a particular body segment, by the length\of each part being experienced as 1 "cun". Such a system of measurement can be applied to all individuals regardless of sex, age, or body shape (Fig. I-3).

Longitudinal Measurement of the Head: The distance between anterior hairline and posterior hairline is 12 cun. The distance between the posterior hairline and Dazhui (Du 14) is 3 cun. The distance between the anterior hairline and glabella is 3 cun.

Transverse Measurement of the Head: The distance between the two mastoid processes is 9 cun.

Longitudinal Measurement of the Chest and Abdomen: Proportional measurement on the chest is based on either the ribs or the intercostal spaces. The distance between the centre of the umbilicus and the sternocostal angle is 8 cun. The distance between the centre of the umbilicus and the upper border of the symphysis pubis is 5 cun.

Transverse Measurement of the Chest and Abdomen: The distance between the two nipples is 8 cun. However, the midclavicular lines are referred to in women.

Longitudinal Measurement on the Back: This is determined on the basis of the locations of the spinous processes of the vertebral column.

Transverse Measurement on the Back: The distance between the medial border of the scapula and the posterior midline is 3 cun.

Longitudinal Measurement on the Upper Extremities: The distance between the end of the anterior axillary fold and the transverse cubital crease is 9 cun. The distance between the transverse cubital crease and the transverse carpal crease is 12 cun.

Longitudinal Measurement of the Lower Extremities: On the lateral side, the distance between the prominence of the greater trochanter and the middle of the patella is 19 cun. The distance between the middle of the patella and the tip of the lateral malleolus is 16 cun. The distance between the tip of the lateral malleolus and the bottom of the foot is 13 cun. On the medial side, the distance between the upper border of the symphysis pubis and the medial epicondyle of the femur is 18 cun. The distance between the lower border of the medial condyle of the tibia and the tip of the medial malleolus is 13 cun (Fig. I-4).

II. According to Anatomical Landmarks

The skeleton, muscles and limbs of the human body form some special prominences and depressions on the exterior. The distribution of the points in meridians is closely related to these landmarks, which can be employed as an aid to point location.

A. Fixed Landmarks

There are some fixed landmarks which can be directly referred to when locating

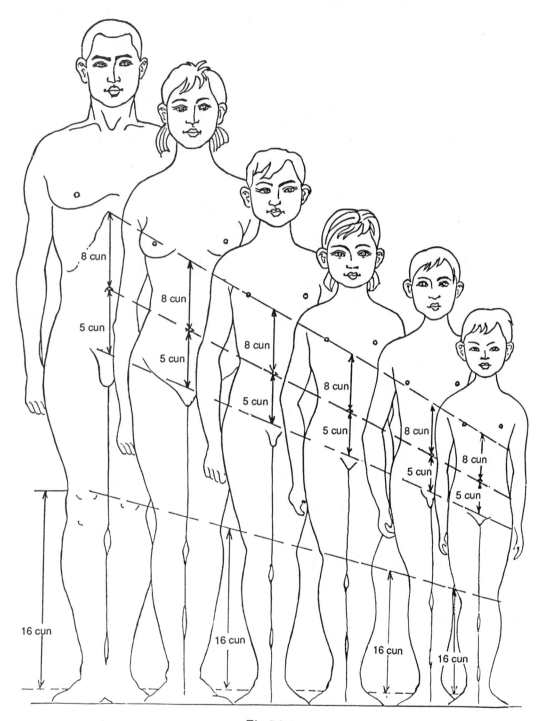

Fig. I-3

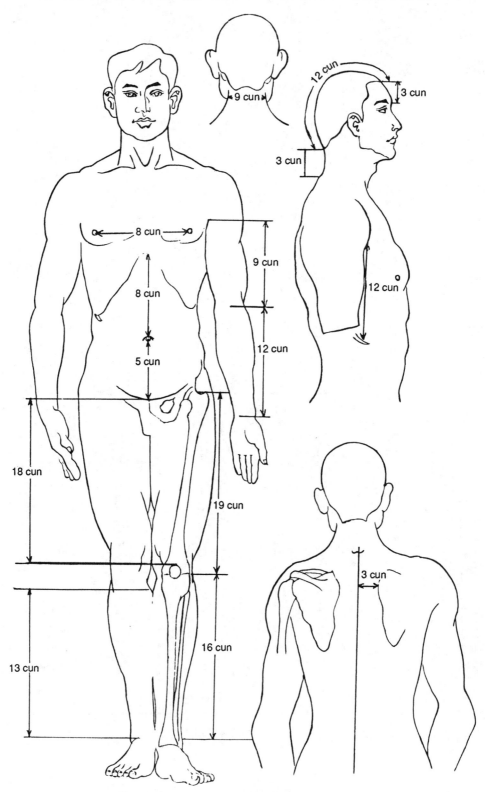

Fig. I-4

points. Zanzhu (U.B.2), for example, is located at the medial end of the eyebrow. Sizhukong (S.J.23) is at the lateral end of the eyebrow. Shuigou (Du 26, or Renzhong) is in the philtrum. Yangxi (L.I.5) is in the depression between the tendons of the m. extensor pollicis longus and the brevis. Qiuxu (G.B.40) is in the depression anterior and inferior to the external malleolus, etc.

B. Motional Landmarks

Motional landmarks suitable for point location are those landmarks which only appear when a specific body posture is adopted. For example, two depressions are apparent on the shoulder when the arm is in full abduction. The anterior depression is Jianyu (L.I.15) while the posterior one is Jianliao (S.J.14). Below the zygomatic arch, there is a prominence when the mouth is opened, but a depression appears when the mouth is closed. This is the location for Xiaguan (St.7).

C. Equivalent Landmarks

Such landmarks occur bilaterally and are used in locating points which lie between them. For example, Dazhui (Du 14) is at the midpoint of the line between the two acromions. Shenzhu (Du 12) is the midpoint of the line between the tops of the two scapular spines. Zhiyang (Du 9) is the midpoint of the line between the lower borders of the arch of ribs. Yaoyangguan (Du 13) is at the midpoint of the line between the upper border of both posterior iliac spines. And Shangzhong (Ren 17) is at the midpoint between the two nipples.

III. Finger Measurement

The length and breadth of certain part(s) of a patient's fingers are taken as a criterion for locating points. When trying to use finger measurement, doctors should also refer to the height and age of the patient. Generally, three methods are often applied in terms of the finger measurement.

A. Middle Finger Measurement

The distance between the two ends of the creases of the interphalangeal joints of the middle finger is taken as 1 cun (Fig. I-5). *Compendium of Acupuncture* (*Zhenjiu Dacheng*) states, "Put the tips of the thumb and middle finger together to form a ring shape, and the distance between the two ends of the creases of the interphalangeal joints of the middle finger is actually 1 cun." Middle finger measurement is apt to the transverse measurement for locating points on the back.

B. Thumb Measurement

The breadth of the thumb is considered as 1 cun, equal to that of the proportional measurement. This method is often used for locating points that are close to each other (Fig. I-6).

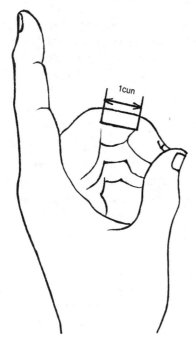

Fig. I-6

Fig. I-5

C. Four-finger Measurement

The breadth formed by the four (index, middle, ring and little) fingers is considered as 3 cun (Fig. I-7). Such a method is also known as one-fu method (一扶法). The book *Liji* states, " 'One-fu' refers to putting four fingers together excluding the thumb". In the old Chinese language, "fu" (扶) was equal to "fu" (夫) in usage. Therefore, one-fu method at the present time is often written as " 一夫法 " rather than " 一扶法 ". This method is commonly used for the vertical measurement for locating points on the abdominal region as well as the transverse measurement for locating points on the back.

The proportional divisions on the lower part of the body are comparatively longer than those of the upper part of the body. To some extent, the application of finger measurement is also relative. For example, the breadth formed by index and middle fingers is considered as 2 cun, if applied for location

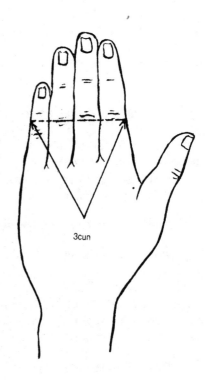

Fig. I-7

of points of the upper part of the body; but 1.5 cun only, if applied for the location of points on the lower part of the body. The breadth formed by the index, middle and ring fingers is considered as 3 cun for the vertical measurement on the upper part of the body. For the vertical measurement in the lower part of the body, the 3 cun length exactly refers to the four-finger measurement.

Finger measurement is relatively often applied in the clinic because people have different height, body shape, age, etc. Practically, it should by no means be against the proportional measurement. That is to say that the finger measurement is used in accordance with the proportional measurement.

IV. Simple Measurement

Simple measurement here indicates those methods commonly used in practice for point location, as in the following examples:

A. To locate Tianfu (Lu.3), raise the arm so that the tip of the nose touches the upper arm;

B. To locate Lieque (Lu.7), interlock the thumbs and index fingers of both hands, with the index finger of one hand touching the styloid process of the other;

C. To locate Laogong (P.8) between the 2nd and 3rd metacarpal bones, make a loose fist with the tip of the middle finger touching the 1st transverse crease in the centre of the palm;

D. To locate Fengshi (G.B.31), lower both hands so that the tip of the middle finger touches the lateral aspect of the thigh;

E. To locate Jianjing (G.B.21), put the operator's hand on the shoulder of the patient, with the first transverse crease of the wrist coinciding with the lower border of the scapular spine, the thumb touching the lower border of C. 7 and the rest of the four fingers on the shoulder, with the middle finger slightly flexed. The spot where the tip of the middle finger touches is the point;

F. To locate Zhangmen (Liv.13), lower the upper arm with the elbow flexed in vertical angle; the spot where the end of the elbow touches is the point; and

G. To locate Baihui (Du 20), fold the ears forward and take a vertical line from their tips to the top of the head.

Section 4 THE CONCEPT AND SIGNIFICANCE OF SPECIFIC POINTS

The specific points are those which have special curative properties affecting the whole body. TCM practitioners in history all paid great attention to the application of these points. Specific points do not exist in isolation, but within the 12 regular meridians or the eight extra meridians. They are grouped under certain names according to their different indications. Each of them is distinguished by its own special therapeutic properties.

I. The Five Shu Points

The Five Shu Points are located along the 12 regular meridians, between the elbow and the tips of the fingers, or the knee and the tips of the toes. They are respectively called Jing-well, Ying-spring, Shu-stream, Jing-river and He-sea points. These names liken the flow of qi along the meridians to the movement of water, from weak to strong, and from well to sea. This is intended to explain that the flow of qi in the meridians plays varied roles at different places along its course. The names and concepts of the Five Shu Points are described as follows:

The Jing-well points (井) are where the qi emerges as if the water starts to bubble. These points are also known as the root points of the 12 regular meridians, because they are located on the sides of nails or the tips of fingers and toes. For example, Shaoshang (Lu. 11) and Shangyang (L.I.1), which are indicated in fullness sensation in the chest.

The Ying-spring points (荥) are where the qi of the meridians starts to flow, as if water has just started to trickle from a spring. The flow of qi is slightly stronger than at the Jing-well points. The Ying-spring points are located between metacarpal (metatarsal) bones, e.g. Yuji (Lu.10) and Erjian (L.I.2), which are indicated in febrile diseases.

The Shu-stream points (输) are where the qi of the meridian flourishes, like the water of a stream irrigating fields. They are located in the areas proximal to the wrist and ankle joints, e.g. Taiyuan (Lu.9) and Taixi (K.3), which are indicated in painful joints and heaviness of the body.

The Jing-river points (经) are where the qi of the meridian increases in abundance, like the water of a river on which boats can travel. They are located at areas proximal and distal to the wrists and ankles or above the wrist joints. For example, Jingqu (Lu.8) and Yangxi (L.I.5) which are indicated in cough, shortness of breath and common cold, with or without fever.

The He-sea points (合) are where the qi of the meridian flourishes like the water merging into the sea. Hence, the qi of the meridian is at its strongest and deepest status. They are located mostly near the elbow and knee joints. For example, Chize (Lu.5) and Quchi (L.I.11), which can be used to treat asthma caused by derangement of qi.

Clinically, Jing-well points are used for coma, syncope and shock; Ying-spring points for febrile diseases; Shu-stream points for painful joints; Jing-river points for sore throat and He-sea points for gastrointestinal disorders.

The Five Shu Points of the 12 Regular Meridians

Point Names	Jing-well (wood)	Ying-spring (fire)	Shu-stream (earth)	Jing-river (metal)	He-sea (water)
Meridians					
The Lung meridian	Shaoshang (L.11)	Yuji (Lu.10)	Taiyuan (Lu.9)	Jingqu (Lu.8)	Chize (Lu.5)
The Large Intestine Meridian	Shangyang (L.I.1)	Erjian (L.I.2)	Sanjian (L.I.3)	Yangxi (L.I.5)	Quchi (L.I.11)
The Stomach Meridian	Lidui (St.45)	Neiting (St.44)	Xiangu (St.43)	Jiexi (St.41)	Zusanli (St.36)
The Spleen Meridian	Yinbai (Sp.1)	Dadu (Sp.2)	Taibai (Sp.3)	Shangqiu (Sp.5)	Yinlingquan (Sp.9)

The Heart Meridian	Shaochong (H.9)	Shaofu (H.8)	Shenmen (H.7)	Lingdao (H.4)	Shaohai (H.3)
The Small Intestine Meridian	Shaoze (S.I.1)	Qiangu (S.I.2)	Houxi (S.I.3)	Yanggu (S.I.5)	Xiaohai (S.I.8)
The Urinary Bladder Meridian	Zhiyin (U.B.67)	Foot-Tonggu (U.B.66)	Shugu (U.B.65)	Kunlun (U.B.60)	Weizhong (U.B.40)
The Kidney Meridian	Yongquan (K.1)	Rangu (K.2)	Taixi (K.3)	Fuliu (K.7)	Yingu (K.10)
The Pericardium Meridian	Zhongchong (P.9)	Laogong (P.8)	Daling (P.7)	Jianshi (P.5)	Quze (p.3)
The Sanjiao Meridian	Guanchong (S.J.1)	Yemen (S.J.2)	Hand-Zhongzhu (S.J.3)	Zhigou (S.J.6)	Tianjing (S.J.10)
The Gall Bladder Meridian	Foot-Qiaoyin (G.B.44)	Xiaxi (G.B.43)	Foot-Linqi (G.B.41)	Yangfu (G.B.38)	Yanglingquan (G.B.34)
The Liver Meridian	Dadun (Liv.1)	Xingjian (Liv.2)	Taichong (Liv.3)	Zhongfeng (Liv.4)	Ququan (Liv.8)

II. The Twelve Yuan (Source) Points

Each of the 12 regular meridians has a Yuan (Source) point near the wrist or ankle joints of the four extremities through which the vital energy of the zangfu organs passes and to some extent accumulates. "Yuan" (源) means origin, and refers to the source of vital energy through which the pathological changes of zangfu organs are manifested. The chapter on the Nine Needles and the Twelve Sources of the book *Lingshu* states, "The twelve Yuan (source) points are indicated in disorders of the internal organs." The vital energy of the twelve regular meridians is closely associated with the Sanjiao which generalizes the functional activities of the stomach, spleen and kidney and is the manifestation of the function of vital energy. Vital energy, originating from the congenital qi of the kidneys, is transported all over the body. It goes to the exterior, interior, superior and inferior parts of the body, following the courses of the meridians and maintaining vital functions of the human body. This process is maintained by the Sanjiao. Clinically, Yuan (source) points are of great significance in treating diseases of the internal organs. Puncturing the Yuan (source) points stimulates the vital energy of the regular meridians, regulates the functional activities of the internal organs, reinforces antipathogenic factors and eliminates pathogenic factors. This method of treating diseases deals principally with the root causes. The Yuan (source) point from the affected meridian is often combined with the Luo (connecting) point of the internally-externally related meridians in use. This is known as the combination of the main point (Yuan) and the accompanying point (Luo), or simply the combination of the Yuan (source) point and the Luo (connecting) point. Functionally, the Lung Meridian of Hand-Taiyin and the Large Intestine Meridian of Hand-Yangming are internally-externally related. The Yuan (source) point from the primarily affected meridian is combined with the Luo (connecting) point of its externally-internally related meridian. For example, if the Lung Meridian of Hand-Taiyin (interior) becomes diseased, sore throat, cough and asthma will occur. Taiyuan (Lu.9) is chosen as the main point and Pianli (L.I.6) is chosen as the accompanying one in the prescription. If the Large Intestine Meridian of Hand-Yangming (exterior) becomes diseased, e.g. toothache, Hegu (L.I.4), the Yuan (source) point of the Large Intestine Meridian of Hand-Yangming, and Lieque (Lu.7), the Luo (connecting) point of the Lung Meridian of Hand-Taiyin are prescribed.

Clinically, research has shown that pathological changes of the zangfu organs are often manifested at the twelve Yuan (source) points. For example, tenderness at a Yuan (source) point often indicates pathological changes of the associated meridian and the internally related organ.

In researching the meridian over the last few decades, Yuan (source) points were used as the key points to detect changes of cutaneous electrical resistance and to examine the condition of qi and blood of the twelve regular meridians. It was discovered that a significantly accurate estimation of the nature of many zangfu disorders could be made by using these methods.

The 12 Yuan (source) points are within the category of the Five Shu Points. Each Yang meridian has its own Yuan (source) point which is located between the Shu-stream point and the Jing-well point. The 6 Yin meridians do not have separate Yuan (source) points, their Shu-stream points being concurrently the Yuan (source) points, i.e. the Yuan (source) points and Shu-stream points of Yin meridians are actually the same.

The Twelve Yuan (Source) Points

Yuan (source) Points	Meridians
Taiyuan (Lu.9)	The Lung Meridian of Hand-Taiyin
Hegu (L.I.4)	The Large Intestine Meridian of Hand-Yangming
Guanchong (St. 42)	The Stomach Meridian of Foot-Yangming
Taibai (Sp.3)	The Spleen Meridian of Foot-Taiyin
Shenmen (H.7)	The Heart Meridian of Hand-Shaoyin
Hand-Wangu (S.I.4)	The Small Intestine Meridian of Hand-Taiyang
Jinggu (U.B.64)	The Urinary Bladder Meridian of Foot-Taiyang
Taixi (K.3)	The Kidney Meridian of Foot-Shaoyang
Daling (P.7)	The Pericardium Meridian of Hand-Jueyin
Yangchi (S.J.4)	The Sanjiao Meridian of Hand-Shaoyang
Qiuxu (G.B.40)	The Gall Bladder Meridian of Foot-Shaoyang
Taichong (Liv.3)	The Liver Meridian of Foot-Jueyin

III. The Fifteen Luo (Connecting) Points

"Luoxue" (络穴), meaning to connect, is a point where a collateral starts to connect a definite pair of Yin and Yang meridians which are externally-internally related. The 12 regular meridians, externally-internally related in pairs, are linked together by the Luo (connecting) points in order. This establishes a continuous system for the circulation of qi and blood through the 12 regular meridians, as to warm and nourish the entire body. Each of the 12 regular meridians has a Luo (connecting) Point as well as Jiuwei (Ren 15), the Luo (connecting) point of the Ren Meridian (connecting with the abdomen), Changqiang (Du 1), the Luo (connecting) point of the Du Meridian (connecting with the head), and Dabao (Sp.21), the Luo (connecting) point of the major collateral of the spleen (connecting with the hypochondriac region), a total of 15. The Spleen Meridian of Foot-Taiyin has another Luo (connecting) point Dabao (Sp.21) in addition to its original one, Gongsun (Sp.4). This is because the four extremities all acquire vital energy from the stomach. As this can not be obtained directly, the help of the spleen is required. The spleen helps the stomach to transport fluids to the five zang organs and the four extremities through its major collateral which governs both Yin and Yang collaterals of the body. Each of the 15 collaterals has its own course and distribution. Each of them has its own pathological manifestations. Consequently, the Luo (connecting) points are as important as the other specific points.

The Luo (connecting) points are all located below the elbow or knee, where the collaterals of the Yin meridians connect with their respective Yang meridians, and the collaterals of the Yang Meridians connect with their respective Yin meridians. Thus, the respective Yin and Yang meridians are internally-externally related by Luo (connecting) points. The fifteen collaterals are the major ones of the fourteen meridians, with the addition of the small collaterals, superficial ones and the tertiary ones which are divided from, governed by and dominated by the major ones. The Luo (connecting) points are locations at which the qi of the twelve regular meridians converges. Jiuwei (Ren 15), the Luo (connecting) point of the Ren Meridian, dominates the collaterals of the Yin merdians; Changqiang (Du 1), the Luo (connecting) point of Du Meridian, governs the collaterals of Yang Meridians; and Dabao (Sp.21), the Luo (connecting) point of the major collateral of the spleen, governs both the collaterals and blood vessels of the whole body. The concept of the spleen's function in keeping the blood circulation inside the vessels and preventing it from extravasation was based on the above understanding.

All of the fifteen collaterals are the passages through which qi and blood are transported into the zangfu organs and tissues of the body. An injury of the collaterals will inhibit the circulation of qi and blood, giving rise to stagnation of qi and coagulation of blood.

Clinically, Luo (connecting) points are often combined with Yuan (source) points in the treatment of diseases. Observations of the collaterals can sometimes be used as a diagnostic aid. For example, observation of the thenar collateral for diagnostic purposes. The chapter on meridians in the book *Lingshu* says, "The fifteen collaterals are sometimes visable in patients suffering from Shi conditions; but are not apparent in those patients affected by Xu syndromes. Such differences vary from person to person, due to particularity of the collaterals and varying degrees of experience among observers." "When collaterals are observed, the colour blue suggests cold and pain, while red suggests heat in the body. For example, over-riding blue at the thenar collateral implies cold in the stomach; over-riding red means heat in the stomach; complete blackness implies prolonged stagnation; a mixture of red, blue and green means invasion of pathogenic cold and heat; and light green denotes qi deficiency." "Pricking at particular collaterals to cause some bleeding once every other day can regulate Xu and Shi conditions in certain diseases."

The application of Luo (connecting) points in general is summarized in the table "Distribution and Indications of the Fifteen Luo (connecting) Points". For example, Waiguan (S.J.5) is used with reducing method for acute elbow pain and an excessive condition of the collaterals of the Shaoyang meridians; Tongli (H.5) is applied with reinforcing method for difficult speech and aphonia due to weakness of qi, or a deficient condition of the collaterals of the Shaoyin meridians. Luo (connecting) points are often applied in the treatment of various chronic diseases involving the internal impairment or accumulation of pathological substances such as stagnant qi, coagulation of blood, phlegm, damp, etc. Pathogenic qi may reach a collateral through a meridian, because "meridians are involved at the onset of diseases whilst collaterals are involved in the chronic cases."

Distribution & Indications of the Fifteen Luo (Connecting) Points

Luo (Connecting) Points	Locations	Connected Meridians	Indications	
			Excess	Deficiency
Lieque (Lu.7)	0.5 cun above wrist joint	large intestine meridian	feverish palm and wrist	shortness of breath frequent urination
Tongli (H.5)	0.5 cun above wrist joint	small intestine meridian	fullness in the chest	difficult speech
Neiguan (P.6)	2 cun above wrist joint	Sanjiao meridian	cardiac pain	restlessness
Zhizheng (S.I.7)	5 cun above wrist joint	heart meridian	motor impairment	warts
Pianli (L.I.6)	3 cun above wrist joint	lung meridian	toothache, deafness	cold in teeth, chest fullness
Waiguan (S.J.6)	2 cun above wrist joint	pericardium meridian	spasm of elbow	motor impairment of the elbow
Feiyang (U.B.58)	7 cun above ankle joint	kidney meridian	nasal obstruction, pain in back and head	epistaxis
Guanming (G.B.37)	5 cun above ankle joint	liver meridian	syncope	Wei syndrome
Fenglong (St.40)	8 cun above ankle joint	spleen meridian	sore throat, aphonia, mania	foot drop
Gongsun (Sp.4)	1 cun posterior to medial malleolus	stomach meridian	sudden abdominal pain, diarrhea	edema
Dazhong (K.4)	near the heel	urinary bladder meridian	restlessness, dysuria	lumbar pain
Ligou (Liv.5)	5 cun above ankle joint	Gall bladder meridian	prolapse of uterus, hernia	itching genitalia
Jiuwei (Ren 15)	7 cun above umbilicus	connecting with abdomen	abdominal pain	itching in abdominal region
Changqiang (Du 1)	between anus and coccyx	connecting with head	spinal rigidity	dizziness, heavy head
Dabao (Sp.21)	6 cun below axilla	connecting with hypochondrium	general pain	general weakness

IV. The Back-shu and Front-mu Points

The Back-shu (shu) are the points on the back where qi of the respective zangfu organs is infused. They are located on either side of the vertebral column, in close proximity to the spinal ganglia and their respective zangfu organs, hence the name Back-shu points. Each of the zangfu organs has a Back-shu point, as does the Sanjiao, a total of twelve.

Front-mu Points (Mu) are the points on the chest and abdomen where qi of the respective zangfu organs is infused. They are located on the chest and abdomen in close proximity to their respectively related zangfu organs, hence the name Front-mu points. Each of the zangfu organs and the Sanjiao has the Front-mu point, twelve in all.

In the application of the Back-shu and Front-mu points, consideration is given to their respective Yang and Yin characteristics. Front-mu points are located on the ventral Yin aspect of the body while the Back-shu points are on the dorsal Yang aspect. The qi of the Back-shu and Front-mu points communicates directly with their related zangfu organs. Clearly, the Back-shu and Front-mu points constitute an important group of specific points. A feature in the distribution of these points is that the level of the Front-mu points on the abdomen corresponds to that of the Back-shu points on the back, both Front-mu and Back-shu points being located at almost the same level as their respectively related zangfu organs. As well as being the points at which the qi of the respective zangfu organs is infused, they are also the places where the pathogenic factors can lodge, causing diseases of either the zangfu organs or of the body surface. In the light of the above, it can be seen that the Front-mu and Back-shu points are of great significance in the physiology, pathology, diagnosis and treatment of diseases.

The Back-shu points are located on the first line of the Urinary Bladder Meridian of Foot-Taiyang on the back, 1.5 cun lateral to the Du Meridian. They are the places through which the qi of the Du Meridian communicates with the urinary bladder meridian and then infuses into the specific internal organs. Points on the first and second lines of the Urinary Bladder Meridian of Foot-Taiyang have similar indications to those points of the Du Meridian and Huatuo Jiaji points located at the same level. This demonstrates a close relationship between the Back-shu points and the spinal ganglia. Further, as regards location, the more superior an internal organ is, the higher the corresponding Back-shu point will be; and vice versa. For example, the lung is the most superior organ among the zangfu; consequently, its related point, Feishu (U.B.13), is the highest among the Back-shu points. The urinary bladder is the most inferior organ, its related point Pangguangshu (U.B.28) is also the lowest among the Back-shu points.

The Front-mu points are also in close proximity to their corresponding internal organs. For example, the Front-mu point of the lung Zhongfu (Lu.1) is the highest whilst Zhongji (Ren 3), the Front-mu point of the urinary bladder, is the lowest. Front-mu and Back-shu points are not necessarily points from their corresponding meridians. Their special influence is due to their close proximity to their corresponding internal organs, rather than their location on specific meridians. Among the Front-mu points, only three are situated on their corresponding meridians, namely Zhongfu (Lu.1), Riyue (G.B.24) and Qimen (Liv.14). None of the Back-shu points is from its corresponding meridian except Pangguangshu (U.B.28), the Back-shu point of the urinary bladder. Therefore, the distribution of the Back-shu and Front-mu points is another unique characteristic.

Back-shu and Front-mu points are not only important in the treatment of the diseases of the internal organs, but are also of clinical significance in the diagnosis of zangfu disorders. When any of the zangfu organs malfunctions, positive reactions such as sensitivity or tenderness will be manifested at the corresponding Back-shu or Front-mu points. Palpation of the sensitive points can be a useful aid to diagnosis. Stimulating techniques such as acupuncture, moxibustion or massage may be applied to these points to relieve disorders of their corresponding organs. For instance, injection of streptomycin in a small dosage at Feishu (U.B.13) or Zhongfu (Lu.1), the Back-shu and Front-mu points of the lung, may help patients suffering from active tuberculosis to build up resistance against the diseases. Puncturing Dachangshu (U.B.25) and Tianshu (St.25), the Back-shu and Front-mu points of the large intestine, may help alleviate the symptoms and signs of acute bacillary dysentery, repeated treatments resulting in a negative stool culture. Puncturing or applying moxa to the corresponding Front-mu points is especially effective in dealing with lingering disorders of the internal organs.

Disorders of both Yin meridians and the five zang organs are sometimes manifested at the Back-shu points on the Yang aspect of the body, and disorders of the Yang meridians and the six fu organs are sometimes manifested at the Front-mu points on the Yin aspect of the body. When Yang is diseased, Yin is also involved, and vice versa. So Back-shu points are often prescribed for disorders of the zang organs, while the Front-mu points are often prescribed for disorders of the fu organs in the clinic. Such an application of Back-shu and Front-mu points is also known as "expelling Yin disorders from Yang meridians, and expelling Yang disorders from Yin meridians".

The chapter Genjiepian of the book *Lingshu* states, "The key to applying acupuncture therapy is to master the method of regulating Yin and Yang." Puncturing the corresponding Back-shu and Front-mu points simply regulates the balance between Yin and Yang, so as to either force the pathogenic factors out of the body or treat internal disorders of the zangfu organs. For example, the Lung Meridian of Hand-Taiyin is a Yin meridian. When it is affected, Feishu (U.B.13) can be applied. The Stomach Meridian of Foot-Yangming is a Yang meridian. When it is affected, Zhongwan (Ren 12) can be used.

Besides, Back-shu points can also be applied for dealing with disorders of the five sense organs. For example, Ganshu (U.B.18) is often used for eye disorders because the liver opens into the eye; Shenshu (U.B.23) for disorders of the ear because the kidney opens into the ear; Feishu (U.B.13) for nasal disorders, because the lung opens into the nose; and Xinshu (U.B. 15) for oral or tongue ulceration because the heart opens into the tongue and the tongue is the mirror of the heart, etc.

Back-shu & Front-mu Points of Internal Organs

Zangfu organs	Back-shu points	Locations	Front-mu points	Locations
lung	Feishu (U.B.13)	1.5 cun lateral to lower border of T3	Zhong fu (Lu.1)	1 cun below Yunmen (Lu.2)
pericardium	Jueyinshu (U.B.14)	1.5 cun lateral to lower border of T4	Shanzhong (Ren 17)	midpoint between the two nipples
heart	Xinshu (U.B.15)	1.5 cun lateral to lower border of T5	Juque (Ren 14)	6 cun above the umbilicus
liver	Ganshu (U.B. 18)	1.5 cun lateral to lower border of T9	Qimen (Liv. 14)	2 ribs below the nipples

gall bladder	Danshu (U.B. 19)	1.5 cun lateral to lower border of T10	Riyue (G.B.24)	1 rib below the Qimen (Liv. 14)
spleen	Pishu (U.B.20)	1.5 cun lateral to lower border of T11	Zhangmen (Liv.13)	end of the 11th rib
stomach	Weishu (U.B.21)	1.5 cun lateral to lower border of T12	Zhongwan (Ren12)	4 cun above the umbilicus
Sanjiao	Sanjiaoshu (U.B.22)	1.5 cun lateral to lower border of L1	Shimen (Ren 15)	2 cun below the umbilicus
kidney	Shenshu (U.B. 23)	1.5 cun lateral to lower border of L2	Jingmen (G.B.25)	end of the 12th rib
large intestine	Dachangshu (U.B.25)	1.5 cun lateral to lower border of L3	Tianshu (St. 25)	2 cun lateral to umbilicus
small intestine	Xiaochangshu (U.B. 27)	1.5 cun lateral to lower border of L4	Guangyuan (Ren 4)	3 cun below umbilicus
urinary bladder	Pangguangshu (U.B.28)	1.5 cun lateral to lower border of L5	Zhongji (Ren 3)	4 cun below the umbilicus

V. The Eight Influential Points

The Influential Points are eight important points where qi of the respective body tissues is infused into the body surface, namely zang, fu, qi, blood, tendons, vessels, bones and marrow. "Hui" (会) means influential in particular. The earliest record of the Eight Influential Points is found in the book *Nanjing: Question Forty-five*.

The Eight Influential Points regulate the function of the zangfu organs, promote the circulation of qi and blood, release tendons and nourish marrow.

Zhangmen (Liv.13), the Influential Point of zang organs;
Zhongwan (Ren 12), the Influential Point of the fu organs;
Shanzhong (Ren 17), the Influential Point of qi;
Geshu (U.B.17), the Influential Point of blood;
Yanglingquan (G.B.34), the Influential Point of tendons;
Taiyuan (Lu.9), the Influential Point of the vessels;
Dashu (U.B.11), the Influential Point of the bones; and
Xuanzhong (G.B.39), the Influential Point of the marrow.

Respective Influential Points can be selected for treating disorders associated with the above eight parts of the body. Explanation of the actions of the Eight Influential Points are as follows:

Zhangmen (Liv.13) is the Influential Point of zang organs and is also the Front-mu point of the spleen. The functional activities of the five zang organs originate from spleen qi. This point can be used in the treatment of disorders of zang organs, such as spleenomegaly, hepatomegaly, hypochondriac pain or jaundice.

Zhongwan (Ren 12) is the Influential Point of the fu organs and is also the Front-mu point of the stomach. The functional activities of the six fu organs originate from stomach qi. This point can be used for treating disorders of the six fu organs such as epigastric distention, abdominal pain, constipation or diarrhea, as well as some other gastrointestinal disorders.

Shanzhong (Ren 17) is the Influential Point of qi, being located in the centre of the chest where Zong qi is formed (Zong qi is the qi of the thorax, formed from respiratory qi and food essence). Internally, this point is in close proximity to the lung, the organ which dominates qi. This point, also called Upper-Qihai, can be used for treating disorders of qi derangement such as chest pain, shortness of breath, asthma and hiccup.

Geshu (U.B.17) is the Influential Point of blood, being located between Xinshu (heart point) and Ganshu (liver point). The liver stores blood while the heart dominates blood. This point is situated between the two organs and has the function to promote the manufacture of blood. It is used for treating disorders of blood such as anemia, stasis of blood, bloody vomiting, bloody stool or cough with bloody sputum.

Yanglingquan (G.B. 34) is the Influential Point of the tendons and is also the He-sea point of the Gall Bladder Meridian of Foot-Shaoyang. The gall bladder and the liver are internally-externally related organs. The liver dominates the tendons. Besides, Yanglingquan (G.B.34) is below the knee joint, the convergent place of the tendons. It is used for treating disorders such as spasm and painful tendons, hemiplegia or numbness.

Taiyuan (Lu.9) is the Influential Point of vessels. Taiyuan (Lu.9), also the Yuan (source) point of the Lung Meridian of Hand-Taiyin, is located at cunkou (at the wrist where the pulse is palpated). The lung is associated with the pulses and cunkou is the major converging place of the qi of the vessels. This point can be used for treating disorder of the vessels, such as vasculitis, acrotism and arteriosclerosis.

Dashu (U.B.11), lateral to the spinal column, is the Influential Point of bones. Bone arises from marrow while marrow flows down to Dashu (U.B.11) from the brain, and further to the bones and joints. This point, the convergent place of qi of the bones, is located superior to all of the Back-shu points. It can be used for treating disorders of the bones such as pain in the shoulder, scapula or back.

Xuanzhong (G.B.39) is the Influential Point of marrow. It was considered in ancient times that marrow was a part of the bones. Marrow is thought of as helping the growth of bones. Thus, it is an essential factor in the ability to walk normally. It is used in the treatment of disorders of the marrow, such as myo-asthenia and anemia.

The Eight Influential Points

	Point Names	Locations	Indications
zang	Zhangmen (Liv.13)	at the end of the 11th rib	disorders of the zang organs
fu	Zhongwan (Ren 12)	4 cun above the umbilicus	disorders of the fu organs
qi	Shanzhong (Ren 17)	between the two nipples	respiratory disorders and the disorders due to qi derangement
blood	Geshu (U.B.17)	1.5 cun lateral to lower border of T 7.	blood diseases and gynecological diseases
tendons	Yanglingquan (G.B.34)	anterior and inferior to head of fibula	disorders of joints, tendons and muscles
vessels	Taiyuan (Lu.9)	at the lateral end of the transverse crease of wrist	disorders of the blood
bones	Dashu (U.B.11)	1.5 cun lateral to Dazhui (Du 14)	disorders of the bones
marrow	Xuanzhong (G.B.39)	3 cun above the external malleolus	disorders of the bone marrow and brain marrow

Clinically, the Influential Points can be used as main points, secondary points being prescribed according to the varying symptoms and signs. For example, Taiyuan (Lu.9), as the main point, could be used in combination with Neiguan (P.6) and Shanzhong (Ren 17) for treating acrotism. Geshu (U.B.17), as the main point, could be used in combination with Xuehai (Sp.10) and Qihai (Ren 6) for treating chronic hemorrhage. Palpation of the Influential Points can also be a useful aid to diagnosis, tenderness at a given point indicating a disorder of the related tissue.

VI. The Eight Confluent Points

The Eight Confluent Points are points of the 12 meridians, located on the four extremities and in connection with the Eight Extra Meridians. Their function is to regulate the circulation of the qi and blood of the 8 extra meridians, which communicates with the qi and blood of the 12 regular meridians at these points, hence the term: the Eight Confluent Points.

The earliest record of their use dates back to *Zhenjiu Zhinan* (*A Guide to Acupuncture*) written by Dou Hanqian during the late years of the Jin Dynasty and early years of the Yuan Dynasty.

The clinical application of the Eight Confluent Points is based on the theory of communication with the 8 extra meridians described above.

The Chong Meridian communicates with Gongsun (Sp.4): One branch of Chong Meridian arises from the pubic region and descends along the medial side of the lower limb with the Kidney Meridian of Foot-Shaoyin, going to the posterior aspect of the medial malleolus when it further divides into two sub-branches. One goes to the sole, connecting with Gongsun (Sp.4), while the other goes to the dorsum of the foot where it communicates with Taichong (Liv.3). The upper part of the Chong Meridian passes through the abdominal and thoracic regions, connecting with the heart and stomach. Consequently, Gongsun (Sp.4) is indicated in disorders of the heart, chest and stomach due to derangement of qi of the Chong Meridian.

The Yinwei Meridian communicates with Neiguan (P.6): The Yingwei Meridian originates from Zhubin (K.9), then ascends through the abdominal and thoracic regions. It is involved in disorders of the heart and stomach. Neiguan (P.6) is located on the Pericardium Meridian of Hand-Jueyin which connects with the Sanjiao meridian, and is also an important point for treating disorders of the heart and stomach.

The Du Meridian communicates with Houxi (S.I.3): The course of the Du Meridian runs along the posterior midline, its qi communicates with the Back-shu points of the Urinary Bladder Meridian of Foot-Taiyang. Houxi (S.I.3) comes from the Small Intestine Meridian of Hand-Taiyang, which links with the Urinary Bladder Meridian of Foot-Taiyang. It connects with the Du Meridian at Jingming (U.B.1), again at Dazhui (Du 14), and consequently the qi of the Du Meridian may be regulated by puncturing Houxi (S.I.3). The course of the Small Intestine Meridian of Hand-Taiyang passes through the neck, ear, shoulder and scapula, so Houxi (S.I.3) can also be applied in disorders of the above areas.

The Yangqiao Meridian communicates with Shenmai (U.B.62): The Yangqiao Meridian starts from Shenmai (U.B.62) of the Urinary Bladder Meridian of Foot-

Taiyang, so the qi of the Yangqiao Meridian may be regulated by puncturing Shenmai (U.B.62). Also, the Yangqiao Meridian passes through the shoulder, neck, posterior of the ear and inner canthus of the eye. So, Shenmai (U.B.62) is indicated in disorders occurring in these areas.

The Dai Meridian communicates with Foot-Linqi (G.B.41): The points being on the course of the Dai Meridian, including Foot-Linqi (G.B.41), are all from the Gall Bladder Meridian of Foot-Shaoyang. The qi of each of these meridians always communicates with the other. The course of the Gall Bladder Meridian of Foot-Shaoyang ascends through the axilla, shoulder, neck, ear, cheek and outer canthus, so Foot-Linqi (G.B.41) is indicated for disorders in these areas, as well as for regulating the qi of the Dai Meridian.

The Yangwei Meridian communicates with Waiguan (S.J.5): Waiguan (S.J.5) comes from the Sanjiao Meridian of Hand-Shaoyang which links with the Gall Bladder Meridian of Foot-Shaoyang at the outer canthus. The Yangwei Meridian starts from Jinmen (U.B.63) below the external malleolus and ascends along the Gall Bladder Meridian of Foot-Shaoyang to the shoulder, neck, posterior region of the ear and cheek. The qi of the Yangwei Meridian has been shown empirically to be influenced by puncturing Waiguan (S.J.5) which is also indicated for disorders of the above areas.

The Ren Meridian communicates with Lieque (Lu.7): Both Ren Meridian and the Lung Meridian of Hand-Taiyin travel through the chest and throat. Lieque (Lu.7) comes from the Lung Meridian of Hand-Taiyin. Thus, qi of the Ren Meridian can be regulated by puncturing Lieque (Lu.7) which is indicated for disorders of the chest, diaphragm and throat.

The Yinqiao Meridian communicates with Zhaohai (K.6): The Yinqiao Meridian, starting from Zhaohai (K.6), ascends together with the Kidney Meridian of Foot-Shaoyin through the chest, diaphragm and throat. The qi of Yinqiao Meridian can be regulated by needling Zhaohai (K.6), which is also indicated for disorders of the chest and throat.

Appropriate use of the eight Confluent Points can often enhance the therapeutic effect of the points used. For example, Neiguan (P.6) and Gongsun (Sp.4) are selected for abdominal distention, anorexia, vomiting, acid regurgitation, etc. This is because Gongsun (Sp.4) communicates with the Chong Meridian, and Neiguan (P.6) communicates with Yinwei Meridian. Gongsun (Sp.4) also communicates with Neiguan (P.6) by the merging of the courses of the meridians in the heart, chest and stomach areas.

Lieque (Lu.7) and Zhaohai (K.6) are combined to treat dryness in the nose and throat, cough, asthma and chest pain. This is because the Ren Meridian communicates with Lieque (Lu.7) and the Yinqiao Meridian communicates with Zhaohai (K.6) by the merging of the two meridians in the chest, diaphragm and lung. Such selections of points from both the upper and lower parts of the body produce harmonious effects in acupuncture therapy. It is also an example of the acupuncture principle of using a small number of well selected points to achieve the best therapeutic effect.

In *Zhenjiu Dacheng* (*Compendium of Acupuncture & Moxibustion*) which appeared in the Ming Dynasty, the use of the eight Confluent Points was known as the "method of treating disease according to the ebb and flow of qi of the eight points". This was associated with "The Eight Diagrams and Nine Tones Theory", which stressed the importance of the date and the hour of the treatment with reference to the heavenly stems and earthly branches. This system was referred to as "The Eight Magic Turtle Techniques". The selection of points on the basis of the variations of the Yin and Yang using the Eight-Diagram Theory (Bagua), as well as the application of the theory of opening and closing of these points on specific dates and at particular hours, is a further development of the clinical use of the eight Confluent Points.

The Eight Confluent Points

Confluent Points	Communicating Meridians	Indications (Portions of the Body)
Gongsun (Sp. 4)	Chong Meridian	heart, chest and stomach
Neiguan (P.6)	Yinwei Meridian	
Houxi (S.I.3)	Du Meridian	neck, shoulder, ear and inner canthus
Shenmai (U.B.62)	Yangqiao Meridian	
Foot-Linqi (G.B.41)	Dai Meridian	neck, shoulder, cheek, ear and outer canthus
Waiguan (S.J.5)	Yangwei Meridian	
Lieque (Lu.7)	Ren Meridian	throat, chest and diaphragm
Zhaohai (K.6)	Yinqiao Meridian	

VII. The Sixteen Xi (Cleft) Points

The Xi (cleft) Points are the places where the qi of the meridian is deeply converged. Each of the 12 regular meridians has a Xi (cleft) Point on the extremity, as do the Yinwei, Yangwei, Yinqiao and Yangqiao Meridians, 16 in all. Xi (cleft) Points are located below the elbows and knees except for Liangqiu (St.34) which is superior to the knee. They constitute another group of important points apart from the Five-shu Points.

Early records of Xi (cleft) Points date back to *Zhenjiu Jiayi Jing* (*A Classic of Acupuncture and Moxibustion*). Xi (cleft) Points are used for treating acute disorders of their related internal organs as well as of the areas supplied by the meridians. Needling these points can regulate the circulation of qi and blood in the diseased areas.

The Sixteen Xi (Cleft) Points

Meridians	Xi (Cleft) Points	Indications
Lu. Meridian of Hand-Taiyin	Kongzui (Lu.6)	hemorrhoid bleeding, hemoptysis, shortness of breath
L.I. Meridian of Hand-Yangming	Wenliu (L.I.7)	toothache, common cold, hemorrhoids
St. Meridian of Foot-Yangming	Liangqiu (St.34)	epigastric pain
Sp. Meridian of Foot-Taiyin	Diji (Sp.8)	acute diarrhea
H. Meridian of Hand-Shaoyin	Yinxi (H.6)	cardiac pain, insomnia and mental mania
S.I. Meridian of Hand-Taiyang	Yanglao (S.I.6)	blurring of vision and tinnitus

U.B. Meridian of Foot-Taiyang	Jinmen (U.B.63)	infantile convulsions and systrema
K. Meridian of Foot-Shaoyin	Shuiquan (K.5)	dysmenorrhea, prolapse of uterus
P. Meridian of Hand-Jueyin	Ximen (P. 4)	cardiac pain, palpitation, hypochondriac pain
S.J. Meridian of Hand-Shaoyang	Huizong (S.J.7)	pain in the heart area, enteritis
G.B. Meridian of Foot-Shaoyang	Waiqiu (G.B.36)	mania with emotional excitement and insanity with emotional depression
Liv. Meridian of Foot-Jueyin	Foot-Zhongdu (Liv.6)	hernia, uterine bleeding
Yangqiao Meridian	Fuyang (U.B.59)	acute diarrhea, sciatica, numbness, lumbar pain
Yinqiao Meridian	Jiaoxin (K.8)	orchialgia, amenorrhea, night sweating
Yangwei Meridian	Yangjiao (G.B.35)	chest pain, numbness of the lower extremites
Yinwei Meridian	Zhubin (K.9)	relieving pathogenic qi, hernia and beriberi

They also have the function to alleviate acute pain of the internal organs. For example, puncturing Liangqiu (St.34) for acute gastric pain; Kongzui (Lu.6) for acute bronchial hemoptysis; Shuiquan (K.5) for dysmenorrhea; Ximen (P.4) for cardiac pain and furuncle; Foot-Linqi (Liv.6) for swelling and pain of the testis, etc. The Xi (cleft) Points can also be used to treat acute sprain, points being selected from meridians passing through the injured area.

Clinically, combination of the Xi (cleft) Points and the Eight Influential Points can often enhance the therapeutic effect of the acupuncture treatment, e.g. Liangqiu (St.34) and Zhongwan (Ren 12) for severe epigastric pain; Kongzui (Lu.6) and Shanzhong (Ren 17) for cough and hiccup with difficult breathing.

Observation of Xi (cleft) Points can sometimes be of help in diagnosing acute disorders. Often there is a reactive spot at a Xi (cleft) Point when a particular organ or meridian is affected, e.g. tenderness can be felt at Ximen (P.4) in case of acute pleurisy; or at Liangqiu (St.34) in case of acute mastitis.

VIII. The Lower He-sea Points

Lower He-sea Point is the cover term referring to the Lower He-sea points of the three Yang meridians of the hand located in the lower extremities of the body as well as He-sea points of the three Yang meridians of the foot, 6 in all. The lower He-sea points of the three Yang meridians of the hand are located on the courses of the Stomach Meridian of Foot-Yangming and the Urinary Bladder Meridian of Foot-Taiyang, viz, Shangjuxu (St.37), Xiajuxu (St.39) and Weiyang (U.B.39). The He-sea points of the three Yang meridians of the foot coincide with the last of the Five-shu Points, viz, Zusanli (St.36), Weizhong (U.B.40) and Yanglingquan (G.B.34).

The three Yang meridians of the hand have their own Lower He-sea points: Shangjuxu (St.37), Xiajuxu (St.39) and Weiyang (U.B.39) as well as their He-sea points on the upper extremities, viz, Quchi (L.I.11), Xiaohai (S.I.8) and Tianjing (S.J.10). This is because both the large and small intestines pertain to the lower jiao, and functionally are connected with the stomach. The Sanjiao itself is a conceptional fu organ dominating the whole body. Inferiorly, it connects with urinary bladder. The qi of each of the three Yang meridians of the hand diverges into its specific fu organ at certain points along the three Yang meridians of the foot, the qi of the three meridians being the most abundant. The three Yang meridians of the foot all start from the head and travel through the body trunk down to the foot. Thus, the three Yang meridians of the foot contain all the He-sea points of the six fu organs:

Shangjuxu (St.37), the Lower He-sea point of the large intestine;

Xiajuxu (St.39), the Lower He-sea point of the small intestine;

Weiyang (U.B.39), the Lower He-sea point of the Sanjiao;

Zusanli (St.36), the He-sea point of the stomach;

Weizhong (U.B.40), the He-sea point of the urinary bladder; and

Yanglingquan (G.B.34), the He-sea point of the gall bladder.

The application of the Lower He-sea points has been given great attention throughout the history of TCM. Lower He-sea points can be applied independently because of their unique therapeutic effect in dealing with disorders of the six fu organs. For example, Shangjuxu (St.37) has an excellent effect in dealing with inflammation, stopping pain, relieving fever and stopping dysentery, when used for treating acute dysentery and acute appendicitis. There have been many reports concerning using the Lower He-sea points in surgery and internal medicine to deal with abdominal distention and pain.

Lower He-sea Points of Six Fu Organs

Fu Organs	Meridians	Lower He-sea Points
stomach	St. Meridian of Foot-Yangming	Zusanli (St.36)
large intestine	L.I. Meridian of Hand-Yangming	Shangjuxu (St.37)
small intestine	S.I. Meridian of Hand-Taiyang	Xiajuxu (St.39)
urinary bladder	U.B. Meridian of Foot-Taiyang	Weizhong (U.B.40)
Sanjiao	S.J. Meridian of Hand-Shaoyang	Weiyang (U.B.39)
gall bladder	G.B. Meridian of Foot-Shaoyang	Yanglingquan (G.B.34)

IX. Coalescent Points

The courses of the meridians in the body do not always travel in parallel lines, but emerge in a system with many complicated changes of directions and crossings. Two, three or even more meridians may intersect at one point, thus allowing the qi to circulate vertically and horizontally throughout the body. These crossing points are regarded as coalescent points. There are 94 such points at intersections in the meridian system, here including the 8 extra meridians as well as the 12 regular meridians. The earliest record of these points appears in the book *Suwen*.

Coalescent Points of the Yin Meridians

Meridians Points	Ren.	Sp.	Lu.	Liv.	Peri.	K.	H.	Yin-wei	Ying-qiao	Chong.
Chengjiang (Ren 24)	O									
Lianquan (Ren 23)	O							+		
Tiantu (Ren 22)	O							+		
Shangwan (Ren 13)	O									
Zhongwan (Ren 12)	O									
Xiawan (Ren 10)	O	+								
Ab-Yinjiao (Ren 7)	O									+
Guanyuan (Ren 4) o	O	+		+		+				
Zhongji (Ren 3) o	O	+		+		+				
Qugu (Ren 2)	O			+						
Huiyin (Ren 1)	O									+
Sanyinjiao (Sp.6)		O		+		+				
Chongmen (Sp.12)		O		+						
Fushe (Sp.13)		O		+				+		
Daheng (Sp.15)		O						+		
Fuai (Sp.16)		O						+		
Zhongfu (Lu.1)		+	O							
Zhangmen (Liv.13)				O						
Qimen (Liv.14)		+		O				+		
Tianchi (P.1)					O					
Henggu (K.11)						O				+
Dahe (K.12)						O				+
Qixue (K.13)						O				+
Siman (K.14)						O				+
Ab-Zhongzhu (K.15)						O				+
Huanshu (K.16)						O				+
Shangqu (K.17)						O				+
Shiguan (K.18)						O				+
Yindu (K.19)						O				+
Ab-Tonggu (K.20)						O				+
Youmen (K.21)						O				+
Zhaohai (K.6)						O			+	
Jiaoxin (K.8)						O			+	
Zhubin (K.9)						O		+		

Coalescent Points of the Yang Meridians

Meridians Points	Du.	U.B.	S.I.	G.B.	S.J.	St.	L.I.	Yang-wei	Yang-qiao	Dai.
Shenting (Du 24)	O	+				+				
Renzhong (Du 26)	O					+	+			

	1	2	3	4	5	6	7	8	9	10
Baihu (Du 20)	O	+								
Naohu (Du 17)	O	+								
Fengfu (Du 16)	O							+		
Yamen (Du 15)	O							+		
Dazhui (Du 14)	O	+	+	+	+	+	+			
Taodao (Du 13)	O	+								
Changqiang (Du 1)	O									
Jingming (U.B.1)		O	+			+				
Dashu (U.B.11)		O	+							
Fengmen (U.B.12)	+	O								
Fufen (U.B.41)		O	+							
Fuyang (U.B.59)		O							+	
Pushen (U.B.61)		O							+	
Shenmai (U.B.62)		O							+	
Jinmen (U.B.63)		O						+		
Naoshu (S.I.10)		O						+	+	
Binfeng (S.I.12)		O	+	+		+				
Quanliao (S.I.18)		O		+						
Tinggong (S.I.19)		O	+	+						
Tongziliao (G.B.1)		+	O	+						
Shangguan (G.B.3)			O	+	+					
Hanyan (G.B.4)			O	+	+					
Xuanlu (G.B.6)			O	+	+					
Qubin (G.B.7)		+	O							
Shuaigu (G.B.8)		+	O							
Fubai (G.B.10)		+	O							
H-Qiaoyin (G.B.11)		+	O							
H-Wangu (G.B.12)		+	O							
Benshen (G.B.13)			O					+		
Yangbai (G.B.14)			O					+		
H-Linqi (G.B.15)		+	O					+		
Muchuang (G.B.16)			O					+		
Zhengying (G.B.17)			O					+		
Chenglin (G.B.18)			O					+		
Naokong (G.B.19)			O					+		
Fengchi (G.B.20)			O					+		
Jianjing (G.B.21)			O					+		
Riyue (G.B.24)			O					+		
Daimai (G.B.26)			O.							+
Wushu (G.B.27)			O							+
Weidao (G.B.28)			O							+
F-Juliao (G.B.29)			O						+	
Huantiao (G.B.30)		+	O							
Yangjiao (G.B.35)			O					+		

Tianliao (S.J.15)					O			+	
Jiaosun (S.J.20)			+	O		+			
Yifeng (S.J.17)			+	O					
E-Heliao (S.J.22)		+	+	O					
Chengqi (St.1)					O			+	
N-Juliao (St.3)					O			+	
Dicang (St.4)					O	+		+	
Touwei (St.8)			+		O		+		
Xiaguan (St.7)			+		O				
Qichong (St.30)					O				
Binao (L.I.14)						O			
Jianyu (L.I.15)						O		+	
Jugu (L.I.16)						O		+	
Yingxiang (L.I.20)					+	O			

Note:

a) "O" stands for the pertaining meridian; "+" stands for the meridian being crossed;

b) Du Meridian and the Stomach Meridian of Foot-Yangming cross at Chengjiang (Ren 24);

c) The Stomach Meridian of Foot-Yangming and the Small Intestine Meridian of Hand-Taiyang cross at Shangwan (Ren 13);

d) Du Meridian crosses at Huiyin (Ren 1);

e) The Kidney Meridian of Foot-Shaoyin crosses at Zhangmen (Liv. 13);

f) The Kidney Meridian of Foot-Shaoyang also crosses at Tianchi (P.1).

Due to the fact that the courses of several meridians may cross at the same coalescent point, one coalescent point can be used for treating disorders involving several meridians. For example, Dazhui (Du 14) has the effect of regulating the circulation of qi of the whole body and is consequently applied for dispelling pathogenic-heat and causing sweating, because the three Yang Meridians of both foot and hand all cross at this point. Sanyinjiao (Sp.6) can be used to treat disorders of the three Yin meridians of the foot, since all three cross here. Coalescent points may be specially applied when a disorder involves more than two meridians, e.g. selecting Huantiao (G.B.30), the coalescent point of the Gall Bladder Meridian of Foot-Shaoyang and the Urinary Bladder Meridian of Foot-Taiyang, for treating rheumatic pain at the lateroposterior aspect of the thigh.

However, if the area of a particular coalescent point is affected, points from the meridians passing through this coalescent point can be used.

For example, Tinggong (S.I.19) in the ear region is the coalescent point of the Small Intestine Meridian of Hand-Taiyang, the Sanjiao Meridian of Hand-Shaoyang and the Gall Bladder Meridian of Foot-Shaoyang. Thus, when dealing with disorders of the ear, in addition to using Tinggong (S.I.19) as a local point, distal points may be selected from the above three meridians. Again, the three Yin meridians of the foot cross at Zhongji (Ren 3) and Guanyuan (Ren 4), so points below the knee from these three meridians can be used for treating disorders of the lower abdominal region.

Most of the specific points are located below the elbow or knee except for the Back-shu points, Front-mu points, the Eight Confluent points, some of the Eight Influential points and many of the 94 coalescent points. All points below the elbow on the three Yin meridians of the hand are specific points without exception. For example, those from the Lung Meridian of Hand-Taiyin:

Shaoshang (Lu.11) is the Jing-well point of the meridian;

Yuji (Lu.10) is the Ying-spring point of the meridian;

Taiyuan (Lu.9) is concurrently the Shu-stream, Influential point of vessels and the Yuan-source point of the meridian;

Jingqu (Lu.8) is the Jing-river point of the meridian;

Lieque (Lu.7) is the Luo-connecting point of the meridian and the Confluent point communicating with the Ren Meridian;

Kongzui (Lu.6) is the Xi-cleft point of the meridian; and

Chize (Lu.5) is the He-sea point of the meridian.

Most of the points below the knee from the three Yang meridians of the foot are specific points. For example, those of the Stomach Meridian of Foot-Yangming:

Lidui (St.45), the Jing-well point of the meridian;

Neiting (St. 44), the Ying-spring point of the meridian;

Xiangu (St.43), the Shu-stream point of the meridian;

Chongyang (St.42), the Yuan-source point of the meridian;

Jiexi (St.41), the Jing-river point of the meridian;

Fenglong (St.40), the Luo-connecting point of the meridian;

Xiajuxu (St.39), the Lower He-sea point of the Large Intestine Meridian of Hand-Yangming; and

Zusanli (St.36), the He-sea point of the meridian.

Points below the elbow and knee have occupied a very important position in the clinical application of acupuncture since ancient times. This is due to the fact that these points are able to deal with disorders manifested at different parts of the body. This forms the basis for an understanding of the specific points and their functions.

Section 5   THE FUNCTIONS OF REGULAR POINTS

Regular points are located along the courses of the meridians, which internally pertain to and link with the zangfu organs, and externally communicate with the body surface. Thus, regular points, zangfu organs, qi and blood are all closely related. The regular points, forming the main component of acupuncture points, have the following functions:

I. Physiologically: Infusion of Qi and Blood

The meridians are the passages through which both qi and blood circulate continuously, the regular points being the places along the main courses of the meridians where qi and blood are infused. The book *Suwen on Concise Explanations* states, "The regular points on the surface of the body communicate internally with the meridians to regulate the nutrient and defensive systems, and superficially with the pores of the skin, where it meets the air and the external environment." Puncturing these points may promote the circulation of qi and blood, so as to maintain the normal physiological functions of the body.

II. Pathologically: Manifestation of Disease

Once the physiological functions of the body are impaired, some abnormal reactions will often occur at specific points. Sometimes such a reaction can be felt subjectively as tenderness or subcutaneous nodules. For example, a large proportion of patients develop tenderness at Zusanli (St.36) when they suffer from gastric disorders. Similarly, most patients affected by pulmonary disorders experience tenderness at Zhongfu (Lu.1). Abnormal reactions occurring at other points, though not evident to the patient, can be detected by an increase of electrical conductivity and a decrease of bioloelectric resistance, demonstrable by measuring the relative skin conductivity at the locations. They are referred to as "effected points" or "good conduction points." Due to the close relationship between these points and the internal zangfu, abnormal changes at them are of great significance in clinical diagnosis and the guidance of treatment. There is a saying in TCM: "Where there is a disorder with associated tenderness at a given point, changes in the nature of the disorder will be reflected at that point." The knowledge that pathological changes of zangfu organs can be manifested at points along the meridians, often serves as an aid to diagnosis. When abnormal changes at these points are seen to have been corrected after needling, the related pain to the disorder will often be alleviated as well.

III. Therapeutically: The Treatment and Prevention of Disease

Acupuncture therapy, based on the meridian theory, aims at treating and preventing disease by needling or applying moxa to points. Stimulating points will regulate the overall balance of the qi and blood of the meridians, regulate Yin and Yang, build up anti-pathogenic factors and dispel pathogenic factors. Selection of points along the course of meridians according to the differentiation of symptoms and signs, is based on the theory that "a point is indicated in disorders occurring at places supplied by its pertaining meridians." This means that the places supplied by the course of a particular meridian, constitute the range of locations, the diseases of which may be treated by points on that particular meridian. The Lung Meridian of Hand-Taiyin, for example, pertains to the lung. Its course passes through the lung, respiratory tract and throat, and also communicates with the nose. The superficial conduit emerges at Zhongfu (Lu.1) and descends along the anteromedial aspect of the arm. Points from this meridian are mainly indicated in disorders of the respiratory system and the areas supplied by the course of the meridian.

The Pericardium Meridian of Hand-Jueyin passes through the chest region and runs along the midline of the medial aspect of the arm to the tip of the middle finger. Points from this meridian are mainly indicated in disorders of the cardivascular system and diseases occurring along the course of the meridian. In general, the functions of regular points, in both the treatment and prevention of disease, are as follows:

A. Common Therapeutic Properties—Dealing with Local Disorders

This refers to the functions of regular points in dealing with both local and adjacent disorders, e.g. Fengchi (G.B.20) is indicated in local headache as well as in adjacent eye disorders. Zhongwan (Ren 12) is indicated in local gastric disorders and adjacent duodenal problems. Ermen (S.J.21), Tinggong (S.J.19) and Tinghui (S.J.17) are all indicated in ear disorders. Chengqi (St.1), Sibai (St.2), Jingming (U.B.1) and Zanzhu (U.B.2) are all indicated in eye disorders. And Zhongwan (Ren 12), Jianli (Ren 11), Liangmen (St.21) and Xiawan (Ren 10) are all indicated in gastric disorders.

B. Special Therapeutic Properties—Dealing with Remote Disorders

This function is divided into two sub-categories.

First, in addition to their local and adjacent indications, regular points on the four extremities are indicated in remote disorders occurring along the courses of the meridians, such as diseases of the facial region, head, body trunk and internal organs. This is especially true of points located below the elbows and knees, being referred to as "the distal functions of the regular points", e.g.

Zusanli (St.36) and Shangjuxu (St.37) are not only indicated in disorders of the lower extremities, but also in gastrointestinal ones. In addition, these two points can promote the digestive function and strengthen both the immunity and body resistance against disease.

Neiguan (P.6) and Jianli (P.5), apart from their indications for local pain, are indicated in chest pain, hypochondriac pain, and disorders of the cardiovascular system;

Hegu (L.I.4) is indicated in disorders of the head and facial region;

Weizhong (U.B.40) in lumbar pain; and

Lieque (Lu.7) is indicated in headache.

This concept was summarized in the Song of the Four Points: "Zusanli (St.36) is needled for abdominal disorders; Weizhong (U.B.40) in conditions affecting the lower back; Lieque (Lu.7) in disorders of the neck and head; and Hegu (L.I.4) for the problems of the face and mouth."

On the basis of the Song of the Four Points, additions were made, "select Neiguan (P.6) for disorders of the heart and chest; Sanyinjiao (Sp.6) for pain on the lower abdomen; Ahshi Points for local pain and Renzhong (Du 26) for emergencies (i.e. resusitation)."

Secondly, some points have their own unique therapeutic properties, e.g.

Zhiyin (U.B.67) can adjust abnormal position of the fetus;

Guanyuan (Ren 4), Qihai (Ren 6) and Zusanli (St. 36) reinforce the body constitution; and

Renzhong (Du 26), Suliao (Du 25) and Huiyin (Ren 1) jointly activate breathing.

Also, there is another type of unique property among some of the points, i.e. mutual reinforcing or mutual constraining. For example:

Combination of Dazhui (Du 14), Quchi (L.I.11) and Hegu (L.I.4) produces a superior effect in dispelling fever;

Combination of Renzhong (Du 26), Shixuan (Extra) and Yongquan (K.1) can help restore consciousness;

Combination of Taixi (K.3) and Sanyinjiao (Sp.6) is effective in treating insomnia;

and Neijuan (P.6) can stabilize irregular heart beat. But this particular function of Neiguan (P.6) is reduced if it is used in combination with Jiaoxin (K.8).

Apart from these unique properties, a particular point may also influence several zangfu organs, or the dysfunction of several zangfu organs can be regulated by needling the same point, e.g.

Needling Zusanli (St.36) not only strengthens immunity and resistance against disease, but also regulates the functions of the digestive and respiratory systems. On the other hand, points such as Zusanli (St.36), Quchi (L.I.11), Taichong (Liv.3), Hegu (L.I.4), Neiguan (P.6) and Sanyinjiao (Sp.6) all have the function to reduce the blood pressure. Thus, a point may possess a variety of functions in addition to its unique properties.

C. The Two-way Regulating Function of Regular Points

Practice has shown that regular points also possess a two-way regulating function. This is to say, puncturing a particular point may result in either tonification or sedation, depending on whether the condition is one of excess or deficiency. This means that a hypoactivity or hyperactivity of a particular organ may be regulated by choosing the same point for either condition. For example,

Neiguan (P.6) may either slow down the heart beat in the case of tachycardia, or speed it up in the case of bradycardia;

Hegu (L.I.4) may cause sweat in fever with anhidrosis, or stop sweating in fever with hidrosis; and

Tianshu (St.25) may either stop diarrhea or dispel constipation.

Such two-way regulating functions of points may be manifested either in localized conditions, or in diseases affecting the general constitution.

In conclusion, a thorough understanding of the physiological functions, pathological changes and the therapeutic properties of points, is an invaluable guide to effective clinical practice. Furthermore, such an understanding of the properties of the points will be helpful in the development of a clearer perspective into the nature of the meridian system as a whole.

Section 6   GENERALITY AND PARTICULARITY OF INDICATIONS

The indications of regular points, formed on the basis of individual meridians, usually match the diseases that may possibly occur in the given meridian. Although the points of the whole body have their own curative properties, those of the same meridian by and large share some generality. For example, points of the Lung Meridian of Hand-Taiyin have the effect to deal with disorders involving the lung and throat; while the points of the Stomach Meridian of Foot-Yangming have a common effect in the treatment of gastrointestinal disorders. The generality of the indications of the points of the same meridian is also manifested by the fact that the points of the same meridian are indicated in the same or similar disorders occurring in two or three meridians. For example, in addition to the disorders of their own meridians, the points of either the Heart Meridian of Hand-Shaoyin or the Pericardium Meridian of Hand-Jueyin are indicated in mental disorders, the common disorders of the two meridians. Moreover, they are also indicated in the chest disorders, the common disorders of the three Yin meridians of the hand.

The Three Yin Meridians of the Hand
(Fig. I-12)

Indications Meridians	Particularity	Generality I	Generality II
The Lung Meridian of Hand-Taiyin	disorders of the lung and throat		
The Pericardium Meridian of Hand-Jueyin	disorders of the heart and stomach	mental illness	chest disorders
The Heart Meridian of Hand-Shaoyin	heart disorders		

The Three Yang Meridians of the Hand
(Fig. I-8, I-13)

Indications Meridians	Particularity	Generality I	Generality II
The Large Intestine Meridian of Hand-Yangming	disorders of the forehead, nose, mouth and teeth		
The Sanjiao Meridian of Hand-Shaoyang	pain in the temporal and hypochondriac regions	ear disorders	eye disorders, disorders of the throat and febrile diseases
The Small Intestine Meridian of Hand-Taiyang	mental illness and those of the occipital and scapular regions		

The Three Yang Meridians of the Foot
(Fig. I-8, I-9, I-10, I-11, I-14, I-15, I-16)

Indications Meridians	Particularity	Generality I	Generality II
The Stomach Meridian of Foot-Yangming	disorders of the forehead, mouth, teeth and gastrointestinal disorders		
The Gall Bladder Meridian of Foot-Shaoyang	disorders of the temporal region, ear and hypochondriac region	eye disorders	mental illness and febrile diseases
The Urinary Bladder Meridian of Foot-Taiyang	disorders of the occipital region, back and lumbar region		

The Three Yin Meridians of the Foot
(Fig. I-9, I-11, I-17)

Indications Meridians	Particularity	Generality
The Spleen Meridian of Foot-Taiyin	disorders of the spleen and stomach	
The Liver Meridian of Foot-Jueyin	liver disorders, disorders of the reproductive organs	
The Kidney Meridian of Foot-Shaoyin	disorders of the kidney and lung	disorders of the urinary and reproductive systems

The Du and Ren Meridians
(Fig. I-8, I-9, I-10)

Indications Meridians	Particularity	Generality
Du Meridian	windstroke, coma, emergency cases, febrile diseases and facial disorders	
Ren Meridian	restoring Yang qi from collapse, and general tonification	mental disorders, disorders of the mouth, teeth, throat, chest, lung, spleen, stomach, intestines and the urinary bladder, leukorrhea and menstrual problems

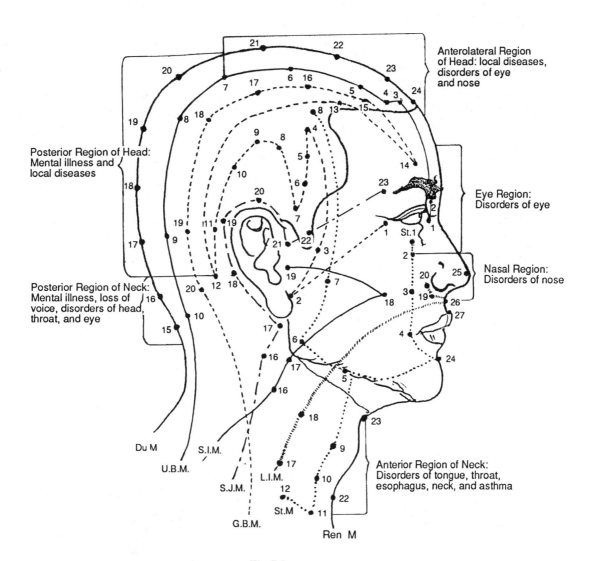

Fig. I-8

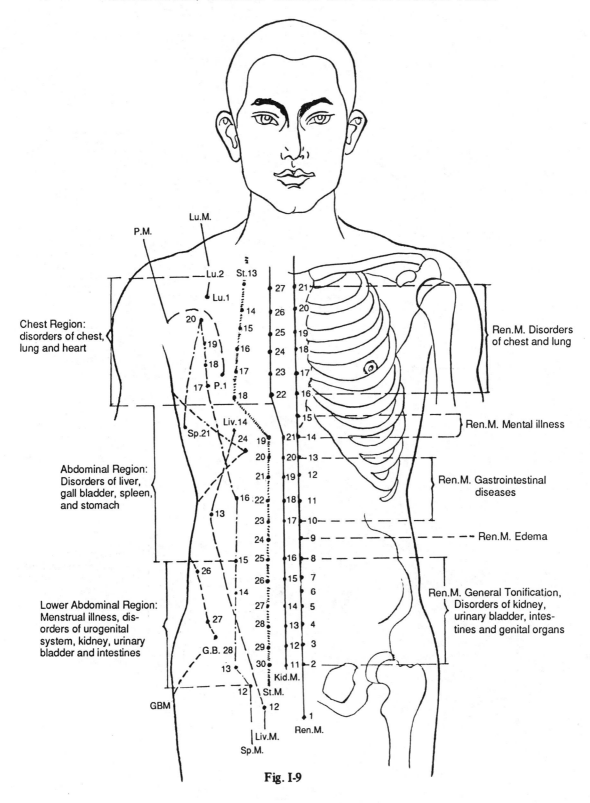

Fig. I-9

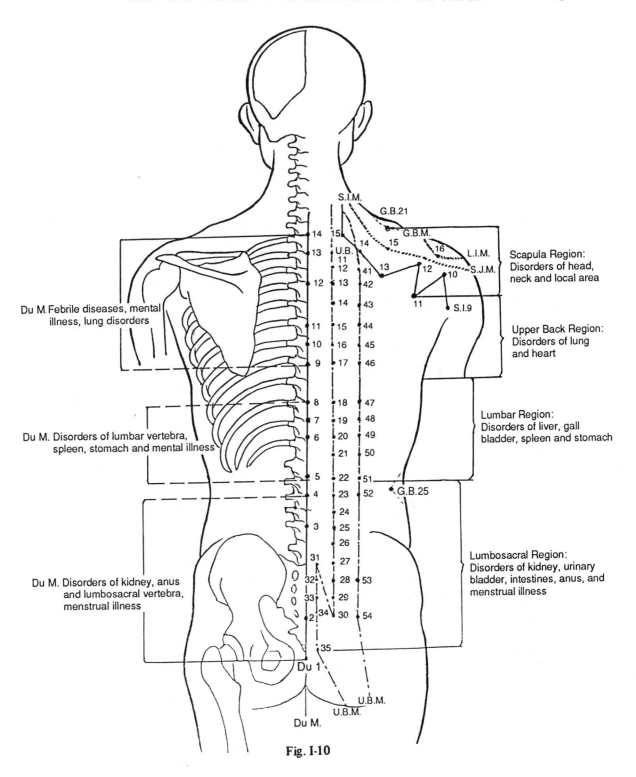

Fig. I-10

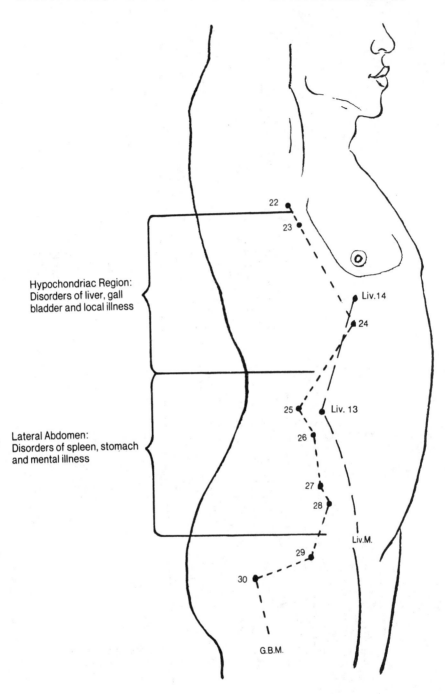

Hypochondriac Region:
Disorders of liver, gall
bladder and local illness

Lateral Abdomen:
Disorders of spleen, stomach
and mental illness

Fig. I-11

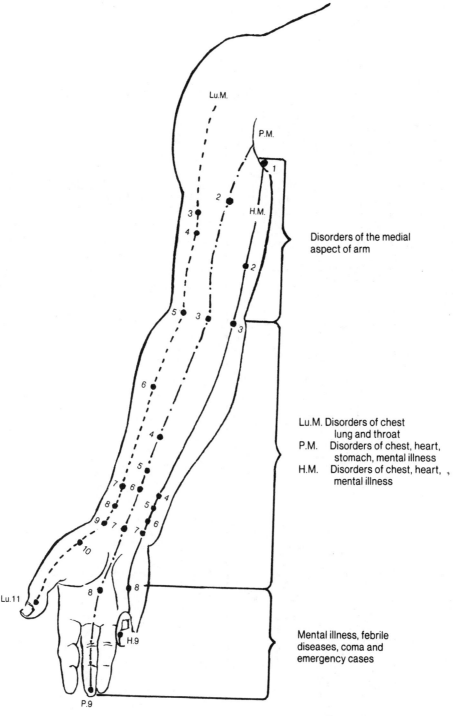

Disorders of the medial
aspect of arm

Lu.M. Disorders of chest
        lung and throat
P.M.   Disorders of chest, heart,
        stomach, mental illness
H.M.   Disorders of chest, heart,
        mental illness

Mental illness, febrile
diseases, coma and
emergency cases

Fig. I-12

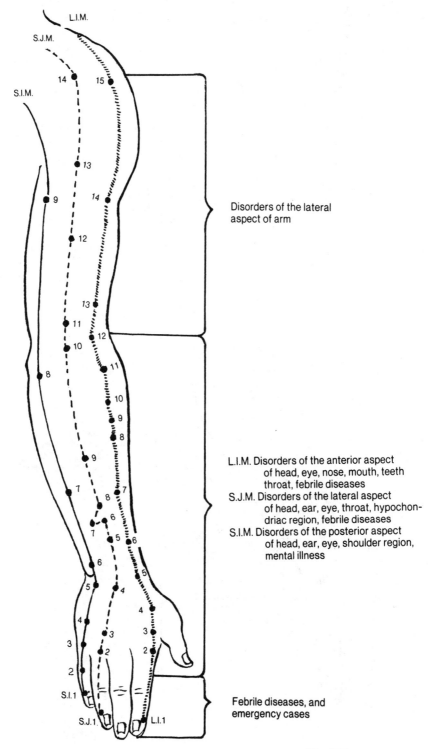

Disorders of the lateral aspect of arm

L.I.M. Disorders of the anterior aspect of head, eye, nose, mouth, teeth throat, febrile diseases

S.J.M. Disorders of the lateral aspect of head, ear, eye, throat, hypochondriac region, febrile diseases

S.I.M. Disorders of the posterior aspect of head, ear, eye, shoulder region, mental illness

Febrile diseases, and emergency cases

Fig. I-13

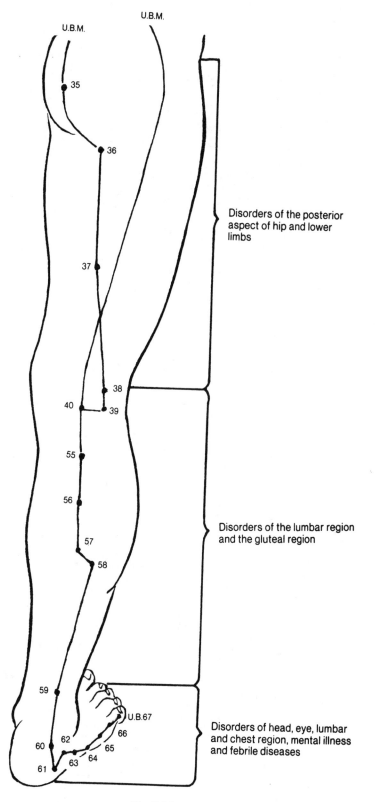

Fig. I-14

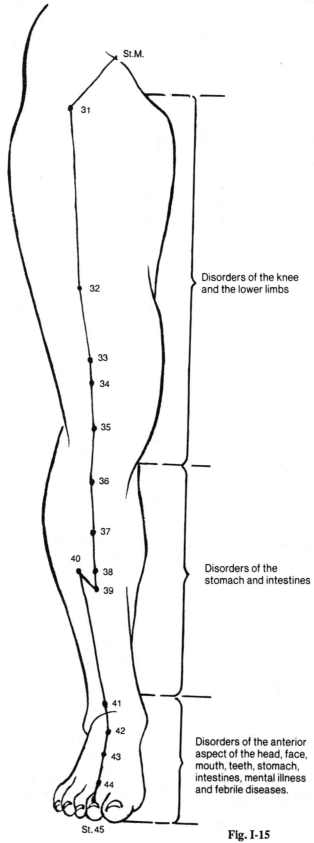

St.M.

31

32

33

34

35

36

37

40

38

39

41

42

43

44

St. 45

Disorders of the knee and the lower limbs

Disorders of the stomach and intestines

Disorders of the anterior aspect of the head, face, mouth, teeth, stomach, intestines, mental illness and febrile diseases.

Fig. I-15

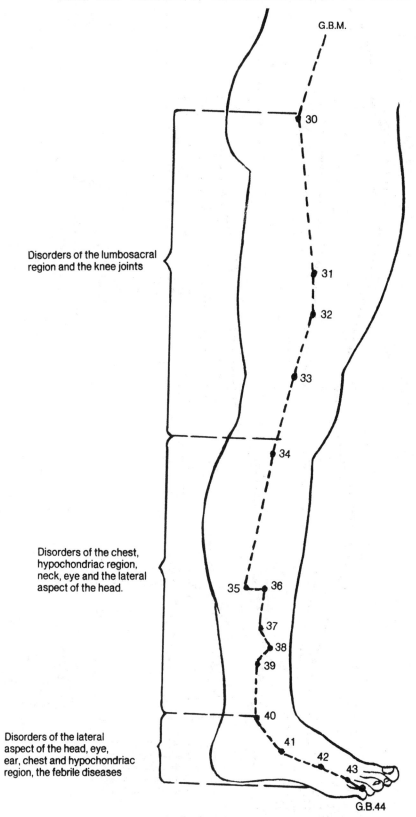

Disorders of the lumbosacral region and the knee joints

Disorders of the chest, hypochondriac region, neck, eye and the lateral aspect of the head.

Disorders of the lateral aspect of the head, eye, ear, chest and hypochondriac region, the febrile diseases

G.B.M.

30
31
32
33
34
35 36
37
38
39
40
41
42
43
G.B.44

Fig. I-16

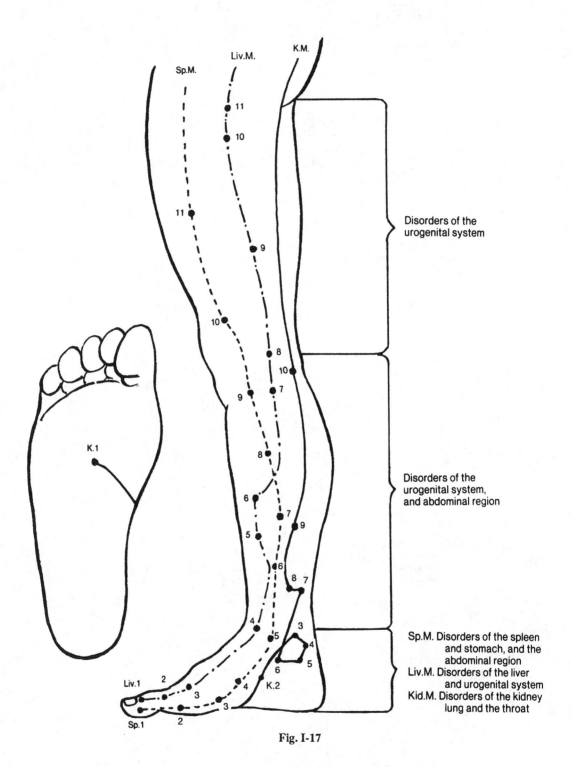

Fig. I-17

PART TWO
The Fourteen Meridians

Chapter I

THE THREE YIN MERIDIANS OF THE HAND

Section 1   THE LUNG MERIDIAN OF HAND-TAIYIN

I. The Meridian

General Indications: The points from this meridian are mainly indicated in disorders of the respiratory system such as cough, asthma, hemoptysis, chest pain, sore throat, respiratory failure and in local disorders occurring along the course of the meridian.

Course of the Meridian:

(1) The Lung Meridian of Hand-Taiyin originates from middle jiao, running downward to connect with the large intestine. (2) Winding back, it goes along the upper orifice of the stomach. (3) Passes through the diaphragm. (4) Enters the lung, its pertaining organ. (5) From the portion of the lung communicating with the throat, it emerges transversely at Zhongfu (Lu.1). (6) Descending along the medial aspect of the upper arm, it passes in front of Heart Meridian of Hand-Shaoyin and the Pericardium Meridian of Hand-Jueyin. (7) Reaches the cubital fossa. (8) Then it descends continuously along the medial aspect of the forearm. (9) Arrives at the medial side of the styloid process of the radius above the wrist, where it enters *cunkou* (the place for pulse palpation). (10) Passing the thenar eminence. (11) It goes along its radial border. (12) Ending at the medial side of the tip of the thumb (Shaoshang, Lu.11). (13) The branch proximal to the wrist emerges from Lieque (Lu. 7). (14) Runs directly to the radial side of the tip of the index finger (Shangyang L.I.1) where it links with the Large Intestine Meridian of the Hand-Yangming (Fig. II-1).

Related Zangfu organs:

This meridian starts from the middle jiao (spleen and stomach), pertains to the lung and connects with the large intestine.

II. The Points

There are altogether 11 points along this meridian on either side. Nine of them are located on the upper limb and 2 on the anteriolateral aspect of the chest. The starting point is Zhongfu (Lu.1) and the terminating point is Shaoshang (Lu.11).

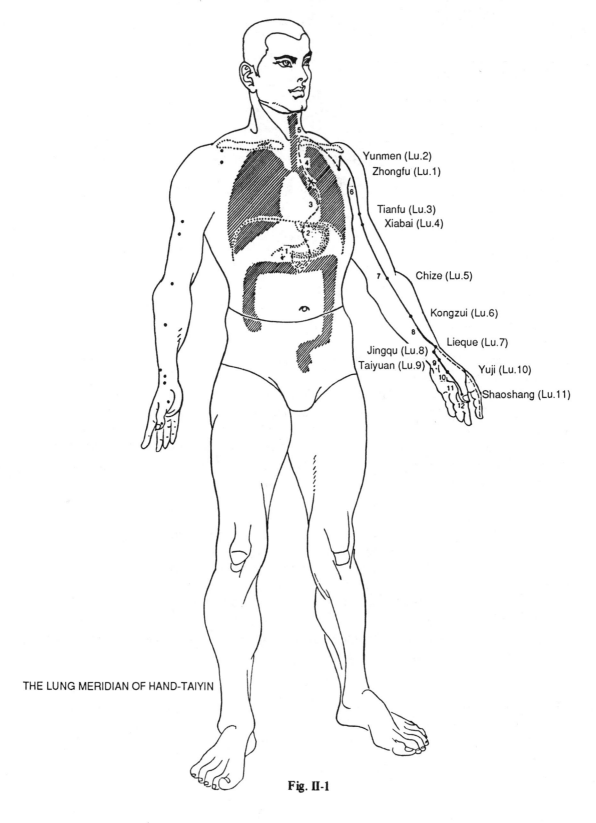

Yunmen (Lu.2)
Zhongfu (Lu.1)

Tianfu (Lu.3)
Xiabai (Lu.4)

Chize (Lu.5)

Kongzui (Lu.6)

Lieque (Lu.7)

Jingqu (Lu.8)
Taiyuan (Lu.9)

Yuji (Lu.10)

Shaoshang (Lu.11)

THE LUNG MERIDIAN OF HAND-TAIYIN

Fig. II-1

Analytical Display of the Course of the Meridian

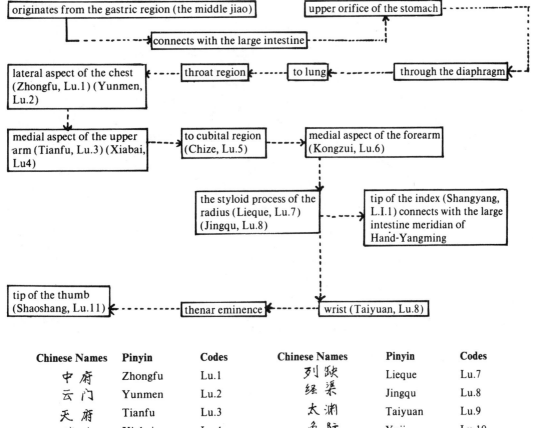

Chinese Names	Pinyin	Codes	Chinese Names	Pinyin	Codes
中 府	Zhongfu	Lu.1	列 缺	Lieque	Lu.7
云 门	Yunmen	Lu.2	经 渠	Jingqu	Lu.8
天 府	Tianfu	Lu.3	太 渊	Taiyuan	Lu.9
侠 白	Xiabai	Lu.4	鱼 际	Yuji	Lu.10
尺 泽	Chize	Lu.5	少 商	Shaoshang	Lu.11
孔 最	Kongzui	Lu.6			

ZHONGFU (Lu. 1)中 府 MU   (CENTRAL MANSION)

"Zhong" (中) refers to the qi of the middle jiao. "Fu" (府) denotes the place where the qi of the meridian converges. This point is the place where the qi of both the Lung Meridian of Hand-Taiyin and the Spleen Meridian of Foot-Taiyin converges. The qi of the middle jiao goes upwards to the lung and gathers here to form the starting point of this meridian, hence the name Zhongfu (Central Mansion).

Location:

At the level with the 3rd rib above the nipple, 6 cun lateral to the Ren Meridian. When a person stands or sits with arms akimbo, one deltoid depression will appear at the lower border of the lateral extremity of the clavicle. The centre of the depression is

---

Note: Points marked with asterisks are the most commonly used ones, and are consequently dealt with in detail.

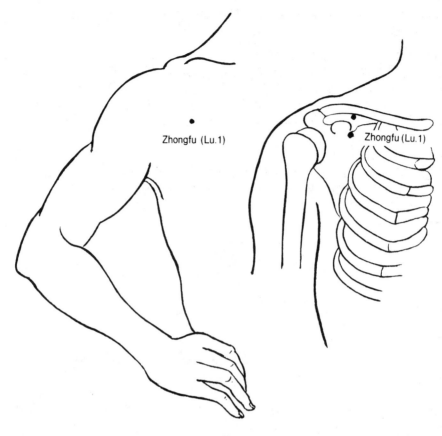

Zhongfu (Lu.1)

Zhongfu (Lu.1)

Fig. II-2

Yunmen (Lu.2). One cun directly below, at the level of the intersoctal space is the point (Fig. II-2).

Indications:

Pain in the upper chest, cough and asthma.

Clinical Application:

Zhongfu (Lu.1) is the Front-mu point of the lung and has the effect of eliminating heat and regulating qi circulation.

Combinations:

With Neiguan (P.6), Shangzhong (Ren 17) and Tiantu (Ren 22) for treating asthma; with Feishu (U.B.13) and Kongzui (Lu.6) for relieving asthma; and with Shaochong (H.9) for treating chest pain.

Method:

Puncture 0.5-1 cun deep obliquely or horizontally towards the lateral aspect of the chest. Moxibustion is applicable. Deep or perpendicular insertion towards the medial aspect of the chest is contraindicated in order to prevent the occurrence of pneumothorax.

Needling Sensations:

Soreness and distention in the shoulder, radiating towards the neck and upper chest.

YUNMEN (LU.2) 云 门 (DOOR OF CLOUD)

"Yun" (云) means cloud. "Men" (门) means a gate. The name "Yunmen" is derived by likening the qi and blood of the human body to a cloud, high in the sky, which nourishes everything on the earth below. The qi and blood of the meridians firstly emerges from Yunmen (Lu.2) to circulate to Qimen (Liv.14), the last point of the Liver Meridian of Foot-Jueyin. Hence the name Yunmen (Door of Cloud).

Location:
One cun directly above Zhongfu (Lu.1) and two fingers' width lateral to the midpoint of the lower border of the clavicle, where there appears a depression (Fig. II-3).

Indications:
Similar to those of Zhongfu (Lu.1)

Method:
Puncture 0.5-1 cun obliquely or horizontally towards the lateral aspect of the chest. Moxibustion is applicable.

TIANFU (LU.3) 天府 (HEAVENS' MANSION)

The lung, considered as being the heavens (Tian, 天) above the earth, is taken as being the superior cover of the rest of the zangfu organs. Also, the lung is the mansion (Fu, 府) of the qi of the body. Furthermore, pulmonary qi converges at this point, hence the name Tianfu (Heavens' Mansion).

Location:
The distance between the end of the axillary fold and the transverse cubital crease is 9 cun. The point is 3 cun below the anterior end of the axillary fold. One simple way to locate the point is to ask the patient to extend his arm. The place where the tip of the nose touches is the point (Fig. II-4).

Indications:
Asthma and epistaxis.

Method:
Puncture perpendicularly 0.5-1 cun deep.

XIABAI (LU. 4) 侠白 (PRESSING WHITE)

"Xia" (侠) means to press and "bai" (白) means white. In ancient times, when locating the point, black ink was applied to both nipples, then the arms were pressed against the chest. The ink marked the location of the point on the medial aspect of the upper arm. This point at the side of the lung is represented by metal and white, according to the theory of the five elements and the five colours. Hence the name Xiabai (Pressing White).

Location:
One cun below Tianfu (Lu.3). Both Tianfu (Lu.3) and Xiabai (Lu.4) are located in the radial groove of the m. biceps brachii. (Fig. II-4).

Indications:
Cough, asthma, and dysmasesis.

Method:

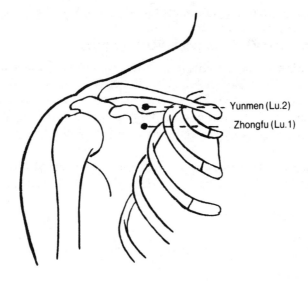

Fig. II-3

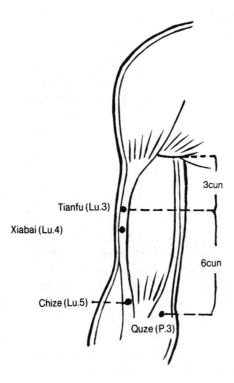

Fig. II-4

Puncture perpendicularly 0.5-1 cun deep. Moxibustion is applicable.

CHIZE (LU. 5) 尺泽 "HE"   (ONE-FOOT MARSH)

The ancient Chinese considered the length from the transverse cubital crease to the wrist crease to be 1 "chi" (one of the units of length measurement in the old system). The forearm is called the "chi" portion. "Ze" (泽) means marsh or a shallow pond. This point, the He-sea point of the meridian, is represented by the concept of water, which gathers in a marsh or pond. Hence the name Chize (One-foot Marsh).

Location:

At the midpoint of the transverse cubital crease, on the radial side of the tendon of m. biceps brachii (Fig. II-5).

Indications:

Cough, asthma, hemoptysis, sore throat, swelling and pain of the upper arm and tidal fever.

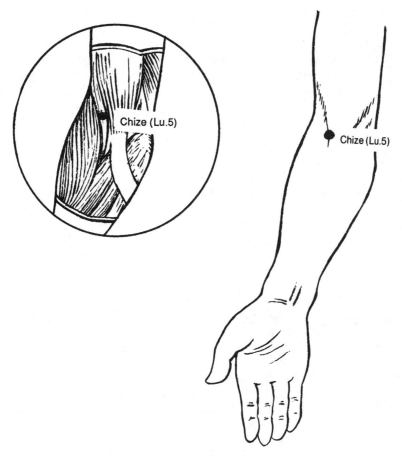

Fig. II-5

Clinical Application:

Chize (Lu.5), the He-sea point of the meridian, has the effect of eliminating pulmonary heat and stopping the ascending of pulmonary qi.

Combinations:

With Quchi (L.I.11) and Hegu (L.I.4) for treating wandering Bi syndrome and motor impairment of the elbow and arm;

With Tiantu (Ren 22) for treating cough;

With Shaoze (S.I.1) for treating restlessness; and

It can also be used to deal with vomiting and diarrhea due to acute gastroenteritis, by bleeding the point with a three-edged needle.

Method:

Puncture perpendicularly about 1 cun deep.

Needling Sensations:

Soreness, numbness and distention, radiating towards the lateral border of the forearm and down to the thumb.

KONGZUI (LU.6)孔最"XI"   (SUPREME PASSAGE)

"Kong" (孔) means a passage. "Zui" (最) means the best, or something supreme. It was believed in ancient times that this point had the best effect in treating febrile disease with no sweat. Nevertheless, this point can also help the lung disperse qi and dominate the opening and closing of the pores. Hence the name Kongzui (Supreme Passage).

Location:

Seven cun above the transverse crease of the wrist on the linking from Chize (Lu.5) to Taiyuan (Lu.9), or 5 cun below Chize (Lu.5) (Fig. II-6).

Indications:

Cough, asthma, hemoptysis, sore throat, pain in the forearm, aphonia and bleeding hemorrhoids.

Clinical Application:

Kongzui (Lu.6), the Xi-cleft point of the Lung Meridian of Hand-Taiyin, has the effect of eliminating pathogenic heat, reducing upward perversion of pulmonary qi and

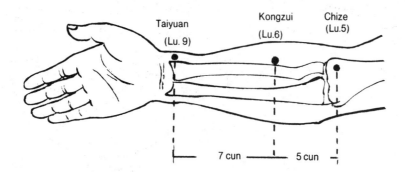

Fig. II-6

stopping bleeding.

Combinations:

With Feishu (U.B.13), Tiantu (Ren 22) and Dazhui (Du 14) for treating high fever, cough and chest pain;

With Hegu (L.I.4) for fever with anhidrosis;

With Feishu (U.B.13) and Quchi (L.I.11) for hemoptysis; and

With Tianrong (S.I.17) and Hegu (L.I.4) for sore throat.

Method:

Puncture perpendicularly about 0.5-1 cun deep.

Needling Sensations:

Soreness, numbness and distention, radiating towards the hand.

LIEQUE (Lu.7) 列缺 "⊗" "∧"   (DIVERGENT BREACH)

"Lie" (列), the same as "lie" (裂) in ancient times, means the state of being divergent or separated. "Que" (缺) means a breach in a utensil. The point is above the wrist at the styloid process of the radius, which was considered as the breach of the arm, and is also the Luo-connecting point of the meridian from which a branch diverges. Hence the name Lieque (Divergent Breach).

Location:

Make the index finger and thumb of one hand cross the index finger and thumb of the other with one index finger pointing at the styloid process of the other. The point is located in the depression where the tip of the index finger touches, that is to say, at the distal point of the styloid process. (Fig. II-7)

Indications:

One-sided headache, sore throat, cough, asthma, deviation of mouth and eye,

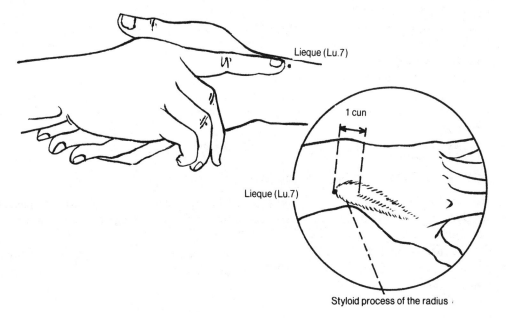

Fig. II-7

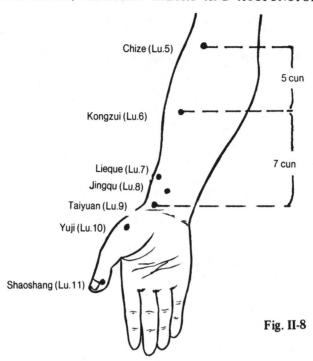

Chize (Lu.5)

5 cun

Kongzui (Lu.6)

7 cun

Lieque (Lu.7)
Jingqu (Lu.8)
Taiyuan (Lu.9)
Yuji (Lu.10)

Shaoshang (Lu.11)

Fig. II-8

toothache, neck pain and impairment of the wrist joint.

Clinical Application:

Lieque (Lu.7) is the Luo-connecting point of the meridian and one of the eight confluent points communicating with the Ren meridian. It has the effect of removing the pathogenic wind, dispersing pulmonary qi and relieving sore throat.

Combinations:

With Zhaohai (K.6) for cough, asthma and sore throat due to deficiency of both the lung and kidney; and

With Houxi (S.I.3) for treating neck rigidity.

Method:

Puncture obliquely upwards 0.5-1 cun deep. Moxibustion is applicable.

Needling Sensations:

Soreness and distention, radiating towards the elbow.

JINGQU (LU.8) 经渠 "θ"   (PASSAGE OF MERIDIAN QI)

Jingqu (Lu.8) is the Jing-river point of the lung meridian and an important passage for the flow of qi in this meridian, hence the name Jingqu (Passage of Meridian Qi).

Location:

On the medial aspect of the top of the styloid process of the radius, that is to say at the "guan" position ("Cun, Guan and Chi" are the three divisions of the region for pulse palpation). (Fig. II-8)

Indications:

Cough, chest pain, sore throat and wrist pain.

Method:

Puncture perpendicularly 0.3-0.5 cun in depth, pushing aside the radial artery.

TAIYUAN (LU.9)太渊 "⊖" "⅄"   (DEEP POND)

"Tai" (太) means something extreme. "Yuan" (渊) means deep or deep water where fish gather. Also, it means the source of a spring. This point, at the "cun" position, is concurrently the Yuan-source point, Shu-stream point and the Influential point of vessels, the qi of vessels being considered to converge there, hence the name Taiyuan (Deep Pond).

Location:

On the radial side of the large multangular bone, in the depression on the radial side of the radial artery, above the 1st transverse crease of the wrist. (Fig. II-8)

Indications:

Cough, asthma, sore throat and acrotism.

Method:

Push aside the radial artery and puncture perpendicularly 0.3-0.5 cun deep. Better effect can be achieved if the needle is inserted immediately beside the wall of the blood vessels.

YUJI (LU.10)鱼际 (THENAR EMINENCE)

"Yu" (鱼、) means fish and "ji" (际) means margin. This point is at the junction of the red and white skin near the 1st metacarpal joint of the thumb. The prominence of the muscle here is similar to the junction of the red and white skin of the fish belly, hence the name Yuji (Thenar Eminence). (Fig. II-8)

Indications:

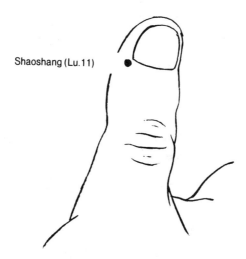

Shaoshang (Lu.11)

Fig. II-9

Indications:

Cough, hemoptysis and aphonia.

Method:

Puncture perpendicularly 0.3-0.8 cun deep. Moxibustion is applicable.

SHAOSHANG (LU.11) " ⊙ " (YOUNG SHANG)

The names of most points at the tips of the fingers contain the character "shao" (少) which forms part of the name of the most terminating points. It means something small, young or primary. The lung is represented by metal. "Shang" (商) is one of the five notes of ancient Chinese five-tone scale*, also represented by the metal. Thus, "shang" (商) here actually refers to lung. Shaoshang (Lu.11) is the last point of the meridian, where qi of the meridian is least abundant. Also, it is the Jing-well point of the meridian where qi starts to bubble. Hence the name Shaoshang (Young Shang).

Location:

0.1 cun posterior to the corner of the nail on the radial side of the thumb. (Fig. II-9)

Clinical Applications:

Shaoshang (Lu.11), the Jing-well point of the meridian, has the effect to eliminate pulmonary heat, clear the throat and restore Yang qi from collapse. It is often used for emergency cases.

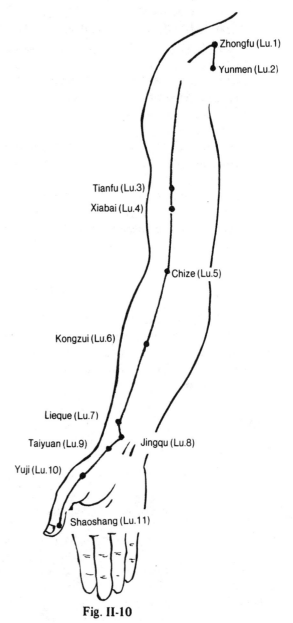

Fig. II-10

Specific Points of the Meridian

Points	Specific Names
Zhongfu Lu.1	Mu
Chize Lu.5	He (water)
Jingqu Lu.8	⊖ (metal)
Taiyuan Lu.9	夫 (earth)
Yuji Lu.10	～ (fire)
Shaoshang Lu.11	⊙ (wood)
Kongzui Lu.6	Xi
Lieque Lu.7	⊗

*The five notes of ancient Chinese five-tone scale are "gong (宮), shang (商), jiao (角), zhi (徵) and yu (羽)."

Combinations:
With Renzhong (Du 26) and Zusanli (St.36) for syncope, coma and shock;
With Hegu (L.I.4) and Neiting (St.44) for acute tonsillitis; and
With moxa cones at this point for epistaxis and epilepsy.
Method:
Puncture shallowly 0.1 cun deep by pricking to cause bleeding.
Needling Sensations:
Slight pain in the local area.

III. Summary

This meridian starts from the middle jiao (spleen and stomach), pertains to the lung, and connects with the large intestine. There are altogther 11 points from this meridian on either side of the body (Fig. II-10).

Indications of Points of the Lung Meridian

Point Names	locations	Indications	Regional Indications
Zhongfu (Lu.1)	6 cun lateral to anterior midline, at the inferior border of the clavicle, level with the lateral end of the 2nd rib	Cough and chest pain	
Yunmen (Lu.2)	6 cun lateral to the anterior midline, at the lower border of the clavicle	Cough and chest pain	Chest pain
Tianfu (Lu.3)	On the medial aspect of the upper arm, 3 cun below the anterior end of the axillary fold, in the radial groove of the m. biceps brachii	Cough and epistaxis	
Xiabai (Lu.4)	1 cun below Tianfu (Lu.1)	Nausea, gastric pain and cough	
Chize (Lu.5)	On the transverse cubital crease at the lateral border of tendon of m. biceps brachii	Tidal fever, asthma, sore throat, vomiting and diarrhea	
Kongzui (Lu.6)	5 cun below Chize (Lu.5) on the linking line between Chize (Lu.5) and Taiyuan (Lu.9)	Cough and hemoptysis	
Lieque (Lu.7)	In the depression of the styloid process of the radius, 1.5 cun above the transverse crease of the wrist	Sore throat, dry mouth and headache	Disorders of throat, lung and chest
Jingqu (Lu.8)	In the depression of the styloid process of the radius, 1 cun above the transverse crease of the wrist	Cough and headache	

Taiyuan (Lu.9)	In the depression distal to the styloid process of the radius above the wrist	Acrotism, pectoral pain, suffocating sensation in the chest
Yuji (Lu.10)	At the midpoint of the border of the thenar eminence	Cough and asthma
Shaoshang (Lu.11)	.1 cun posterior to the lateral side of the finger nail	Pharyngeal swelling in febrile diseases, syncope.

Section 2   THE HEART MERIDIAN OF HAND-SHAOYIN

I. The Meridian

General Indications:

Points from this meridian are mainly indicated in psychoses, neuroses and disorders of the cardiavascular system, e.g. mental disorders, epilepsy, insomnia, tachycardia, bradycardia, arrhythmia, and angina pectoris, etc.

Course of the Meridian:

(1) The Heart Meridian of Hand-Shaoyin starts from the heart. Emerging, it spreads over the "heart system," i.e. the vessels connecting the heart with the other zangfu organs. (2) It passes through the diaphragm to connect with the small intestine. (3) The ascending portion of the meridian from the "heart system" (4) runs alongside the esophagus (5) to connect with the "eye system," i.e. the tissues connecting with the eyeball. (6) The straight portion of the meridian from the "heart system" goes upward to the lung, (7) then turns downward and emerges from the axilla (Jiquan, H.1). From there it goes along the posterior border of the medial aspect of the upper arm, behind the Lung Meridian of Hand-Taiyin and the Pericardium Meridian of Hand-Jueyin, (8) down to the cubital fossa. (9) It descends along the posterior border of the medial aspect of the forearm to the pisiform region, proximal to the palm (10) and enters the palm. (11) Then, it follows the medial aspect of the little finger to its tip (Shaochong, H.9) and links with the Small Intestine Meridian of Hand-Taiyang (Fig. II-11).

Related Zangfu Organs:

Pertaining to the heart, connecting with the small intestine and passing through the lung.

II. The Points

There are altogether 9 points from this meridian on either side. Eight of them are distributed on the medial aspect of the arm, and one on the lateral aspect of the chest. Jiquan (H.1) is the starting point and Shaochong (H.9) is the terminating one.

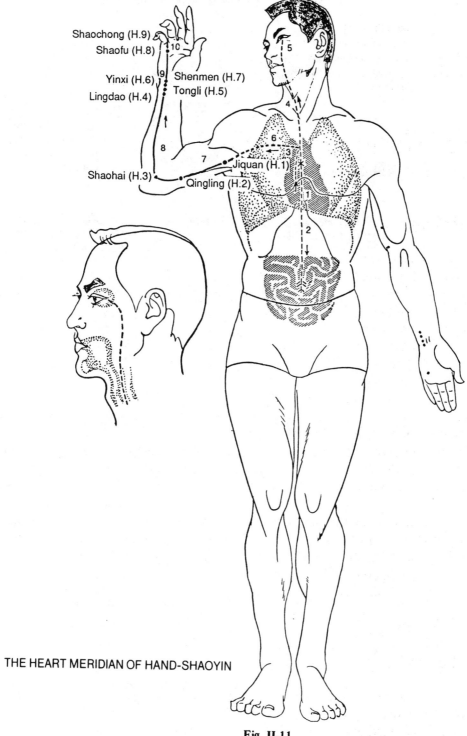

Shaochong (H.9)
Shaofu (H.8)
Yinxi (H.6)
Lingdao (H.4)
Shenmen (H.7)
Tongli (H.5)
Shaohai (H.3)
Jiquan (H.1)
Qingling (H.2)

THE HEART MERIDIAN OF HAND-SHAOYIN

Fig. II-11

Analytical Display of the Course of the Meridian

Starting from the heart	pertaining to the heart system (vessels connecting the heart with other zangfu organs)	passing through the diaphragm	connecting with the small intestine
brain			
eye throat	side of the esophagus lung	axilla (Jiquan, H.1)	posterior border of the medial aspect of the upper arm (Qingling, H.2; Shaohai, H.3)
connecting with the Small Intestine Meridian of Hand-Taiyang	tip of the medial aspect of the small finger	palm (Shaofu, H.8)	the pisiform region (Lingdao, H.4; Tongli, H.5; Yinxi, H.6 and Shenmen, H.7)

Chinese Names	Pinyin	Codes	Chinese Names	Pinyin	Codes
极泉	Jiquan	H.1	阴郄	Yinxi	H.6
青灵	Qingling	H.2	神门	Shenmen	H.7
少海	Shaohai	H.3	少府	Shaofu	H.8
灵道	Lingdao	H.4	少冲	Shaochong	H.9
通里	Tongli	H.5			

JIQUAN (H.1) 极泉 (RUNNING SPRING)

"Ji" (极) means the ending place or fast running, here referring to the highest point in the axillary area. "Quan" (泉) means a spring. The heart dominates blood circulation in the vessels, likened in this case to the flow of a spring. The point is located in the centre of the axilla where the axillary artery can be palpated. The blood circulation here is fast and strong, like water flowing from a spring, hence the name Jiquan (Running Spring). (Fig. II-12, 18).

Indications:

Pain in the hypochondriac region, dry throat and scrofula.

Method:

Puncture perpendicularly or obliquely 0.3-0.5 cun deep, avoiding the artery. Moxibustion is applicable.

QINGLING (H.2) 青灵 (GREEN EFFECT)

"Qing" (青) refers to the colour green, which in the TCM diagnosis denotes pain. "Ling" (灵) represents the image that the effect of this point is all-curative. This point is effective in the treatment of pain occurring in the head, arm, heart or chest, hence the name Qingling (Green Effect).

Location:

Three cun above the lateral epicondyle of the humerus, i.e. 3 cun above Shaohai

(H.3), in the groove medial to m. biceps brachii.(Fig. II-12)

Indications:

Headache, pain in the shoulder, arm, chest or hypochondriac region.

Method:

Puncture perpendicularly 0.5-1 cun deep. Moxibustion is applicable.

SHAOHAI (H.3) 少 海 "HE"   (YOUNG SEA)

"Shao" (少) here refers to the Heart Meridian of Hand-Shaoyin.

"Hai" (海) means sea. The heart dominates the blood circulation in the vessels. Qi is the most abundant at this point, as though waters were converging into the sea. Also, it is the He-sea point of the meridian, hence the name Shaohai (Young Sea).

Location:

At the medial end of the transverse cubital crease, with the elbow flexed. Alternatively, if the elbow is only slightly flexed, the point is located at the midpoint between the process of the medial epicondyle of the humerus and Quchi (L.I.11) (Fig. II-12, 13, 14).

Indications:

Pain in the heart area, hand tremor, numbness of the arm, pain and swelling of the lymphatic glands in the axilla and hypochondriac pain.

Clinical Application:

Shaohai (H.3), the He-sea point of the meridian, has the effect to dispel pathogenic heat from the heart, calm the mind, resolve phlegm and stop pain.

Combinations:

With Hegu (L.I.4) and Neiting (St. 44) for treating sore throat and toothache;

With Houxi (S.I.3) for hand tremor;

With Quchi (L.I.11) for painful elbow and numbness in the hand.

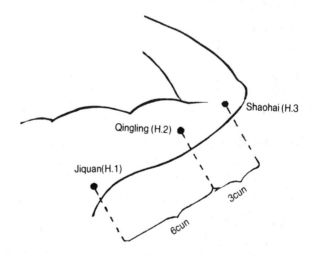

Fig. II-12

Method:
Puncture perpendicularly about 1 cun deep. Moxibustion is applicable.
Needling Sensations:
Soreness, numbness and distention, radiating towards the palm.
Explanation of Fig. II-14;
The small head of the ulna is divided into 3 equal parts for locating Lingdao (H.4), Tongli (H.5) and Yinxi (H.6).

Lingdao (H.4) is level with the root of the small head of the ulna, i.e. 1.5 cun above Shenmen (H.7).

Tongli (H.5) is level with the midpoint of the small head of the ulna, i.e. 1 cun above Shenmen (H.7).

Yinxi (H.6) is level with the top of the small head of the ulna, i.e. 0.5 cun above Shenmen (H.7). All three are located on the radial side of the tendon of m. flexor carpi ulnaris. They are similar in actions, dealing with mental diseases, pain in the heart area, sore throat, painful wrist and arm, and sudden loss of voice. Yinxi (H.6) also has the effect to eliminate internal heat due to deficiency. The depth of insertion for these points is 0.5-0.8 cun.

LINGDAO (H.4)灵道 ⊖ (MIND PASSAGE)

"Ling" (灵) refers to spirit, soul or mind. "Dao" (道) means path or passage. The point, the Jing-river point of this meridian, is likened to a passage leading to the heart, which is in turn considered to dominate the mind. It is indicated in mental diseases and

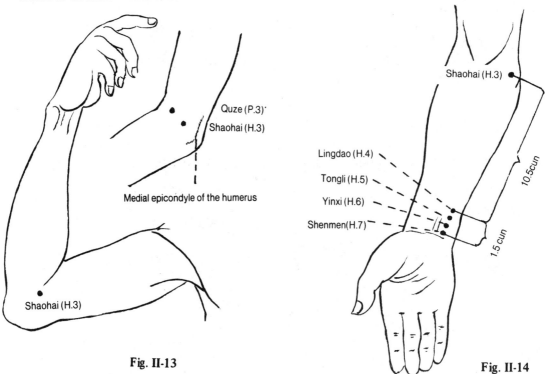

Fig. II-13   Fig. II-14

heart disorders. Hence the name Lingdao (Mind Passage). Moxibustion is applicable. (Fig. II-14)

TONGLI (H.5) 通里 ∧ (INNER COMMUNICATION)

"Tong" (通) means leading to or passing through. "Li" (里) means interior, referring to the internal-external relationship between the heart and small intestine meridians in particular. It is the Luo-connecting point of this meridian, from which its collateral starts to connect with the Small Intestine Meridian of Hand-Taiyang, thus relating the two meridians internally and externally. Hence the name Tongli (Inner Communication). It produces good results in dealing with aphonia in hysteria, hoarseness and bradycardia. Moxibustion is applicable. (Fig. II-14)

YINXI (H.6) 阴都 XI (YIN CREVICE)

"Yin" (阴) means Yin, as opposite to Yang, and here refers to the Heart Meridian of Foot-Shaoyin. "Xi" (都) means a hole or a crevice, and refers to the Xi-cleft point of this meridian, where qi and blood converge. Hence the name Yinxi (Yin crevice). It is indicated in bone steaming (i.e. afternoon fever, night sweating), epistaxis, palpitation and cardiac pain. Moxibustion is applicable. (Fig. II-14)

SHENMEN (H.7) 神门 &O   (SPIRITUAL GATE)

"Shen" (神) means spirit or mind, referring to the heart's function of dominating mental activities and housing the mind. "Men" (门) means a gate or door. This point from the Heart Meridian of Hand-Shaoyin is likened to a gate through which the qi of the heart comes and goes. Hence the name Shenmen (Spiritual Gate).

Location:

In the depression on the ulnar side of the tendon of m. flexor carpi ulnaris, on the 2nd transverse crease of the wrist (Fig. II-14, 15).

Indications:

Insomnia, poor memory, palpitation, cardiac pain and hysteria.

Clinical Application:

Shenmen (H.7) is the Shu-stream point and Yuan-source point of this meridian. It has the effect to calm the mind and heart and remove obstruction from the meridian.

Combinations:

With Fengchi (G.B.20) and Baihui (Du 20) for treating neurasthenia, poor memory and insomnia;

With Neiguan (P.6) and Xinshu (U.B.15) for angina pectoris.

Method:

Puncture perpendicularly 0.3-0.5 cun deep. Moxibustion is applicable.

Needling Sensations:

Numbness in the local area.

SHAOFU (H.8) 少府 ～ (YOUNG MANSION)

"Shao" (少) means small or young and refers to the Meridian of Hand-Shaoyin. "Fu" (府) means a gathering place. This point is in the small bony gap of the metacarpal bones where the qi of the heart meridian gathers. Hence the name Shaofu (Young Mansion).

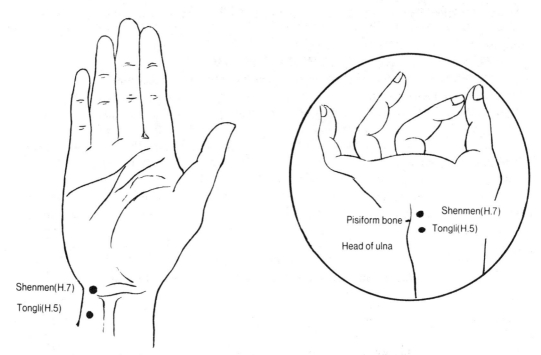

Fig. II-15

Location:
Between the 4th and 5th metacarpal bones, level with Laogong (P.8) (Fig. II-16).
Indications:
Palpitation, chest pain, spasmodic pain of the little finger and feverish sensation in the palm.
Method:
Puncture perpendicularly 0.3-0.5 cun deep. Moxibustion is applicable.

SHAOCHONG (H.9) 少冲 ⊖ (SMALL FORT)

"Shao" (少) means small or young again, referring to this meridian. "Chong" (冲) can be interpreted as meaning an important fort. It is the point where the qi and blood of the meridian start to flourish. It is the Jing-well point of the Heart Meridian of Hand-Shaoyin where qi bubbles out and flows into the arm. Hence the name Shaochong (Small Fort).

Location:
0.1 cun posterior to the medial corner of the nail of the little finger (Fig. II-16,17).
Indications:
Palpitation, chest pain, febrile disease and coma.
Clinical Application:
Shaochong (H.9) is the Jing-well point of this meridian. It has the effect to restore Yang qi from collapse, and is often used for emergency cases.

Combinations:
With Renzhong (Du 26), Zusanli (St.36) and Zhongchong (P.9) for treating sun-stroke, shock and syncope.
Method:
Puncture shallowly 0.1 cun deep by pricking to cause bleeding.
Needling Sensations:
Slight pain in the local area.

III. Summary

The Heart Meridian of Hand-Shaoyin pertains to the heart and connects with the small intestine. There are altogether 9 points from this meridian on either side of the body (Fig. II-19).

Indications of Points of the Meridian According to Locations

Point Names	Locations	Indications	Regional Indications
Jiquan H.1	In the centre of the axillary where the axilla artery is palpated	Chest pain	
Qingling H.2	3 cun above Shaohai (H.3), on the line linking Jiquan (H.1) and Shaohai (H.3)	Arm and shoulder pain with motor impairment	
Shaohai H.3	At the medial end of the transverse cubital crease	Swelling of the lymphatic glands in the axilla; hand tremor	Cardiac pain, palpitation, chest disorders, mental disorders and febrile diseases
Lingdao H.4	1.5 cun above the medial end of the transverse crease of the wrist	Cardiac and epigastric pain	
Tongli H.5	1 cun above medial end of the transverse crease of the wrist	Tongue rigidity, hysteria	
Yingxi H.6	0.5 cun above the medial end of the transverse crease of the wrist	Night sweating	
Shenmen H.7	On the medial end of the transverse crease of the wrist	Insomnia, tachycardia, arrythmia	
Shaofu H.8	Between the 4th and 5th metacarpal bones	Arrhythmia, angina pectoris, toothache	
Shaochong H.9	0.1 cun posterior to the radial corner of the little finger	Coma in febrile diseases, angina pectoris	

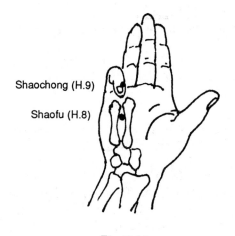

Fig. II-16

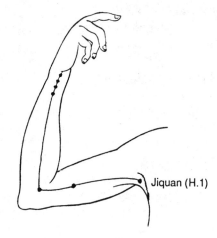

Fig. II-18

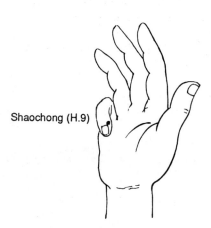

Fig. II-17

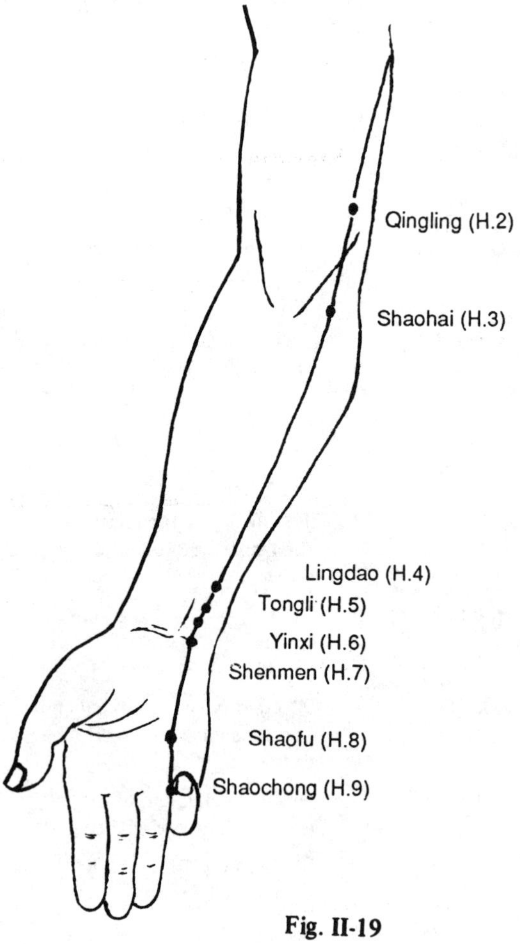

Specific Points of the Meridian

Shaohai H.3   He (water)

Lingdao H.4 $\ominus$ (metal)

Shenmen H.7   ♀ (earth)

Shaofu H.8 $\sim$ (fire) O

Shaochong H.9   ☉ (wood)

Yinxi H.6   Xi

Tongli H.5   A

Qingling (H.2)

Shaohai (H.3)

Lingdao (H.4)
Tongli (H.5)
Yinxi (H.6)
Shenmen (H.7)

Shaofu (H.8)

Shaochong (H.9)

Fig. II-19

Section 3   THE PERICARDIUM MERIDIAN OF HAND-JUEYIN

I. The Meridian

General Indications:

Points from this meridian are mainly indicated in disorders of the cardiovascular system, epigastric pain, nausea, vomiting, psychic disorders and syncope.

Course of the Meridian:

(1) The Pericardium Meridian of Hand-Jueyin originates from the chest where it enters its pertaining organ, the pericardium.(2) It descends through the diaphragm (3) to the abdomen, connecting successively with the upper, middle and lower jiao (i.e. Triple Heater). (4) Another branch arising from the chest runs inside the chest, (5) emerges from the costal region at a point 3 cun below the anterior axillary fold (Tianchi, P.1) (6) and ascends to the axilla. (7) Following the medial aspect of the upper arm, it runs downwards between the Lung Meridian of Hand-Taiyin and the Heart Meridian of Hand-Shaoyin (8) to the cubital fossa, (9) further downward along the forearm between the tendons of m. palmaris longus and m. flexor carpi radialis, (10) and enters into the palm (11) until it reaches to its tip, Zhongchong (P.9). (12) Another branch rises from the palm at Laogong (P.8) (12), runs along the ring finger to its tip (Guangchong, S.J.1) and links with the Sanjiao Meridian of Hand-Shaoyang. (Fig. II-20)

Analytical Display of the Course of the Meridian

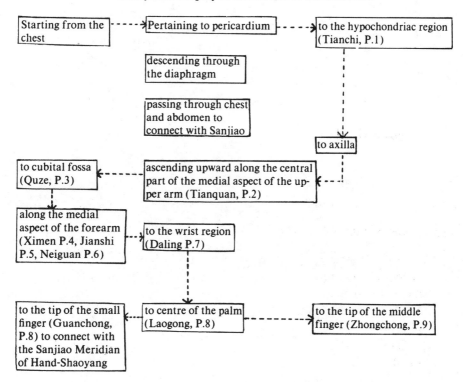

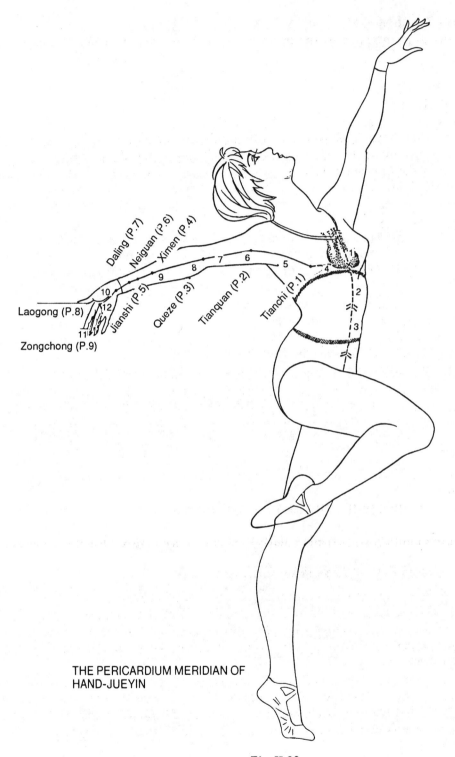

THE PERICARDIUM MERIDIAN OF
HAND-JUEYIN

Fig. II-20

Related Zangfu organs:
This meridian pertains to the pericardium and connects with the Sanjiao (Triple Heater)

II. The Points

There are altogether nine points on this meridian, among which eight are distributed along the central line of the palmar aspect of the upper limb and one on the lateral side of the breast. Tianchi (P.1) is the starting point and Zhongchong (P.9) is the terminating point.

Point Names	Pinyin	Codes	Point Names	Pinyin	Codes
天池	Tianchi	P.1	内关	Neiguan	P.6
天泉	Tianquan	P.2	大陵	Daling	P.7
曲泽	Quze	P.3	劳宫	Laogong	P.8
郄门	Ximen	P.4	中冲	Zhongchong	P.9
间使	Jianshi	P.5			

TIANCHI (P.1) 天池 (CELESTIAL POND)

"Tian" (天) means celestial, but here refers to the upper part of the body in general. In ancient times, physicians referred to the upper part as "tian," heaven, and the lower part as "di," earth. "Chi" (池) means a pond from which water flows. The point is beside the breast from which milk flows via the nipple, as though a pond inside. Hence the name Tianchi (Celestial Pond).

Location:
One cun lateral to the nipple on the level of the 4th intercostal space (Fig. II-21).

Indications:
Fullness sensation in the chest and hypochondriac pain.

Method:
Puncture obliquely or perpendicularly 0.3-0.5 cun deep. Moxibustion is applicable.

TIANQUAN (P.2) 天泉 (CELESTIAL SPRING)

"Tian" (天) bears the same meaning as mentioned above. "Quan"(泉) means a spring, here refers to the qi and blood of the meridian. This point is on the superior aspect of the upper arm at the level of the nipple. The qi and blood of the meridian descend from this point like water from a spring, hence the name Tianquan (Celestial Spring).

Location:
At the same level as Tianchi (P.1) and Tianxi (Sp.18), in the muscular belly of biceps brachii, 2 cun below the anterior axillary crease. Have the patient raise his arm close to the ear lobulus auriculae. The place where the midpoint of the lower border of the lobulus auriculae touches the upper arm is the point (Fig. II-22).

Indications:
Cardiac pain and pain in the arm and hypochondriac region.

Method:

Puncture perpendicularly 1-1.5 cun deep. Moxibustion is applicable.

QUZE (P.3) 曲泽   "HE" (CURVED POND)

"Qu" (曲) means something curved, but refers to the flexion of the elbow in this context. "Ze" (泽) means marsh, usually more extensive and shallower than a pond ("chi" in Chinese). It is the He-sea point of the Pericardium Meridian of Hand-Jueyin, represented by water. The elbow is flexed when locating this point, hence the name Quze (Curved Pond).

Location:

At the midpoint of the transverse crease from cubital fossa to Chize (Lu.5), on the ulnar side of the m. biceps brachii (Fig. II-23).

Indications:

Epigastric pain, cardiac pain, vom-

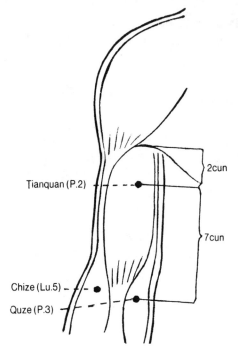

Fig. II-22

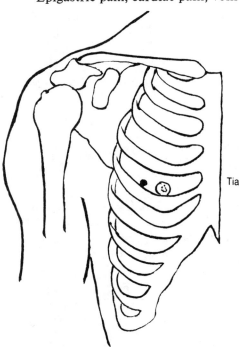

Tianchi (P.1)

Fig. II-21

iting, palpitation, restlessness, irascibility, elbow pain, arm pain and hand tremor.

Clinical Application:

Quze (P.3), the He-sea point of this meridian, has the effect to regulate circulation of qi and blood in the meridian, dispel pathogenic heat and dampness, release pain and stop diarrhea.

Combinations:

With Neiguan (P.6) and Daling (P.7) for cardiac pain;

With Weizhong (U.B.40) for stopping bleeding or vomiting and diarrhea in acute enteritis or high fever due to sunstroke.

Method:

Puncture perpendicularly 1-1.5 cun deep, or prick to cause bleeding at the vein.

Needling Sensations:

Soreness and numbness, radiating down to the middle finger.

XIMEN (P.4) 郗门 "XI" (CLEFT GATE)

"Xi" (郗) means a cleft, viz, the cleft point where qi and blood of this meridian converge. "Men" (门) likens the point to a gate through which the qi and blood of the Pericardium Meridian of Hand-Jueyin may pass in and out. Hence the name Ximen (Cleft Gate).

Location:

Five cun above the first transverse crease of the wrist (Fig. II-24).

Indications:

Chest pain and palpitation.

Method:

Puncture perpendicularly 0.5 cun deep. Moxibustion is applicable.

JIANSHI (P.5) 间使 "—ᘓ—" (INNER MESSENGER)

"Jian" (间) refers to a gap between the two. "Shi" (使) means mes-

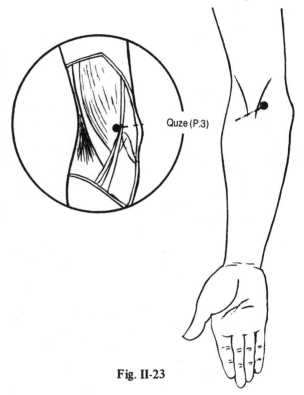

Quze (P.3)

Fig. II-23

senger. This point, located between the tendons of m. palmaris longus and m. flexor carpi radialis, has the effect to transport qi in the meridian, hence the name Jianshi (Inner Messenger).

Another name for this point is ghost passage, the concept being that in the treatment of mental diseases, its action is like that of a ghost, working inside the disease.

Location:

Three cun above the midpoint of the transverse crease of the wrist, between the tendons of m. palmaris longus and m. flexor carpi radialis (Fig. II-24, 25, 26).

Indications:

Angina pectoris, palpitation, vomiting, phrenospasm, hysteria, hypertension, epilepsy and infantile convulsions.

Clinical Application:

Jianshi (P.5), the Jing-river point of this meridian, has the effect to tranquilize the heart and mind, activate qi and blood circulation, pacify the stomach and dispel phlegm.

Combinations:

With Houxi (S.I.3), Baihui (Du 20) and Hegu (L.I.4) for epilepsy;

With Xinshu (U.B.15) and Shaofu (H.8) for angina pectoris and palpitation.

Method:

Puncture perpendicularly for 0.5-1 cun deep. Moxibustion is applicable.

Note: The distance between the transverse cubital crease and the first transverse palmar crease is 12 cun. Ximen (P.4), Jianshi (P.5), Neiguan (P.6) and Daling (P.7) are located between the tendons of m. palmaris longus and flexor carpi radialis. These four points are mainly indicated in cardiac pain and palpitations.

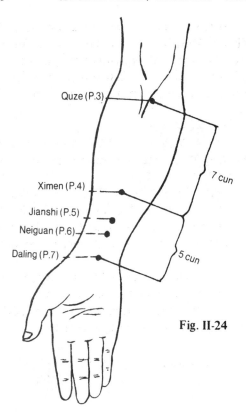

Fig. II-24

Needling Sensations:

Soreness and numbness, radiating towards the middle finger.

NEIGUAN (P.6)内关 " 八 " " ⊗ " (INNER PASS)

"Nei" (内) means interior, opposite to exterior. "Guan" (关) refers to the area lateroposterior to *cunkou* (the place for pulse palpation), meaning the passage where the qi of the meridian comes in and out, hence the name Neiguan (Inner Pass).

Location:

Two cun above the midpoint of the transverse crease of the wrist, between the tendons of m. palmaris longus and m. flexor carpi radialis (Fig. II-24, 25, 26, 27).

Indications:

Palpitation, angina pectoris, hypochondriac pain, epigastric pain, vomiting, coma, morning sickness, insomnia, dizziness and vertigo.

Clinical Application:

Neiguan (P.6), the Luo-connecting point of this meridian, and one of the eight

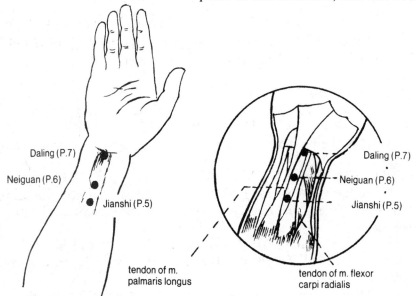

Fig. II-25

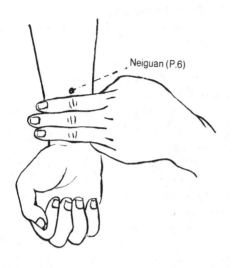

Fig. II-26

Confluent Points communicating with the Yinwei Meridian, is commonly used for disorders of the cardiovascular system. It has the effect to regulate qi circulation and pacify the stomach, calm the heart and mind, and cease pain.

Combinations:

With Xinshu (U.B.15) and Jueyinshu (U.B.14) for releasing angina pectoris and palpitation;

With Renzhong (Du 26), Baihui (Du 20) and Zusanli (St.36) for coma and shock;

With Gongsun (Sp.4) and Zusanli (St.36) for disorders involving both gastric and chest areas.

The point Neiguan (P.6) is also commonly used for acupuncture anesthesia in pneumonectomy and pericardiotomy. Needling Neiguan (P.6) can reinforce insufficient blood supply in the arteria coronaria.

Method:

Puncture perpendicularly 0.5-1 cun deep. Moxibustion is applicable.

Needling Sensations:

Numbness radiating to the finger.

DALING (P.7)大陵 " 俞 " " O " (BIG MOUND)

"Da" (大) means something lofty or big. "Ling" (陵) means a high place, but here refers to the process of the carpal bone. The point is posterior to the carpal bone, hence the name Daling (Big Mound).

Location:

In the depression at the middle of the 1st transverse crease of the wrist, between the tendons of m. palmaris longus and m. flexor carpi radialis (Fig. II-24, 25).

Indications:

Palpitation, epigastric pain, vomiting, fever due to Yin deficiency, and pain in the heel.

Clinical Application:

Daling (P.7), the Shu-stream point and Yuan-source point of this meridian, has the effect to calm the heart and mind and pacify the stomach.

Combinations:

With Shenmen (H.7), Renzhong (Du 26) and Baihui (Du 20) for mental diseases;

With Neiguan (P.6) and Xinshu (U.B.15)

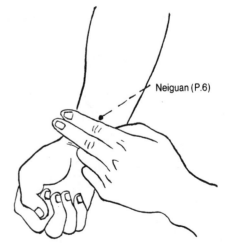

Fig. II-27

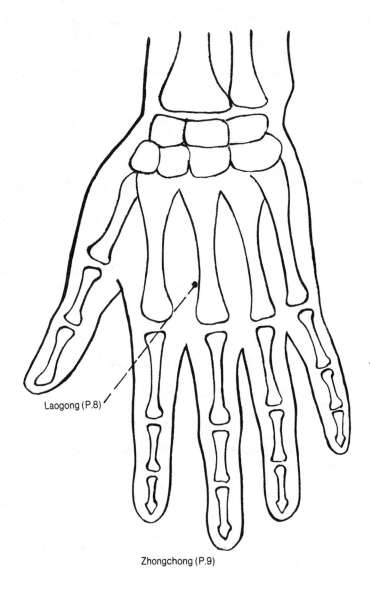

Laogong (P.8)

Zhongchong (P.9)

Fig. II-28

for diseases of the heart.
    Method:
Puncture perpendicularly 0.5-0.8 cun deep. Moxibustion is applicable.

LAOGONG (P.8)劳宫 " ⌒ "   (LABOURING PALACE)

    "Lao" (劳) means to labour. "Gong" (宫) means a palace. The human hand is the organ of labour. This point in the centre of the palm is from the Pericardium Meridian

_____

    Note: A new point, called "Yatong" (toothache point) or "Zhizhang" (palm), was recently added between the 3rd and 4th metacarpophalangeal joints, 1 cun distal to the transverse crease of the wrist.

of Hand-Jueyin, the pericardium being the palace of the heart (the emperor). Hence the name Laogong (Labouring Palace).

Location:

Between the 2nd and 3rd metacarpal bones, proximal to the metacarpophalangeal joints, on the radial side of the 3rd metacarpal bone (Fig. II-28, 29).

Indications:

Cardiac pain, profuse sweating of the hands, hand tinea, mental mania, epilepsy, mouth ulceration and foul breath.

ZHONGCHONG (P.9) 中冲 " ⊙ " (CENTRAL FORT)

"Zhong" (中), meaning centre, refers to the centre of the tip of the middle finger. "Chong" (冲) means a fort, i.e. a place where there is an abundant flow of qi and blood. Hence the name Zhongchong (Central Fort).

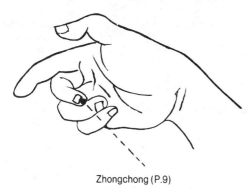

Zhongchong (P.9)

Fig. II-29

Location:

In the centre of the tip of the middle finger, 0.1 cun distal to the tip of the finger nail (Fig. II-28, 29).

Indications:

Coma, sunstroke, cardiac pain, febrile disease, stiffness of the tongue with difficult speech, infantile convulsions, morbid crying of a baby at night, feverish sensation in the palm and abdominal pain.

Clinical Application:

Zhongchong (P.9), the Jing-well point of the Pericardium Meridian of Hand-Jueyin, has the effect to remove obstruction from the collaterals, resuscitate the unconscious and restore Yang qi from collapse.

Combinations:

With Renzhong (Du 26) and Neiguan (P.6) for syncope and loss of consciousness due to windstroke;

With Shangyang (L.I.1) and Shaoshang (Lu.11) by bleeding to alleviate fever due to exogenous pathogenic invasion;

With Guanchong (S.J.1) for aphonia with tongue rigidity.

Method:

Puncture perpendicularly 0.1 cun deep by pricking to cause bleeding.

Needling Sensations:

Mild pain in the local area.

III. Summary

This meridian pertains to the pericardium and connects with the Sanjiao (Fig. II-30).

Specific Points of the Meridian

Quze (P.3)	He (water)	Zhongchong (P.9)	☉ (wood)
Jianshi (P.5)	⊖ (metal)	Neiguan (P.6)	V ⊗
Daling (P.7)	⚡ (earth)	Ximen (P.4)	Xi
Laogong (8)	⌇ (fire)		

Point Indications of the Pericardium Meridian According to Locations

Point Names	Locations	Indications	Regional Indications
Tianchi P.1	1 cun lateral to the nipple, on the level of the 4th intercostal space	Fullness sensation in the chest, chest pain	Chest pain, fullness sensation in the chest, pain in the heart area
Tianquan P.2	In the centre of the medial aspect of the upper arm, 2 cun below the axillary fold		
Quze P.3	On the transverse crease of the elbow at the ulnar border of the tendon of m. biceps brachii	Vomiting, diarrhea, hand tremor	Pain in the heart area, nausea, vomiting, mental diseases, febrile diseases spasm of the upper limbs

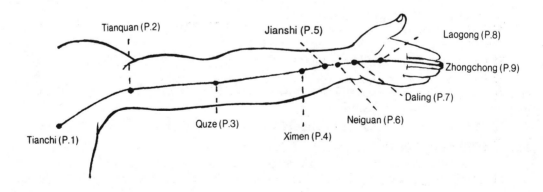

Fig. II-30

Ximen P.4	Between the tendons of m. palmaris longus and m. flexor carpi radialis, 7 cun directly below Quze (P.3) or 5 cun above Daling (P.7)	Tachycardia, bradycardia, arrhythmia
Jianshi P.5	Between the previously mentioned two tendons, 3 cun above the transverse crease of the wrist in the medial aspect of the forearm	Tachycardia, angina pectoris
Neiguan P.6	Between the two above-mentioned tendons, 1 cun below Jianshi (P.5)	Arrhythmia, angina pectoris, shock, gastric pain
Daling P.7	Between the two above-mentioned tendons, at the midpoint of the transverse crease proximal to the palm	Tachycardia, hypochondriac pain
Laogong P.8	At the posterior border of the metacarpo-phalangeal joints, between the 3rd and 4th metacarpal bones	Psychoses, aphthae
Zhongchong P.9	Midpoint of the tip of the middle finger	Syncope, angina pectoris

Section 4 SUMMARY OF THE LOCATIONS OF SOME POINTS FROM THE THREE YIN MERIDIANS OF THE HAND

I. Finger Tips

Tips of fingers, corners of finger nails (Fig. II-31, 32):
Zhongchong (P.9): at the tip of the middle finger,
Shaochong (H.9) and Shaoshang (Lu.11): at the roots of the finger nails,
Shaochong (H.9): at the root of the radial corner of the small finger nail,
Shaoshang (Lu.11): at the root of the radial corner of the thumb nail.

II. Metacarpophalangeal Joints

The following points are located proximal to the metacarpophalangeal joints (Fig. II-33):
Yuji (Lu.10): proximal to the 1st metacarpophalangeal joint, on the medial border of the 1st metacarpal bone,
Laogong (P.8): proximal to the 2nd and 3rd metacarpophalangeal joints,
Shaofu (H.8): proximal to the 4th and 5th metacarpophalangeal joints, between the 4th and 5th metacarpal bones.

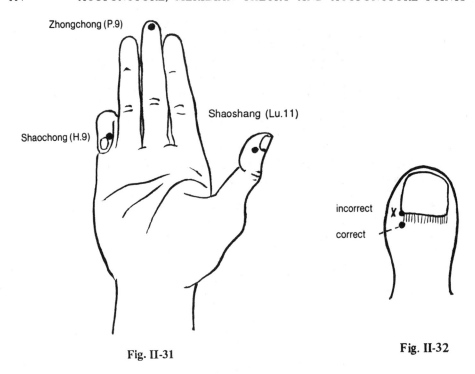

Fig. II-31   Fig. II-32

III. Wrist Region

Two bones, two tendons and one transverse crease (Fig. II-34)⊦)

The two bones refer to the large multangular bone and the pisiform bone. The two tendons refer to the tendons of m. palmaris longus and m. flexor carpi radialis. The transverse crease refers to the 1st transverse crease proximal to the wrist.

Taiyuan (Lu.9): at the lower border of the radial side of the great multangular bone,

Shenmen (H.7): on the radial side of the pisiform bone,

Daling (P.7): between the tendons of m. palmaris longus and m. flexor carpi radialis.

IV. Forearm

Borders of bones, borders of tendons and between the tendons:

Borders of bones refer to the border of the radius and border of the styloid process of radius (Fig. II-35, Fig. II-36).

Jingqu (Lu.8): at the highest point of the styloid process of the radius on the palmar side,

Kongzui (Lu.6): on the ulnar border of the radius, 7 cun proximal to the 1st transverse crease of the wrist.

Shenmen (H.7), Yinxi (H.6), Tongli (H.5) and Lingdao (H.4) are all located on the radial border of the tendon of m. flexor carpi ulnaris. Daling (P.7), Neiguan (P.6), Jianshi (P.5) and Ximen (P.4) are all located between the tendons of m. palmaris longus and m. flexor carpi radialis (Fig. II-36).

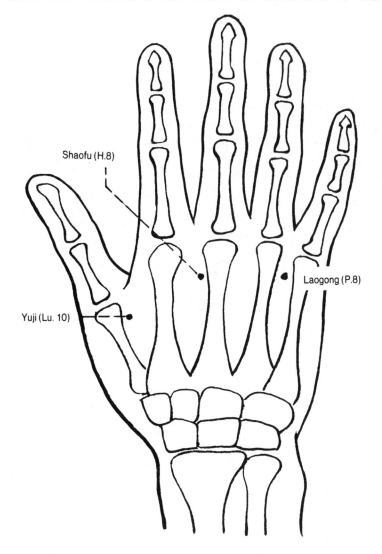

Shaofu (H.8)

Laogong (P.8)

Yuji (Lu. 10)

Fig. II-33

V. Elbow

Transverse crease, end of transverse crease and borders of the two tendons (Fig. II-37, 38).

Chize (Lu.5) and Quze (P.3): on the transverse cubital crease, but

Chize (Lu.5) is on the radial border of the tendon of m. biceps brachii; Quze (P.3) is on the ulnar border of the tendon of m. biceps brachii

Shaoze (H.3): at the ulnar end of the tranverse cubital crease when the elbow is flexed.

VI. Upper Arm

One muscle and two muscular grooves (Fig. II-39).

One muscle refers to m. biceps brachii. Two muscular grooves refer to the radial groove and ulnar groove of m. biceps brachii.

Tianquan (P.2): on the m. biceps brachii, 2 cun inferior to the anterior axillary fold,

Tianfu (Lu.3) and Xiabai (Lu.4): 4 cun inferior to the anterior axillary fold,

Qingling (H.2): in the ulnar groove of m. biceps brachii, 3 cun above the medial epicondyle of the humerus.

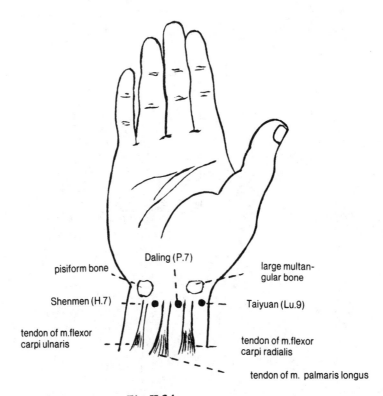

Fig. II-34

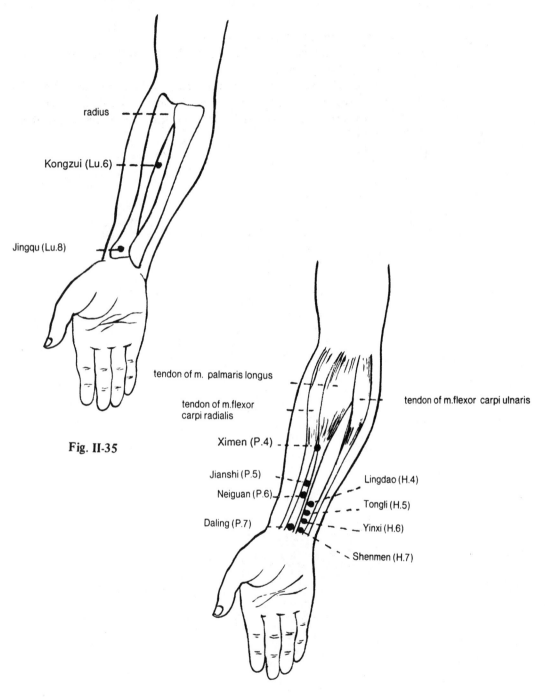

radius

Kongzui (Lu.6)

Jingqu (Lu.8)

tendon of m. palmaris longus

tendon of m.flexor
carpi radialis

Fig. II-35

Ximen (P.4)

Jianshi (P.5)

Neiguan (P.6)

Daling (P.7)

tendon of m.flexor carpi ulnaris

Lingdao (H.4)

Tongli (H.5)

Yinxi (H.6)

Shenmen (H.7)

Fig. II-36

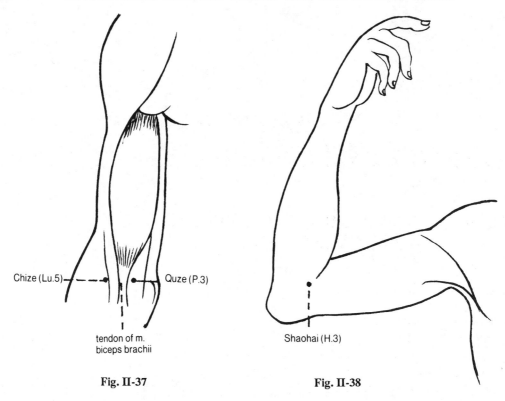

Chize (Lu.5) — — — — Quze (P.3)

tendon of m.
biceps brachii

Fig. II-37

Shaohai (H.3)

Fig. II-38

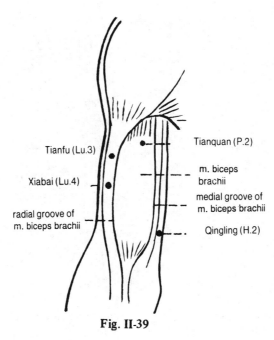

Tianfu (Lu.3)   Tianquan (P.2)

m. biceps
brachii

Xiabai (Lu.4)   medial groove of
                                 m. biceps brachii

radial groove of
m. biceps brachii   Qingling (H.2)

Fig. II-39

Chapter II

THE THREE YANG MERIDIANS OF THE HAND

Section 1   THE LARGE INTESTINE MERIDIAN OF HAND-YANGMING

I. The Meridian

General Indications:

Points from this meridian are mainly indicated in facial disorders, disorders of the five sense organs, disorders of the throat, teeth, mouth and neck, and disorders of the lateral aspect of the upper extremities.

Course of the Meridian:

(1) The Large Intestine Meridian of Hand-Yangming starts from the tip of the index finger (Shangyang, L.I.1). (2) It runs upwards along the radial side of the index finger, passes through the interspace of the 1st and 2nd metacarpal bones (Hegu, L.I.4) and dips into the depression between the tendons of m. extensor pollicis longus and brevis. (3) Following the lateral anterior aspect of the forearm, (4) it reaches the lateral side of the elbow, (5) ascends along the lateral anterior aspect of the upper arm (6) to the highest point of the shoulder (Jianyu, L.I.15), (7) proceeds along the anterior border of the acromion (8) and goes up to 7th cervical vertebra (Dazhui, Du 14). (9) It descends to the supraclavicular fossa (10) to connect with the lung, (11) passes through the diaphragm (12) and enters the large intestine, its pertaining organ. (13) The branch from the supraclavicular fossa runs upward to the neck, (14) passes through the cheek (15) and enters the gums of the lower jaw. (16) It curves around the upper lip and crosses the opposite meridian at the philtrum. From this point, the left meridian goes to the right and the right meridian goes to the left one, to either side of the nose (Yingxiang, L.I.20), where the Large Intestine Meridian links with the Stomach Meridian of Foot-Yangming (Fig. II-40).

Related Zangfu Organs:

Pertaining to the large intestine, connecting with the lung and passing through the mouth, lower teeth and nose.

The coalescent points of the Large Intestine Meridian of Hand-Yangming:
Bingfeng (S.J.12), Dicang (St.4), Dazhui (Du 14) and Renzhong (Du 26).

Note: The lower He-sea point of the Large Intestine Meridian of Hand-Yangming is Shangjuxu (St.37).

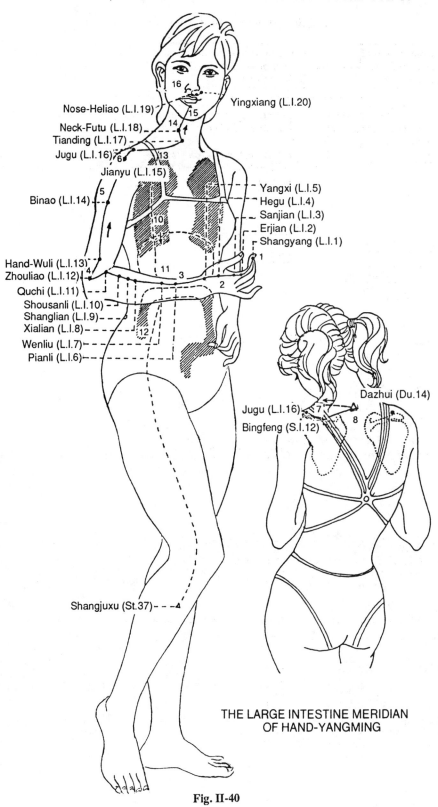

Nose-Heliao (L.I.19)
Yingxiang (L.I.20)
Neck-Futu (L.I.18)
Tianding (L.I.17)
Jugu (L.I.16)
Jianyu (L.I.15)
Binao (L.I.14)
Yangxi (L.I.5)
Hegu (L.I.4)
Sanjian (L.I.3)
Erjian (L.I.2)
Shangyang (L.I.1)
Hand-Wuli (L.I.13)
Zhouliao (L.I.12)
Quchi (L.I.11)
Shousanli (L.I.10)
Shanglian (L.I.9)
Xialian (L.I.8)
Wenliu (L.I.7)
Pianli (L.I.6)

Jugu (L.I.16)
Dazhui (Du.14)
Bingfeng (S.I.12)

Shangjuxu (St.37)

THE LARGE INTESTINE MERIDIAN
OF HAND-YANGMING

Fig. II-40

Analytical Display of the Course of the Meridian

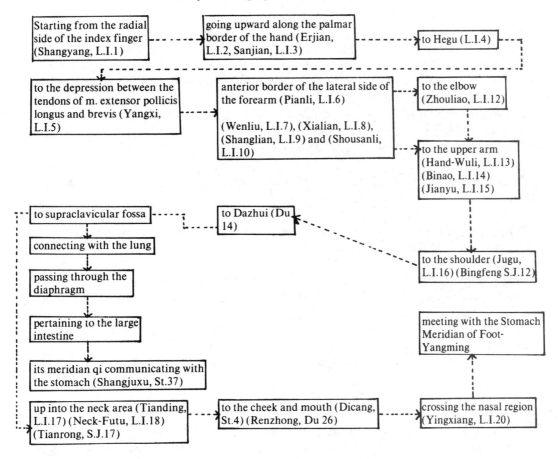

II. The Points

There are 20 points on this meridian, among which 15 are distributed on the radial border of the lateral aspect of the upper arm and 5 on the neck and facial region. The starting point is Shangyang (L.I.1) and the terminating point is Yingxiang (L.I.20).

Point Names	Pinyin	Codes	Point Names	Pinyin	Codes
商	Shangyang	L.I.1		Quchi	L.I.11
二间	Erjian	L.I.2		Zhouliao	L.I.12
三间	Sanjian	L.I.3		Shouwuli	L.I.13
合谷	Hegu	L.I.4		Binao	L.I.14
阳溪	Yangxi	L.I.5		Jianyu	L.I.15
偏历	Pianli	L.I.6		Jugu	L.I.16
温溜	Wenliu	L.I.7		Tianding	L.I.17
下廉	Xialian	L.I.8		Neck-Futu	L.I.18
上廉	Shanglian	L.I.9		Nose-Heliao	L.I.19
手三里	Shousanli	L.I.10		Yingxiang	L.I.20

*SHANGYANG (L.I.1) 商阳 " ⊙" (YANG SHANG)

"Shang" (商) is one of the five notes of the ancient five-tone scale and is represented by metal. "Shangyang" 商阳) refers to yang of Shangyang (L.I.1). Shangyang (L.I.1) and Shaoshang (Lu.11) are the Jing-well points respectively of the Large Intestine Meridian of Hand-Yangming and the Lung Meridian of Hand-Taiyin. The Large Intestine Meridian of Hand-Yangming, represented by metal, is a Yang meridian and the Lung Meridian of Hand-Taiyin, also represented by metal, is a Yin meridian. These two meridians are internally-externally related. The qi of the Yin meridian transforms from Shaoshang to Shangyang, i.e. from the metal point of the Yin meridian to the metal point of the Yang meridian, and further disperses, hence the name Shangyang (Yang Shang).

Location:

On the radial side of the index finger, 0.1 cun posterior to the corner of the nail (Fig. II-41, 42).

Indications:

Febrile diseases, sore throat, loss of consciousness, toothache, numbness of the fingers, parotitis and encephalemia.

Clinical Application:

Shangyang (L.I.1), the Jing-well point and the point used for emergency cases, has the effect to resuscitate the unconscious, dispel heat and relieve swelling.

Combinations:

With Renzhong (Du 26), Baihui (Du 20) and Neiguan (P.6) for loss of consciousness due to windstroke and shock;

With Shaoshang (Lu.11) and Hegu (L.I.4) for sore throat.

ERJIAN (L.I.2) 二间 "〜 " (THE 2ND PLACE)
SANJIAN (L.I.3) 三间 " ♀ " (THE 3RD PLACE)

"Er" (二) means two and "San" (三)means three. "Jian" (间) refers to a fixed area. These two points are the 2nd and 3rd as well as the Ying-spring and Shu-stream points of the Large Intestine Meridian of Hand-Yangming. They are located respectively in the two depressions on either side of the 2nd metacarpophalangeal joint on the radial aspect (Fig. II-42, 43).

Indications:

Similar in indications, being indicated in toothache, blurring of vision, sore throat and febrile diseases.

Method:

Puncture these two points 0.3-0.5 cun deep. Moxibustion is applicable.

Needling Sensations:

Slight pain is often felt in the local area.

*HEGU (L.I.4) 合谷 " ⊙ " (CONVERGING VALLEY)

"He" (合) means to converge and "gu" (谷) refers to valley where a spring flows to joint a stream. In ancient times, the parts of the body where muscles converged in abundance were referred to as "gu" (valley), while those parts where there were less muscles were referred to as "xi" (a small stream). In this context, "gu" is bigger and shallower than "xi". Here "he" refers to the place where muscles converge. Also, when

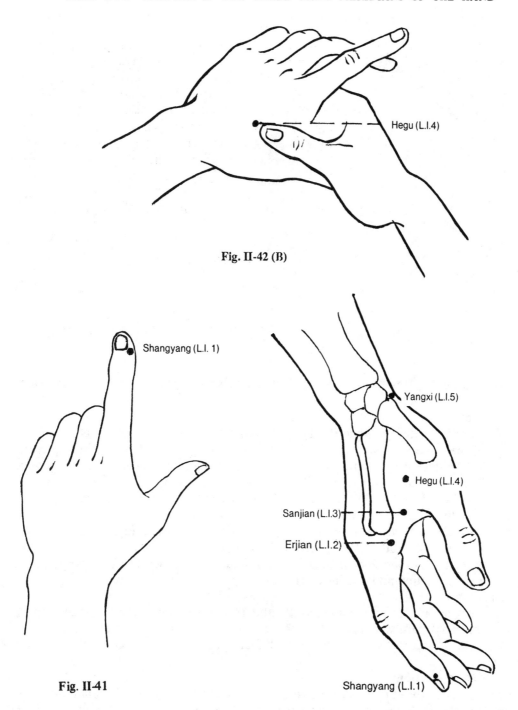

Fig. II-42 (B)

Shangyang (L.I. 1)

Yangxi (L.I.5)

Hegu (L.I.4)

Sanjian (L.I.3)

Erjian (L.I.2)

Shangyang (L.I.1)

Fig. II-41

Fig. II-42 (A)

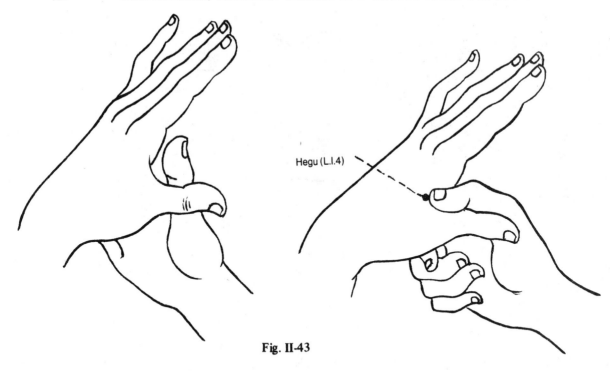

Hegu (L.I.4)

Fig. II-43

the thumb and index fingers are separated, it is similar to a deep valley, hence the name Hegu (Converging Valley).

Location:

This point is located between the 1st and 2nd metacarpal bones. It can be located by following three methods: 1) Open the thumb and index finger, then put the transverse crease of the thumb of one hand on the midpoint of the extended margin between the thumb and index finger of the other. The place to which the tip of the thumb extends is Hegu (L.I.4) (Fig. II-42-45); 2) a perpendicular crease will appear if the thumb and index finger are tightened, alongside of which there is a muscular process. The point is on the top of the muscle level with the end of the perpendicular crease; and 3) with the thumb and index finger separated, the point will be half way along the line linking the conjunction of the 1st and 2nd metacarpal bones and the midpoint of the margin of the web between the thumb and the index finger.

Indications:

Disorders of the facial region, mouth and throat, e.g. headache, toothache, nasal obstruction, facial paralysis, redness of the eye and sore throat. It is also indicated in common cold, dysmenorrhea, hemorrhoids, finger spasm, hidrosis and paralysis of the upper limb.

Clinical Application:

Hegu (L.I.4), the Yuan-source point of the Large Intestine Meridian of Hand-Yangming and one of the four general points, has the effect to sedate pain, eliminate heat, calm the mind, remove obstruction from the collaterals, relieve superficial syndromes and dispel exogenous wind.

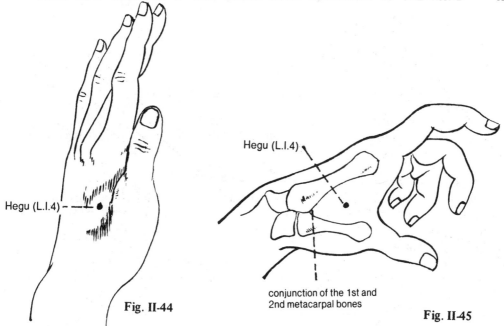

Hegu (L.I.4)

Hegu (L.I.4)

conjunction of the 1st and
2nd metacarpal bones

Fig. II-44

Fig. II-45

Combinations:

With Fengchi (G.B.20), Dazhui (Du 14) and Quchi (L.I.11) for fever due to common cold. Strong stimulation is suggested so as to force the patient to sweat slightly. Usually, the body temperature can be reduced within half an hour;

With Dazhui (Du 14), Quchi (L.I.11) and Zusanli (St.36) for good therapeutic results in patients suffering from aleucemia. The curative effect often reaches its climax within three hours;

With Quchi (L.I.11), Xuehai (Sp.10) and Dazhui (Du 14) for urticaria;

With Taiyang (extra) for upper toothache;

With Jiache (St.6) for lower toothache;

With Sanyinjiao (Sp.6) to facilitate delivery and for the treatment of amenorrhea;

With Jianyu (L.I.15), Quchi (L.I.11), Shousanli (L.I.10) and Waiguan (S.J.5) for weakness of the upper limb due to paralysis.

Method:

Puncture perpendicularly 0.5-1 cun deep. Moxibustion is applicable.

Needling Sensations:

Numbness and soreness, radiating towards the index finger.

YANGXI (L.I.5)阳溪 (YANG STREAM)

"Yang" (阳) refers to Yang meridian. "Xi" (溪) refers to a stream between two hills. As was mentioned previously, "xi" also refers to a part of the body where there are less muscles. When the thumb is tilted up, the point is in the depression on the medial aspect of the wrist, as though in a stream between two hills, hence the name Yangxi (Yang Stream).

Location:

Yangxi (L.I.5), the Jing-river point of the Large Intestine Meridian of Hand-Yangming, is located in the depression between tendons of m. extensor pollicis longus and brevis. This depression is commonly known as the snuff box (Fig. II-42).

Indications:

Headache, redness of the eye, sore throat and painful wrist.

Method:

Puncture perpendicularly 0.3-0.5 cun deep. Moxibustion is applicable.

Figure II-46 shows the locations of points on the linking between Yangxi (L.I.5) and Quchi (L.I.11).

PIANLI (L.I.6) 偏历 " ∧ " (DIVERGENT PASSAGE)

"Pian" (偏) means something away from. "Li" (历) means to pass through. The collateral of the Large Intestine Meridian of Hand-Yangming emerges from this point and diverges to connect with the Lung Meridian of Hand-Taiyin, hence the name Pianli (Divergent Passage).

Location:

Three cun above Yangxi (L.I.5) on the lateral side of the radius (Fig. II-46).

Indications:

Redness of the eyes, tinnitus, soreness and pain of the arm.

Method:

Puncture perpendicularly 0.5-1 cun deep. Moxibustion is applicable.

WENLIU (L.I.7) 温溜 "XI" (WARMING THE MERIDIAN)

"Wen" (温) means warming. "Liu" (溜) means to flow into. This point has the effect to warm up the meridian and dispel cold, hence the name Wenliu (Warming the Meridian). It is the Xi-cleft point of the Large Intestine Meridian of Hand-Yangming.

Location:

Two cun above Pianli (L.I.6) on the lateral side of the radius (Fig. II-46).

Indications:

Borborygmus, abdominal pain, headache and soreness and pain of the shoulder.

Method:

Puncture perpendicularly 0.5-1 cun deep. Moxibustion is applicable.

XIALIAN (L.I.8) 下廉 (INFERIOR MARGIN OF RHOMBUS)

"Xia" (下) means inferior or lower. "Lian" (廉) refers to the margin or edge of a rhombus. When the elbow is flexed to make a loose fist, a muscular prominence appears here in the form of a rhombus.

The upper and lower margins are respectively called: upper "lian" and lower "lian", hence the name Xialian (Inferior Margin).

Location:

Three cun above Wenliu (L.I.7) and 4 cun below Quchi (L.I.11) lateral to the radius (Fig. II-46).

Indications:

Dizziness and vertigo, headache and painful elbow.

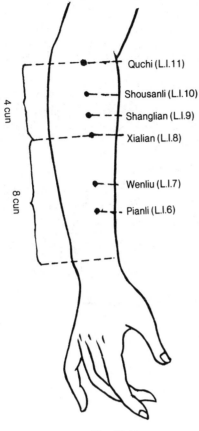

Quchi (L.I.11)

Shousanli (L.I.10)

Shanglian (L.I.9)

Xialian (L.I.8)

Wenliu (L.I.7)

Pianli (L.I.6)

4 cun

8 cun

Fig. II-46

Method:

Puncture perpendicularly 0.8-1.5 cun deep. Moxibustion is applicable.

SHANGLIAN (L.I.9) 上廉 (SUPERIOR MARGIN OF RHOMBUS)

Location:

One cun above Xialian (L.I.8) and 3 cun below Quchi (L.I.11) lateral to the radius (Fig.II-46).

Indications:

Headache, shoulder pain, numbness in the arm and paralysis of the body.

Method:

Puncture perpendicularly 0.8-1.5 cun deep. Moxibustion is applicable.

*SHOUSANLI (L.I.10) 手三里 (THREE LI FROM ZHOULIAO)

"Li" (里) means a residential quarter, or measuring unit in the old times. "San" (三) means three. Also, the distance between the point Shousanli (L.I.10) and Zhouliao (L.I.12) is three cun, hence the name Shousanli (Three Li from Zhouliao). Furthermore, this point corresponds anatomically to Zusanli (St. 36, Three Li of the Foot).

Location:

Two cun above Quchi (L.I.11) on the lateral side of the radius. Flex the elbow when locating this point (Fig. II-46, 47).

Indications:

Pain in the arm and shoulder, numbness of the upper limbs, hypertension, parotitis, poor digestion, abdominal pain, diarrhea,. back pain and toothache.

Clinical Application:

This point has the effect to remove obstruction from meridians and collaterals, sedate pain, dispel wind and promote gastrointestinal functions.

Combinations:

With Jianyu (L.I.15), Quchi (L.I.11), Waiguan (S.J.5) and Hegu (L.I.4) for shoulder pain and numbness in the upper limb;

With Zusanli (St.36) for gastrointestinal disorders.

Method:

Puncture perpendicularly 1 cun deep. Moxibustion is applicable.

Needling Sensations:

The needling sensation usually radiates to the hand.

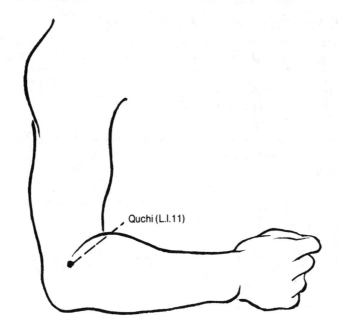

Quchi (L.I.11)

Fig. II-48

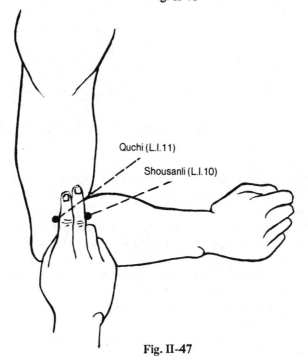

Quchi (L.I.11)

Shousanli (L.I.10)

Fig. II-47

*QUCHI (L.I.11) 曲池 **"HE" (CURVED POND)**

"Qu" (曲) means to flex the elbow. The depression in which this point lies is likened to a pond "Chi" (池) when the elbow is flexed. Hence the name Quchi (Curved Pond).

Location:

On the lateral side of the transverse crease of the elbow, approximately midway between Chize (Lu.5) and the lateral epicondyle of the humerus (Fig.II-46, 47, 48).

Indications:

Febrile diseases, hypertension, headache, hemiplegia, swelling of the arm, puritis, urticaria and irregular menstruation.

Clinical Application:

This point, the He-sea point of the Large Intestine Meridian of Hand-Yangming, can disperse exogenous wind, relieve superficial syndromes and regulate the circulation of qi and blood. It is also one of the points for general tonification.

Combinations:

With Dazhui (Du 14), Waiguan (S.J.5), Fengchi (G.B.20) and Taiyang (Extra) for treating invasion of the body by wind-cold, headache, and fever;

With Renying (St.9) and Zusanli (St.36) for hypertension;

With Dazhui (Du 14), Zusanli (St.36) and Xuehai (Sp.10) for urticaria and itching of the skin;

With Zusanli (St.36) and Neiguan (P.6) for gastrointestinal disorders.

Method:

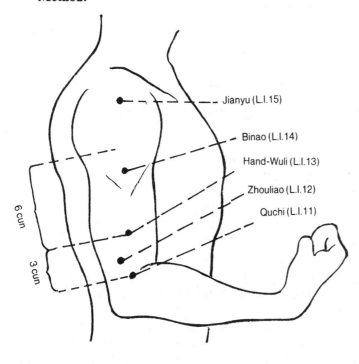

Jianyu (L.I.15)

Binao (L.I.14)

Hand-Wuli (L.I.13)

Zhouliao (L.I.12)

Quchi (L.I.11)

6 cun

3 cun

Fig. II-49

Puncture perpendicularly 1-1.5 cun deep.

Needling Sensations:

Soreness and distention, radiating along the inside of the arm towards the hand.

ZHOULIAO (L.I.12) 肘髎 **(ELBOW CREVICE)**

"Zhou" (肘) means elbow. "Liao" (髎) refers to a depression beside a bony process or a tiny gap. This point is superior to the lateral epicondyle of the humerus, hence the name Zhouliao (Elbow Crevice).

Location:

One cun above the lateral epicondyle of the humerus when the elbow is flexed (Fig.II-49).

Indications:

Pain in the elbow and arm, and numbness in the upper limb.
Method:
Puncture perpendicularly 0.8-1.5 cun deep. Moxibustion is applicable.

SHOUWULI (L.I.13)手五里 (FIVE UNITS FROM THE LATERAL EPICONDYLE OF THE HUMERUS)

"Li" (里) refers to cun measurement in ancient times. "Wu" (五) means five. This point is five cun superior to the lateral epicondyle of the humerus, hence the name Shouwuli, or Hand-Wuli (Five Units from the Lateral Epicondyle of the Humerus).
Location:
On the medial border of the humerus, 3 cun above Quchi (L.I.11), on the line between Quchi (L.I.11) and Jianyu (L.I.15) (Fig. II-49).
Indications:
Painful elbow or arm and scrofula.
Method:
Puncture 0.8-1.5 cun deep. Moxibustion is applicable.

*BINAO (L.I.14)臂臑(MEDIAL SIDE OF THE UPPER ARM)

"Bi" (臂) means the upper arm. "Nao" (臑) refers to the medial aspect of the upper arm. This point is above the intersection of the humerus and the anteroinferior border of m. deltoideus, on the line connecting with Quchi (L.I.11) and Jianyu (L.I.15), hence the name Binao (Medial Side of the Upper Arm).
Location:
On the radial side of the humerus, superior to the lower end of m. deltoideus, on the line connecting with Quchi (L.I.11) and Jianyu (L.I.15) (Fig.II-49).
Indications:
Painful shoulder joint, neck rigidity, scrofula and eye disorders.
Clinical Application:
This point is often used for acupuncture analgesia. It has the effect to help the lung to disperse qi and remove obstruction from collaterals.
Method:
Puncture perpendicularly or obliquely 1.2 cun deep. Penetrate Binao (L.I.14) towards Jianyu (L.I.15) in pneumonectomy for analgesic purposes. Moxibustion is applicable.
Needling Sensations:
Deep radiation of needling sensation into the muscle.

JIANYU (L.I.15)肩髃 (SHOULDER BLADE)

"Jian" (肩) means shoulder. "Yu" (髃) refers to the scapula. This point is near the scapula and is indicated in shoulder disorders, hence the name Jianyu (Shoulder Blade).
Location:
In the middle of the upper portion of m. deltoideus. When the arm is in full abduction, the point is in the anterior of the two depressions which appear at the anterior border of the acromioclavicular joint. The point in the posterior depression is Jianliao (S.J.14). When the arm is lowered, Jianyu (L.I.15) will be just inferior to the anterior

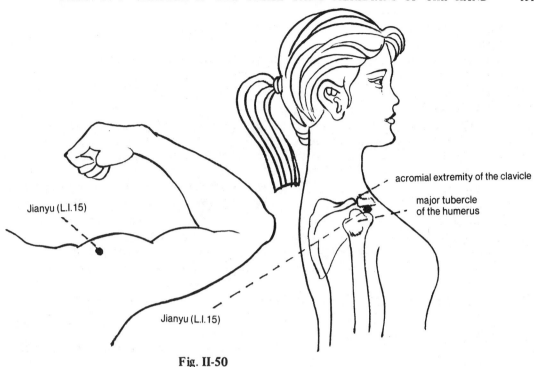

acromial extremity of the clavicle

major tubercle of the humerus

Jianyu (L.I.15)

Jianyu (L.I.15)

Fig. II-50

border of the acromion (Fig. II-49, 50).

Indications:

Pain in the upper arm, pain in the shoulder joint, hemiplegia of the upper limb and neck rigidity.

Clinical Application:

Jianyu (L.I.15), the Confluent Point of the Large Intestine Meridian of Hand-Yangming and Yangqiao Meridian, has the effect to activate blood circulation, disperse wind, promote qi and blood circulation and relieve joint pain.

Combinations:

With Quchi (L.I.11), Hegu (L.I.4) and Waiguan (S.J.5) for paralysis of the upper limb;

With Jianliao (S.J.15) for frozen shoulder.

Method:

Puncture perpendicularly or obliquely 1.5 cun deep. Moxibustion is applicable.

Needling Sensations:

Soreness and distention, radiating towards fingers.

JUGU (L.I.16) 巨骨 (HUGE BONE)

"Ju" (巨) means something huge or big. "Gu" (骨) means bone. "Jugu" here refers to the clavicle. This point on the lateral end of the shoulder bears a heavy load when a person carries something on the shoulder, hence the name Jugu (Huge Bone).

Location:

In the depression formed by the acromion and the scapular spine (Fig. II-51).

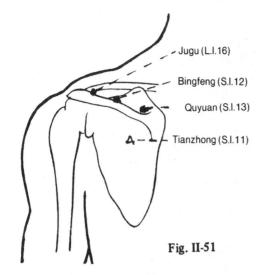

Fig. II-51

Indications:

Pain in the shoulder and arm, scrofula and limited movement of the arm.

Method:

Puncture perpendicularly 0.5-1 cun deep.

TIANDING (L.I.17) 天鼎 (CELESTIAL VESSEL)

"Ding" (鼎) refers to one of the cooking vessels with two loop handles and three legs used in the ancient times. Its top was round in shape and was likened to heavens (Tian, 天). Man's head, at the top of the body, is also likened to "tian" (celestial). The ears are the images of the two handles of "ding" (cooking vessel). There is one prominence on either side of this point indicating the point Dazhui (Du 14), the spinal process of 7th cervical vertebra, creating the image of the three legs of the cooking vessel, hence the name Tianding (Celestial Vessel).

Location:

One cun inferior to Neck-Futu (L.I.18) at the posterior border of the m. sternocleidomastoideus (Fig. II-52).

Indications:

Hoarseness, hiccup, sore throat and scrofula.

Method:

Puncture perpendicularly 0.5-0.8 cun deep. Moxibustion is applicable.

NECK-FUTU (L.I.18) 扶突 (THREE-CUN PROMINENCE)

Four fingers' width was called a "fu" (扶) in the old times, one "fu" being equal to three proportional cun. "Tu" (突) means a prominence. This point is at the midpoint of the m. sternocleidomastoideus, three cun lateral to Adam's apple, hence the name Neck-Futu (Three-cun Prominence) (Fig. II-52).

It is called Neck-Futu (L.I.18) so as to differentiate it from Femur-Futu (St.32).

Indications:

Cough, asthma, sore throat, hoarseness and phrenospasm.

Method:

Puncture perpendicularly 0.5-0.8 cun deep. Moxibustion is applicable.

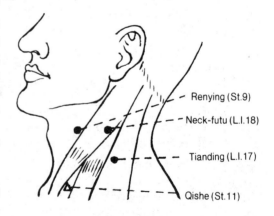

Fig.II-52

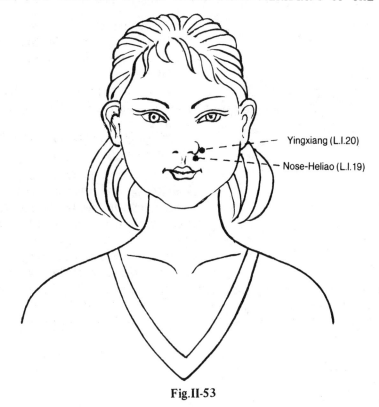

Fig.II-53

NOSE-HELIAO (L.I.19)禾髎 (GRAIN SEAM)

"He" (禾) means grain. "Liao" (髎) refers to a crevice near a depression in a bone. This point is inferior to the nose which can smell food and superior to the mouth which can eat it. Hence the name Heliao (Grain Seam). However, it is called Nose-Heliao so as to differentiate it from Ear-Heliao (S.J.22).

Location:
At the medial side of the ala nasi, 0.5 cun lateral to Renzhong (Du 26) (Fig.II-53).
Indications:
Nasal obstruction, deviation of the mouth and epistaxis.
Method:
Puncture perpendicularly 0.4-0.5 cun deep.

*YINGXIANG (L.I.20)迎香 (WELCOME FRAGRANCE)

"Ying" 迎) means to welcome. "Xiang" (香) means fragrance. It is the last point of the meridian which is internally-externally related to the Lung Meridian of Hand-Taiyin. The lung has its opening in the nose and Yingxiang (L.I.20) is indicated in nasal obstruction and loss of the sense of smell. Needling Yingxiang (L.I.20) helps the lung to perform its dispersing function, so that the nose can smell fragrant scents again, hence the name Yingxiang (Welcome Fragrance).

Location:

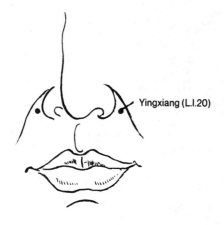

Yingxiang (L.I.20)

Fig.II-54

In the nasolabial groove, at the level of the midpoint of the lateral border of the ala nasi (Fig. II-53).

Indications:

Nasal obstruction, epistaxis, acute and chronic rhinitis, facial paralysis and biliary ascariasis.

Clinical Application:

Yingxiang (L.I.20), the crossing point of the Large Intestine Meridian of Hand-Yangming and the Stomach Meridian of Foot-Yangming, has the effect to dispel pathogenic heat and remove nasal obstruction.

Combinations:

With Shangxing (Du 23), Yingtang (Extra) and Hegu (L.I.4) for rhinitis, nasal obstruction and sinusitis;

With Sibai (St.2) for biliary ascariasis;

With Dicang (St.4) and Jiache (St.6) and Xiaguan (St.7) for facial paralysis.

Method:

Puncture perpendicularly or obliquely towards the ala nasi or the root of the nose 0.3-0.8 cun deep.

Needling Sensations:

Slight pain in the local area.

III. Summary

The Large Intestine Meridian of Hand-Yangming pertains to the large intestine and connects with the lung (Fig.II-54,55).

Specific Points of the Meridian

Quchi, L.I.11 He (earth)   Sanjian, L.I.3 (wood)
Shangyang, L.I.1. (metal)   Pianli, L.I.6
Yangxi, L.I.5 (fire)   Erjian, L.I.2 (water)
Hegu, L.I.14   Wenliu, L.I.7 Xi

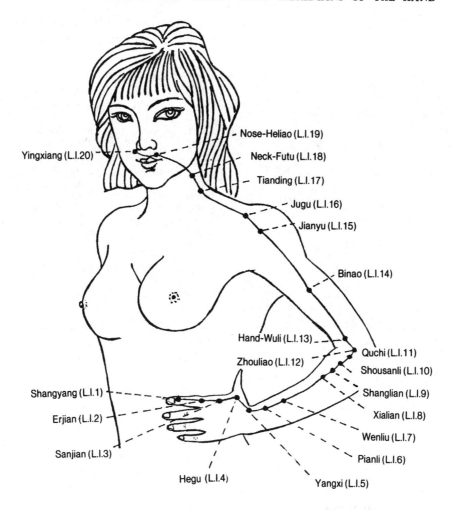

Yingxiang (L.I.20)

Nose-Heliao (L.I.19)

Neck-Futu (L.I.18)

Tianding (L.I.17)

Jugu (L.I.16)

Jianyu (L.I.15)

Binao (L.I.14)

Hand-Wuli (L.I.13)

Zhouliao (L.I.12)

Quchi (L.I.11)

Shousanli (L.I.10)

Shanglian (L.I.9)

Xialian (L.I.8)

Wenliu (L.I.7)

Pianli (L.I.6)

Yangxi (L.I.5)

Shangyang (L.I.1)

Erjian (L.I.2)

Sanjian (L.I.3)

Hegu (L.I.4)

Fig.II-55

Point Indications of the Large Intestine Meridian According to Locations

Point Names	Locations	Indications	Regional Indications
Shangyang L.I.1	On the radial side of the tip of the index finger, 0.1 cun posterior to the corner of the finger nail	Loss of consciousness, high fever and finger numbness	
Erjian L.I.2	In the anterior depression on the radial side of the metacarpophalangeal joint	Blurring of vision, toothache	Toothache, sore throat, nasal obstruction, common cold, local pain in the upper limb

Sanjian L.I.3	In the posterior depression on the radial side of the metacarpophalangeal joint	Toothache, sore throat	
Hegu L.I.4	Between the 1st and 2nd metacarpal joints, proximal to the midpoint of the 2nd metacarpal bone	Common cold, headache, toothache	
Yangxi L.I.5	In the depression on the radial side of the wrist joint	Headache, toothache, pain in the wrist	
Pianli L.I.6	3 cun above Yangxi (L.I.5)	Puffiness, pain in the forearm, epistaxis	Paralysis of the upper limb
Wenliu L.I.7	5 cun above Yangxi (L.I.5)	Borborygmus, abdominal pain, stomatitis	
Xialian L.I.8	8 cun above Yangxi (L.I.5), or 4 cun below Quchi (L.I.11)	Headache, abdominal pain, mastitis	
Shanglian L.I.9	9 cun above Yangxi, (L.I.5), or 3 cun below Quchi (L.I.11)	Hemiplegia, abdominal pain, numbness of hand	
Shousanli L.I.10	10 cun above Yangxi (L.I.5) or 2 cun below Quchi (L.I.11)	Painful arm and shoulder, paralysis of the upper limb	
Quchi L.I.11	Midpoint between Chize (Lu.5) and the lateral epicondyle of humerus	Common cold, hypertension, paralysis of the upper limb	
Zhouliao L.I.12	1 cun laterosuperior to Quchi (L.I.11)	Painful elbow, numbness and paralysis of the upper limb	
Hand-Wuli L.I.13	3 cun directly above Quchi (L.I.11)	Painful elbow and arm, scrofula	
Binao L.I.14	7 cun above Quchi (L.I.11), inferior to the m. deltoideus	Painful elbow and upper arm, paralysis of the upper limb	
Jianyu L.I.15	At the midpoint of the upper border of the m. deltoideus	Pain in the shoulder joint, paralysis of the upper limb	Local disorders of the upper limb
Jugu L.I.16	In the depression between the acromial extremity of the clavicle and the scapular spine	Pain in the shoulder and arm	
Tianding L.I.17	1 cun below Neck-Futu (L.I.18), at the posterior border of the m. sternocleidomastoideus	Throat problems	
Neck-Futu L.I.18	3 cun lateral to Adam's apple	Hoarseness, difficult swallowing	Throat problems
Nose-Heliao L.I.19	Directly below the lateral margin of the nostril, level with Renzhong (Du 26)	Syncope, locked jaws	
Yingxiang L.I.20	In the nasolabial groove, at the level of the midpoint of the lateral border of ala nasi	Nasal obstruction, nasal discharge, deviation of eye and mouth	Disorders of the nasal region

Section 2   THE SMALL INTESTINE MERIDIAN OF HAND-TAIYANG

I. The Meridian

General Indications:

Points from this meridian are mainly indicated in deafness, tinnitus, pain and stiffness of the neck and back, pain of the scapular region and disorders along the ulnar side of the upper extremities.

Course of the Meridian:

(1) The Small Intestine Meridian of Hand-Taiyang starts from the ulnar side of the tip of the little finger (Shaoze, S.I.1). (2) Following the ulnar side of the dorsum of the hand, it reaches the wrist where it passes over the styloid process of the ulna. (3) Ascending along the posterior aspect of the forearm, it runs along the posterior border of the lateral aspect of the upper arm (4) to the shoulder joint. (5) Circling around the scapular region, (6) it meets the Du Meridian on the superior aspect of the shoulder at Dazhui (Du 14). (7) Then turning downward to the supraclavicular fossa, (8) it connects with the heart. (9) It continues to descend along the esophagus, (10) passes through the diaphragm, (11) reaches the stomach, (12) and finally enters the small intestine, its pertaining organ.

The branch from the supraclavicular fossa:

(13) A branch rises from the supraclavicular fossa, (14) ascends to the neck, (15) and further to the cheek. (16) It continues to pass the outer canthus (17) and enters the ear (Tinggong, S.I.19).

The branch from the cheek:

(18) A branch comes from the cheek, runs upward to the infraorbital region (Quanliao, S.I.18) and further to the lateral side of the nose. (19) On reaching the inner canthus (Jingming, U.B.1) it links with the Urinary Bladder Meridian of Foot-Taiyang (Fig. II-56).

Ralated Zangfu Organs:

This meridian pertains to the small intestine, connects with the heart and links with the stomach.

Coalescent Points:

Fufen (U.B.41), Dashu (U.B.11), Jingming (U.B.1), Tongziliao (G.B.1), Ear-Heliao (S.J.22), Jiaosun (S.J.20), Shangzhong (Ren 17), Shangwan (Ren 13), Zhongwan (Ren 12) and Dazhui (Du 14).

II. The Points

There are altogether 19 points on this meridian on either side. Among them, 8 are distributed along the ulnar side of the posterior aspect of the forearm, the remaining 11 being located on the shoulder, neck and facial area. The starting point is Shaoze (S.I.1)

Note: The Small Intestine Meridian has an Inferior He-sea Point Xiajuxu (St.39).

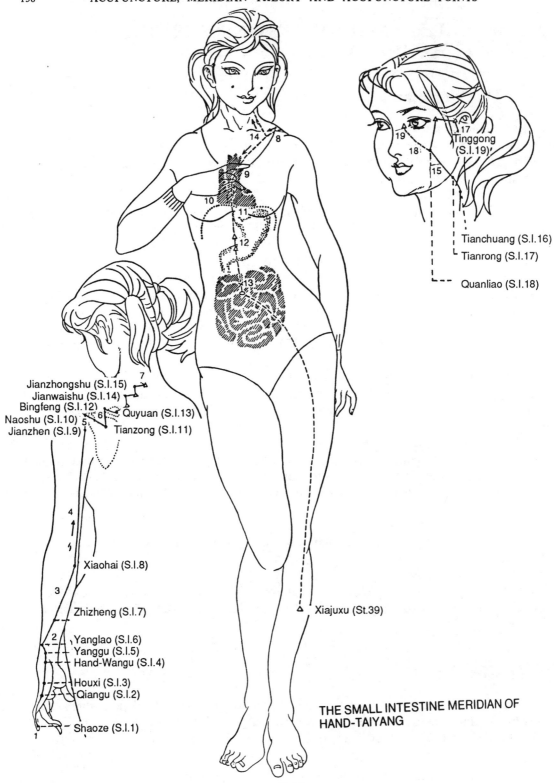

Tinggong (S.I.19)

Tianchuang (S.I.16)

Tianrong (S.I.17)

Quanliao (S.I.18)

Jianzhongshu (S.I.15)
Jianwaishu (S.I.14)
Bingfeng (S.I.12)
Naoshu (S.I.10)
Jianzhen (S.I.9)

Quyuan (S.I.13)

Tianzong (S.I.11)

Xiaohai (S.I.8)

Zhizheng (S.I.7)

Yanglao (S.I.6)
Yanggu (S.I.5)
Hand-Wangu (S.I.4)

Houxi (S.I.3)
Qiangu (S.I.2)

Shaoze (S.I.1)

Xiajuxu (St.39)

THE SMALL INTESTINE MERIDIAN OF
HAND-TAIYANG

Fig.II-56

and the terminating point is Tinggong (S.I.19)

Analytical Display of the Course of the Meridian

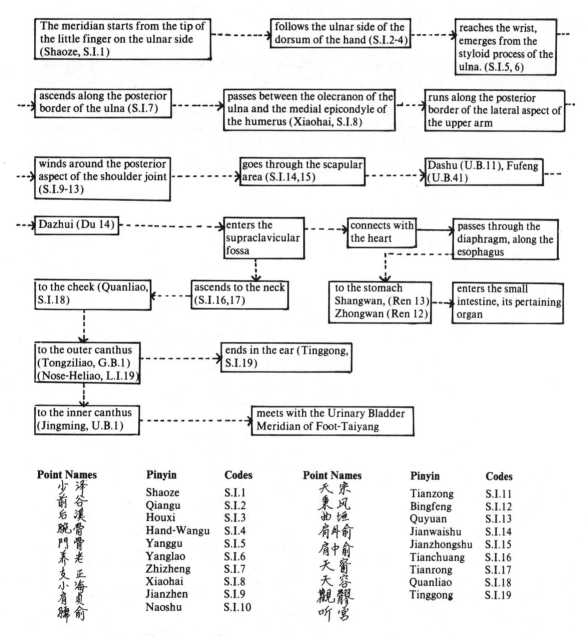

Point Names	Pinyin	Codes	Point Names	Pinyin	Codes
	Shaoze	S.I.1		Tianzong	S.I.11
	Qiangu	S.I.2		Bingfeng	S.I.12
	Houxi	S.I.3		Quyuan	S.I.13
	Hand-Wangu	S.I.4		Jianwaishu	S.I.14
	Yanggu	S.I.5		Jianzhongshu	S.I.15
	Yanglao	S.I.6		Tianchuang	S.I.16
	Zhizheng	S.I.7		Tianrong	S.I.17
	Xiaohai	S.I.8		Quanliao	S.I.18
	Jianzhen	S.I.9		Tinggong	S.I.19
	Naoshu	S.I.10			

SHAOZE (S.I.1) 少泽 " ⊙ " (SMALL MOISTENING)

"Shao" 少 meaning small, here refers to the Small Intestine Meridian. The point is located on the tip of the little finger, level with Shaochong (H.9). It is also the Jing-Well point of this meridian and "Jing-Well" is considered to be moistening, "Ze" (泽). The circulation of the qi and blood of the meridian at the point is minimal, similar to water lying dormant in a well, hence the name Shaoze (Small Moistening).

Location:

On the ulnar side of the little finger, about 0.1 cun posterior to the corner of the nail (Fig. II-57).

Indications:

Febrile diseases, lactation deficiency, syncope, mastitis and cloudness of the cornea. It is also one of the points used for emergency cases.

Clinical Application:

This is the Jing-Well point of the Small Intestine Meridian of Hand-Taiyang. It has the effect to activate the circulation of the qi and blood of the meridian and collaterals, restore consciousness, and promote lactation.

Combinations:

With Rugen (St.18), Shanzhong (Ren 17) and Hegu (L.I.4) for lactation deficiency and mastitis.

Method:

Puncture 0.1 cun deep by pricking to cause bleeding.

Needling Sensations:

Pain around the local area.

QIANGU (S.I.2) 前谷 " ～ " (FRONT VALLEY)

"Qian"(前) means front. Here it refers to the anterior part of the fifth metacarpophalangeal joint. "Gu" (谷) means a valley, a narrow stretch of land between hills.

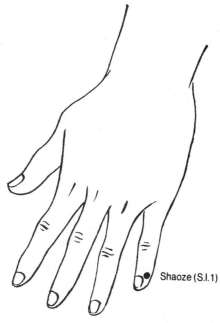

Here it illustrates the location of the point with reference to Houxi (Back Stream, S.I.3), hence the name Qiangu (Front Valley).

Location:

When a loose fist is made, the point is distal to the fifth metacarpophalangeal joint, on the ulnar end of the transverse crease, at the junction of the red and white skin (Fig. II-58).

Indications:

Headache, eye pain, sore throat, distention and fullness of the chest, febrile diseases without sweating, lactation deficiency after delivery and numbness of the fingers.

Method:

Puncture perpendicularly 0.3-0.5 cun deep.

HOUXI (S.I.3) 后溪 "昂㇆" (BACK STREAM)

Shaoze (S.I.1)

Fig.II-57

"Hou" (后) means back or behind."Xi" (溪) means stream. Because the point is just behind the small head of the 5th metacarpal bone on the end of the transverse crease of the palm, it is higher than Qiangu (S.I.2). Besides, the location of the point is the place where the muscles start to become more abundant, like water accumulating to form a stream, hence the name Houxi (Back Stream).

Location:

When a loose fist is made, the point is on the lateral side of the hypothenar eminence at the end of the transverse crease, proximal to the head of the 5th metacarpal bone (Fig.

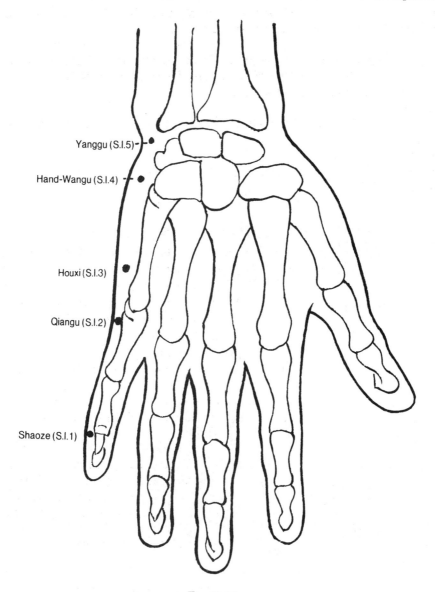

Fig. II-58

II-59).

Indications:

Headache, neck rigidity and sprain, intercostal neuralgia, contracture and twitching of the elbow, arm, and fingers.

Clinical Application:

Houxi (S.I.3) is the Shu-Stream point of this meridian, and also one of the eight confluent points connecting with the Du Meridian. Needling it can calm the mind and soothe the heart, dispel heat and clear the throat.

Combinations:

With Shenmai (U.B.62) for headache;

With Fengchi (G.B.20), Fengfu (Du 16) and Baihui (Du 20) for neck rigidity or neck sprain;

With Sanjian (L.I.3) for contracture and twitching of the fingers (penetrating the needle from one point to the other).

Method:

Puncture perpendicularly 0.5-1 cun deep.

Needling Sensations:

Numbness extending downwards to the little finger.

HAND-WANGU (S.I.4) 腕骨 " 〇 "
(WRIST BONE)

"Wan" (腕) means the wrist. "Gu" (骨) means bone. The point is found near the pisiform bone, which is pronounced "Wandougu". The name of the wrist also has a similar sound being pronounced "Wan", hence the name Wangu (Wrist Bone).

Location:

On the ulnar side of the hand, in the depression distal to the pisiform bone (Fig. II-59).

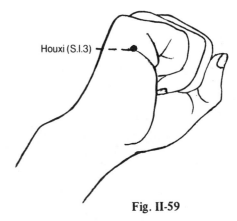

Houxi (S.I.3)

Fig. II-59

Indications:

Febrile diseases without sweating, headache, pain of the shoulder, arm and neck, wrist pain and jaundice.

YANGGU (S.I.5) 阳谷 " 〇 " **(YANG VALLEY)**

"Yang" (阳) is the opposite of "Yin" (阴). Here it refers to the Yang side, the lateral aspect being considered Yang and the medial aspect, Yin. "Gu" (谷) means a valley. The point is in the depression formed by the junction of the styloid process of the ulna and the triquetrous bone, hence the name Yanggu (Yang Valley).

Location:

At the ulnar end of the transverse crease of the dorsum of the wrist, in the depression

---

Note: Shaoze (S.I.1), Qiangu (S.I.2), Houxi (S.I.3), Hand-Wangu (S.I.4), and Yanggu (S.I.5) are all on the junction of the red and white skin.

between the styloid process of the ulna and the triquetral bone (Fig .II-58).
Indications:
Deafness, tinnitus, dizziness, eye pain and pain of the shoulder, arm and wrist.

YANGLAO (S.I.6) 养老   "XI" (BENEFITING THE AGED)

"Yang" (养) means to benefit. "Lao" (老) refers to old age. The point is mainly indicated in blurring of vision, deafness, pain of the shoulder, lower back pain, difficulty in sitting and rising, as well as motor impairment. Needling the point can alleviate the above problems in the aged, reinforce the body constitution and promote longevity. Hence the name Yanglao (Benefiting the Aged).
Location:
In the depression behind the styloid process of the ulna. When locating the point, ask the patient to put the palm facing the chest and rotate outwards so that the palm turns upward. The point is in the bony cleft on the radial side of the styloid process of the ulna (Fig. II-60).
Indications:
Hypoposia, pain of the elbow, shoulder and back, soreness of the shoulder area, occipital headache, intercostal neuralgia and appendicitis.
Clinical Application:
It is the "Xi-Cleft" point of this meridian and has the effect to benefit the liver, brighten the eye, pacify the stomach and promote the function of the collaterals.
Combinations:
With Geshu (U.B.17), Guangming (G.B.37) and Fengchi (G.B.20) for treating hypoposia;

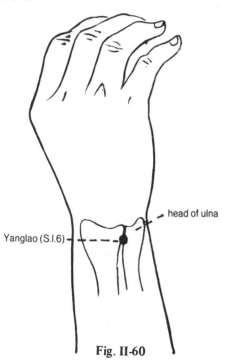

Yanglao (S.I.6)

head of ulna

Fig. II-60

With Neiguan (P.6) for hiccup.
Method:
Puncture perpendicularly or obliquely 0.5-0.8 cun deep.
Needling Sensations:
Numbness, soreness or distention going upwards or downwards along the course of the meridian.

ZHIZHENG (S.I.7) 支正   " ∧ " (MERIDIAN'S BRANCH)

"Zhi"(支) means a branch of a meridian. "Zheng" (正) means major, large or more important meridian, referring to the Heart Meridian of Hand-Shaoyin. A branch emerges from the Small Intestine Meridian at this point to connect with the Heart Meridian, the key organ of the internal zang-fu and shows greater significance than the small intestine. Hence the name Zhizheng (Meridian's Branch).
Location:

Five cun proximal to Yanggu (S.I.5), on the line joining Yanggu (S.I.5) and Xiaohai (S.I.8), at the medial side of the ulna (Fig. II-61).

Indications:

Febrile diseases, headache, blurring of vision, pain of the elbow, forearm and fingers.

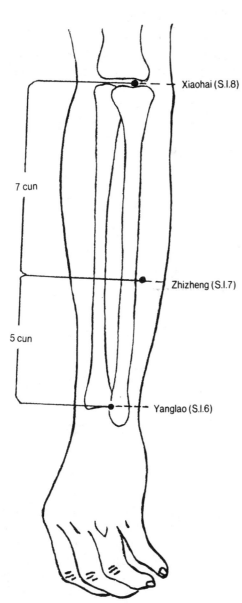

Xiaohai (S.I.8)

Zhizheng (S.I.7)

7 cun

5 cun

Yanglao (S.I.6)

Fig. II-61

Method:

Puncture perpendicularly 0.5-0.8 cun deep.

XIAOHAI (S.I.8)小海 "HE" (SMALL SEA)

"Xiao" (小) means small, here referring to the Small Intestine Meridian. "Hai" (海) means sea. At this point, the qi of the meridian becomes most abundant, similar to the confluence of rivers into a sea. The small intestine is a place to receive the food, partially digested by the stomach. Its lower portion goes downward to the large intestine while its upper portion connects with the stomach, known as the sea of the water and grain. Hence the name Xiaohai (Small Sea).

Location:

Posterior to the medial epicondyle of the humerus, in the groove near the ulnar nerve (Fig. II-61).

Indications:

Headache, pain of the neck, shoulder, elbow and forearm, paralysis of the ulnar nerve, deafness and tinnitus.

Clinical Application:

As it is the "He-Sea" point of the Small Intestine Meridian of Hand-Taiyang, it has the effect to eliminate wind, restore consciousness, remove obstruction from the meridian and stop pain.

Combinations:

With Hegu (L.I.4) and Taichong (Liv.3) for neck pain;

With Taiyang (extra) for headache.

Method:

Puncture perpendicularly 0.3-0.5 cun deep.

Needling Sensations:

Numbness going towards the little finger.

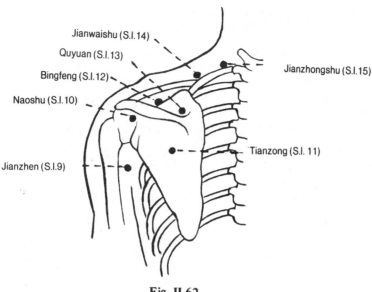

Fig. II-62

*JIANZHEN (S.I.9) 肩貞 (SHOULDER NORMALIZATION)

"Jian" (肩) means the shoulder. "Zhen" (貞) means to be normal, or the opposite of abnormal. This point is indicated in shoulder pain and difficulty in lifting the arm. It can promote the body resistance in order to dispel the exogenous pathogenic factors, promote the functional activity of the shoulder joint and restore it to normal. Hence the name Jianzhen (Shoulder Normalization).

Location:

One cun directly above the posterior end of the axillary fold when the arm is abducted (Fig. II-62).

Indications:

Apart from the above-mentioned conditions, it is also used to treat tinnitus, toothache and febrile diseases.

Clinical Application:

This point has the effect to remove obstruction from the meridians, invigorate the collaterals and eliminate wind.

Combinations:

With Jianyu (L.I.15) and Jianliao (S.J.14) for shoulder joint pain.

Method:

Puncture perpendicularly 1.5 cun deep.

Needling Sensations:

Soreness and distention of the shoulder region.

*NAOSHU (S.I.10) 臑俞 (POINT OF HUMERUS)

The upper portion of the humerus is called "Nao" (臑). "Shu" (俞) means a site through which the qi of the meridian is transported to the body surface, namely the point.

Note: The following points are all punctured either perpendicularly or obliquely about 0.5-0.8 cun deep.

It is located inferoposterior to the acromion below Jugu (L.I.16) at the upper portion of the humerus. Hence the name Naoshu (Point of Humerus).

Location:

It is directly above the posterior axillary fold, in the depression inferolateral to the scapular spine. When locating the point, place the thumb on point Jianzhen (S.I.9) and push upward along the skin until an obstruction is felt. At this stage, the point lies under the tip of the thumb.

Soreness can also be felt when the point is pressed (Fig. II-62).

Indications:

Frozen shoulder, scrofula and pain around the shoulder.

Clinical Application:

The point has the effect to remove obstruction from the collaterals and stop pain.

Combinations:

With Jianzhen (S.I.9), Jianyu (L.I.15), Quchi (L.I.11) and Waiguan (S.J.5) for pain of the shoulder and arm.

Method:

Puncture perpendicularly or obliquely 1-1.5 cun deep.

Needling Sensations:

Soreness in the shoulder region.

TIANZONG (S.I.11) 天 宗 (HEAVENLY CONVERGENCE)

"Tian" (天) means heavens, referring to the upper portion of the body. "Zong" (宗) means convergence. The lung is thought of as the superior cover of the zangfu organs, connecting with the natural heavens through its window, the nose. Consequently, the lung is sometimes also referred to as "heavens." The point is situated above the lung, where the qi and blood of the small intestine meridian leading to the pulmonary area converges. Hence the name Tianzong (Heavenly Convergence).

Location:

In the centre of the infrascapular fossa, 1 cun directly below the mid-point of the infrascapular spine (Fig II-62).

Indications:

Pain and soreness of the shoulder and the arm.

BINGFENG (S.I.12) 秉 风 (WIND RECEIVER)

"Bing" (秉) means to receive and accept something. "Feng" (风) means the wind, here referring to exogenous pathogenic wind. The adjacent area may easily be affected by exogenous pathogenic wind, which makes the point valuable in the treatment of wind related conditions. Hence the name Bingfeng (Wind Receiver).

Location:

In the centre of the suprascapular fossa, directly above Tianzong (S.I.11) (Fig. II-62).

Indications:

Shoulder and arm pain.

QUYUAN (S.I.13) 曲 垣 (CURVED WALL)

"Qu" (曲) means curved. "Yuan" (垣) means a section of low wall. The point is situated in the depression above the scapular spine, which looks like a low curved wall, hence the name Quyuan (Curved Wall).

Location:
In the depression on the medial aspect of the suprascapular fossa (Fig. II-62).

Indications:
Aching of the shoulder, back and arm.

JIANWAISHU (S.I.14)肩外俞 (POINT BESIDE THE SCAPULA)

"Jianwai" (肩外) means outside the scapula on the shoulder, referring to the point not being located on the scapula, though close to it. "Shu" (俞) here means a point. The point is superior to the medial border of the scapula, unlike the previous two points which are located on it. Hence the name Jianwaishu (Point Beside the Scapula).

Location:
Three cun lateral to the lower border of the spinous process of the 1st thoracic vertebra (Fig. II-62).

Indications:
Neck rigidity, pain of the shoulder and back.

JIANZHONGSHU (S.I.15)肩中俞 (CENTRAL SHOULDER POINT)

"Jian" (肩) means the shoulder, or the shoulder area. "Zhong" (中) means centre and refers to the midpoint on the line joining Jianjing (G.B.21) and Dazhui (Du 14). "Shu" (俞) means a point. Hence the name Jianzhongshu (Central Shoulder Point).

Location:
Two cun lateral to Dazhui (Du 14) (Fig. II-62).

Indications:
Cough, asthma, bloody vomiting, pain of the shoulder and back.

TIANCHUANG (S.I.16) 天窗 (CELESTIAL WINDOW)

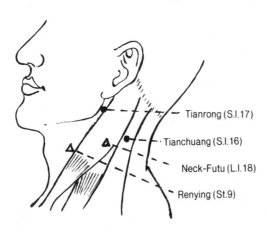

Fig. II-63

"Tian" (天) means heavens or celestial region, here referring to the upper portion of the body, the head and neck in particular. "Chuang" (窗) means an opening or a window and here refers to the ears. This point can be used to treat deafness and remove obstruction sensation from the ear, as though by opening a window. Hence the name Tianchuang (Celestial Window).

Location:
3.5 cun lateral to the Adam's apple and 0.5 cun posterior to Neck-Futu (L.I.18), on the posterior border of m. sternocleidomastoideus. When locating the point, ask the patient to place the

midpoint of the margin of the web between the thumb and the index finger against the Adam's apple. The point is where the tip of the index finger touches (Fig. II-63).

Indications:

Sore throat, swelling of the cheek, deafness, tinnitus, aphasia and aphonia.

Method:

Puncture perpendicularly about 0.5-1 cun deep.

*TIANRONG (S.I.17) 天容 (CELESTIAL APPEARANCE)

"Tian" (天) again means the celestial area, referring to the upper portion of the body, but in this case the head in particular. "Rong" (容) means appearance. In ancient times, women usually wore the ear rings which would often touch the point area. Furthermore, this point is commonly used to treat cosmetic problems affecting the neck and face. Hence the name Tianrong (Celestial Appearance).

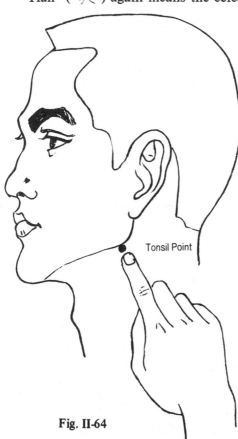

Tonsil Point

Fig. II-64

Location:

Posterior to the angle of the mandible, in the depression at the anterior border of m. sternocleidomastoideus. When locating this point, have the patient place the midpoint of the margin of the web between the index finger and the thumb against the centre of the hyoid bone. The point is where the tip of the thumb touches (Fig. II-64).

Indications:

Deafness, tinnitus, sore throat, swelling of the throat, pain and swelling of the neck.

Biantao (the Tonsil Point) is sometimes called Front-Tianrong. It is located in front of the carotid artery, interior and anterior to the mandibular angle.

Indications:

Similar to Tianrong (S.I.17).

Method:

Puncture both of them perpendicularly about 0.5-1 cun deep.

QUANLIAO (S.I.18) 顴 髎 (ZYGOMATIC CREVICE)

"Quan" (顴) means the zygoma. "Liao" (髎) means a bone crevice. The point is in the depression below the highest place of the zygoma, hence the name Quanliao (Zygomatic Crevice).

Location:

Directly below the outer canthus, in the depression on the lower border of the

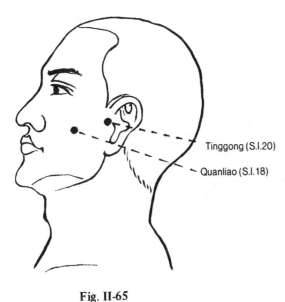

Fig. II-65

zygoma (Fig. II-65).

Indications:

Facial paralysis, toothache, trigeminal neuralgia and twiching of the eyelids.

Clinical Application:

This point is the coalescent point of the Small Intestine Meridian of Hand-Taiyang and the Sanjiao Meridian of Hand-Shaoyang. It has the effect to relieve the pain and calm the mind. It is a commonly selected point for acupuncture anesthesia in craniocerebral operations.

Combinations:

With Taiyang (Extra), Sizhukong (U.B.2), Dicang (St.4) and Jiache (St.6) for spasm of the facial nerves and facial paralysis.

Method:

Puncture perpendicularly 0.5-1 cun deep.

Needling Sensations:

Numbness and distention in the local area.

*TINGGONG (S.I.19) 听 宫 (HEARING PALACE)

"Ting" (听) means hearing. "Gong" (宫) means a palace, or a very important place. The point is in front of the tragus and can restore the hearing function. Hence the name Tinggong (Hearing Palace).

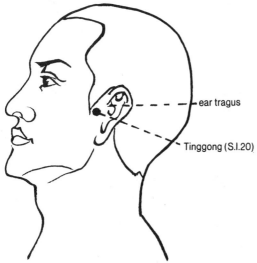

Fig. II-66

Location:

In front of the ear, posterior to the mandibular joint, at the level of the tip of the tragus where a depression is formed when the mouth is slightly opened (Fig. II-66).

Indications:

Deafness, tinnitus, otitis media and toothache.

Clinical Application:

It is a coalescent point of the Small Intestine Meridian of Hand-Taiyang and the Gall Bladder Meridian of Foot-Shaoyang. It has the effect to remove the obstruction from the related meridians and the collaterals, promote the hearing function, calm and benefit the mind.

Combinations:

With Yifeng (S.J.17) and Hand-Zhongzhu (S.J.3) for tinnitus and deafness,
With Hegu (L.I.4), Yifeng (S.J.17) and Waiguan (S.J.5) for otitis media.

III. Summary

The Small Intestine Meridian of Hand-Taiyang pertains to the Small Intestine, connects with the Heart, and links with the Stomach. It passes through the esophagus, eye, ear and the nose. There are 19 points on either side (Fig. II-67).

The Specific Points of the Meridian
Point Indications of the Small Intestine Meridian

Xiaohai	S.I.8	He-Sea Earth	Shaoze	S.I.1	⊙ Metal
Yanggu	S.I.5	↶ Fire	Wangu	S.I.4	O
Houxi	S.I.3	↟ Wood	Yangliao	S.I.6	Xi
Qiangu	S.I.2	∼ Water	Zhizheng	S.I.7	∧

According to Locations

Point Names	Locations	Indications	Regional Indications
Shaoze S.I.1	0.1 cun posterior to the corner of the nail, on the ulnar side of the little finger	Febrile diseases, loss of consciousness, lactation deficiency	Head, neck, ear, eye and throat problems, febrile diseases, mental illness
Qiangu S.I.2	In the depression distal to the 5th metacarpophalangeal joint	Pain of the neck and headache	
Houxi S.I.3	Superior to the end of the transverse crease of the palm when a loose fist is made	Neck rigidity, neck sprain	
Hand-Wangu S.I.4	In the depression between the base of the 5th metacarpal bone and the pisiform bone	Weakness of the wrist, contracture of the fingers	
Yanggu S.I.5	In the depression between the styloid process of the ulna and the triquetrous bone	Febrile diseases without sweating, epilepsy	
Yanglao S.I.6	In the bony cleft on the radial side of the styloid process of the ulna	Neck sprain, pain of the back and the eye diseases	
Zhizheng S.I.7	5 cun directly above Yanggu (S.I.5)	Pain of the fingers, neck, and back problems	Local diseases and local problems
Xiaohai S.I.8	In the depression between the olecranon and the medial epicondyle of the humerus	Diseases of the shoulder and back, upper abdominal diseases	

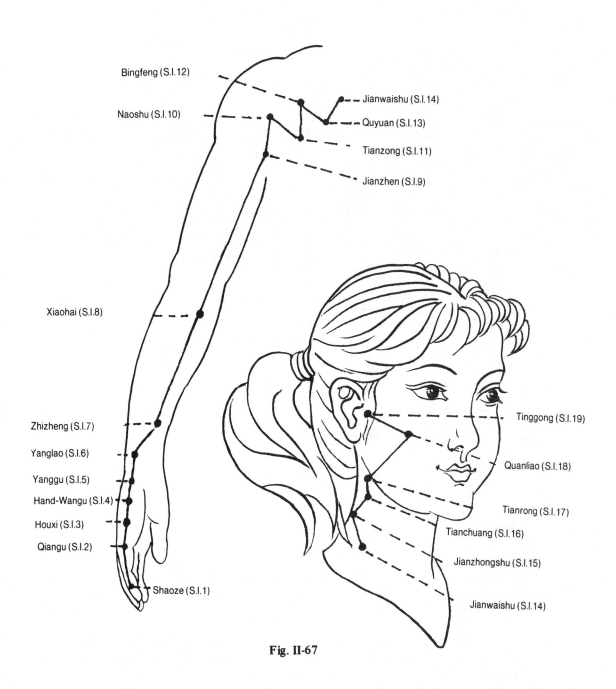

Bingfeng (S.I.12)

Naoshu (S.I.10)

Jianwaishu (S.I.14)

Quyuan (S.I.13)

Tianzong (S.I.11)

Jianzhen (S.I.9)

Xiaohai (S.I.8)

Zhizheng (S.I.7)

Yanglao (S.I.6)

Yanggu (S.I.5)

Hand-Wangu (S.I.4)

Houxi (S.I.3)

Qiangu (S.I.2)

Shaoze (S.I.1)

Tinggong (S.I.19)

Quanliao (S.I.18)

Tianrong (S.I.17)

Tianchuang (S.I.16)

Jianzhongshu (S.I.15)

Jianwaishu (S.I.14)

Fig. II-67

Jianzhen S.I.9	1 cun above the end of the posterior axillary fold	Diseases around the shoulder and the back	
Naoshu S.I.10	In the depression inferior and lateral to the scapular spine	Diseases around the shoulder and the back	
Tianzhong S.I.11	1 cun below the midpoint of the lower border of the scapular spine	Shoulder and back diseases, lactation deficiency	
Bingfeng S.I.12	In the centre of the suprascapular fossa	Shoulder and back diseases	
Quyuan S.I.13	On the medial extremity of the suprascapular fossa	Diseases of the scapular region	
Jianwaishu S.I.14	3 cun lateral to Taodao (Du 13)	Diseases on the neck and scapular region	
Jianzhongshu S.I.15	2 cun lateral to Dazhui (Du 14)	Asthma, cough, diseases of the shoulder and back	Diseases of the shoulder and scapular regions
Tianchuang S.I.16	Level with Adam's Apple, on the posterior border of m. sternocleidomastoideus	Sore throat, and throat itching	
Tianrong S.I.17	Posterior to the mandibular angle, on the anterior border of m. sternocleidomastoideus	Deafness, tinnitus, throat itching	Diseases of the ear, mouth, tooth and throat
Quanliao S.I.18	Directly below the outer canthus, in the depression on the lower border of the zygoma	Facial paralysis and trigeminal neuralgia	
Tinggong S.I.19	Half-way between the mid-point of the tragus and the mandibular joint	Facial paralysis, deafness and tinnitus	

Section 3   THE SANJIAO MERIDIAN OF HAND-SHAOYANG

I. The Meridian

General Indications:

Points from the Sanjiao Meridian of Hand-Shaoyang are mainly indicated in deafness, tinnitus, sore throat, eye disorders, febrile diseases, disorders of the head, temporal region and the posterior aspect of the upper extremities.

Course of the Meridian:

(1) It originates from the tip of the ring finger (Guanchong, S.J.1). (2) Running upwards between the 4th and 5th metacarpal bones, (3) it goes along the dorsal aspect of the wrist, (4) to the lateral aspect of the forearm between the radius and ulna. (5) It ascends, passing through the olecranon, (6) along the lateral aspect of the upper arm (7) and reaches the shoulder. It meets Dazhui (Du 14) at the lower border of the spinous process of the 7th cervical vertebra, (8) passes behind the Gall Bladder Meridian of Foot-Shaoyang. (9) Passing over the supraclavicular fossa, (10) it enters the chest at Shanzhong (Ren 17) to connect with the pericardium. (11) It then descends through the

diaphragm to the abdomen, to connect with the upper, middle and the lower Jiao, i.e. the Sanjiao (triple heater), its pertaining organ.

(12) The branch from the chest: It runs upwards, (13) emerges from the supraclavicular fossa, (14) ascends to the neck, (15) curves around the posterior border of the ear (16) to the superior aspect of the ear, (17) turns downwards to the cheek and terminates in the infraorbital region.

(18) The Auricular branch: It arises from the retroauricular region and enters the ear. Emerging in front of the ear, it crosses the previous branch at the cheek and (19) reaches the lateral end of the eyebrow (Sizhukong, S.J.23), at the outer canthus (Tongziliao, G.B.1) to link with the Gall Bladder Meridian of Foot-Shaoyang (Fig. II-68).

Analytical Display of the Course of the Meridian

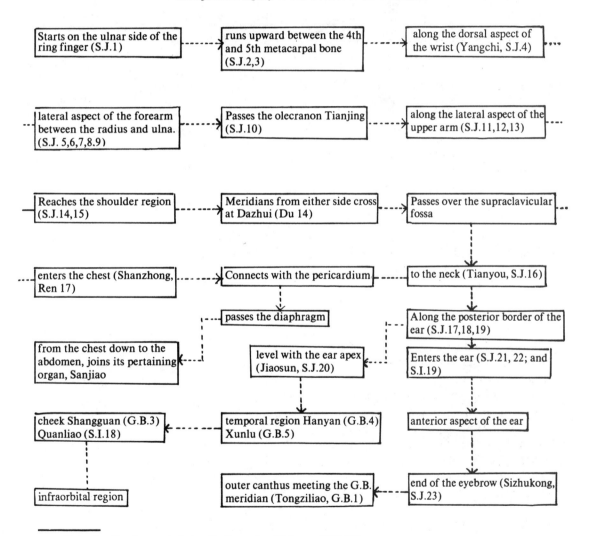

Note: Sanjiao has an inferior He-Sea point Weiyang (U.B.39).

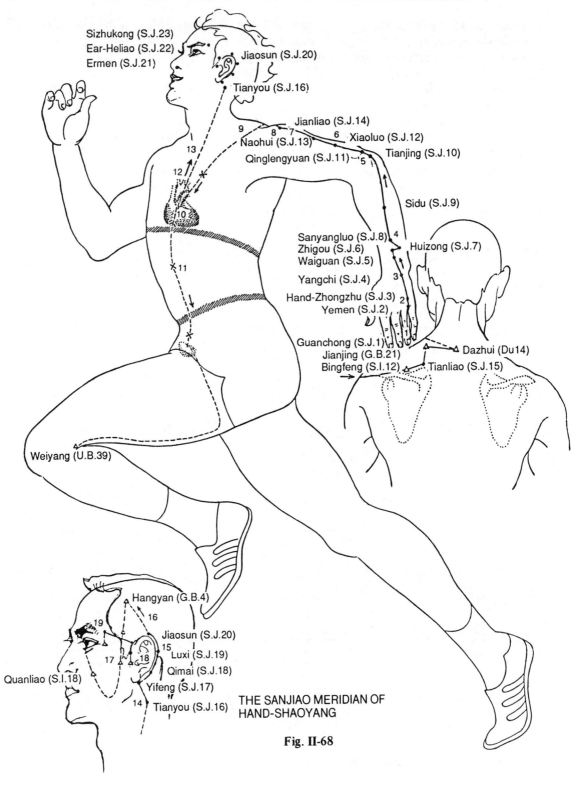

Sizhukong (S.J.23)
Ear-Heliao (S.J.22)
Ermen (S.J.21)
Jiaosun (S.J.20)
Tianyou (S.J.16)
Jianliao (S.J.14)
Naohui (S.J.13)
Xiaoluo (S.J.12)
Qinglengyuan (S.J.11)
Tianjing (S.J.10)
Sidu (S.J.9)
Sanyangluo (S.J.8)
Huizong (S.J.7)
Zhigou (S.J.6)
Waiguan (S.J.5)
Yangchi (S.J.4)
Hand-Zhongzhu (S.J.3)
Yemen (S.J.2)
Guanchong (S.J.1)
Jianjing (G.B.21)
Dazhui (Du14)
Bingfeng (S.I.12)
Tianliao (S.J.15)
Weiyang (U.B.39)

Hangyan (G.B.4)
Jiaosun (S.J.20)
Luxi (S.J.19)
Qimai (S.J.18)
Yifeng (S.J.17)
Quanliao (S.I.18)
Tianyou (S.J.16)

THE SANJIAO MERIDIAN OF
HAND-SHAOYANG

Fig. II-68

Related Zangfu Organs:

The Sanjiao Meridian of Hand-Shaoyang pertains to the upper, middle, and the lower jiao, i.e. the triple-heater, and connects with the pericardium.

Coalescent Points of the Meridian:

Bingfeng (S.I.12), Tinggong (S.I.19), Quanliao (S.I.18), Jianjing (G.B.21), Shangguan (G.B.3), Hanyan (G.B.4), Tongziliao (G.B.1). Dazhui (Du 14) and Weiyang (U.B.39).

II. The Points

The Sanjiao Meridian of Hand-Shaoyang has 23 points on either side of the body. Among them, 13 are located on the mid-line of the posterior aspect of the upper limb, the other 10 being located on the neck or head. The starting point is Guanchong (S.J.1), and the terminating point is Sizhukong (S.J.23)

Point Names	Pinyin	Codes	Point Names	Pinyin	Codes
关 冲	Guanchong	S.J.1	臑 会	Naohui	S.J.13
液 门	Yemen	S.J.2	肩 髎	Jianliao	S.J.14
中 渚	Hand-Zhongzhu	S.J.3	天 髎	Tianliao	S.J.15
阳 池	Yangchi	S.J.4	天 牖	Tianyou	S.J.16
外 关	Waiguan	S.J.5	翳 风	Yifeng	S.J.17
支 沟	Zhigou	S.J.6	瘈 脉	Qimai	S.J.18
会 宗	Huizong	S.J.7	颅 息	Luxi	S.J.19
三 阳 络	Sanyangluo	S.J.8	角 孙	Jiaosun	S.J.20
四 渎	Sidu	S.J.9	耳 门	Ermen	S.J.21
天 井	Tianjing	S.J.10	耳 和 髎	Ear-Heliao	S.J.22
清 冷 渊	Qinglengyuan	S.J.11	絲 竹 空	Sizhukong	S.J.23
消 泺	Xiaoluo	S.J.12			

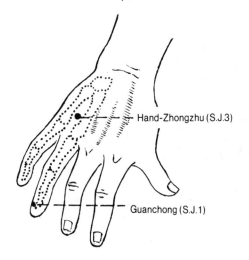

Fig. II-69

*GUANCHONG (S.J.1) 关冲 " ⊙ " (ESSENTIAL PASS)

"Guan" (关) means a pass, a narrow way over or through the mountains. "Chong" (冲) means essential or important, but here referring to the vigorous flow of the qi and blood of the meridian at this point. The area between Shaochong (H.9) and Zhongchong (P.9) is like an important pass between the two forts, hence the name Guanchong (Essential Pass).

Location:

On the lateral side of the ring finger, 0.1 cun posterior to the corner of the nail (Fig. II-69, 70).

Indications:

Headache, redness of the eye, sore throat and

infantile indigestion.

Clinical Application:

It is the Jing-well point of the Sanjiao Meridian of Hand-Shaoyang and has the effect to eliminate heat and soothe the throat.

Combinations:

With Renzhong (Du 26), Neiguan (P.6) and Shixuan (Extra 30) for coma, loss of the consciousness and sunstroke;

With Yamen (Du 15) for stiffness of the tongue.

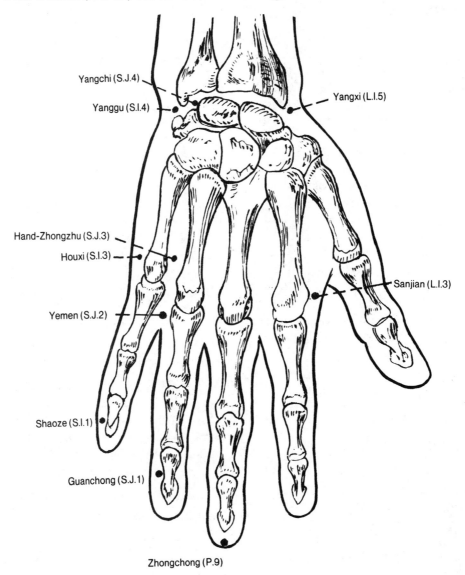

Fig. II-70

Method:

Puncture shallowly about 0.1 cun deep to cause bleeding.

Needling Sensations:

Slight pain in the local area.

YEMEN (S.J.2) 液门 " ～ " (FLUID GATE)

"Ye" (液) means water or fluid. "Men" (门) means gate. The Sanjiao regulates and controls the circulation of the body fluid and is referred to as the chief palace of the body fluid. Consequently, many of the names of points from this meridian are associated with water: e.g. Fluid Gate (Yemen, S.J.2), Mid Islet (Hand-Zhongzhu S.J.3), Four Rivers (Sidu, S.J.9), and Cooling Gulf (Qinglengyuan, S.J.11), etc. This point, represented by water, is the Ying-Spring point of the meridian, where the substantial qi of the body fluid passes in and out. Hence the name Yemen (Fluid Gate) (Fig. II-70).

Location:

When a loose fist is made, the point is in the depression of the web between the 4th and 5th metacarpophalangeal joints.

Indications:

Headache, blurring of vision, deafness, tinnitus, aching of the forearm and sore throat.

Method:

Puncture perpendicularly about 0.3-0.5 cun deep.

*HAND-ZHONGZHU (S.J. 3) 中渚 " 个 " (MID ISLET)

"Zhong" (中) means middle. "Zhu" (渚) means a small piece of land surrounded by water, or a small islet. The point is directly above Yemen (S.J.2), midway between the 4th and 5th metacarpal bones. Hence the name Zhongzhu (Mid Islet).

Location:

On the dorsum of the hand between the 4th and 5th metacarpal bones, in the depression 1 cun above the mid-point of the line joining the 4th and 5th metacarpophalangeal joints (Fig. II-69, 70).

Indications:

Deafness, tinnitus, headache, sore throat, numbness of the hand and motor impairment of the fingers.

Clinical Application:

The point is the Shu-Stream point of the Sanjiao Meridian of Hand-Shaoyang. It can be used to restore consciousness, tonify the brain, regulate qi and relieve stagnation of qi.

Combinations:

With Yifeng (S.J.17), Tianrong (S.I.19), Tinghui (G.B.2) and Ermen (S.J.21) for tinnitus and deafness;

With Taixi (K.3) for sore throat;

With Tianliao (S.J.14) and Shousanli (L.I.10) for shoulder pain.

Method:

Puncture perpendicularly 0.3-0.5 cun deep.

Needling Sensations:

Numbness radiating to the ring finger.

*YANGCHI (S.J. 4) 阳池 " ○ " (POND OF YANG)

The dorsal aspect of the wrist is considered as being the "Yang" (阳) side, points there being from the Yang meridians. "Chi" (池) means a depression. The point is in the depression on the Yang side of the wrist, hence the name Yangchi (Pond of Yang). It is one of the three Yang points of the wrist, Yanggu (S.I.5) and Yangxi (L.I.5) being the other two.

Location:

On the transverse crease of the wrist in the depression between the tendons of m. extensor digiti minimi and digitorum communis (Fig. II-70, 74).

Indications:

Pain in the wrist, shoulder and arm, thirst due to diabetes and deafness. The book *Qixiao Lianfang* (*Special Indications and Well Tried Prescriptions*) records another point between Yangchi (S.J.4) and Yangxi (L.I.5) which is called "Zhongquan" (Middle Spring). Its indications are identical to those of Yangchi (S.J.4).

Clinical Application:

It is the Yuan-Source point of the Sanjiao Meridian of Hand-Shaoyang, having the effect to relax the tendons, remove obstruction from the meridians and collaterals, eliminate the heat and alleviate exterior syndromes.

Combinations:

With Quchi (L.I.11), Hegu (L.I.4) and Waiguan (S.J.5) for pain of the elbow and wrist area;

With Yifeng (S.J.17) and Ermen (G.B.2) for deafness;

With Lianquan (Ren.23) for thirst due to the diabetes.

Method:

Puncture perpendicularly or slightly oblique 0.3-0.5 cun deep.

Needling Sensations:

The needling reaction goes downwards to the middle finger.

*WAIGUAN (S.J.5) 外关 " ∧ " (EXTERIOR PASS)

"Wai" (外) means exterior and here refers to the lateral side of the forearm. "Guan" (关) means a pass. The meridian arrives here from the wrist as though entering a narrow way or a pass. Besides, it is the Luo-Connecting point of this meridian, from which a branch connects with the Pericardium Meridian of Hand-Jueyin on the medial aspect of the forearm. It is also directly opposite to Neiguan (P.6) (Interior Pass), hence the name Waiguan (Exterior Pass).

Location:

Two cun above the mid-point of the transverse crease of the wrist, between the radius and the ulna (Fig, II-71, 72, 74).

Indications:

Febrile diseases, one-side headache, deafness, tinnitus, hypochondriac pain, neck sprain, mumps, motor impairment of the upper extremities and pain of the joints.

Clinical Application:

It is the Luo-Connecting point of the Sanjiao Meridian of Hand-Shaoyang, connect-

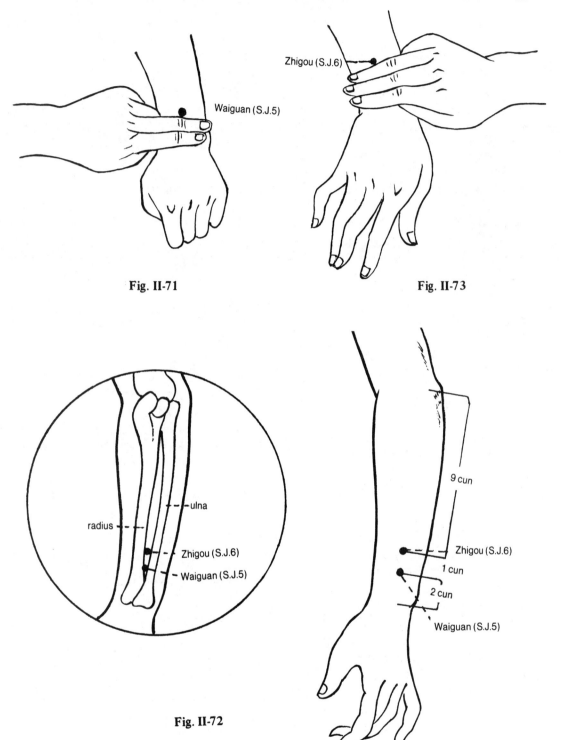

Waiguan (S.J.5)

Fig. II-71

Zhigou (S.J.6)

Fig. II-73

radius

ulna

Zhigou (S.J.6)

Waiguan (S.J.5)

Fig. II-72

9 cun

Zhigou (S.J.6)

1 cun

2 cun

Waiguan (S.J.5)

ing with the Pericardium Meridian of Hand-Jueyin. It is also one of the eight Confluent points, influencing the Yangwei Meridian. It is used to remove obstructions from the meridian and collaterals, eliminate wind and relieve exterior syndromes.

Combinations:

With Dazhui (Du 14), Quchi (L.I.11) and Hegu (L.I.4) for common cold with fever;

With Jianyu (L.I.15), Quchi (L.I.11), Shousanli (L.I.10) and Hegu (L.I.4) for paralysis of the upper limbs.

Method:

Puncture perpendicularly 0.5-1 cun deep.

Needling Sensations:

Numbness may radiate to the index, middle or ring finger.

ZHIGOU (S.J.6) 支 沟 " 𝓐 " (LIMB DITCH)

"Zhi" (支) refers here to the upper limb. "Gou" (沟) means a narrow groove or ditch. The point is located in the narrow space between the ulna and radius, where the qi of the meridian flows like water in a ditch, hence the name Zhigou (Limb Ditch).

Location:

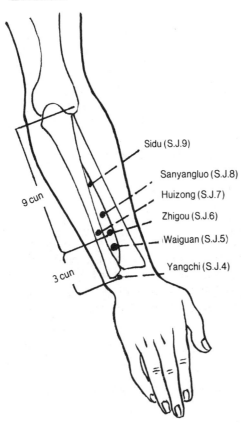

Sidu (S.J.9)

Sanyangluo (S.J.8)

Huizong (S.J.7)

Zhigou (S.J.6)

Waiguan (S.J.5)

Yangchi (S.J.4)

9 cun

3 cun

Fig. II-74

One cun directly above Waiguan (S.J.5), between the ulna and radius.

Indications:

Constipation, hypochondriac pain, soreness and pain of the arm and shoulder, sore throat and somnolence (Fig. II-72, 73, 74).

Clinical Application:

It is the Jing-River point of the Sanjiao Meridian of Hand-Shaoyang, having the effect to remove obstructions, restore consciousness, invigorate the collaterals, disperse coagulation of blood and regulate the zangfu organs.

Combinations:

With Renzhong (Du 26), Zhongchong (P.9) and Hegu (L.I.4) for loss of consciousness due to windstroke;

With Yanglingquan (G.B.34) for hypochondriac pain;

With Zusanli (St.36), Tianshu (St.25) and Dazhui (Du 14) for habitual constipation.

Method:

Puncture perpendicularly 1 cun deep.

Needling Sensations:

Numbness and distention radiating around the point.

HUIZONG (S.J.7) 会宗 "Xi" (JOIN AND CONVERGE)

"Hui" (会) means to meet or to join. "Zong" (宗) means to converge. The flow of the qi of the Sanjiao Meridian coming from Zhigou (S.J.6) converges at this point before progressing to the next point, Sanyangluo (S.J.8), hence the name Huizong (Join and Converge).

Location:
One cun lateral to Zhigou (S.J.6) on the medial side of the ulna (Fig. II-74).
Indications:
Deafness, epilepsy and aching of the arm.
Method:
Puncture perpendicularly about 1-1.5 cun deep.
Needling Sensations:
Radiate downwards along the course of the meridian.

SANYANGLUO (S.J.8) 三阳络 (THREE YANG CONNECTING)

"Sanyang" (三阳) refers to the three Yang meridians of the hand. "Luo" (络) means to link or connect. The three yang meridians of the hand are connected at the point, hence the name Sanyangluo (Three Yang Connecting). This point corresponds to Sanyinjiao (Sp.6) (Three Yin Crossing), in the lower limb.

Location:
One cun above Zhigou (S.J.6), between the ulna and radius (Fig. II-74).
Indications:
Sudden deafness, sudden hoarseness, toothache and pain of the upper limbs.
Method:
Puncture perpendicularly 1-1.5 cun deep.
Needling Sensations:
The needling reaction radiates either upwards or downwards along the course of the meridian.

SIDU (S.J.9) 四渎 (FOUR RIVERS)

"Si" (四) is four. "Du" (渎) means river or canal. In ancient times people called the Yangtze, Yellow, Huai, and Ji Rivers, the great four rivers of the world (They are the four longest rivers in China). The Sanjiao is considered to be the official of the waters, having the function to maintain the water passages and keep water flowing freely, like the waters of the four great rivers. It is located above Sanyangluo (S.J.8), from which the qi of the meridian can be thought of as irrigating a large area. Hence the name Sidu (Four Rivers).

Location:
Four cun above Zhigou (S.J.6), or 5 cun below the olecranon (Fig. II-74).
Indications:
Deafness, toothache, sudden hoarseness, pain of the forearm and one-sided headache.
Method:
Puncture perpendicularly 1-1.5 cun deep.

Note: From Fig. II-74 we can see that the points Sanyangluo (S.J.8), Waiguan (S.J.5) and Huizong (S.J.7) are located 1 cun above, 1 cun below and 1 cun lateral to Zhigou point (S.J.6).

Needling Sensations:

It may get either upwards or downwards along the course of the meridian.

*TIANJING (S.J.10) 天 井   "HE" (CELESTIAL WELL)

The upper portion of the body is known as "Tian" (天), heaven. "Jing" (井) means a well, here referring to a depression. The point is located 1 cun superior to the olecranon, in the depression between the tendons, which looks like a pool or well on the top of the mountain. The Sanjiao controls the water passages and keeps water flowing freely, hence the name Tianjing (Celestial Well).

Location:

In the depression about 1 cun superior to the olecranon when the elbow is flexed slightly (Fig.II-75).

Indications:

One-sided headache, pain on the neck, shoulder and arm, and scrofula.

Method:

Puncture perpendicularly 0.5-1 cun deep.

Clinical Application:

It is the "He-Sea" point of the meridian, having the effect to relax the tendons and remove the obstructions from the meridians and collaterals.

Combinations:

With Fengchi (G.B.20) and Dazhui (Du 14) for stiffness of the neck and pain of the back.

Needling Sensations:

Soreness and distension around the elbow joint.

QINGLENGYUAN (S.J. 11) 清冷渊 (COOLING GULF)

"Qing" (清) means cool. "Leng" (冷) means cold. "Yuan" (渊) means a gulf. The point is mainly indicated in diseases of the Sanjiao related with either the retention or accumulation of heat. It is the specific point from this meridian used to eliminate heat and cool the blood. Hence the name Qinglengyuan (Cooling Gulf).

Location:

Two cun proximal to the olecranon (Fig. II-75).

Indications:

Headache, pain of the neck, toothache, pain of the shoulder and back.

Method:

Puncture perpendicularly 1-1.5 cun deep.

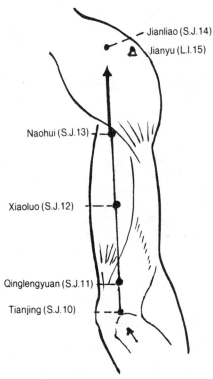

Fig. II-75

XIAOLUO (S.J.12) 消泺 (RELIEVE THIRST)

"Xiao" (消) means to relieve. "Luo" (泺) means thirst, referring to exhaustion of body fluid, consumed by endogenous heat, as in the case of diabetes. As the point is specifically indicated in the treatment of diabetes, it is called Xiaoluo (Relieve Thirst).

Location:

Five cun above the olecranon, 3 cun above Qinglengyuan (S.J.11), in the mid-point of the line joining Naohui (S.J.13) and Qinglengyuan (S.J.11) (Fig. II-75).

Indications:

Diabetes, headache, stiffness of the neck, toothache, pain of the shoulder and back.

Method:

Puncture perpendicularly 1-1.6 cun deep.

NAOHUI (S.J.13) 臑会 (ARM CROSSING)

The upper arm is called "Nao" (臑). "Hui" (会) means crossing or meeting. The point is a crossing point, where the Sanjiao meridian intersects with the Yangwei meridian, hence its name Naohui (Arm Crossing).

Location:

Three cun above Xiaoluo (S.J.12), on the junction of the posterior border of the m. deltoideus and the humerus (Fig. II-75).

Indications:

Soreness and pain of the shoulder and arm, scrofula.

Clinical Application:

Relaxes the tendons, removes obstructions from the meridian and the collaterals, and stops pain.

Combinations:

With Jianyu (L.I.15) and Jianliao (S.J.14) for frozen shoulder.

Method:

Puncture perpendicularly 1-1.5 cun deep.

Needling Sensations:

Distention and soreness radiating along the course of the meridian up and down.

*JIANLIAO (S.J. 14) 肩髎 (SHOULDER CREVICE)

"Jian" (肩) means shoulder, referring to the acromion or the shoulder joint. "Liao" (髎) means bone crevice. This is the last point from the meridian on the shoulder area and is located in a bone depression, hence the name Jianliao (Shoulder Crevice).

Location:

Directly below the lateral and posterior border of the acromion, in the depression which opens when the arm is raised, or 1.3 cun posterior to Jianyu (L.I.15) (Fig. II-75).

Indications:

Heaviness and motor impairment of the shoulder, arm pain.

Clinical Application:

Invigorates the circulation of the blood, disperses the blood coagulation, removes obstruction from the meridians and collaterals and reduces pain.

Combinations:

With Tianzhong (S.I.11) and Yanggu (S.I.5) for arm pain;

Penetrating the needle from Jianliao (S.J.14) to Jianyu (L.I.15) or to Jiquan (H. 1) for treating frozen shoulder.

Method:

Puncture perpendicularly 1-1.5 cun deep towards the shoulder joint.

Needling Sensations:

Soreness and distention around the local area.

*TIANLIAO (S.J.15) 天髎 (CELESTIAL CREVICE)

"Tian" (天), meaning heaven or celestial, refers to the upper portion of the body, in this case to the shoulder region in particular. "Liao" (髎) means a crevice along the border of the tuberosity of the bone, or the depression in a bony cleft. The point is located posterior to the shoulder in the suprascapular fossa, hence the name Tianliao (Celestial Crevice).

Location:

In the depression over the superior angle of the scapula. If the hand is placed

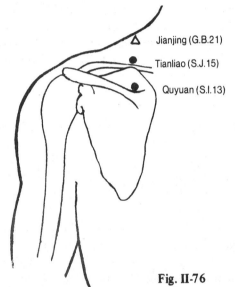

Jianjing (G.B.21)

Tianliao (S.J.15)

Quyuan (S.I.13)

Fig. II-76

naturally on the shoulder of the other side, the point is located where the tip of the middle finger touches, 1.3 cun below Jianjing (G.B.21) (Fig. II-76).

Indications:

Shoulder and elbow pain, stiffness and pain of the neck.

Method:

Puncture perpendicularly 0.6-0.8 cun deep.

TIANYOU (S.J.16) 天牖 (CELESTIAL OPENING)

"Tian" (天), meaning heaven or celestial, again refers to the upper portion of the body, but in this case the neck in particular. "You" (牖) means an opening, or the opening of the head. It is indicated in severe intermittent headache, gout and ear orifice problems, hence the name Tianyou (Celestial Opening).

Location:

At the level of the mandibular angle, on the posterior border of the m. sternocleido-mastoideus (Fig. II-77).

Indications:

Headache, facial swelling, scrofula, neck rigidity and sudden aphonia.

Method:

Puncture perpendicularly 0.5-1 cun deep.

---

*Note: The distances between Jianjing (G.B.21) and Tianliao (S.J.15) and between Tianliao (S.J.15) and Quyuan (S.I.13) are about 1.3 cun.

*YIFENG (S.J.17) 翳风 (EAR-SHIELDING WIND)

"Yi" (翳) originally means a fan made of chicken feathers, the shape of a fan being similar to that of the ear. "Feng" (风) means wind, here implying the noise made by wind. The point is in the depression behind the ear, a place shielded from the wind and is mainly indicated in tinnitus, a wind-like noise in the ear. Hence the name Yifeng (Ear-Shielding Wind).

Location:

Posterior to the lobule of the ear, in the depression between the mandible and mastoid process, where a distinct soreness and distention can be felt on finger pressure (Fig. II-78, 79).

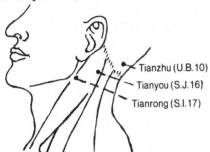

Tianzhu (U.B.10)
Tianyou (S.J.16)
Tianrong (S.I.17)

Fig. II-77

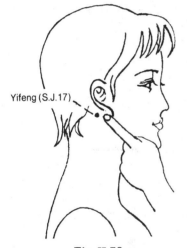

Yifeng (S.J.17)

Fig. II-78

Indications:

Deafness, tinnitus, facial paralysis, parotitis, otitis media and trigeminal neuralgia.

Clinical Application:

It is the crossing point of the Sanjiao Meridian of Hand-Shaoyang and the Gall Bladder Meridian of Foot-Shaoyang. It has the effect to eliminate the wind, remove obstruction from the collaterals and restore the hearing function.

Combinations:

With Ermen (S.J.21), Tinghui (G.B.2) and Hand-Zhongzhu (S.J.3) for tinnitus, deafness and mutism.

With Dicang (St.5), Jiache (St.6), Xiaguan (St.7), Yingxiang (L.I.20) and Hegu (L.I.4) for facial paralysis.

Method:

Puncture perpendicularly about 1 cun deep.

For treating deafness and tinnitus, the tip of the needle is directed upwards;

For sore throat, the tip of the needle should be directed towards the throat,

For insomnia, the needle tip is directed posteriorly;

For facial paralysis, the needle should be directed anteriorly.

Needling Sensations:

Soreness, distention, heaviness, and numbness radiating in the direction of the tip of the needle.

QIMAI (S.J.18) 瘈脉 (CONVULSION VESSEL)

"Qi" (瘈) means convulsion, or spasm. "Mai" (脉) means vessel. It is located on the posterior superficial auricular vein, and can be used to treat infantile convulsion, spasm, etc. Hence the name Qimai (Convulsion Vessel).

Location:

Anterior and posterior to the border of the mastoid process. When locating the point, draw a curved line from Yifeng (S.J.17) to Jiaosun (S.J.20) along the helix. The point lies at the junction of the middle and lower third of the line (Fig. II-79).

Indications:

Headache, tinnitus, infantile convulsion, deafness, vomiting, diarrhea and dysentery.

Method:

Puncture horizontally about 0.3-0.5 cun deep.

LUXI (S.J.19) 颅息 (BRAIN REST)

"Lu" (颅) here refers to the brain or the head. "Xi" (息) means an enforced rest, or stop. This point can relieve headache, treat infantile epilepsy and calm the mind, hence the name Luxi (Brain Rest).

Location:

At the superior and anterior border of the mastoid process, on the junction of the upper and middle third of a curved line drawn from Yifeng (S.J.17) to Jiaosun (S.J.20) along the helix (Fig. II-79).

Indications:

Headache, tinnitus and infantile epilepsy.

Method:

Puncture horizontally about 0.3-0.5 cun deep.

JIAOSUN (S.J.20) 角孙 (CORNER OF COLLATERAL BRANCH)

"Jiao" (角) here means the angle or corner of the skull. "Sun" (孙) refers to the branches of a collateral. The point is located nearly at the corner of the temporal region, directly above the ear apex. A branch of the collateral comes out from the point and curves down to the lower cheek, hence the name Jiaosun (Corner of Collateral

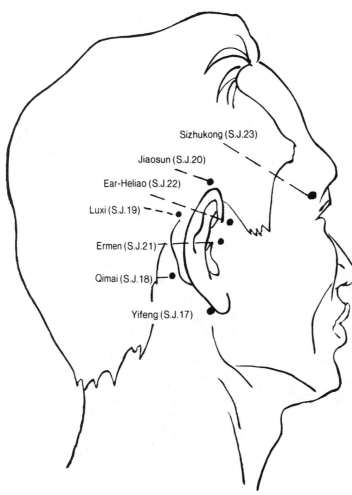

Sizhukong (S.J.23)

Jiaosun (S.J.20)

Ear-Heliao (S.J.22)

Luxi (S.J.19)

Ermen (S.J.21)

Qimai (S.J.18)

Yifeng (S.J.17)

Fig. II-79

Branch).

Location:

Directly above the ear apex, within the hairline when the ear is folded anteriorly (Fig. II-79).

Indications:

Tinnitus, cloudiness of the cornea, swollen gums, dryness of the mouth and lips and stiffness of the neck.

Method:

Puncture horizontally about 0.3-0.5 cun deep.

ERMEN (S.J.21) 耳 门 (EAR GATE)

"Er" (耳) means ear. "Men" (门) means gate. The point is just in front of the ear, and is mainly indicated in ear disorders, hence the name Ermen (Ear Gate).

Location:

In the depression anterior to the supratragic notch. When the mouth is open, a small depression is formed just anterior to the upper process of the tragus (Fig. II-79, 80).

Indications:

Tinnitus, deafness, otitis media, one-sided headache, pain of the cheek, clicking of the mandibular joint and toothache.

Clinical Application:

The point has the effect to remove the obstruction from the meridians and collaterals, promote the hearing function and benefit the brain.

Combinations:

With Tinggong (G.B.2), Tinghui (S.I.19), Yifeng (S.J.17) and Hand-Zhongzhu (S.J.3) for tinnitus, deafness and otitis media;

With Yamen (Du 15) for the deafness and hysteria.

Method:

Puncture perpendicularly about 0.8 cun deep or obliquely 1-1.5 cun deep with the mouth open. Usually the needle is penetrated from Ermen (S.J.21) towards Tinggong (G.B.2) or Tinghui (S.I.19) when treating tinnitus, deafness or otitis media.

Needling Sensations:

Soreness, numbness, distension and heaviness, radiating towards the ear drum.

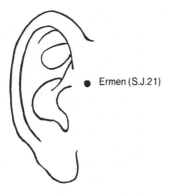

Fig. II-80

EAR-HELIAO (S.J.22) 耳和髎 (NORMALIZING CREVICE)

Here "ear" (耳) is added to the name in order to differentiate the point from Nose-Heliao (L.I.19). "He" (和) means normal function. There is an ancient saying: "Normal function of the nose distinguishes odour from odour; normal function of the mouth tastes the five flavours; the normal function of the ear hears the five sounds; and normal function of the eye sees the five colours". "Liao" (髎) refers to a bony cleft or crevice. Needling this point can restore the functions of the ear, nose, eye and mouth to normal. Hence the name Ear-Heliao (Normalizing Crevice).

Location:

One cun anterior to the root of the auricle at the level of the outer canthus, on the posterior aspect of the superficial artery (Fig. II-79).

Indications:

Headache, heaviness sensation of the head, tinnitus, lock jaw, swelling of the neck and deviation of the mouth.

Method:

Puncture obliquely or horizontally 0.3-0.5 cun deep, avoiding the artery.

SIZHUKONG (S.J.23) 丝竹空 (BAMBOOLEAF DEPRESSION)

"Sizhu" (丝竹) means a tiny, thin bamboo leaf, here referring to the eyebrow. "Kong" (空) means a depression. The point is located in the depression at the lateral end of the eyebrow, hence the name Sizhukong (Bambooleaf Depression).

Location:

It is opposite to Zhanzhu (U.B.2) from the Urinary Bladder Meridian of Foot-Taiyang, located at the other end of the eyebrow.

Indications:

Headache, redness and pain of the eye, blurring of vision, twitching of the eyelids, toothache and epilepsy.

Method:

Puncture horizontally 0.5-1 cun subcutaneously.

III. Summary

The Sanjiao Meridian of Hand-Shaoyang pertains to Sanjiao (the triple heater), connects with the pericardium and passes through the ear and eye. There are 23 points on either side of the body. (Fig. II-81, 82).

Point Indications of the Sanjiao Meridian According to Locations

Point Names	Locations	Indications	Regional Indications
Guanchong S.J.1	On the lateral side of the ring finger, about 0.1 cun posterior to the corner of the nail	Sore throat, conjunctivitis	Diseases of the eye, ear, head, pharynx and larynx; febrile diseases
Yemen S.J.2	On the web between the ring finger and the little finger	Swelling of the dorsum of the hand, malaria	
Hand-Zhongzhu S.J.3	1 cun posterior to the web between the ring and the little fingers	Deafness, tinnitus, febrile diseases	
Yangchi S.J.4	Mid-point of the transverse dorsal wrist crease	Deafness, pain of the wrist	

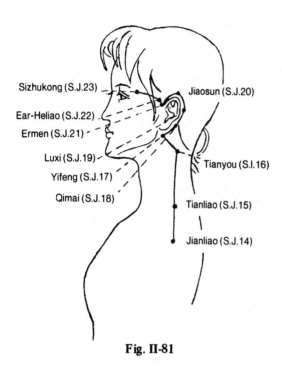

Sizhukong (S.J.23)
Jiaosun (S.J.20)
Ear-Heliao (S.J.22)
Ermen (S.J.21)
Luxi (S.J.19)
Tianyou (S.I.16)
Yifeng (S.J.17)
Qimai (S.J.18)
Tianliao (S.J.15)
Jianliao (S.J.14)

Fig. II-81

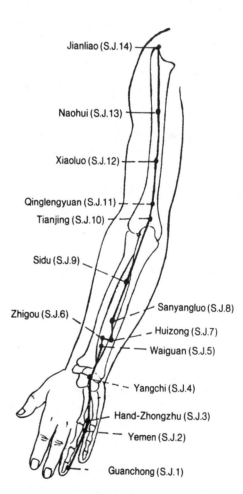

Jianliao (S.J.14)
Naohui (S.J.13)
Xiaoluo (S.J.12)
Qinglengyuan (S.J.11)
Tianjing (S.J.10)
Sidu (S.J.9)
Zhigou (S.J.6)
Sanyangluo (S.J.8)
Huizong (S.J.7)
Waiguan (S.J.5)
Yangchi (S.J.4)
Hand-Zhongzhu (S.J.3)
Yemen (S.J.2)
Guanchong (S.J.1)

Fig. II-82

The Specific Points from the Meridian

Tianjing	(S.J.10)	He Earth
Zhihou	(S.J.6)	⊘ Fire
Hand-Zhongzhu	(S.J.3)	O Wood
Yemen	(S.J.2)	∧ ⊗ Water
Guanchong	(S.J.1)	Metal
Yangchi	(S.J.4)	
Waiguan	(S.J.5)	
Huizong	(S.J.7)	

Point	Location	Indications	
Waiguan S.J.5	2 cun posterior to the transverse crease of the wrist, between the two bones	Fever, one-sided headache, tinnitus	
Zhigou S.J.6	1 cun above Waiguan (S.J.5)	Hypochondriac pain, constipation	
Huizhong S.J.7	1 finger breadth lateral to Zhigou (S.J.6) on the ulnar side	Asthma, fullness of the chest, deafness	Diseases of the ear, eye, head, pharynx and larynx; febrile diseases
Sanyangluo S.J.8	1 cun above Zhigou (S.J.6)	Deafness, aphasia	
Sidu S.J.9	4 cun above Zhigou (S.J.6)	Deafness, pain of the arm	
Tianjing S.J.10	In the depression superior and posterior to the olecranon	Chest pain	
Qinglengyuan S.J.11	1 cun above Tianjing (S.J.10)	Elbow pain, pain of the arm and shoulder	
Xiaoluo S.J.12	Mid-way between Qinglengyuan (S.J.11) and Naohui (S.J.13)	Headache, dizziness, pain of the arm	
Naohui S.J.13	On the posterior border of the m. deltoideus	Shoulder pain, goiter	Local disorders
Jianliao S.J.14	When the arm is raised, the point is in the depression posterior and inferior to the acromion	Pain of the shoulder and lateral aspect of the arm	
Tianliao S.J.15	Mid-way between Jianjing (G.B.21) and Quyuan (S.I.13) on the superior angle of the scapula	Deafness, febrile diseases	
Tianyou S.J.16	About 1 cun below the mastoid process	Neck rigidity	
Yifeng S.J.17	Posterior to the ear lobule in the depression between the mandible and mastoid process	Deafness, tinnitus, facial paralysis	
Qimai S.J.18	In the centre of the mastoid process and lateral to the root of the auricle	Deafness, tinnitus	Disorders of the head, ear, eye, and face
Luxi S.J.19	Mid-way between Qimai (S.J.18) and Jiaosun (S.J.20)	Hypochondriac pain, deafness, tinnitus	
Jiaosun S.J.20	Directly above the ear apex within the temporal hairline	Headache, neck rigidity	
Ermen S.J.21	In the depression anterior to the supratragic notch	Deafness, tinnitus	
Ear-Heliao S.J.22	1 cun superior and anterior to Ermen (S.J.21)	Headache, heaviness sensation of the head, tinnitus	
Sizhukong S.J.23	On the lateral end of the eyebrow	One-sided headache, redness and pain of the eye	

Section 4 SUMMARY OF THE LOCATIONS OF SOME POINTS FROM THE THREE YANG MERIDIANS OF THE HAND

I. Finger tips: Locations of points are at the posterior corner of the nail (Fig.II-83).

Shangyang (L.I.1): On the radial side of the index finger, posterior to the corner of the nail.
Guanchong (S.J.1): On the ulnar side of the ring finger, posterior to the corner of the nail.
Shaoze (S.I.1) On the ulnar side of the little finger, posterior to the corner of the nail.

II. Metacarpophalangeal joints: Locations of points are either distal or proximal to the joints (Fig. II-84).

Large Intestine Meridian: Erjian (L.I.2) and Sanjian (L.I.3) are at the radial side of the 2nd metacarpophalangeal joint, the former being distal to it and the latter being proximal.

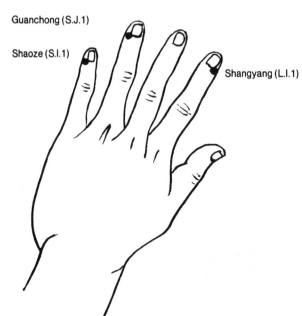

Guanchong (S.J.1)

Shaoze (S.I.1)

Shangyang (L.I.1)

Fig. II-83

Sanjiao Meridian: Yemen (S.J.2) and Hand-Zhongzhu (S.J.3) are between the 4th and 5th metacarpal bones, but the former being distal to the metacarpophalangeal joints and the later, proximal.

Small Intestine Meridian: Qiangu (S.I.2) and Houxi (S.I.3) are on the ulnar side of the 5th metacarpophalangeal joint, the former being distal to it and the latter being proximal.

III. Wrist Joint: Locations of points are in the depression between the tendons and bones (Fig. II-85, 86, 87).

Yangxi (L.I.5): Between the trapezium and the radius, and between the tendons of m. extensor pollicis longus and brevis.

Yangchi (S.I.4): Between the lunate bone and the ulna, and between the tendons of m. extensor digiti minimi and tendons of m. extensor digitorum communis.

Yanggu (S.I.5): Between the styloid process of the ulna and the triquetrous bone.

IV. On the Forearm: Locations of points are along, between or on the both sides of the bones (Fig. II-88, 89, 90).

Small Intestine Meridian: Zhizheng (S.I.7), on the medial aspect of the ulna.

Sanjiao Meridian: Waiguan (S.J.5), Zhigou (S.J.6), Huizong (S.J.7), Sanyangluo

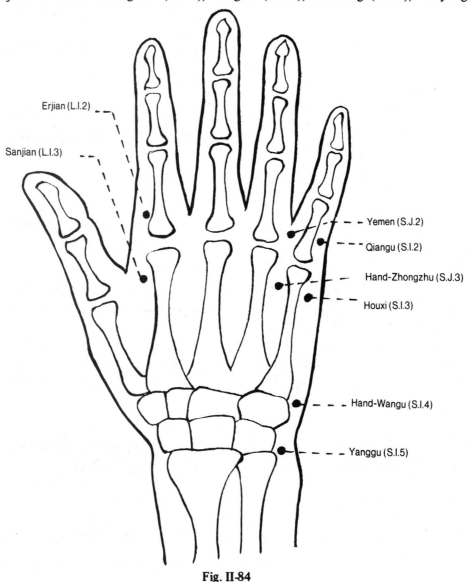

Fig. II-84

(S.J.8) and Sidu (S.J.9) are all between the radius and the ulna, Huizong (S.J.7) being on the radial side of the ulna.

Large Intestine Meridian: Pianli (L.I.6), Wenliu (L.I.7) and Xialian (L.I.8) are on the lateral side of the radius, Shanglian (L.I.9), Shousanli (L.I.10) and Quchi (L.I.11) are on the medial side of the radius.

V. The Elbow Joint Area: Locations of points are with reference to the end of the transverse cubital crease and the olecranon (Fig. II-90, 91, 92, 93).

Quchi (L.I.11) is on the lateral end of the transverse cubital crease when the elbow is flexed.

Xiaohai (S.I. 8) is between the olecranon and the medial epicondyle of the humerus.

Tianjing (S.J.10) is 1 cun superior to the olecranon.

VI. The Upper Arm: Locations of points are from the anterior or the posterior aspect of m. deltoideus and the humerus (Fig. II-94).

Binao (L.I.14) is on the junction of the anterior and inferior border of m. deltoideus and the humerus.

Naohui (S.J.13) is on the junction of the posterior and inferior border of m. deltoideus and humerus.

VII. The Shoulder Joint: Locations of points are on either the anterior or posterior aspect to the clavicle and the acromion (Fig II-95).

Jianyu (L.I.15) is in the depression directly below the anteroinferior border of the clavicle and acromion. Jianliao (S.J.14) is in the depression posteroinferior to the acromion and the clavicle.

VIII. On the Scapular Region: Location of points are above or below the middle of the scapular spine (Fig. II-96).

Bingfeng (S.I.12): 1 cun above the upper border,

Tianzong (S.I.11): 1 cun below the lower border,

Naoshu (S.I.10): 1 cun within the lower border of the lateral extremity of the scapular spine, and

Quyuan (S.I.13): 1 cun lateral to the upper border of the medial extremity of the

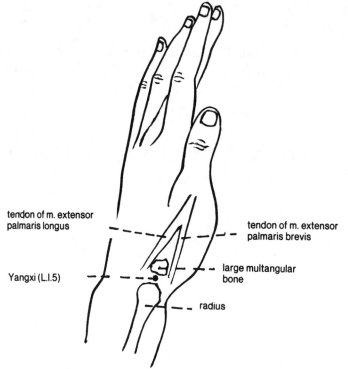

tendon of m. extensor
palmaris longus

tendon of m. extensor
palmaris brevis

large multangular
bone

Yangxi (L.I.5)

radius

Fig. II-85

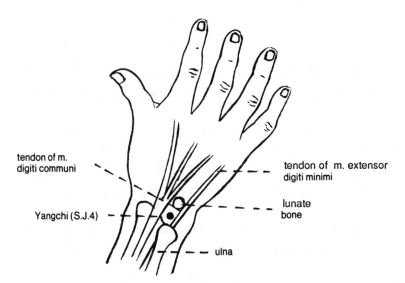

tendon of m.
digiti communi

tendon of m. extensor
digiti minimi

lunate
bone

Yangchi (S.J.4)

ulna

Fig. II-86

scapular spine.

IX. On the Neck: Locations of points are around the prominence, the angle and the muscle. Here the prominence refers to the Adam's apple, the angle is the mandibular angle and the muscle is m. sternocleidomastoideus (Fig. II-97).

On the line level with the Adam's apple:
Neck-Futu (L.I.18) is on the m. sternocleidomastoideus,
Tianchuang (S.I.16) is at the posterior border of the m. sternocleidomastoideus.
On the line level with the mandibular angle:
Tianrong (S.I.17) is at the anterior border of the m. sternocleidomastoideus,
Tianyou (S.J.16) is at the posterior border of the m. sternocleidomastoideus.

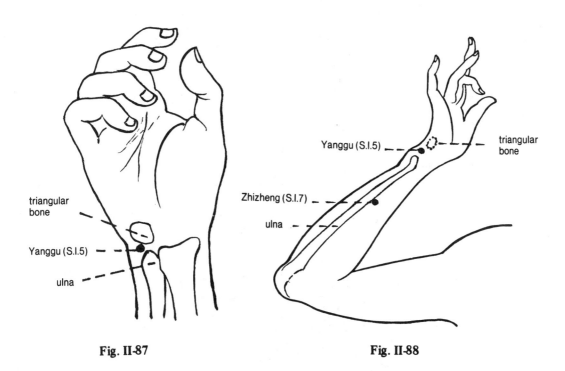

Fig. II-87   Fig. II-88

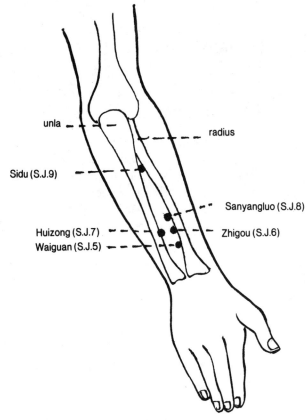

Fig. II-89

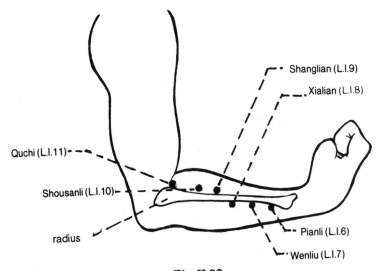

Fig. II-90

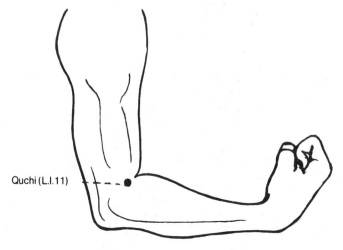

Quchi (L.I.11)

Fig. II-91

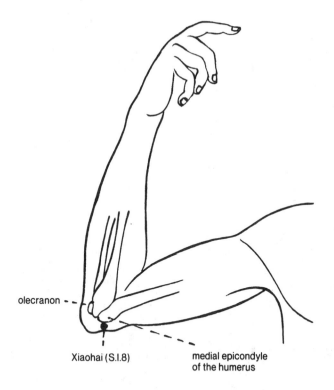

olecranon

Xiaohai (S.I.8)

medial epicondyle
of the humerus

Fig. II-92

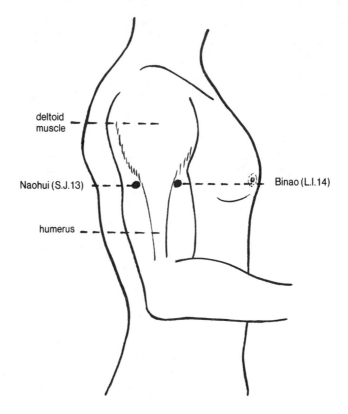

Fig. II-94

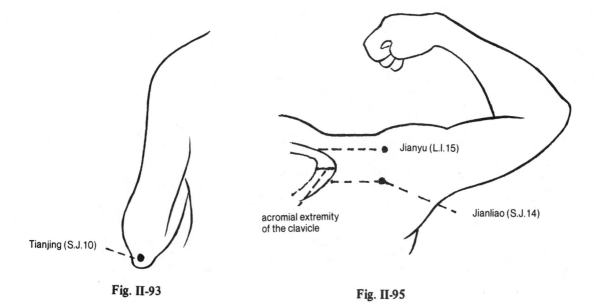

Fig. II-93

Fig. II-95

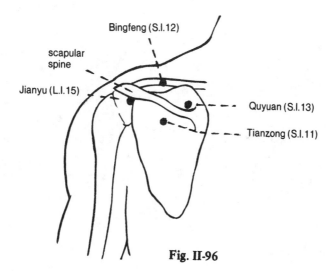

Fig. II-96

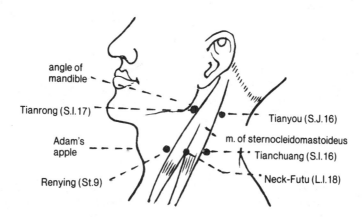

Fig. II-97

Chapter III

THE THREE YANG MERIDIANS OF THE FOOT

Section 1 THE STOMACH MERIDIAN OF FOOT-YANGMING

I. The Meridian

General Indications:

The points from this meridian are mainly indicated in diseases and disorders of the stomach and intestines, as well as diseases and problems of the head, facial area, eye, nose, mouth, teeth and the anterior aspect of the lower extremities.

Course of the Meridian:

(1) The Stomach Meridian of Foot-Yangming starts from the lateral side of the ala nasi (Yingxiang, L.I.20). It ascends to the bridge of the nose, (2) where it meets the Urinary Bladder Meridian of Foot-Taiyang (Jingming U.B.1). (3) Turning downwards along the lateral side of the nose (Chengqi, St. 1), (4) it enters the upper gums. (5) Re-emerging, it curves around the lips (6) and descends to meet the Ren Meridian at the mentolabial groove (Chengjian, Ren 24). (7) It then runs posterolaterally across the lower cheek at Daying (St.5), (8) winding along the angle of the mandible (Jiache, St.6). (9) It ascends in front of the ear and crosses Shangguan (G.B.3) of the Gall Bladder Meridian of Foot-Shaoyang (10) and follows the anterior hairline, (11) to the forehead, Touwei (St.8).

The Facial Branch:

(12) The branch emerging in front of Daying (St.5) runs downwards to Renying (St.9), goes along the throat and (13) enters the supraclavicular fossa. (14) Descending, it passes through the diaphragm, (15) enters the stomach, its pertaining organ, and connects with the spleen.

The straight portion of the meridian: Arising from the supraclavicular fossa (16) it runs downward, passes through the nipple, (17) descends by the umbilicus and enters Qichong (St.30) on the lateral side of the lower abdomen.

The Branch from the lower orifice of the stomach:

(18) It comes out of the lower orifice of the stomach and descends inside the abdomen to join the previous portion of the meridian at Qichong (St.30). (19) It runs downward passing Biguan (St.31) (20), and further through Femer-Futu (St.32), (21) until it reaches the knee. (22) It continues downwards along the anterior border of the lateral aspect of the tibia, (23) passes through the dorsum of the foot, (24) and reaches the lateral side of the tip of the 2nd toe (Lidui, St.45).

The Tibial Branch:

(25) It emerges from Zusanli (St.36), 3 cun below the knee, where it goes further downwards along the anterior aspect of the leg, passes through the dorsum of the foot (26) and enters the lateral side of the middle toe.

The Branch from the dorsum of the foot:

(27) It arises from Chongyang (43) and terminates at the medial side of the tip of the big toe (Yinbai, Sp 1), where it links with the Spleen Meridian of Foot-Taiyin, (Fig.II-98)

Analytical Display of the Course of the Meridian

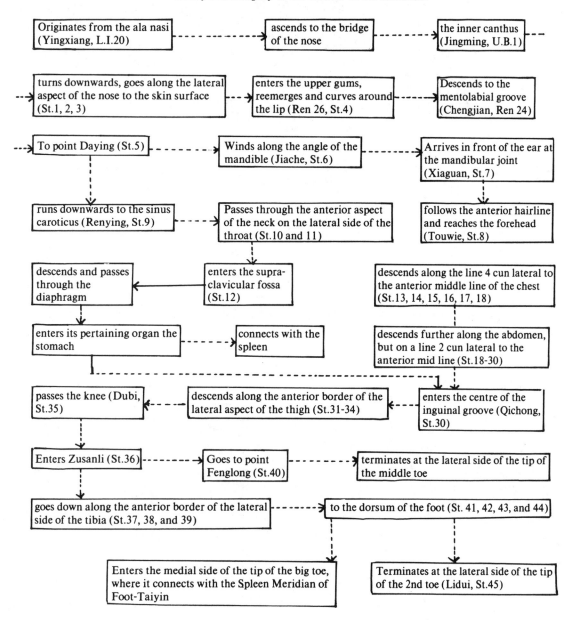

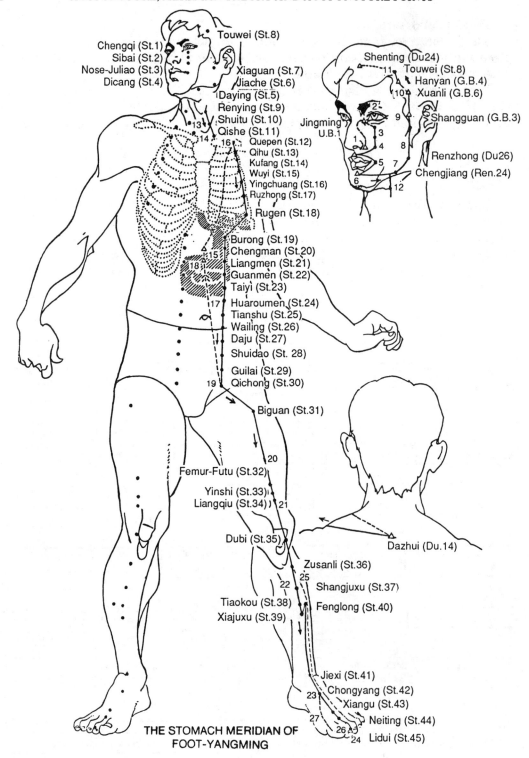

Chengqi (St.1)
Sibai (St.2)
Nose-Juliao (St.3)
Dicang (St.4)
Touwei (St.8)
Xiaguan (St.7)
Jiache (St.6)
Daying (St.5)
Renying (St.9)
Shuitu (St.10)
Qishe (St.11)
Quepen (St.12)
Qihu (St.13)
Kufang (St.14)
Wuyi (St.15)
Yingchuang (St.16)
Ruzhong (St.17)
Rugen (St.18)
Burong (St.19)
Chengman (St.20)
Liangmen (St.21)
Guanmen (St.22)
Taiyi (St.23)
Huaroumen (St.24)
Tianshu (St.25)
Wailing (St.26)
Daju (St.27)
Shuidao (St. 28)
Guilai (St.29)
Qichong (St.30)
Biguan (St.31)
Femur-Futu (St.32)
Yinshi (St.33)
Liangqiu (St.34)
Dubi (St.35)
Zusanli (St.36)
Shangjuxu (St.37)
Tiaokou (St.38)
Xiajuxu (St.39)
Fenglong (St.40)
Jiexi (St.41)
Chongyang (St.42)
Xiangu (St.43)
Neiting (St.44)
Lidui (St.45)

Shenting (Du24)
Touwei (St.8)
Hanyan (G.B.4)
Xuanli (G.B.6)
Shangguan (G.B.3)
Jingming
U.B.1
Renzhong (Du26)
Chengjiang (Ren.24)

Dazhui (Du.14)

THE STOMACH MERIDIAN OF FOOT-YANGMING

Fig. II-98

Related Zangfu Organs:

The Stomach Meridian of Foot-Yangming pertains to the stomach, connects with the spleen and it is related to both the large and small intestines.

Coalescent Points of This Meridian:

Yingxiang (L.I.20), Jingming (U.B.1), Shangguan (G.B.3), Xuanli (G.B.6), Hanyan (G.B.4), Renzhong (Du 26), Mouth-Yingjiao (Du 28), Shenting (Du 24), Dazhui (Du 14), Chengjian (Ren 24) and Zhongwan (Ren 12).

II. The Points

There are 45 points on this meridian located bilaterally. Fifteen of them are on the anterior border of the lateral aspect of the lower limb, while the remaining 30 are on the abdomen, chest, face and head. The first point is Chengqi (St.1) and the last point is Lidui (St.45)

Point Names	Pinyin	Codes	Point Names	Pinyin	Codes
承泣	Chengqi	St.1	滑肉门	Huaroumen	St.24
四白	Sibai	St.2	天枢	Tianshu	St.25
巨髎	Nose-Juliao	St.3	外陵	Wailing	St.26
地仓	Dicang	St.4	大巨	Daju	St.27
大迎	Daying	St.5	水道	Shuidao	St.28
颊车	Jiache	St.6	归来	Guilai	St.29
下关	Xiaguan	St.7	气冲	Qichong	St.30
头维	Touwei	St.8	髀关	Biguan	St.31
人迎	Renying	St.9	伏兔	Femur-Futu	St.32
水突	Shuitu	St.10	阴市	Yinshi	St.33
气舍	Qishe	St.11	梁丘	Liangqiu	St.34
缺盆	Quepen	St.12	犊鼻	Dubi	St.35
气户	Qihu	St.13	足三里	Zusanli	St.36
库房	Kufang	St.14	上巨虚	Shangjuxu	St.37
屋翳	Wuyi	St.15	条口	Tiaokou	St.38
膺窗	Yingchuang	St.16	下巨虚	Xiajuxu	St.39
乳中	Ruzhong	St.17	丰隆	Fenglong	St.40
乳根	Rugen	St.18	解溪	Jiexi	St.41
不容	Burong	St.19	冲阳	Chongyang	St.42
承满	Chengman	St.20	陷谷	Xiangu	St.43
梁门	Liangmen	St.21	内庭	Neiting	St.44
关门	Guanmen	St.22	厉兑	Lidui	St.45
太乙	Taiyi	St.23			

CHENGQI (St.1) 承泣 (HOLD TEARS)

"Cheng" (承) means to hold. "Qi" (泣) means tear. When crying, tears run down to the point area. It is indicated in lacrimation due to exposure to wind, and restrains tears, hence the name Chengqi (Hold Tears).

Location:

Have the patient to look straight ahead. The point is located between the eyeball and the midpoint of the infraorbital ridge, 0.7 cun directly below the pupil. (Fig.II-99)

Indications:

Myopia, redness with swelling and pain of the eyes, twitching of the facial muscles, night blindness, optic atrophy and lacrimation when exposed to wind.

Clinical Application:

This point is a coalescent point of the Stomach Meridian of Foot-Yangming, the Yangqiao Meridian and Ren Meridian. It has the effect to dispel wind, smooth the circulation of qi and blood of the meridians and collaterals, reduce fire and brighten the

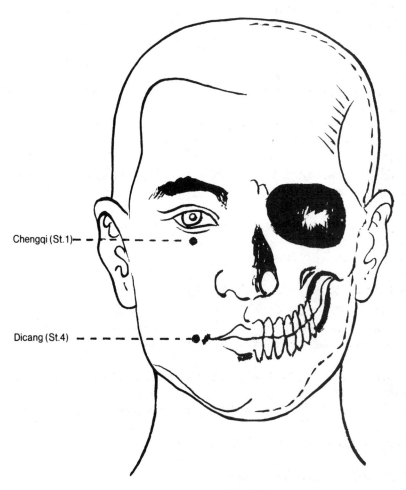

Chengqi (St.1)

Dicang (St.4)

Fig. II-99

eye.

Combinations:

With Fengchi (G.B.20), Taiyang (Extra), Quchi (L.I.11) and Taichong (Liv.3) for treating glaucoma,

With Fengchi (G.B.20), Taiyang (Extra), Jingming (U.B.1), Ganshu (U.B.18), Shenshu (U.B.23) and Hegu (L.I.4) for optic atrophy.

Method:

Puncture obliquely about 1 cun towards the inner canthus, Jingming (U.B.1); or puncture perpendicularly 1-1.5 cun deep along the infraorbital ridge (the inferior aspect of the eye ball).

Needling Sensations:

Soreness and distention at the local area.

SIBAI (St.2) 四 白 (ALL BRIGHTENING)

"Si" (四) here refers to all directions. "Bai" (白) means brightening. This point is under the eye, the organ of vision, and is mainly indicated in eye disorders, such as blurring of vision, redness of the eye and itching with slight corneal opacity. It can also brighten the eye, hence the name Sibai (All Brightening).

Location:

One cun directly below the pupil when looking directly ahead, in the depression at the infraorbital foramen (Fig.II-100)

Clinical Application:

The point has the effect to dispel wind, smooth the circulation of qi and blood in the collaterals, relax the tendons and muscles and stop pain.

Combinations:

With Xiaguan (St.7), Dicang (St.4), Jiache (St.6), Quanliao (S.I.18) and Hegu (L.I.4) for facial paralysis and twitching of the facial muscles.

Method:

Puncture either obliquely or perpendicularly about 0.3-0.5 cun deep.

Needling Sensations:

Soreness and distention all over the face.

NOSE-JULIAO (St.3) 巨 髎 (BIG CREVICE)

"Ju" (巨) means big. "Liao" (髎) refers to a bone crevice or the depression of a bony cleft. The point is in the depression below the zygomatic process, where there is a big crevice in the bone, hence the name Juliao (Big Crevice).

Location:

Directly below the pupil at the level of the lower border of the ala nasi (Fig.II-101).

Indications:

Deviation of the mouth and eyes, twitching of the eyelids, toothache, rhinitis.

Method:

Puncture perpendicularly about 0.3-0.5 cun deep.

DICANG (St.4) 地 仓 (EARTH GRANARY)

"Di" (地) means earth. "Cang" (仓) means a place for storing grain. The Earth provides man with various kinds of crops which are taken as food via mouth and stored in the stomach, as though in a granary. The point is close to the mouth, hence the name Dicang (Earth Granary).

Location:

0.4 cun lateral to the corner of the mouth (Fig.II-100).

Indications:

Deviation of the eyes and mouth, salivation, twitching of the eyelids and trigeminal neuralgia.

Clinical Application:

The point is a coalescent point of the Yangming Meridians of both foot and hand with the Yangqiao Meridian. It can dispel wind, smooth the circulation of qi and blood in the collaterals and stop pain.

Combinations:

With Jiache (St.6) and Hegu (L.I.4) for facial paralysis, salivation and trigeminal neuralgia,

With Houxi (S.J.3) for twitching of the mouth.

Method:

Puncture obliquely towards either the direction of Chengjiang (Ren 24) or the direction of Jiache (St.6) about 1-2 cun deep.

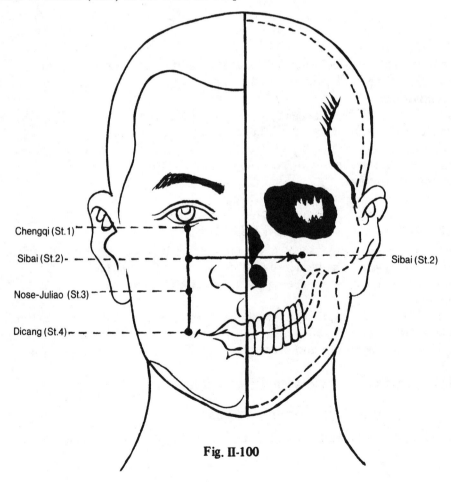

Chengqi (St.1)

Sibai (St.2)

Nose-Juliao (St.3)

Dicang (St.4)

Sibai (St.2)

Fig. II-100

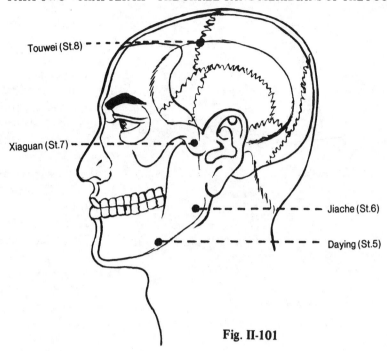

Fig. II-101

Puncture obliquely towards either the direction of Chengjiang (Ren 24) or the direction of Jiache (St.6) about 1-2 cun deep.
Needling Sensations:
Localized distention and heaviness.

DAYING (St.5) 大 迎 (GREAT MEETING)

"Da" (大) means big or great. "Ying" (迎) has two meanings, one referring to the mandible. The other refers to the meeting at this point of branches from Chengqi (St.1) and Touwei (St.8), before descending to the next point, Renying (St.9). Also the Yangming Meridians are considered as the Big Meridians containing most abundant qi and blood, hence the name Daying (Great Meeting).
Location:
1.3 cun anteroinferior to the mandibular angle (Fig.II-101).
Indications:
Deviation of the mouth, toothache and swelling of the cheek.
Method:
Avoid the artery when needling this point, and care should be taken to prevent bleeding, especially when giving warming needle treatment. Puncture perpendicularly about 0.3-0.5 cun deep.

JIACHE (St.6) 颊 车 (JAW VEHICLE)

"Jia" (颊) means the lateral aspect of the face or the mandible. The mandible was called the Jaw Vehicle Bone "Jiachegu" (颊车骨) in the ancient times. It holds the lower teeth and keeps them moving when chewing food. The point is located on the jaw, close

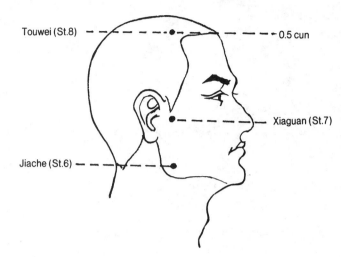

Fig. II-102

to the mandibular angle, hence the name Jiache (Jaw Vehicle).

Location:

One finger-breadth antero-superior to the lower mandibular angle where m. masseter attaches at the prominence of the muscle when the teeth are clenched. There is a depression in the muscle which can be detected by finger pressure (Fig. II-102).

Indications:

Toothache, deviation of the mouth, trismus, parotitis and trigeminal neuralgia.

Clinical Application:

The point has the effect to eliminate the heat, ease pain and decrease the secretion of saliva.

Combinations:

With Chengjiang (Ren 24) and Hegu (L.I.4) for trismus,

With Hegu (L.I.4) and Yifeng (S.J.17) for parotitis.

Method:

Puncture perpendicularly 0.3-0.5 cun deep, or obliquely 1-2 cun deep.

Needling Sensations:

Soreness, distention and heaviness in the local area.

XIAGUAN (St.7) 下 关 (LOWER HINGE)

"Xia" (下) means the lower part. "Guan" (关) here means the joint, or hinge. The point is located at the lower part of the junction between the superior maxillary bone and the mandible, which acts as a hinge and allows the mandible to move. Hence the name Xiaguan (Lower Hinge).

Location:

In the depression at the lower border of the zygomatic arch. This depression can be felt when the mouth is closed, a prominence appearing when the mouth is opened (Fig.II-102).

Indications:

Toothache, deviation of the mouth and the eyes, trigeminal neuralgia, arthritis of the mandibular joint, tinnitus and deafness.

Clinical Application:

This point is the coalescent point of the Yangming Meridian of Foot and the Shaoyang Meridian of Foot. It has the effect to dispel wind, smooth the circulation of qi and blood of the collaterals and ease pain and otorrhea.

Combinations:

With Ermen (S.J.21), Tinggong (S.I.19), Yifeng (S.J.17) and Waiguan (S.J.5) for deafness, tinnitus and pain in the ear,

With Jiache (St.6) and Hegu (L.I.4) for toothache,

With Dicang (St.4), Quanliao (S.I.18), Yingxiang (L.I.20), Jiache (St.6), and Hegu (L.I.4) for facial paralysis.

Method:

Puncture perpendicularly about 0.5-1 cun deep.

Needling Sensations:

Local distention and soreness, radiating to the whole mandibular area.

TOUWEI (St.8) 头 维   (HEAD CORNER)

"Tou" (头) means the head. "Wei" (维   ) means the corner of something. The point is at the corner of the forehead, 0.5 cun within the anterior hairline, hence the name Touwei (Head Corner).

Location:

Extend a vertical line from the mid-point of the eyebrow to the area 0.5 cun within the anterior hairline. Make a horizontal line from this position to intersect with another vertical line drawn along the anterior temple hairline in front of the ear. The point lies on this intersection (Fig.II-102).

Indications:

One-sided headache, ophthalmalgia, blurring of vision, lacrimation when exposed to wind and twitching of the eyelids.

Clinical Application:

This is the coalescent point of the Stomach Meridian of Foot-Yangming and the Gall Bladder Meridian of Foot-Shaoyang. It has the effect to dispel wind, eliminate fire, ease pain and brighten the eye.

Combinations:

With Shuaigu (G.B.8), Baihui (Du 20) and Taiyang (Extra) for treating one-sided headache.

Method:

Puncture horizontally about 0.5-1 cun deep.

Needling Sensations:

Distention and heaviness in the local area.

RENYING (St.9) 人迎   (MAN PULSE)

"Ying" (迎   ) here means throbbing or palpitation. The point is just lateral to the Adam's apple on the common carotid artery where the pulse can be palpated. "Ren" (人) means man, but here it refers to the "Man Position" or middle region in the theory of "three regions and nine modes for pulse taking". The book *Suwen* "On the Three Regions and Nine Modes for Pulse Taking" divides the body into three regions, each having its own pulse, which is further subdivided into three positions (modes). The pulse regions are known as the upper pulse, the middle pulse and the lower pulse, or the heaven, man and earth pulses. The three levels in each pulse region are also known as the upper, middle and lower levels or the heaven, man and earth modes, referring respectively to the floating, medium and sinking pulses. The point lies on the pulse of the man region (on the neck below the head), hence the name Renying (Man Pulse).

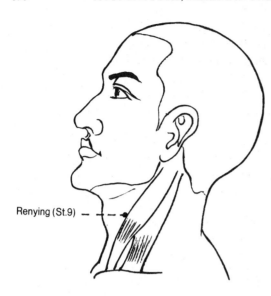

Renying (St.9)

Fig. II-103

Location:

It is posterior to the common carotid artery, on the anterior border of m. sternocleidomastoideus, at the level of the tip of the Adam's apple. Many doctors locate this point on the superior aspect of the junction of sinus caroticus (Fig.II-103).

Indications:

Sore throat, hoarseness, asthma, goiter, hypertension, lymphadenitis and difficulty in swallowing.

Clinical Application:

It is a coalescent point of the Stomach Meridian of Foot-Yangming and the Gall Bladder Meridian of Foot-Shaoyang. It has the effect to remove obstructions from the meridians and collaterals, regulate the circulation of qi and blood, dispel heat and relieve asthma.

Combinations:

With Quchi (L.I.11) and Zusanli (St.36) for hypertension. With Baihui (Du 20), Renzhong (Du 26), Neiguan (P.6), Taichong (Liv.3), Geshu (U.B.17), Pishu (U.B.20) and Ganshu (U.B.18) for hypotension.

Method:

Puncture perpendicularly about 0.3-0.5 cun deep with the index finger pressing on the sinus caroticus. Avoid touching the common carotid artery.

Needling Sensations:

Soreness and distention around the point area.

SHUITU (St.10) 水突、 (WATER PROMINENCE)

"Shui" (水) means water, but here refers to the fluid of the body. "Tu" (突) means a prominence or process. The point is inferolateral to the Adam's apple and there may appear a prominence when one swallows, forcing the local tissues to move up and down. Hence the name Shuitu (Water Prominence).

Location:

Near the thyroid gland, about 1 cun directly below Renying (St.9) on the anterior border of m. sternocleidomastoideus (Fig.II-104).

Indications:

Sore throat, cough, hiccup, regurgitation, asthma and scrofula.

Method:

Puncture perpendicularly about 0.3-0.5 cun deep.

QISHE (St.11) 气 舍 (QI RESIDENCE)

"Qi" (气) means air, but here it refers to Zong Qi (the qi stored in the thorax), which is formed by the combination of the respiratory qi (Qing Qi) and essence of water

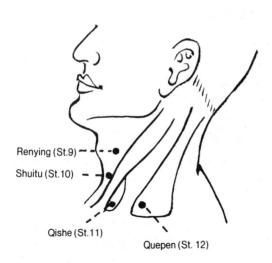

Renying (St.9)

Shuitu (St.10)

Qishe (St.11)

Quepen (St. 12)

Fig. II-104

and grain (Gu Qi). "She" (舍) means a residential quarter. This point is the residence of Zong Qi. It is indicated in cough, regurgitation, hiccup and disorders related to the Zongqi, hence the name Qishe (Qi Residence).

Location:

At the superior border of the clavicle, between the sternal head and clavicular head of m. sternocleidomastoideus.

Indications:

Sore throat, cough, hiccup, regurgitation, asthma and scrofula.

Method:

Puncture perpendicularly about 0.3-0.5 cun deep.

QUEPEN (St.12) 缺 盆 **(BROKEN BASIN)**

"Que" (缺) means broken. "Pen" (盆) means a depression. The point is in the centre of the supraclavicular fossa, which in ancient times was called Quepen, meaning a broken basin. Hence the name Quepen (Broken Basin).

Location:

In the centre of the supraclavicular fossa, 4 cun lateral to the Ren Meridian (Fig.II-104).

Indications:

Sore throat, cough, hiccup, regurgitation, asthma and scrofula.

Method:

Puncture perpendicularly about 0.3-0.5 cun deep.

*QIHU (St.13) 气 戶 **(QI PLACE)**

"Qi" (气) means the qi of the upper jiao. "Hu" (戶) means a living place. The point is above the upper part of the lung, at the level of the point Yunmen (Lu.2). It is the place where the qi of the upper jiao infuses at the body surface, hence the name Qihu (Qi Place).

Location:

On the lower border of the clavicle, 4 cun lateral to the anterior mid-line (Fig.II-105).

Indications:

---

*Note: The following 6 points on the chest area are mainly indicated in distention and pain of the chest and hypochondriac region, cough, asthma, upward disturbance of qi, and purulent sputum. Ruzhong (St.17) only serves as a landmark for locating the other points on the chest and the abdomen. Rugen (St.18), apart from the above-mentioned indications, is also indicated in mastitis and lactation deficiency. The points on the chest, Qihu (St.13), Kufang (St.14), Wuyi (St.15), Yingchuang (St.16), Ruzhong (St.17) and Rugen (St.18) are all located in the intercostal spaces, in the order from the first to the sixth ribs, on the mammillary line, 4 cun lateral to the anterior mid-line. All points on the chest area are unsuitable for deep insertion. Usually they are punctured obliquely about 0.5-0.8 cun deep or subcutaneously about 1-2 cun deep (Fig.II-105).

It is a commonly-selected point for treating the hiccup. (See above note.)

KUFANG (St.14) 庫房   (STORE HOUSE)

"Ku" (庫) means to store. "Fang" (房) means a house. The qi of the lung from Qihu (St.13) enters the deep part of the lung and is stored at this point, hence the name Kufang (Store House).

Location:
In the first intercostal space, 4 cun lateral to the anterior midline (Fig.II-105).
Indications:
See above note.

WUYI (St.15) 屋翳   (HOUSING FAN)

"Wu" (屋) means house. This point is located over the middle portion of the lung, where the qi arrives from the deeper part and is likened to a residence for qi. "Yi" (翳) originally means a fan made of chicken feather. The point is located on either side of the chest, which is likened to a fan. Hence the name Wuyi (Housing Fan).

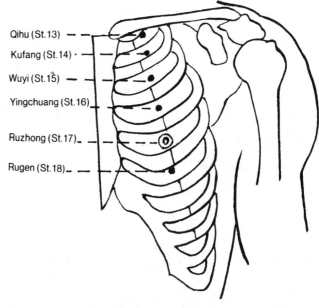

Location:
In the 2nd intercostal space, 4 cun lateral to the anterior midline (Fig.II-105).
Indications:
See above note.

YINGCHUANG (St.16) 膺窗 (CHEST WINDOW)

"Ying" (膺) is an ancient Chinese word for chest. "Chuang" (窗) means a window, through which qi or light may enter. Needling the point can relieve fullness or obstruction in the chest, disperse stagnation and regulate

Fig. II-105

qi circulation, as though opening the window of a house. Hence the name, Yingchuang (Chest Window).

Location:
In the 3rd intercostal space, 4 cun lateral to the anterior midline. (Fig.II-105).
Indications:
See above note.

*RUZHONG (St.17) 乳中 (BREAST CENTRE)

---

*Note: This point has no therapeutic application, being used only as a landmark.

"Ru" (乳) means breast. "Zhong" (中) means middle or centre. The point is in the middle of the nipple, hence the name Ruzhong (Breast Centre).

RUGEN (St.18)乳根   (BREAST ROOT)

"Ru" (乳) means breast. "Gen" (根) means the root or base of something. The point is in the lower part of the breast, hence the name Rugen (Breast Root).

Location:

In the 5th intercostal space directly below the nipple or 4 cun lateral to the anterior midline (Fig.II-105).

Indications:

See above note.

Locations:

The distance from the lower border of the sternocostal angle to the centre of the umbilicus is 8 cun, and the 6 points are located 1 cun apart, along a line 2 cun lateral to the anterior midline (Fig.II-106).

Indications:

Gastrointestinal disorders such as epigastric pain, diarrhea, borborygmus, anorexia, abdominal distention and vomiting.

Method:

The depth of the insertion of these 6 points is about 1 cun.

BURONG (St.19)不容   (CONTAINER'S LIMIT)

"Bu" (不) means no. "Rong" (容) means containing. The stomach is a container of water and food and has a certain limit. When the food and water in the stomach reach the level of this point, it will not accept any more. It is indicated in abdominal distention and vomiting due to excessive food intake. Hence the name, Burong (Container's Limit).

Location:

Six cun above the umbilicus, 2 cun lateral to the anterior midline (Fig.II-106).

Indications and Method:

See above note.

CHENGMAN (St.20)承满   (FULL RECEIVING)

"Cheng" (承) means to receive. "Man" (满) means fullness. When the food and water received by the stomach reach the level of this point, the quantity is sufficient. Hence the name, Chengman (Full Receiving). It is very effective in the treatment of indigestion with retention of food and abdominal distention.

Location:

Five cun above the umbilicus, 2 cun lateral to the anterior midline. (Fig.II-106)

Indications and Method:

See above note.

LIANGMEN (St.21)梁门   (GATE OF LIANG)

"Liang" (梁) originally means a beam, but here refers to the Fuliang syndrome,

Note: There are 6 points on the upper part of the abdomen, namely Burong (St.19), Chengman (St.20), Liangmen (St.21), Guanmen (St.22), Taiyi (St.23) and Huaroumen (St.24).

an ancient name of a disease due to the stagnation of qi and blood of the heart. Stagnation of qi and blood involving the heart is known as "Fuliang," 伏梁 ; involving the spleen is called "Piqi," 痞气 ; in the case of the lung, it is called "Xipeng," 息贲 ; of the kidney, "Bentun," 奔豚 ; and if the liver is involved, it is called "Feiqi," 肥气 . The chief manifestations of the "Fuliang" syndrome are: mass between the umbilicus and the lower part of the heart area accompanied by gastric pain, abdominal distention, nausea, vomiting, anorexia and symptoms of the stagnation of both qi and blood. Needling the point can alleviate the above problems, as though opening a door to dispel the disorder. Hence the name, Liangmen (Gate of Liang).

Location:
Four cun above the umbilicus and 2 cun lateral to Zhongwan (Ren 12) (Fig.II-107).
Indications:

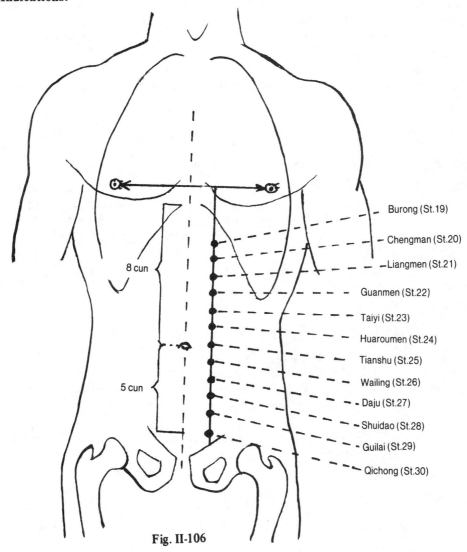

8 cun

5 cun

Burong (St.19)

Chengman (St.20)

Liangmen (St.21)

Guanmen (St.22)

Taiyi (St.23)

Huaroumen (St.24)

Tianshu (St.25)

Wailing (St.26)

Daju (St.27)

Shuidao (St.28)

Guilai (St.29)

Qichong (St.30)

Fig. II-106

Gastric pain, abdominal distention, anorexia, diarrhea and cholecystitis.
Clinical Application:
The point has the effect to pacify the stomach and remove stagnation, strengthen the functional activity of the spleen and regulate qi circulation.
Combinations:
With Zhongwan (Ren 12), Zusanli (St.36), Gongsun (Sp.4) and Neiguan (P.6) for epigastric pain, indigestion and loose stool.

GUANMEN (St.22) 关门 (CLOSED DOOR)

"Guan" (关) means to close. "Men" (门) means door. The point is located at the level with the junction of the stomach and the intestine, and is mainly indicated in poor appetite, as though the door of the stomach had been closed. Hence the name Guanmen (Closed Door).
Location:
Three cun above the umbilicus and 2 cun lateral to the anterior midline (Fig.II-106).
Indications and Method:
See above note.

TAIYI (St.23) 太乙 (GREAT YI)

"Tai" (太) means big, great or important. "Yi" (乙) means one. "Tai Yi" (太乙) refers to the great and endless universe on which the growth and development of all things of this world depend. The spleen and stomach are considered to manufacture the acquired qi, subsequently supplying the congenital qi of the body. The point has the effect to promote the function of both the spleen and stomach, the sources of the body energy. Hence the name Taiyi (Great Yi).
Location:
Two cun above the umbilicus and 2 cun lateral to the anterior midline. (Fig.II-106)
Indications and Method:
See above note.

HUAROUMEN (St.24) 滑肉门 (SMOOTHING FLESH GATE)

"Hua" (滑) means to smooth. "Rou" (肉) means flesh, here referring to the tongue. "Men" (门) means gate. Needling the point promotes the free movement of the tongue in case of rigidity and smoothes the tongue muscle. Hence the name Huaroumen (Smoothing Flesh Gate).
Location:
One cun above the umbilicus and 2 cun lateral to the anterior midline (Fig.II-106).
Indications and Method:
See above note.

Note: There are 6 points on the lower abdominal area, namely Tianshu (St.25), Wailing (St.26), Daju (St.27), Shuidao (St.28), Guilai (St.29) and Qichong (St.30). They are mainly indicated in diseases of the abdomen, the urinary and reproductive systems, such as pain and distention of the lower abdomen, dysuria, borborygmus, diarrhea and irregular menstruation. The distance between the umbilicus to the upper border of symphysis pubis is 5 cun. The points are located 1 cun from each other along a line 2 cun lateral to the anterior midline. The depth of the insertion at these points is about 1-1.5 cun.

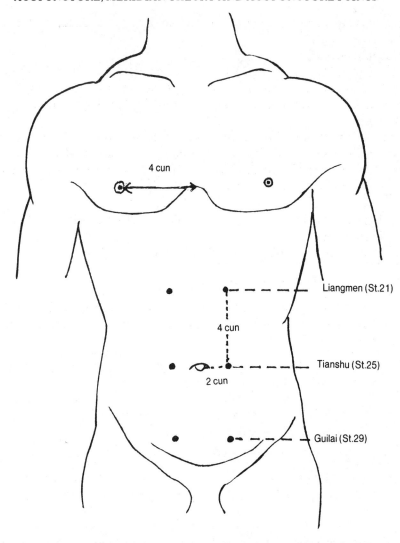

4 cun

4 cun

2 cun

Liangmen (St.21)

Tianshu (St.25)

Guilai (St.29)

Fig. II-107

TIANSHU (St.25) 天 枢 "MU"   (UPPER PIVOT)

"Tian" (天) means heaven, referring here to the upper part of the abdomen. "Shu" (枢) means pivot. The umbilicus divides the abdomen into two parts. The upper one being called "Tian" (heavens), and the lower one "Di" (earth). The point is at the level with the umbilicus, which is considered to be the pivot of the qi function of the stomach and intestines, hence the name Tianshu (Upper Pivot).

Location:

Two cun lateral to the centre of the umbilicus (Fig.II-107).

Indications:

Abdominal distention, abdominal pain, diarrhea, pain around the umbilicus, borborygmus, intestinal obstruction, irregular menstruation, leukorrhea, dysmenorrhea and edema.

Clinical Application:

This is the Front-Mu point of the large intestine and it is one of the most important points in treating digestive system diseases. It has the effect to promote spleen function, pacify the stomach, regulate qi circulation and remove the obstructions.

Combinations:

With Zusanli (St.36) and Zhongwan (Ren 12) for treating intestinal disorders,
With Sanyinjiao (Sp.6) and Guanyuan (Ren 4) for gynecopathy,
With Yinlingquan (Sp.9) and Sanyinjiao (Sp.6) for urinary system diseases, and
With Shangjuxu (St.37) for appendicitis.

Method:

Puncture perpendicularly 1-1.5 cun deep. Shallow insertion is also effective.

Needling Sensations:

Soreness, distention and slight pain of the local area.

WAILING (St.26) 外 陵 (OUTSIDE TOMB)

"Wai" (外) means outside. "Ling" (陵) means a tomb, but here referring to a prominence or process. The point is on the lateral aspect of m. rectus on the abdomen, hence the name Wailing (Outside Tomb).

Location:

One cun below the level of the umbilicus and 2 cun lateral to the anterior midline (Fig.II-106).

Indications and Method:

See above note.

DAJU (St.27) 大 巨 (GREAT AND EXTREME)

"Da" (大) means big or great. "Ju" (巨) means extreme. The point is on the highest and largest prominence of the abdomen, hence the name Daju (Great and Extreme).

Location:

Two cun below the level of the umbilicus and 2 cun lateral to the anterior midline (Fig.II-106).

Indications:

Seminal emission, prospermia, premature ejaculation and dysuria.

Method:

See above note.

SHUIDAO (St.28) 水 道 (WATER PASSAGE)

"Shui" (水) means water. "Dao" (道) means way or passage. The urinary bladder and the small intestine both lie beneath this point, the two organs being considered as water passages, in addition to which, the point is indicated in retention of urine and edema due to disturbance of the water metabolism. Hence the name Shuidao (Water Passage).

Location:

Three cun below the level of the umbilicus and 2 cun lateral to the anterior midline (Fig.II-106).

Indications and Method:

See above note.

*GUILAI (St.29) 归来 (RETURN BACK)

"Gui" (归) means return. "Lai" (来) means back. The point is mainly indicated in prolapse of the uterus, having the effect to invigorate qi and blood circulation. It can also restore normal menstruation and fertility in females, hence the name, Guilai (Return Back).

Location:

Four cun below the level of the umbilicus and 2 cun lateral to the anterior midline at the level of Zhongji (Ren 3) (Fig.II-107).

Indications:

Amenorrhea, irregular menstruation, lower abdominal pain, prolapse of the uterus, pain of the external genitalia and leukorrhea.

Clinical Application:

The point has the effect to dispel heat, ease pain, regulate menstruation and stop leukorrhea.

Combinations:

With Sanyinjiao (Sp.6) and Baihui (Du 20) for leukorrhea and prolapse of the uterus,

With Taichong (Liv.3) for dysmenorrhea and chronic pelvic inflammation.

Method:

Puncture perpendicularly about 1-1.5 cun deep.

Needling Sensations:

Soreness in the local area.

QICHONG (St.30) 气冲 (QI POURING)

"Qi" (气) refers to the vital energy flowing in the meridians at the groin area. "Chong" (冲) means pouring or upward going. The point is in the groin, which is from the abdomen. The point is indicated in upward disturbance of qi, especially in pregnancy (morning sickness). Hence the name Qichong (Qi Pouring).

Location:

Five cun below the level of the umbilicus, 2 cun lateral to the anterior midline (Fig.II-106).

Indications and Method:

See above note.

BIGUAN (St.31) 髀关 (FEMORAL JOINT)

"Bi" (髀) means femur or thigh. "Guan" (关) means pass or joint. The Stomach Meridian of Foot-Yangming arrives at the margin of the thigh from the anterior aspect of the hip joint. The point is close to this joint, hence the name Biguan (Femoral Joint).

Location:

On the line connecting the anterior superior iliac spine and the lateral border of the patella in the depression on the lateral side of m. sartorius when the thigh is flexed, at

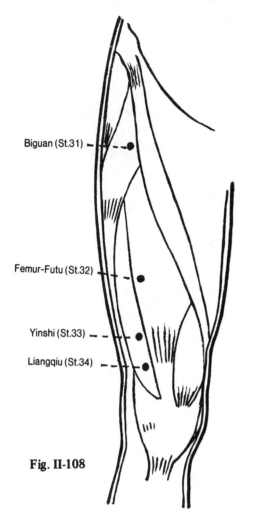

Fig. II-108

Biguan (St.31)

Femur-Futu (St.32)

Yinshi (St.33)

Liangqiu (St.34)

the level of the lower border of the synphysis pubis (Fig.II-108).

Indications:

Pain of the lower back, cold knee joints, muscular atrophy and abdominal pain.

Method:

Puncture perpendicularly about 1-1.2 cun deep.

FEMUR-FUTU (St.32)伏 兔 (HIDDEN RABBIT)

"Fu" (伏) means to lie down or try to hide oneself. "Tu" (兔) means a rabbit. When the leg is extended, a prominence appears in the musculature of the anterior thigh, which is likened here to a hidden rabbit. The point is located on this prominence, hence the name Futu (Hidden Rabbit).

Location:

Six cun above the laterosuperior border of the patella (Fig.II-108).

Indications:

Lower back pain and cold knee joints.

Method:

Puncture perpendicularly about 1-2 cun deep.

YINSHI (St.33)阴市   (YIN STAGNATION)

"Shi" (市) means to gather things together, referring to accumulation of cold, and other Yin pathogenic factors. The point is indicated in cold and stiff knee joints, and needling it can dispel the cold and Yin pathogenic factors. Hence the name Yinshi (Yin Stagnation).

Location:

Three cun above the laterosuperior border of the patella.

Indications:

Lower back pain, cold knee joints, and abdominal distention.

Method:

Puncture perpendicularly about 1-2.5 cun deep.

*LIANGQIU (St.34) 梁 丘 "XI"   (HILL RIDGE)

"Liang" (梁) means ridge, the point being on the upper part of the patella as though on a mountain ridge. "Qiu" (丘) means hill, referring here to a prominence, the point being located just above the knee. Hence the name Liangqiu (Hill Ridge).

Location:

Two cun above the laterosuperior border of the patella, on the line connecting the anterosuperior iliac spine and the laterosuperior corner of the patella. When the leg is extended, a depression appears, in which the point is located (Fig.II-109).

Indications:

Colicky gastric pain due to spasm of the stomach, pain and swelling of the knee (joint), mastitis and motor impairment of the lower extremities.

Clinical Application:

The point is the Xi-Cleft point of the Stomach Meridian of Foot-Yangming. It has the effect to remove obstructions and promote the function of the stomach. Needling this point with strong stimulation can immediately slow down peristalsis of the stomach and intestines.

Combinations:

With Zhongwan (Ren 12), Neiguan (P.6), Gongsun (Sp.4) and Zusanli (St.36) for gastric pain and abdominal pain,

With Dubi (St.35), Xuehai (Sp.10), Zusanli (St.36) and Yinlingquan (Sp.9) for pain and swelling of the knee, and

Fire needling method is applied if there is retention of water or fluid in the knee joint.

Method:

Puncture perpendicularly about 1-1.5 cun deep.

Needling Sensations:

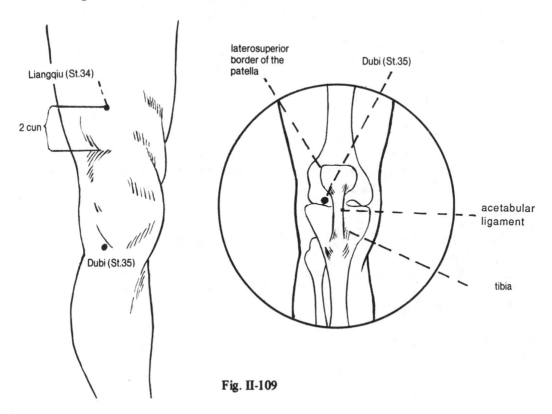

Fig. II-109

The needling reaction radiates towards the knee and the lower part of the leg.

DUBI (St.35)   犊鼻 (OX NOSE)

"Du" (犊) means a young ox or calf. "Bi" (鼻) means nose. The point is in the depression below the lateral aspect of the patella, which, with its bilateral depressions, is similar in appearance to the nose of an ox. Hence the name Dubi (Ox Nose).

Location:

Between the patella and the tibia, lateral to the patella ligament (Fig.II-109, 110).

Indications:

Pain of the knee, numbness of the lower extremities, motor impairment of the knee in flexion and extension, sprain of the knee.

Clinical Application:

The point has the effect to remove obstructions from the meridian, activate the collaterals, eliminate wind, dispel cold, alleviate swelling and ease pain.

Combinations:

With Liangqiu (St.34), Xuehai (Sp.10), Yanglingquan (G.B.34) and Zusanli (St.36) for pain and swelling of the knee.

Method:

Puncture obliquely 0.5-1 cun deep with the needle directed slightly towards the medial aspect of the knee. Penetration of the point through to Neixiyan (Extra) is often applied in the clinic.

Needling Sensations:

Soreness and distention in the deep part of the knee.

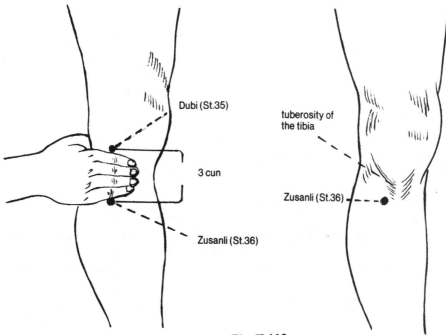

Fig. II-110

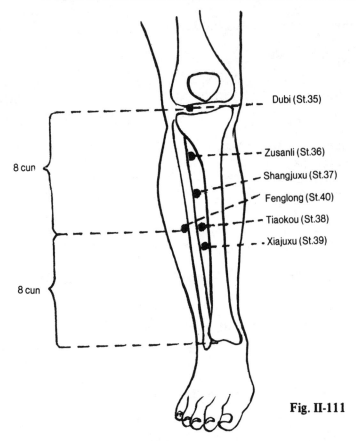

Fig. II-111

*ZUSANLI (St.36) 足 三 里 **"HE"** (THREE LI OF FOOT)

"Zu" (足) means foot. "San" (三) means three. "Li" (里) means reaching to. "Sanli" refers to the location of the point, 3 cun below the previous one, Dubi (St.35). It is the He-Sea point of the Stomach Meridian of Foot-Yangming, the qi and blood of the meridian converging here in abundance. Hence the name Zusanli (Three Li of Foot).

Location:
Three cun directly below Dubi (St.35), 4 finger-breadth downwards and 1 finger breadth from the anterior crest of the tibia. Alternatively, 1 finger breadth lateral to the lower border of the tibial tuberosity (Fig.II-110, 111).

Indications:
This is the chief point for treating the gastrointestinal disorders, such as gastric pain, abdominal distention, indigestion, nausea, vomiting, borborygmus, diarrhea, constipation, dysentery and intestinal obstruction. It can also be used to treat headache, hypertension, insomnia, dizziness, paralysis of the lower extremities, jaundice and lactation deficiency. In addition, it is the most important point for general qi tonification.

Clinical Application:
It is the He-Sea point of the Stomach Meridian of Foot-Yangming, and one of the Four General Tonification Points, having the effect to remove obstructions from the meridians, promote the collaterals, regulate the circulation of the qi and blood, strengthen the body resistance, dispel pathogenic factors and promote the functional activities

of both spleen and stomach. According to some clinical reports, needling the point can increase the contractive function of the stomach when it is in a relaxed condition, relax it in case of spasm or ease spasm of the pylorus. Needling Zusanli (St.36) also can regulate the gastric secretion, increase the free acidity and total acidity of the stomach and promote the secretion of pepsin and gastric lipase. Needling this point may also stimulate contraction of the gall bladder and significantly increase the opsonin of the body, in order to further increase the white blood cell count for strengthening the body immunity.

Combinations:

With Zhongwan (Ren 12), Pishu (U.B.20) and Weishu (U.B.21) for gastric pain;

With Tianshu (St.25), Qihai (Ren 6) and Guanyuan (Ren 4) for abdominal distention, diarrhea, dysentery and constipation, and with Quchi (L.I.11), Hegu (L.I.4) and Sanyinjiao (Sp.6) for hypertension.

Method:

Puncture perpendicularly about 1-2 cun deep.

Needling Sensations:

Soreness, numbness, distention and heaviness, radiating down to the foot.

SHANGJUXU (St.37) 上巨虚 "Õ"   (UPPER LARGE VOID)

"Shang" (上) means upper, referring to the upper portion of the leg. "Ju" (巨) is great or large, here referring to the large intestine. "Xu" (虚) means void. It is the lower He-Sea point of the Large Intestine Meridian and is indicated in stagnation or obstruction giving rise to upward disturbance of qi, which causes stiffness in the chest. Needling the point can regulate the circulation of normal qi, dispel pathogenic qi and resolve stagnant blood, thus alleviating the stiffness and clearing (voiding) the chest. Hence the name Shangjuxu (Upper Large Void).

Location:

Three cun directly below Zusanli (St.36) (Fig.II-111).

Indications:

Borborygmus, diarrhea, abdominal pain, dysentery, constipation and other intestinal disorders.

Clinical Application:

It is the Lower He-Sea point of the Large Intestine Meridian of Hand-Yangming, and is mainly indicated in disorders of the zangfu organs, having the effect to dispel heat and damp and regulate the functional activities of the stomach and intestines.

Combinations:

With Hegu (L.I.4) and Tianshu (St.25) for treating borborygmus and abdominal pain;

With Zhigou (S.J.6) and Quchi (L.I.11) for constipation.

Method:

Puncture perpendicularly about 1-2 cun deep.

Needling Sensations:

Soreness, numbness and distention, radiating towards the dorsum of the foot.

TIAOKOU (St.38) 条口 (NARROW MOUTH)

"Tiao" (条) means a narrow place. "Kou" (口) means mouth. When locating the point, have the patient sit with the heels resting on the ground, but with the toes turned upwards. In this posture, a depression may appear in the muscle at the point area. The depression looks like a narrow mouth, the point being located in that depression, hence the name Tiaokou (Narrow Mouth).

Location:

Two cun below Shangjuxu (St.37), one finger breadth over the crest of the tibia (Fig.II-111).

Indications:

Pain and numbness of the knee and skin, spasm of the gastrocnemius muscles, and shoulder pain.

Method:

Puncture perpendicularly about 2 cun deep.

XIAJUXU (St.39) 下 巨 虚 "Õ"   (LOWER LARGE VOID)

"Xia" (下) means lower, opposite to "Shang" (upper), referring here to the lower portion of the leg. "Ju" (巨) means great or large. "Xu" (虚) means void, referring to the space between the tibia and fibula. The point is located in this space of the lower leg, and it is the lower He-Sea point of the Small Intestine Meridian of Hand-Taiyang, indicated in small intestine disorders, hence the name Xiajuxu (Lower Large Void).

Location:

Three cun below Shangjuxu (St.37), one finger breadth over the crest of the tibia (Fig.II-111).

Indications:

Abdominal pain, mastitis and pain of the lower back.

Method:

Puncture perpendicularly about 2 cun deep.

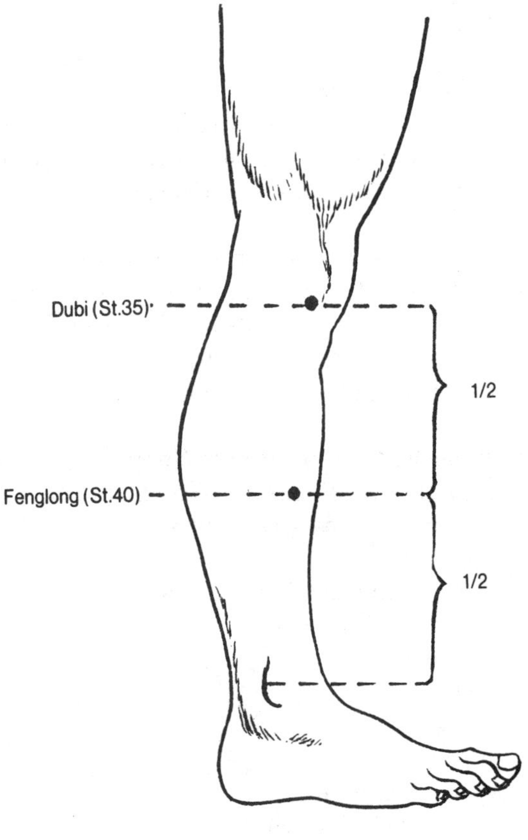

Fig. II-112

FENGLONG (St.40) 丰隆 "∧" (RICH AND PROSPEROUS)

"Feng" (丰) means great and rich. "Long" (隆) means prosperous. The Stomach Meridian of Foot-Yangming has the most abundant qi, blood, and food energy. Also there are abundant muscles around the point area. Hence the name Fenglong (Rich and Prosperous).

Location:

On the lateral lower leg, 8 cun above the external malleolus, or midway along a line connecting Dubi (St.35) and the tip of the external malleolus (Fig.II-112).

Indications:

Asthma, cough, excessive sputum, chest pain, dizziness, vertigo, paralysis of the lower extremities, pain and soreness of the knee and skin.

Clinical Application:

The point is the Luo-Connecting point of the Stomach Meridian of Foot-Yangming, from which a branch emerges to connect with the Spleen Meridian of Foot-Taiyin. Frequent application of moxa to this point can promote the appetite, relieve tiredness and prevent windstroke.

Combinations:

With Taichong (Liv.3) and Fengshi (G.B.31) for hepatitis,

With Shenshu (U.B.23), Huantiao (G.B.30), Fengshi (G.B.31), Yanglingquan (G.B.34), Weizhong (U.B.40), Xuanzhong (G.B.39) and Sanyinjiao (Sp.6) for paralysis of the lower limbs and sequela of infantile palsy,

With Quchi (L.I.11) and Hegu (L.I.4) for chronic lower fever.

Method:

Puncture perpendicularly about 1-2 cun deep.

Needling Sensations:

The needling reaction radiates down to the foot.

*JIEXI (St.41) 解溪 " Ѳ "   (RELIEVE STREAM)

"Jie" (解) means to open or to relieve. "Xi" (溪) means stream or depression. It is on the tarsals in a depression between two tendons. If shoes are laced too tightly, pressure will be felt in this area, which can be relieved by loosening the shoe laces.

Location:

In the middle of the transverse crease of the ankle joint, on the junction of the dorsum of the foot and leg, approximately at the level of the tip of the external malleolus, between the tendons of m. extensor digitorum longus and hallucis longus (Fig. II-113).

Indications:

Headache, dizziness, vertigo, abdominal distention, constipation and ankle pain.

Clinical Application:

This point is the Jing-River point of the Stomach Meridian of Foot-Yangming. It has the effect to regulate the circulation of the qi, remove obstruction and ease pain.

Combinations:

With Liequ (Lu.7) for headache,

With Shuaigu (G.B.8) for dizziness and vertigo, and

With Zusanli (St.36) for abdominal distention.

Method:

Puncture perpendicularly about 0.5-1 cun deep.

Needling Sensations:

The needling reaction radiates down to the toes.

*CHONGYANG (St.42) 冲阳 "O"   (THROBBING YANG)

"Chong" (冲) means throbbing or pouring. "Yang" (阳) is the opposite of Yin, referring to the dorsum of the foot compared with the sole. The pulsation of Fuyangmai

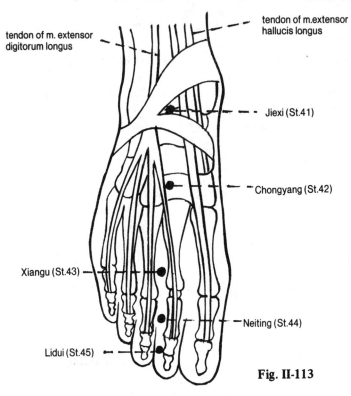

tendon of m. extensor
digitorum longus

tendon of m.extensor
hallucis longus

Jiexi (St.41)

Chongyang (St.42)

Xiangu (St.43)

Neiting (St.44)

Lidui (St.45)

Fig. II-113

(arteria dorsalis pedis) can be easily felt at the point area, hence the name Chongyang (Throbbing Yang).

Location:

1.3 cun down from Jiexi (St.40) where the pulse is palpable. (Fig.II-113)

Indications:

Deviation of the eye and mouth, swelling of the face, upper toothache and gastric pain.

Method:

Puncture perpendicularly about 0.3-0.5 cun deep, avoid the artery when needling this point.

XIANGU (St.43) 陷 谷 " 尺 "   (SINKING VALLEY)

"Xian" (陷) means sinking, referring to a depression. "Gu" (谷) means valley. The point is in a depression between the bones, likened here to a valley between mountains. It can be used to treat abdominal distention, borborygmus and deficiency or sinking of stomach qi, hence the name Xiangu (Sinking Valley).

Location:

In the depression proximal to the junction of the 2nd and 3rd metatarsal bones (Fig.II-113).

Indications:

Swelling of the face and body, distention of the chest, hypochondriac pain, abdominal distention, abdominal pain and borborygums.

Method:

Puncture perpendicularly about 0.5-1 cun deep.

*NEITING (St.44) 内 庭 " 〜 "   (INNER ROOM)

"Nei" (内) means the deep part or the inside. "Ting" (庭) means a residence. The point can be used to treat cold limbs, aversion to noise and the symptoms of reclusive patients who dread noise and tend to stay along inside a room with the door closed. Hence the name Neiting (Inner Room).

Location:

About 0.5 cun proximal to the margin of the web between the 2nd and 3rd toes (Fig.II-114).

Indications:

Tonsillitis, upper toothache, thirst, gastric pain, abdominal pain, dysmenorrhea, insomnia and dysentery.

Clinical Application:

It is the Ying-Spring Point of the Stomach Meridian of Foot-Yangming and has the effect to clear the throat, relax the diaphragm, stop pain and pacify the stomach.

Combinations:

With Hegu (L.I.4) for tonsillitis, laryngitis, pharyngitis, toothache due to wind heat, swelling and pain of the gums,

With Sanyinjiao (Sp.6) for dysmenorrhea,

With Zusanli (St.36) and Yinlingquan (Sp.9) for abdominal distention and pain, and

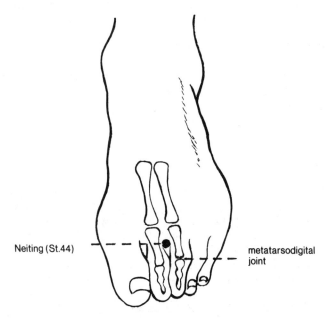

Fig. II-114

With Shenmen (H.7) for insomnia.

LIDUI (St.45) 厉 兑 "O"   (FUNDAMENTAL DOOR)

"Li" (厉) means strict, but here it refers to the stomach in particular. "Dui" (兑)
is one of the Eight Diagrams for Divination (Bagua,   八 卦), meaning the door. The
point is the Jing-Well point of the Stomach Meridian of Foot-Yangming, and one of the
important places through which the qi must pass, hence the name Lidui (Fundamental
Door).
Location:
On the lateral side of the 2nd toe, about 0.1 cun posterior to the corner of the nail.
Indications:
Toothache, foreign body sensation on the throat, abdominal distention and dream-
disturbed sleep.
Method:
Puncture obliquely about 0.1 cun deep or prick to cause bleeding.

III. Summary

The Stomach Meridian of Foot-Yangming pertains to the stomach, connects with the
spleen and is associated with the large and small intestines. It links with the nose, eye,
mouth, upper teeth and breast. There are 45 points on either side of the body (Fig. II-
115).

The Specific Points from the Stomach Meridian of Foot-Yangming

Zusanli	St.36	He Earth	Tianshu	St.25	Mu
Jiexi	St.41	O Fire	Shangjuxu	St.37	Ö
Chongyang	St.42	O	Xiajuxu	St.39	O
Xiangu	St.43	朵 Wood	Fenglong ↑	St.40	∧
Neiting	St.44	~ Water	Liangqiu	St.34	Xi
Lidui	St.45	⊖ Metal			

Point Indications of Stomach Meridian of Foot-Yangming
According to Locations

Point Names	Locations	Indications	Regional Indications
Chenqi St.1	Between the eyeball and the infraorbital ridge	Eye diseases	
Sibai St.2	In the depression of the infraorbital foramen	Facial paralysis and trigeminal neuralgia	Diseases of the head and facial region
Nose-Juliao St.3	Directly below Sibai (St.2) at the lower border of ala nasi	Facial paralysis and trigeminal neuralgia	

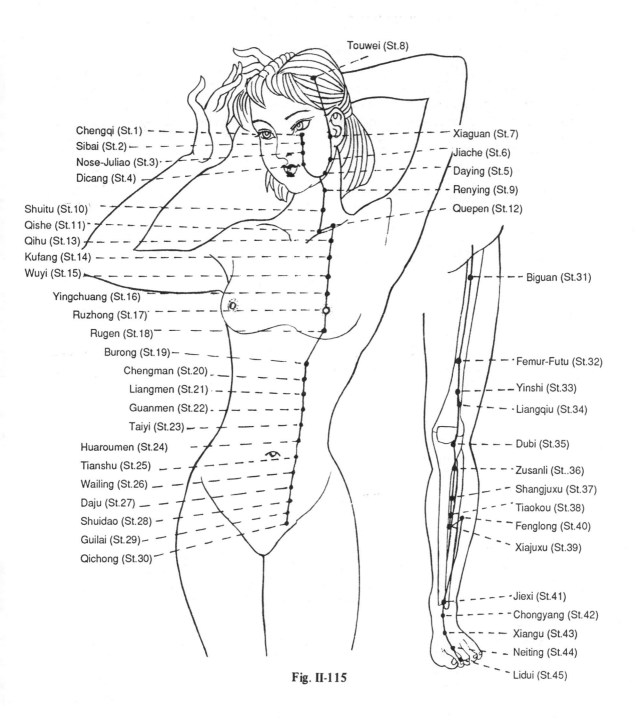

Touwei (St.8)

Chengqi (St.1)
Sibai (St.2)
Nose-Juliao (St.3)
Dicang (St.4)

Shuitu (St.10)
Qishe (St.11)
Qihu (St.13)
Kufang (St.14)
Wuyi (St.15)

Yingchuang (St.16)
Ruzhong (St.17)
Rugen (St.18)
Burong (St.19)
Chengman (St.20)
Liangmen (St.21)
Guanmen (St.22)
Taiyi (St.23)
Huaroumen (St.24)
Tianshu (St.25)
Wailing (St.26)
Daju (St.27)
Shuidao (St.28)
Guilai (St.29)
Qichong (St.30)

Xiaguan (St.7)
Jiache (St.6)
Daying (St.5)
Renying (St.9)
Quepen (St.12)

Biguan (St.31)

Femur-Futu (St.32)
Yinshi (St.33)
Liangqiu (St.34)

Dubi (St.35)

Zusanli (St..36)
Shangjuxu (St.37)
Tiaokou (St.38)
Fenglong (St.40)
Xiajuxu (St.39)

Jiexi (St.41)
Chongyang (St.42)
Xiangu (St.43)
Neiting (St.44)
Lidui (St.45)

Fig. II-115

Dichang St.4	0.4 cun lateral to the corner of the mouth	Facial paralysis and salivation	
Daying St.5	Anterior to the angle of the mandible, on the anterior border of m. masseter	Trigeminal neuralgia	
Jiache St.6	In the depression at the prominence of m. masseter	Toothache	
Xiaguan St.7	In the depression at the lower border of the zygomatic arch, anterior to the condyloid process of the mandible	Toothache, arthritis of the mandibular joint	
Touwei St.8	0.5 cun within the anterior hairline at the corner of the forehead	Headache, dizziness, vertigo	
Renying St.9	At the level of the tip of the Adam's apple, on the anterior border of m. sternocleidomastoideus	Hypertension, sore throat	
Shuitu St.10	Midway between Renying (St.9) and Qishe (St.11)	Asthma, sore throat	
Qishe St.11	At the superior border of the medial end of the clavicle	Asthma, thyroid enlargement	Diseases of throat, neck and chest regions, disorders of the lung
Quepen St.12	Directly above the nipple in the midpoint of the supraclavicular fossa	Asthma, cough, scrofula	
Qihu St.13	At the midpoint of the lower border of the clavicle	Cough, asthma, hiccup	
Kufang St. 14	In the 1st intercostal space, on the mammillary line	Cough, asthma, fullness of the chest and hypochondriac region	
Wuyi St.15	In the 2nd intercostal space on the mammillary line	Cough, asthma, intercostal neuralgia	
Yingchuang St.16	In the 3rd intercostal space on the mammillary line	Cough, asthma, fullness and pain in the chest, mastitis	
Ruzhong St.17	In the centre of the nipple, the 4th interostal space	It only serves as a landmark for locating points, no needling or moxibustion	
Rugen St.18	In the 5th intercostal space, directly below the nipple	Lactation deficiency, mastitis	
Burong St. 19	6 cun above the umbilicus, 2 cun lateral to Ren Meridian	Fullness of the abdomen, gastric pain	
Chengman St. 20	5 cun above the umbilicus, 2 cun lateral to the anterior midline	Abdominal distention, borborygmus, poor appetite	Diseases of the stomach and intestine
Liangmen St.21	4 cun above the umbilicus, 2 cun lateral to Ren Meridian	Gastric disorders	
Guanmen St.22	3 cun above the umbilicus, 2 cun lateral to Ren Meridian	Abdominal distention and pain	

Taiyi St.23	2 cun above the umbilicus, 2 cun lateral to Ren Meridian	Irritability, gastrointestinal disorder, poor appetite	
Huaroumen St.24	1 cun above the umbilicus, 2 cun lateral to Ren Meridian	Gastrointestinal disorders, hydroperitoneum	
Tianshu St.25	2 cun lateral to the umbilicus	Chronic and acute diarrhea, acute intestinal paralysis	
Wailing St.26	1 cun below the umbilicus, 2 cun lateral to Ren Meridian	Abdominal pain, diarrhea	
Daju St.27	2 cun below the umbilicus, 2 cun lateral to Ren Meridian	Lower abdominal distention, seminal emission	
Shuidao St.28	3 cun below the umbilicus, 2 cun lateral to Ren Meridian	Chronic pelvic inflammation, retention of urine	Diseases of the reproductive and urinary systems
Guilai St.29	4 cun below the umbilicus, 2 cun lateral to Ren Meridian	Chronic pelvic inflammation, dysmenorrhea, impotence	
Qichong St.30	5 cun below the umbilicus, 2 cun lateral to Ren Meridian	Abdominal distention, irregular menstruation, lower back pain	
Biguan St.31	Directly below the anterior superior iliac spine at the level of the perineum	Disorders of the anterior aspect of the thigh	
Femur-Futu St.32	6 cun above the laterosuperior border of the patella	Diseases in the anterior aspect of the lower limbs	
Yinshi St.33	3 cun above the laterosuperior border of the patella	Coldness of the lower back and thigh, numbness of the lower limbs	Diseases of the thigh and knee joints
Liangqui St.34	2 cun above the laterosuperior border of the patella	Gastric pain, mastitis	
Dubi St.35	In the depression inferolateral to the patella	Diseases of the knee joints and local soft tissues	
Zusanli St.36	3 cun below Dubi (St.35)	Gastrointestinal diseases, hypertension, insomnia, loss of consciousness	
Shangjuxu St.37	6 cun below Dubi (St.35) or 3 cun below Zusanli (St.36)	Appendicitis, chronic or acute diarrhea	Diseases of the stomach and intestines, diseases of the anterior aspect of the lower limbs
Tiaokou St.38	5 cun below Zusanli (St.36), 8 cun below Dubi (St.35) or 2 cun below Shangjuxu (St.37)	Spasm of the calf muscle	
Xiajuxu St.39	6 cun below Zusanli (St.36), 9 cun below Dubi (St.35)	Acute or chronic diarrhea	
Fenglong St.40	8 cun below Dubi (St.35), and 1 finger-breadth lateral to Tiaokou (St.38)	Cough, asthma, excessive sputum, epilepsy	
Jiexi St.41	Midpoint of the anterior transverse crease of the ankle	Cough, asthma, headache, disorders of the lower limbs, local diseases	Diseases of the ankle joint and of dorsum of the foot

Chongyang St.42	At the highest point of the dorsum of the foot	Diseases of the lower limbs and dorsum of the foot	Diseases of the ankle joint and of dorsum of the foot
Xiangu St.43	In the depression distal to the junction of the 2nd and 3rd metatarsal bones	Facial edema, pain and swelling of the dorsum of the foot	
Neiting St.44	0.5 cun proximal to the web of the margin between the 2nd and 3rd toes	Headache, sore throat, toothache	
Lidui St.45	On the lateral side of the 2nd toe, about 0.1 cun posterior to the corner of the nail	Insomnia, hysteria, sore throat	

Section 2 THE URINARY BLADDER MERIDIAN OF FOOT-TAIYANG

I. The Meridian

General Indications

The points of this meridian are mainly indicated in disorders of the eye, neck, back, lumbar and sacral areas, as well as the posterior aspect of the lower limbs. They are also indicated in mental illness and epilepsy. The Back-shu points from the medial line on the back can be used to treat diseases of their corresponding zangfu organs, or disorders of the tissues and organs which are closely related with the functional activities of those zangfu. Points from the lateral line of the meridian on the back can also be used to treat problems of the zangfu organs, but they are mostly used for local conditions. Deep insertion should be avoided on all the Back-shu points from this meridian.

Course of the Meridian:

(1) The Urinary Bladder Meridian of Foot-Taiyang starts from the inner canthus (Jingming, U.B.1). (2) Ascending to the forehead, (3) it joins the Du Meridian at the vertex (Baihui, Du 20).

(4) The temporal branch arises from Baihui (Du 20), running to the temple.

(5) The straight portion of the meridian from the vertex enters and communicates with the brain from the vertex, (6) then emerges and bifurcates into two, descending along the posterior aspect of the neck. (7) Running downwards alongside the medial aspect of the scapula and parallel to the vertebral column, (8) it reaches the lumbar region (9) where it enters the body cavity via the paravertebral muscle, (10) connects with the kidney (11) and joins its pertaining organ, the urinary bladder.

(12) The branch from the lumbar region descends there, and passes through the gluteal area (13) to the popliteal fossa.

(14) Starting from the posterior aspect of the neck, the posterior branch runs straight downwards along the medial border of the scapula. (15) Passing through the gluteal region (Huantiao, G.B.30), (16) it continues downwards along the lateral side

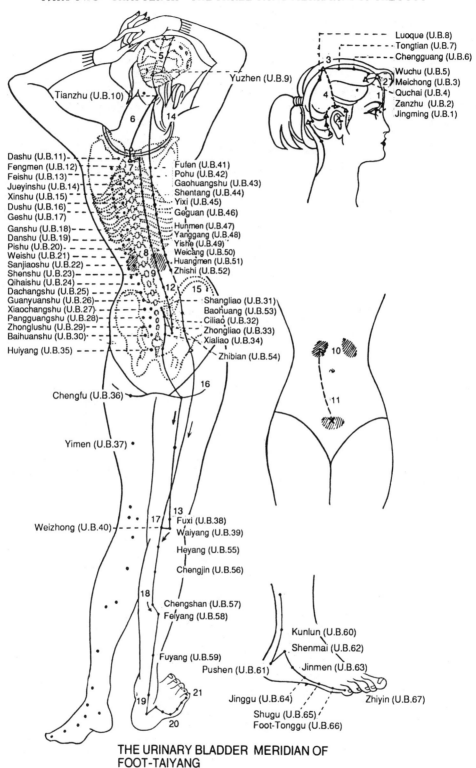

THE URINARY BLADDER MERIDIAN OF FOOT-TAIYANG

Fig. II-116

of the posterior aspect of the thigh, and (17) meets the previous branch descending from the lumbar region in the popliteal fossa.

(18) The straight branch from the popliteal fossa descends along the posterior aspect of the leg, (19) passes posteriorly to the external malleolus. (20) Running along the tuberosity of the 5th metatarsal bone, (21) it reaches the lateral side of the tip of the small toe (Zhiyin, U.B.67), where it links with the Kidney Meridian of Foot-Shaoyin (Fig. II-116).

An Analytical Display of the Course of the Meridian

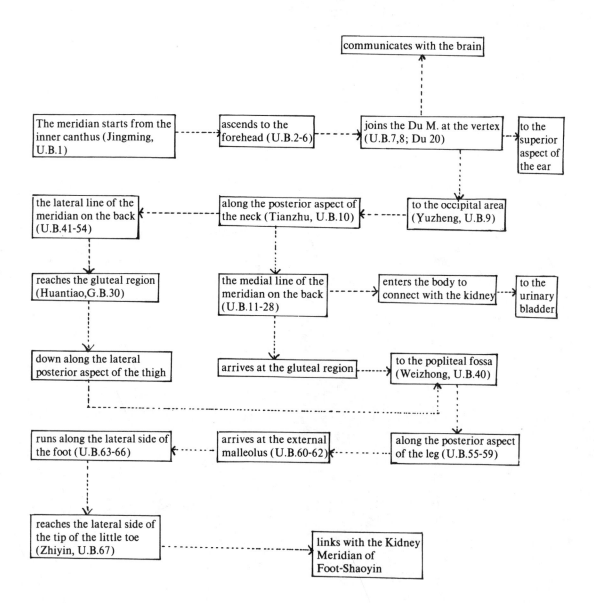

Related Zangfu Organs:

This meridian pertains to the urinary bladder and connects with the kidney.

Coalescent Points of This Meridian:

Head-Linqi (G.B.5), Shuaigu (G.B.8), Tianchong (G.B.9), Fubai (G.B.10), Head-Qiaoyin (G.B.11), Head-Wangu (G.B.12), Qubin (G.B.7), Huantiao (B.B.30), Shenting (Du 24), Naohui (Du 17), Fengfu (Du 16), Dazhui (Du 14), Taodao (Du 13)

II. The Points

There are 67 points on either side of the body along the course of the meridian. Among them, 49 are located on the head, neck, back and lumbar region, beside the Du Meridian. The remaining 18 are distributed along the posterior lateral aspect of the lower limbs and the lateral aspect of the foot. The first point is Jingming (U.B.1) and the last point is Zhiyin (U.B.67).

Name	Pinyin	Code	Name	Pinyin	Code
	Jingming	U.B.1		Huiyang	U.B.35
	Zanzhu	U.B.2		Chengfu	U.B.36
	Meichong	U.B.3		Yinmen	U.B.37
	Quchai	U.B.4		Fuxi	U.B.38
	Wuchu	U.B.5		Weiyang	U.B.39
	Chengguang	U.B.6		Weizhong	U.B.40
	Tongtian	U.B.7		Fufen	U.B.41
	Luoque	U.B.8		Pohu	U.B.42
	Yuzhen	U.B.9		Gaohuang	U.B.43
	Tianzhu	U.B.10		Shentang	U.B.44
	Dashu	U.B.11		Yixi	U.B.45
	Fengmen	U.B.12		Geguan	U.B.46
	Feishu	U.B.13		Hunmen	U.B.47
	Jueyinshu	U.B.14		Yanggang	U.B.48
	Xinshu	U.B.15		Yishe	U.B.49
	Dushu	U.B.16		Weicang	U.B.50
	Geshu	U.B.17		Huangmen	U.B.51
	Ganshu	U.B.18		Zhishi	U.B.52
	Danshu	U.B.19		Baohuang	U.B.53
	Pishu	U.B.20		Zhibian	U.B.54
	Weishu	U.B.21		Heyang	U.B.55
	Sanjiaoshu	U.B.22		Chengjin	U.B.56
	Shenshu	U.B.23		Chengshan	U.B.57
	Qihaishu	U.B.24		Feiyang	U.B.58
	Dachangshu	U.B.25		Fuyang	U.B.59
	Guanyuanshu	U.B.26		Kunlun	U.B.60
	Xiaochangshu	U.B.27		Pushen	U.B.61
	Pangguangshu	U.B.28		Shenmai	U.B.62
	Zhonglüshu	U.B.29		Jinmen	U.B.63
	Baihuanshu	U.B.30		Jinggu	U.B.64
	Shangliao	U.B.31		Shugu	U.B.65
	Ciliao	U.B.32		Foot-Tonggu	U.B.66
	Zhongliao	U.B.33		Zhiyin	U.B.67
	Xialiao	U.B.34			

JINGMING (U.B.1)睛 明 (EYE BRIGHTNESS)

"Jing" (睛   ) refers to the eye. "Ming" (明   ) means bright. This point has the effect to treat eye disorders and to brighten the eye, hence the name Jingming (Eye Brightness).

Location:

0.1 cun superior to the inner canthus, proximal to the medial border of the orbital bone (Fig.II-117,118).

Indications: Myopia, pain and redness of the eye, strabismus, night blindness, optic neuritis, optic atrophy, retinitis, early minor cataract, nervous visual hallucination, etc.

Clinical Application:

This is the coalescent point of the Taiyang meridians of both the foot and hand (the Urinary Bladder Meridian of Foot-Taiyang and the Small Intestine Meridian of Hand-Taiyang), the Stomach Meridian of Foot-Yangming, and the Yinqiao and Yangqiao Meridians. It has the effect to eliminate wind, clear heat and remove obstruction from the collaterals.

Combinations:

With Fengchi (G.B.20) and Chengqi (St.1) for eye disorders, and with Yintang (Extra) and Taiyang (Extra) for redness, swelling and pain of the eye. [Note: in this case, use the three-edged needle to bleed Taiyang (Extra).]

Method:

Puncture perpendicularly about 0.5-1 cun along the orbital wall. It is not advisable to manipulate by lifting, thrusting or rotating, but gentle scraping of the handle is safe. After withdrawal of the needle, press a piece of cotton ball on the needling spot to prevent subcutaneous bleeding. If there is bleeding after needling, apply a cold compress. The hematoma will disappear in approximately one week.

Needling Sensations:

Soreness and distention at the local area.

*ZANZHU 攒 竹 (U.B.2) (GATHERING EYEBROW)

"Zan" (攒) means to gather together, referring to the move-

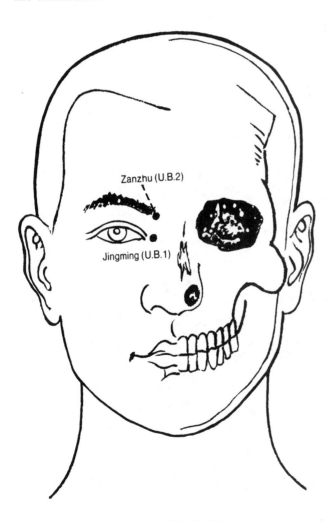

Zanzhu (U.B.2)

Jingming (U.B.1)

Fig. II-117

ment of the eyebrow in the act of frowning. "Zhu" (竹) means bamboo leaves and refers to the shape of the eyebrow; when one frowns, the eyebrow looks like a piece of bamboo leaf. The point is at the medial end of the eyebrow, hence the name Zanzhu (Gathering Eyebrow).

Location:

Superior to Jingming (U.B.1) on the medial end of the eyebrow, where there is a depression which can be detected by finger pressure (Fig. II-117, 118).

Indications:

Headache, blurring of vision, vertigo, pain of the supraorbital region, spasm of the facial muscles, corneal opacity and twitching of the eyelids.

Clinical Application:

This point has the effect to reduce heat and dispel wind, promote the collaterals and brighten the eye.

Combinations:

With Yintang (Extra) and Shangxing (Du 23) for treating the frontal sinusitis,

With Fengchi (G.B.20) for pain of the supraorbital region.

Method:

Puncture either obliquely or horizontally about 0.5-0.8 cun deep.

Needling Sensations:

Distention and soreness around the local area.

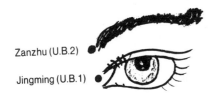

Zanzhu (U.B.2)

Jingming (U.B.1)

Fig. II-118

*MEICHONG (U.B.3) 眉 冲 (EYEBROW POURING)

"Mei" (眉) means eyebrow. "Chong" (冲) means pouring, facing towards or moving towards. In this case, it refers to the course of the meridian, from the previous point at the eyebrow. Hence the name Meichong (Eyebrow Pouring) (Fig.II-119).

Indications:

Headache, dizziness and epilepsy.

QUCHAI (U.B.4) 曲 差 (IRREGULAR TURNING)

"Qu" (曲) means turning or curving. "Chai" (差) means irregular or uneven. The meridian turns abruptly towards the lateral side of the head from Meichong (U.B.3), making a crooked line before arriving at the point. Hence the name Quchai (Irregular

---

Note: The following points are all needled horizontally about 0.3-0.5 cun along the scalp.

Meichong (U.B.3) is directly above Zanzhu (U.B.2) and 0.5 cun within the anterior hairline.

Quchai (U.B.4) is 0.5 cun within the anterior hairline and 1.5 cun lateral to the anterior posterior midline of the head.

Wuchu (U.B.5) is 1 cun within the anterior hairline and 1.5 cun lateral to the anterior posterior midline of the head.

Chengguang (U.B.6), Tongtian (U.B.7) and Luoque (U.B.8) are all on the same line, 1.5 cun lateral to the anterior posterior midline of the head, the distance between adjacent points being 1.5 cun. The tips of the thumb, index and middle fingers may be used to form an equilateral triangle with a distance of 1.5 cun between each of the tips. Place one of the three fingers on Baihui (Du 20), so that the finger to the front touches the point Tongtian (U.B.7) and the finger to the back touches Luoque (U.B.8). A similar method can be used to locate Wuchu (U.B.5) and Chengguang (U.B.6), by placing one of the three fingers on Xinhui (Du 22).

Turning) (Fig.II-119).
Indications:
Frontal headache, nasal obstruction, epistaxis and blurring of vision.

WUCHU (U.B.5) (五处) (THE FIFTH PLACE)

"Wu" (五) means five. "Chu" (处) means place. This is the 5th point on the meridian, hence the name Wuchu (The Fifth Place) (Fig. II-119).
Indications:
Headache, dizziness and vertigo, blurring of vision due to anemia, and epilepsy.

CHENGGUANG (U.B.6) 承光 (TAKING LIGHT)

"Cheng" (承) means to take or to receive. "Guang" (光) means bright. The point is located on the top of the head, where the light of the heaven first strikes the body. The point is also effective in the treatment of eye conditions, promoting the eyesight and thereby letting in the brightness of the outside. Hence the name Chengguang (Taking Light) (Fig. II-119).
Indications:
Headache, blurring of vision and nasal obstruction.

TONGTIAN (U.B.7) 通天 (CONNECTING HEAVEN)

"Tong" (通) means to connect or link with something. "Tian" (天) means heaven or nature. This point is located on the vertex, where it communicates with the qi of the heaven (environmental qi). It can also be used in the treatment of dysfunction of lung qi, such as nasal obstruction, poor sense of smell, etc. And the lung is considered figuratively to be the heaven or cover over the other zangfu organs. Hence the name Tongtian (Connecting Heaven) (Fig. II-119).

Indications:
Headache, blurring of vision and epilepsy.

LUOQUE (U.B.8) 络却 (VESSELS DECLINING)

"Luo" (络), meaning the collaterals, refers to the small vessels, or the congested vessels in the case of conjunctivitis. "Que" (却) means to eliminate or to decline. This point is mainly indicated in pain and redness of the eye, to eliminate the congestion from the vessels. Hence the name Luoque (Vessels Declining) (Fig. II-119).

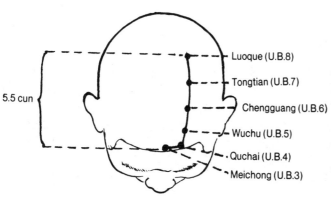

5.5 cun

Luoque (U.B.8)
Tongtian (U.B.7)
Chengguang (U.B.6)
Wuchu (U.B.5)
Quchai (U.B.4)
Meichong (U.B.3)

Fig. II-119

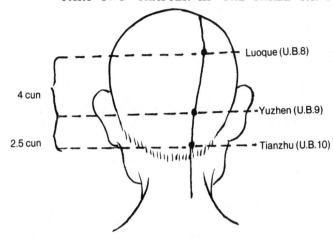

Fig. II-120

YUZHEN (U.B.9)玉枕 (JADE PILLOW)

"Yu" (玉) originally means jade, but here refers to the lung. "Zhen" (枕) means pillow, here referring to the occipital bone. The point is mainly used in the treatment of nasal obstruction, the nose being the orifice of the lung. Hence the name Yuzhen (Jade Pillow) (Fig. II-119).

Location:

1.3 cun lateral to Naohu (Du 17), on the lateral side of the superior border of the external occipital protuberance.

Indications:

Nasal obstruction, pain of the head and neck area, and blurring of vision.

Method:

Puncture horizontally about 0.3-0.5 cun deep.

*TIANZHU (U.B.10) 天柱 (CELESTIAL PILLAR)

"Tianzhu" (天柱) means the pillar supporting the heavens. "Tian" (天), heaven, here refers to head. "Zhu" (柱) means the pillar of a house. The point is lateral to the trapezius muscle, which looks like a pillar supporting the skull. Hence the name Tianzhu (Celestial Pillar) (Fig. II-120).

Location:

In the depression 1.3 cun lateral to Yamen (Du 15), within the posterior hairline on

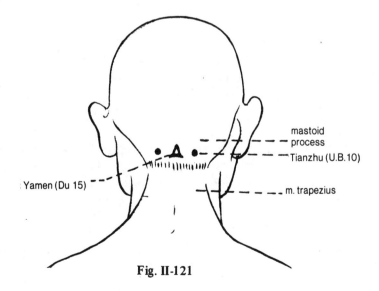

Fig. II-121

the lateral side of the m. trapezius.

Indications:

Headache, neck pain, pain in the shoulder and back, nasal obstruction, neck sprain and insomnia.

Clinical Application:

This point has the effect to eliminate wind, remove obstruction from the collaterals, clear the mind and stop pain. It can maintain good spirits and promote memory if massaged regularly.

Combinations:

With Houxi (S.I.3) and Xuanzhong (G.B.39) for neck sprain,

With Yanglao (S.I.5) for shoulder pain,

With Dazhui (Du14) and Shaoshang (Lu.11) for sore throat.

Method:

Puncture perpendicularly about 0.5-1 cun deep.

Needling Sensations:

Distention and pain at the local area.

*DASHU (U.B.11) 大杼 (BIG SHUTTER)

"Da" (大) is big or great. "Shu" (杼) means the shutter, referring to the 1st thoracic vertebra, which was called the shutter bone in ancient times. The point is at the lateral end of the shutter bone, hence the name Dashu (Big Shutter).

Location:

1.5 cun lateral to the lower border of the spinous process of the 1st thoracic vertebra (Fig. II-122).

Indications:

Headache, pain of the posterior aspect of the neck, back pain, cough and fever.

Clinical Application:

This point has the effect to eliminate pathogenic wind and ease pain. It is one of the Eight Influential points, being associated with bones.

Combinations:

With Dazhui (Du 14), Hegu (L.I.4) and Feishu (U.B.13) in the treatment of cough, asthma and common cold with fever.

*FENGMEN (U.B.12) 风门 (WIND GATE)

"Feng" (风) means wind. "Men" (门) means door or gate, a place for coming in and going out. The point is from the Urinary Bladder Meridian of Foot-Taiyang, which dominates superficial syndromes of the whole body. It is also a place through which pathogenic wind may invade the body. Hence the name Fengmen (Wind Gate).

Location:

1.5 cun lateral to the lower border of the spinous process of the 2nd thoracic vertebra (Fig.II-122).

Indications:

Note: The points from Dashu (U.B.11) to Weishu (U.B.21) are all needled obliquely with the needle being inserted towards the spinal column, about 0.5-0.8 cun. The needling sensations such as soreness and distention are felt around the local area of each point. They often radiate downwards or anteriorly.

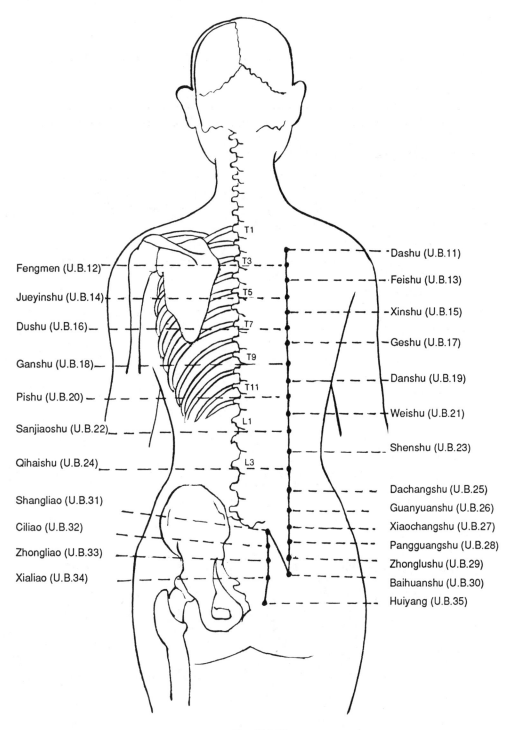

Fengmen (U.B.12)
Jueyinshu (U.B.14)
Dushu (U.B.16)
Ganshu (U.B.18)
Pishu (U.B.20)
Sanjiaoshu (U.B.22)
Qihaishu (U.B.24)
Shangliao (U.B.31)
Ciliao (U.B.32)
Zhongliao (U.B.33)
Xialiao (U.B.34)

Dashu (U.B.11)
Feishu (U.B.13)
Xinshu (U.B.15)
Geshu (U.B.17)
Danshu (U.B.19)
Weishu (U.B.21)
Shenshu (U.B.23)
Dachangshu (U.B.25)
Guanyuanshu (U.B.26)
Xiaochangshu (U.B.27)
Pangguangshu (U.B.28)
Zhonglushu (U.B.29)
Baihuanshu (U.B.30)
Huiyang (U.B.35)

Fig. II-122

Cough, asthma, common cold with fever, headache, pain of the neck and back.

Clinical Application:

This point has the effect to eliminate wind and promote the lung's function in dispersing qi.

Combinations:

With Dazhui (Du 14) and Hegu (L.I.4) in the treatment of common cold with fever, cough and asthma. Cupping is often applied after needling.

FEISHU (U.B.13)肺俞   (LUNG POINT)

"Fei" (肺   ) means lung. "Shu" (俞) means point. This point is close to the lung, and is the place through which the qi of the lung infuses into the body surface. It is mainly indicated in lung disorders due to the invasion of exogenous pathogenic factors. Hence the name Feishu (Lung Point).

Location:

1.5 cun lateral to the lower border of the spinous process of the 3rd thoracic vertebra (Fig.II-122).

Indications:

Cough, asthma, hemoptysis, afternoon fever, night sweating, pain and cold sensations in the back.

Clinical Application:

This point has the effect to dispel heat and promote the lung's function in dispersing qi and stop cough and asthma.

Combinations:

With Tiantu (Ren 22) and Shangzhong (Ren 17) for cough;

With Yingxiang (L.I.20) and Shangxing (Du 24) for reducing nasal discharge.

JUEYINSHU (U.B.14) 厥阴俞 (PERICARDIUM POINT)

"Jueyin" (厥阴) refers to the pericardium. Ancient physicians considered that the pericardium and the lung were closely related to each other. This point, located between Feishu (U.B.13) and Xinshu (U.B.15), is mainly indicated in pericardium disorders. Hence the name Jueyinshu (Pericardium Point).

Location:

1.5 cun lateral to the lower border of the spinous process of the 4th thoracic vertebra (Fig.II-122).

Clinical Application:

This point can be used to treat cough, angina pectoris, suffocating sensation in the chest, nausea and vomiting.

Method:

Puncture obliquely towards the medial aspect about 0.5-0.8 cun.

*XINSHU (U.B.15)心俞   (HEART POINT)

"Xin" (心) means the heart. The point is close to the heart and is the place through which the qi of the heart infuses into the surface of the body. It is mainly indicated in heart disorders, hence the name Xinshu (Heart Point).

Location:

1.5 cun lateral to the lower border of the spinous process of the 5th thoracic vertebra (Fig.II-122).

Indications:

Irritability, palpitation, arrhythmia, forgetfulness, insomnia and nocturnal emission.

Clinical Application:

This point has the effect to benefit the heart, calm the mind and regulate the circulation of qi and blood.

Combinations:

With Shenshu (U.B.23) to treat seminal emission;

With Neiguan (P.6) for treating arrhythmia and angina pectoris; and

With Fengchi (G.B.20), Baihui (Du 20), Zusanli (St.36) and Sanyinjiao (Sp.6) for neurasthenia.

DUSHU (U.B.16) 督俞 (GOVERNOR SHU)

"Du" (督) refers to the Du Meridian (Governor Meridian). The ancient physicians believed that the qi of the Du Meridian infuses into the body surface through this point, hence the name Dushu (Governor Point).

Location:

1.5 cun lateral to the lower border of the spinous process of the 6th thoracic vertebra (Fig.II-122).

Indications:

Heart pain, common cold with fever, abdominal pain and borborygmus.

Method:

Puncture obliquely towards the medial aspect about 0.5-0.8 cun.

*GESHU (U.B.17) 膈俞 (DIAPHRAGM POINT)

"Ge" (膈) means diaphragm. This point is mainly indicated in disorders of the diaphragm such as nausea, vomiting, belching and hiccup. Hence the name Geshu (Diaphragm Point).

Location:

1.5 cun lateral to the lower border of the spinous process of the 7th thoracic vertebra (Fig.II-122).

Indications:

Phrenospasm, esophagospasm, hemoptysis, bloody vomiting, anemia, cough, asthma and urticaria.

Clinical Application:

This is one of the Eight Influential points, being associated with blood. It has the effect to relieve the heaviness in the chest, regulate qi circulation, tonify blood and pacify the stomach. It may be used together with Xuehai (Sp.10) and Quchi (L.I.11) for treating urticaria.

*GANSHU (U.B.18) 肝俞 (LIVER POINT)

"Gan" (肝) means the liver. This point, located close to the liver, is the place through which the qi of the liver infuses into the body surface. It is commonly used to treat liver disorders, hence the name Ganshu (Liver Point).

Location:

1.5 cun lateral to the lower border of the spinous process of the 9th thoracic vertebra (Fig.II-122).

Indications:

Disorders of the liver and gall bladder, hypochondriac pain, lower back pain, epigastric pain, eye diseases, myopia and glaucoma.

Clinical Application:

This point has the effect to clear the mind, brighten the eyes, soothe the liver and pacify the stomach.

Combinations:

With Yanglingquan (G.B.34) for treating diseases of the liver and gall bladder;

With Neiguan (P.6) for chest and hypochondriac pain;

With Zusanli (St.36) for indigestion;

With Xuehai (Sp.10) and Yinlingquan (Sp.9) for anemia;

With Fengchi (G.B.20), Baihui (Du 20) and Shenmen (H.7) for headache, dizziness and insomnia; and

With Shenshu (U.B.23) and Fengchi (G.B.20) for optic atrophy and retinal bleeding.

*DANSHU (U.B.19) 胆俞   (GALL BLADDER POINT)

"Dan" (胆) means gall bladder. This point is close to the gall bladder and is the place through which the qi of the gall bladder infuses into the body surface. It is mainly indicated in diseases of the gall bladder, hence the name Danshu (Gall Bladder Point).

Location:

1.5 cun lateral to the lower border of the spinous process of 10th thoracic vertebra (Fig.II-122).

Indications:

Liver and gall bladder diseases, pain in the chest and hypochondriac region, bitter taste in the mouth, biliary ascariasis, abdominal pain and esophagospasm.

Clinical Application:

This point has the effect to eliminate evil heat from the liver and gall bladder, alleviate heaviness of the chest and regulate qi circulation.

Combinations:

With Sibai (St.2) and Yanglingquan (G.B.34) for biliary ascariasis, severe colic pain or cholelithiasis; and

With Zhigou (S.J.6) for hypochondriac pain.

*PISHU (U.B.20) 脾俞 (SPLEEN POINT)

"Pi" (脾) means spleen. The point is close to the spleen and is the place through which the qi of the spleen infuses into the body surface. It is mainly indicated in diseases of the spleen, hence the name Pishu (Spleen Point).

Location:

1.5 cun lateral to the lower border of the spinous process of the 11th thoracic vertebra (Fig.II-122).

Indications:

Indigestion, abdominal distention, diarrhea, nausea and vomiting, edema, dysentery, anemia, uterine bleeding and urticaria.

Clinical Application:

This point is the place where the qi of the spleen converges. The spleen provides the resources from which the qi and blood of the body are provided. This point has the effect to promote digestion, tonify the spleen, promote the stomach and build up the body constitution. It is the most important point in the treatment of blurring of vision, as well as palpitation due to deficiency of both heart and spleen qi, combined with insufficiency of qi and blood.

Combinations:

With Shenshu (U.B.23) for deficiency of spleen and kidney;

With Weishu (U.B.21) and Zusanli (St.36) for indigestion. Moxibustion applied to this point can increase the production of blood platelets.

*WEISHU (U.B.21) 胃俞 (STOMACH POINT)

"Wei" (胃) means stomach. This point lies close to the stomach and is the place through which the qi of the stomach infuses into the surface of the body. It is mainly indicated in disorders of the stomach, hence the name Weishu (Stomach Point).

Location:

1.5 cun lateral to the lower border of the spinous process of the 12th thoracic vertebra (Fig.II-122).

Indications:

Epigastric pain, pain in the chest and the hypochondriac region, abdominal pain, diarrhea, nausea and vomiting, borborygmus, weakness of the spleen and the stomach.

Clinical Application:

This point has the effect to invigorate the Yang of the stomach, strengthen the function of the spleen and stomach, resolve dampness and remove stagnation.

Combinations:

With Zhongwan (Ren 12), Pishu (U.B.20), Neiguan (P.6), Zusanli (St.36) and Sanyinjiao (Sp.6) in the treatment of acute or chronic gastritis, gastric ulcer and infantile indigestion.

*SANJIAOSHU (U.B.22) 三焦俞 (SANJIAO POINT)

"Sanjiao" (三焦) generalizes the water passages of the body and has a close relationship with the spleen, stomach and kidney. The point is below Pishu (U.B.20) and Weishu (U.B.21), and above Shenshu (U.B.23), the spleen, the stomach and the kidney points. It is considered to be the most important place where the qi of the Sanjiao converges at the body surface. Hence the name Sanjiaoshu (Sanjiao Point). It is mainly indicated in disorders of the Sanjiao.

Location:

1.5 cun lateral to the lower border of the spinous process of the 1st lumbar vertebra (Fig.II-122).

Indications:

Note: As noted, the points from Dashu (U.B.11) to Weishu (U.B.21) are all needled obliquely with the needle being inserted towards the spinal column, about 0.5-0.8 cun. The needling sensations such as soreness and distention are felt around the local area of each point. They often radiate downwards or anteriorly.

Borborygmus, abdominal distention, loose stool with undigested food and lower back pain.

Method:

Puncture perpendicularly 1 cun deep.

*SHENSHU (U.B.23) 肾俞 (KIDNEY POINT)

"Shen" (肾) means kidney. The point is very close to the kidney, and it is the place through which the qi of the kidney infuses into the body surface. It is commonly used to treat disorders of the kidney, hence the name Shenshu (Kidney Point).

Location:

1.5 cun lateral to the lower border of the spinous process of the 2nd lumbar vertebra (Fig.II-122).

Indications:

Lumbago, seminal emission, impotence, enuresis, irregular menstruation, profuse leukorrhea, tinnitus, deafness, edema and urolithiasis.

Clinical Application:

This point has the effect to tonify kidney Yin, strengthen the brain and marrow, benefit the mind, brighten the eye, strengthen the lower back and the knees.

Combinations:

With Ganshu (U.B.18), Xinshu (U.B.15), Fengchi (G.B.20) and Shenmen (H.7) for treating headache with insomnia, forgetfulness and neurasthenia;

With Ganshu (U.B.18), Zhongji (Ren 3), Pangguangshu (U.B.28) and Sanyinjiao (Sp.6) for the diseases related to the urinary and reproductive systems, such as rhinitis, irregular menstruation, seminal emission, impotence, prospermia and dysmenorrhea;

With Huantiao (G.B.30), Fengshi (G.B.31), Baliao (U.B.31-34), Weizhong (U.B.40), Zusanli (St.36) and Xuanzhong (G.B.39) for treating numbness of the lower limbs, paralysis and sciatica; and

With Pishu (U.B.20), Guanyuanshu (U.B.26), Zusanli (St.36) and Sanyinjiao (Sp.6) for treating diabetes.

Many reports have stated that needling Shenshu (U.B.23) bilaterally can significantly invigorate the kidney function in case of rhinitis. Other effects obtained by needling this point are as follows: the secretion of the phenol red (PSP) is much increased, both white and red blood cells in the urine are decreased or eliminated entirely. Blood pressure can be lowered and edema can be alleviated. The results can last from about 2-3 hours to several days, depending on the nature of the conditions.

Method:

Puncture perpendicularly about 1 cun deep, or obliquely towards the spinal column.

Needling Sensations:

Soreness and distention, radiating towards the inferior aspect.

QIHAISHU (U.B.24) 气海俞 (SEA OF QI'S POINT)

This point is closely associated with Qihai (Ren 6) from the Ren Meridian and corresponds to that point. It is indicated in various kinds of disorders due to qi derangement, hence the name Qihaishu (Sea of Qi's Point).

Location:

1.5 cun lateral to the lower border of the spinous process of the 3rd lumbar vertebra (Fig.II-122).

Indications:

Lumbago, dysmenorrhea and hemorrhoid bleeding.

Method:

Puncture perpendicularly about 1 cun deep.

*DACHANGSHU (U.B.25) 大肠俞 (LARGE INTESTINE POINT)

"Dachang" (大肠) means the large intestine. The point is associated with the large intestine and it is the place where the qi of the large intestine infuses into the body surface. It is mainly indicated in diseases of the large intestine, hence the name Dachangshu (Large Intestine Point).

Location:

1.5 cun lateral to the lower border of the spinous process of the 4th lumbar vertebra (Fig.II-122).

Indications:

Lumbago, abdominal pain, diarrhea and borborygmus.

Clinical Application:

This point has the effect to regulate the function of the stomach and intestines, eliminate heat, promote bowel movement, strengthen the lower back and knees, regulate qi circulation and remove stagnation.

Combinations:

With Renzhong (Ren 26) for treating acute lumbar sprain,

With Huantiao (G.B.30) for sciatica,

With Kunlun (U.B.60) for the lumbosacral pain, and

With Zusanli (St.36) and Shangjuxu (St.37) for borborygmus and abdominal pain.

Method:

Puncture perpendicularly about 1-2 cun deep, or obliquely towards the column.

Needling Sensations:

Soreness and distention, radiating down to the anus area.

GUANYUANSHU (U.B.26) 关元俞 (GUANYUAN POINT)

This point is closely associated with Guanyuan (Ren 4) from the Ren Meridian, as its corresponding point. Its indications are the same as those of Guanyuan (Ren 4), hence the name Guanyuanshu (Guanyuan Point).

Location:

1.5 cun lateral to the lower border of the spinous process of the 5th lumbar vertebra (Fig.II-122).

Indications:

Lower back pain, abdominal distention, dysuria and enuresis.

Method:

Puncture perpendicularly about 1 cun deep.

XIAOCHANGSHU (U.B.27) 小肠俞 (SMALL INTESTINE POINT)

This point is close to the small intestine and it is the place where the qi of the small intestine infuses into the body surface. It is a commonly selected point in the treatment of small intestine disorders, hence the name Xiaochangshu (Small Intestine Point).

Location:

1.5 cun lateral to the lower border of the spinous process of the 1st sacral vertebra (Fig.II-122).

Indications:

Lower abdominal pain and distention, dysentery, seminal emission, enuresis and profuse leukorrhea.

Method:

Puncture perpendicularly about 1 cun deep.

PANGGUANGSHU (U.B.28)膀胱俞 (URINARY BLADDER POINT)

Pangguang (膀胱) means urinary bladder.

This point is closed to the urinary bladder and it is the place where the qi of the urinary bladder infuses into the body surface. It is mainly indicated in bladder disorders, hence the name Pangguangshu (Urinary Bladder Point).

Location:

At the level of the 2nd posterior sacral foramen, 1.5 cun lateral to the posterior midline (Fig.II-122).

Indications:

Retention of urine, enuresis, diarrhea and pain of the lumbosacral region.

Clinical Application:

This point is one of the most important points for strengthening kidney Yang, regulating water passages and promoting the functions of the urinary and reproductive systems.

Combinations:

With Shenshu (U.B.23), Guanyuan (Ren 4), Zhongji (Ren 3) and Sanyinjiao (Sp.6) in the treatment of urecystitis, dysuria and enuresis; and

With Weizhong (U.B.40) and Zhibian (U.B.54) for pain of the lower back and knees.

ZHONGLÜSHU (U.B.29)中膂俞 (BACK MUSCLE POINT)

"Lü" (膂) refers to the muslces along either side of the vertebral column. "Zhong" (中) means middle. The point is located approximately at the midpoint of the muscle along the sacral vertebra, hence the name Zhonglushu (Back Muscle Point).

Locations:

1.5 cun lateral to the lower border of the spinous process of the 3rd sacral vertebra (Fig.II-122).

Indications:

Dysentery, or stiffness and pain of the lower back.

Method:

Puncture perpendicularly about 1-1.5 cun deep.

BAIHUANSHU (U.B.30)白环俞 (WHITE RING POINT)

"Bai" (白) means white; and "huan" (环) means a ring made of jade or gold, referring to something valuable or important. The place where the sperm or vital energy is stored is called white ring. Besides, the point is mainly indicated in profuse leukorrhea and seminal emission. Both leukorrhea and sperm are white in colour, hence the name Baihuanshu (White Ring Point).

Location:

At the level of the 4th posterior sacral foramen, 1.5 cun lateral to the posterior midline (Fig.II-122).

Indications:

Profuse leukorrhea, enuresis, irregular menstruation, lower back pain, hip-joint pain and seminal emission.

Method:

Puncture perpendicularly about 1-1.5 cun deep.

THE FOUR LIAO POINTS:

Shangliao (U.B.31) (Upper Crevice)
Ciliao (U.B.32) (Second Crevice)
Zhongliao (U.B.33) (Middle Crevice)
Xialiao (U.B.34) (Lower Crevice)

These four points are respectively located in the 1st, 2nd, 3rd and 4th posterior sacral foramen. "Liao" (髎) means bony crevice, referring to the deep part of the foramen. The four points are situated in the following order: Shangliao (U.B.31) in the 1st foramen, Ciliao (U.B.32) in the 2nd, Zhongliao (U.B.33) in the 3rd and Xialiao (U.B.34) in the lowest one, hence their names (Fig.II-122, 123).

Locations:

The process in the centre of the sacrum at the level of the posterior superior iliac spine is the spinous process of the 1st sacral vertebra. Shangliao (U.B.31) is located in the 1st posterior sacral foramen, midway between the posterior superior iliac spine and the spinous process of the 1st sacral vertebra.

At the upper part of the coccygeal cornua is the sacral cornua, and the sacral hiatus is between the sacral cornua, which is at the same level of the 4th sacral foramen. Place the tip of the index finger between the posterior superior iliac spine and the posterior middle line, the tip of the little finger on the depression just at the lateral superior border of the sacral cornua and the other two fingers in between, so that they are equidistant and in a straight line. Shangliao (U.B.31), Ciliao (U.B.32), Zhongliao (U.B.33) and Xialiao (U.B.34) will be under the tips of the four fingers in the order of index, middle, ring and little fingers.

Indications:

Diseases of the urinary and reproductive systems, such as urgency of micturition, irregular menstruation, profuse leukorrhea, dysuria, dysmenorrhea, pain in the lower back and sciatica.

Method:

Puncture perpendicularly about 1-1.5 cun deep for the four points.

HUIYANG (U.B.35) 会阳 (MEETING OF YANG)

"Hui" (会) means to meet. "Yang" (阳) refers to the Du Meridian and the Urinary Bladder Meridian of Foot-Taiyang. The point is 0.5 cun lateral to the tip of the coccyx. It is the coalescent point of the Urinary Bladder Meridian of Foot-Taiyang and Du Meridian. It is opposite to Huiyin (Meeting of Yin), hence the name Huiyang

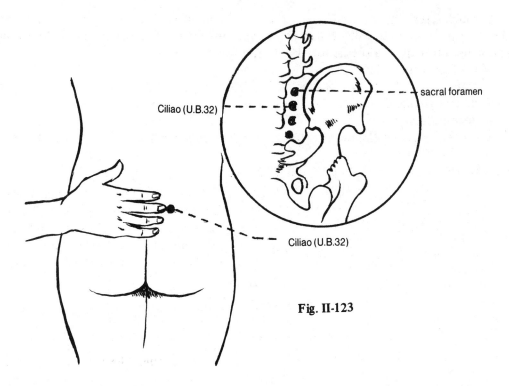

Ciliao (U.B.32)

sacral foramen

Ciliao (U.B.32)

Fig. II-123

(Meeting of Yang).
 Location:
 0.5 cun lateral to the tip of the coccyx.
 Indications:
 Impotence, dysentery, diarrhea, profuse leukorrhea and hemorrhoids (Fig.II-122).
 Method:
 Puncture perpendicularly about 1-1.5 cun deep.

*CHENGFU (U.B.36) 承扶 (HOLD AND SUPPORT)

 "Cheng" (承) means to hold or take. "Fu" (扶) means to support or to hold. The two in combination mean to support and prevent the body from falling down, either with the hands or with crutches. The main indication of this point is to treat the severely painful syndromes of the hip, thigh and lower back, due to invasion of cold. After needling the point, the pain may be alleviated and the patient will soon be able to give up the stick or the help of the others and stand up by himself, hence the name Chengfu (Hold and Support).
 Location:
 At the midpoint of the transverse gluteal fold (Fig.II-125).
 Indications:
 Lower back pain, pain in the hip region, sciatica, constipation and hemorrhoids.
 Clinical Application:
 This point has the effect to invigorate the functional activities of the collaterals and relax the tendons.

Combinations:

With Weizhong (U.B.40) and Zhibian (U.B.54) for treating paralysis, numbness and pain in the lumbar area or the lower extremities,

With Tianshu (St.25) for constipation.

Method:

Puncture perpendicularly about 1-1.5 cun deep.

Needling Sensations:

Soreness, distention and numbness, radiating downwards.

*YINMEN (U.B.37) 殷门 **(THICK RED GATE)**

"Yin" (殷) means something thick and deep or located centrally, but it also refers to large size or the red colour. "Men" (门) means gate. The point is located in the posterior aspect of the thigh, where the muscles are abundant and thick, and is indicated in lumbar sprain and lumbago due to the coagulation of evil blood. Hence, the name Yinmen (Thick Red Gate).

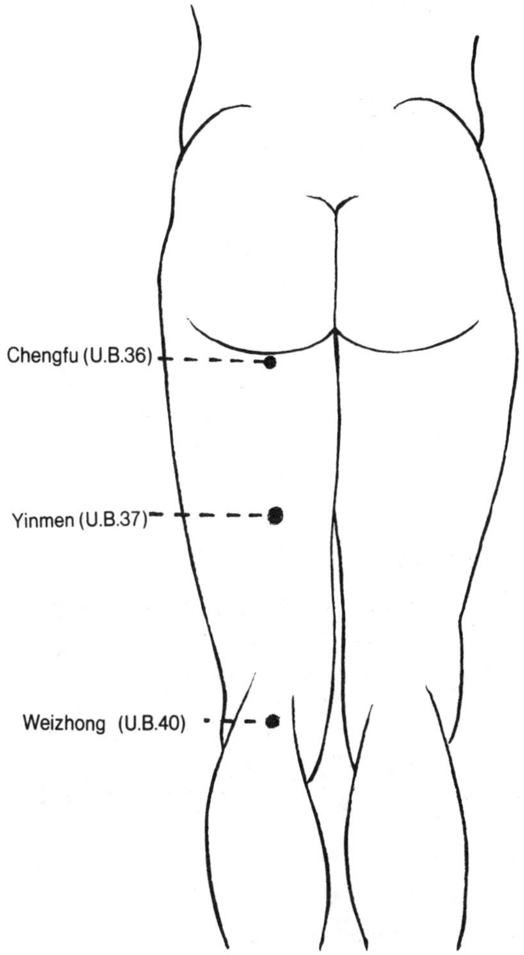

Location:

The line joining the midpoint of the transverse gluteal fold and the midpoint of the transverse crease of the popliteal fossa is about 14 cun long. The point is located on this line 6 cun below the transverse gluteal fold (Fig.II-125).

Indications:

Sciatica, lumbago, occipital headache, paralysis and numbness of the lower extremities.

Clinical Application:

This point has the effect to activate collaterals and relax the tendons.

Combination:

With Kunlun (U.B.60) and Dachangshu (U.B.25) for treating lumbago.

Method:

Puncture perpendicularly 1-2 cun deep.

Needling Sensations:

Soreness and distention, radiating down to the leg.

FUXI (U.B.38) 浮郄 **(FLOATING CLEFT)**

"Fu" (浮) means floating or upward. "Xi" (郄) is a crevice or a cleft. The point is located in the depression above Weiyang (U.B.39), hence the name Fuxi (Floating

Chengfu (U.B.36)

Yinmen (U.B.37)

Weizhong (U.B.40)

Fig. II-125

cleft).

Location:

On the medial side of the tendon of m. biceps femoris, 1 cun above Weiyang (U.B.39) (Fig.II-126).

Indications:

Numbness of the gluteal and femoral regions, and spasm of the tendons in the popliteal fossa.

Method:

Puncture perpendicularly 1-1.5 cun deep.

WEIYANG (U.B.39) 委阳 "Ō" (LATERAL TO POPLITEAL)

"Wei" (委) is an abbreviation of Weizhong (U.B.40), but here refers to the popliteal fossa. "Yang" (阳) refers to the lateral aspect. The point is lateral to Weizhong (U.B.40), hence the name Weiyang (Lateral to Popliteal).

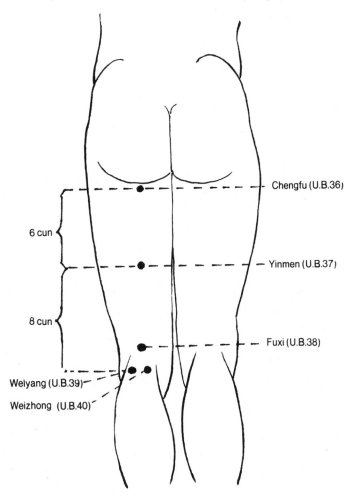

Fig. II-126

Location:

At the level of Weizhong (U.B.40) on the lateral end of the transverse crease of the popliteal fossa, at the medial border of the tendon of m. biceps femoris (Fig.II-126).

Indications:

Pain and stiffness of the lower back, distention and fullness of the lower abdomen, and pain or cramp of the leg and foot.

Method:

Puncture perpendicularly 1-1.5 cun deep.

*WEIZHONG (U.B.40) 委中 "HE" (POPLITEAL CENTRE)

"Wei" (委) originally meant to flex or to bend, and here it refers to the popliteal fossa. "Zhong" (中) means centre. When locating the point, the patient is asked to flex the knee to such an extent where a depression appears in the centre of the popliteal fossa. The point lies in the depression, hence the name "Weizhong" (Popliteal Centre). This point is also sometimes called Weizhongyang.

Location:

At the midpoint of the transverse crease of the popliteal fossa, between the tendons of m. biceps femoris and m. semitendinosus. Some sources record a new point 2 cun above Weizhong (U.B.40), called Weishang (Upper Popliteal) (Fig. II-127).

Indications:

Lower back pain, sciatica, rheumatalgia of the lower extremities, abdominal pain, acute vomiting and diarrhea, sunstroke and contraction of the calf muscle.

Clinical Application:

This point is the He-Sea point of the Urinary Bladder Meridian of Foot-Taiyang and is one of the "Four General Points" frequently used for treating disorders of the lower back. It has the effect to activate the collaterals, relax the tendons, strengthen the lower back and knees, stop vomiting and diarrhea.

Combinations:

With Shenshu (U.B.23), Guanyuanshu (U.B.26), Huantiao (G.B.30), Zusanli (St.36) and Sanyinjiao (Sp.6) for treating sciatica and paralysis of the lower extremities.

Method:

Puncture perpendicularly about 1-1.5 cun deep. Prick with three-edged needle to cause bleeding from the popliteal vein in relieving acute vomiting and diarrhea.

Needling Sensations:

Soreness, numbness and distention, radiating down to the sole.

FUFEN (U.B.41) 附分 (ATTACHED BRANCH)

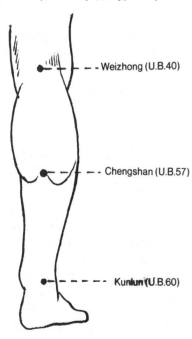

Weizhong (U.B.40)

Chengshan (U.B.57)

Kunlun (U.B.60)

Fig.II-127

"Fu" (附) means lateral or attached; "fen" (分) means a branch. The point is the first point on the 2nd line of the back, lateral and parallel to the 1st line of the meridian, hence the name Fufen (Attached Branch).

Location:

Three cun lateral to the lower border of the spinous process of the 2nd thoracic vertebra, about 4 finger-breadths from the posterior midline (Fig.-II-124).

Indications:

Stiffness and pain of the shoulder, back and neck as well as numbness of the elbow and arm.

Method:

Puncture obliquely about 0.5-0.8 cun deep.

Note: The second line of the Urinary Bladder Meridian of Foot-Taiyang on the back, is 3 cun lateral to the posterior midline. Puncture all points from this line obliquely about 0.5-0.8 cun deep, from Fufen (U.B.41) to Zhishi (U.B.52). Baohuang (U.B.53) can be punctured perpendicularly 1.5 cun deep and Zhibian (U.B.54) 2-3 cun deep.

POHU (U.B.42) 魄戶 (SPIRIT SHELTER)

The point is at the level of Feishu (U.B.13), the lung point. The lung houses the spirit (Po). "Hu" (戶) means shelter. The point is indicated in lung system diseases and has the effect to stop cough and relieve asthma, hence the name Pohu (Spirit Shelter).

Location:

Three cun lateral to the lower border of the spinous process of the 3rd thoracic vertebra (Fig.II-124).

Method:

Puncture obliquely about 0.5-0.8 cun deep.

GAOHUANG (U.B.43) 膏肓 (VITAL ENERGY POINT)

The vital energy produced by the spleen is called "gao" (膏) and the vital energy produced by the kidney is called "huang" (肓). "Gao" and "huang" meet together near the 4th thoracic vertebra where the point is located. The point can be used to treat the diseases due to chronic and prolonged deficiency of both the spleen and kidney, hence the name Gaohuang (Vital Energy Point).

Location:

Three cun lateral to the lower border of the spinous process of the 4th thoracic vertebra (Fig.II-124).

Indications:

Pulmonary tuberculosis, cough, asthma, poor memory and seminal emission.

Method:

Puncture obliquely about 0.5-0.8 cun deep.

SHENTANG (U.B.44) 神堂 (MIND HOUSE)

"Shen" (神) means the mind. "Tang" (堂) means a living place or house. The heart houses the mind and the point is lateral to Xinshu (U.B.15), the heart point. Hence, the name Shentang (Mind House).

Location:

Three cun lateral to the lower border of the spinous process of the 5th thoracic vertebra, having the effect to alleviate heavy sensation of the chest and calm the mind (Fig.II-124).

Method:

Puncture obliquely about 0.5-0.8 cun deep.

YIXI (U.B.45) 譩譆 (YIXI)

"Yixi" (譩譆) means the sound of a sigh. When the point is needled, the patient may sigh, and the doctor may feel throbbing around the point. Hence the name Yixi.

Location:

Three cun lateral to the lower border of the spinous process of the 6th thoracic vertebra (Fig.II-124).

Indications:

Cough, asthma, febrile disease without sweating, and pain of the shoulder or back.

Method:

Puncture obliquely about 0.5-0.8 cun deep.

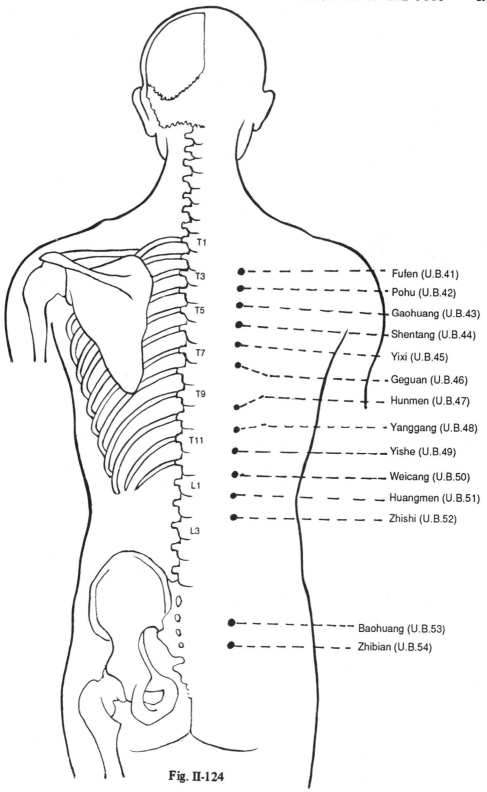

Fufen (U.B.41)
Pohu (U.B.42)
Gaohuang (U.B.43)
Shentang (U.B.44)
Yixi (U.B.45)
Geguan (U.B.46)
Hunmen (U.B.47)
Yanggang (U.B.48)
Yishe (U.B.49)
Weicang (U.B.50)
Huangmen (U.B.51)
Zhishi (U.B.52)

Baohuang (U.B.53)
Zhibian (U.B.54)

Fig. II-124

GEGUAN (U.B.46) 隔关 (DIAPHRAGM PASS)

"Ge" (隔) refers to the diaphragm. "Guan" (关) means pass. The point is lateral to Geshu (U.B.17), the diaphragm point, and is mainly indicated in hiccup, regurgitation, nausea, vomiting and disorders associated with the diaphragm. Hence the name Geguan (Diaphragm Pass).

Location:
Three cun lateral to the lower border of the spinous process of the 7th thoracic vertebra (Fig.II-124).

Indications:
Hiccup, acid regurgitation, nausea, vomiting, belching and difficulty in swallowing.

Method:
Puncture obliquely about 0.5-0.8 cun deep.

HUNMEN (U.B.47) 魂 门 (SOUL GATE)

"Hun" (魂) is the soul and "Men" (门) means a gate. The point is at the level of Ganshu (U.B.18), the liver point. The liver houses the soul and the point is mainly indicated in liver disorders, such as hypochondriac pain, mental diseases, pain in the back, vomiting, etc. Hence the name Hunmen (Soul Gate).

Location:
Three cun lateral to the lower border of the spinous process of the 9th thoracic vertebra. This point has the effect to soothe the liver, remove stagnation of liver qi and pacify the stomach (Fig.II-124).

Method:
Puncture obliquely about 0.5-0.8 cun deep.

YANGGANG (U.B.48) 阳 纲 (KEY LINK OF YANG)

"Yang" (阳) means lateral. "Gang" (纲) originally means the key link, or the commander. The point is from the Urinary Bladder Meridian of Foot-Taiyang. It is lateral to Danshu (U.B.19), the gall bladder point, above Weishu (U.B.21), the stomach point; Sanjiaoshu (U.B.22), the Sanjiao point; Dachangshu (U.B.25), the large intestine point; Xiaochangshu (U.B.27), the small intestine point; and Pangguangshu (U.B.28), the urinary bladder point. These fu organs are also known as Yang organs. The point above them acts as the commander or the key link of the fu organs, hence the name Yanggang (Key Link of Yang).

Location:
Three cun lateral to the lower border of the spinous process of the 10th thoracic vertebra (Fig.II-124).

Indications:
Borborygmus, abdominal pain, jaundice and hepatitis.

YISHE (U.B.49) 意舍 (EMOTION'S RESIDENCE)

"Yi" (意) here means the emotions. "She" (舍) refers to the place of residence. The spleen stores the emotions and the point is at the level of Pishu (U.B.20), the spleen point. Hence the name Yishe (Emotion's Residence).

Location:

Three cun lateral to the lower border of the spinous process of the 11th thoracic vertebra (Fig.II-124).

Indications:

Spleen problems, abdominal distention, borborygmus, poor appetite and those disorders associated with the emotions.

Method:

Puncture obliquely about 0.5-0.8 cun deep.

WEICANG (U.B.50) 胃仓 (STOMACH STOREHOUSE)

"Cang" (仓) means a place to store or to keep things. "Wei" (胃) means stomach. The point is at the level of Weishu (U.B.21), the stomach point, and is mainly indicated in stomach disorders, poor appetite, retention of food, infantile food retention, pain in the back and waist motor impairment. It has the effect to strengthen the spleen and tonify the stomach. Hence the name Weicang (Stomach Storehouse).

Location:

Three cun lateral to the lower border of the spinous process of the 12th thoracic vertebra (Fig.II-124).

Method:

Puncture perpendicularly about 0.5-0.8 cun deep.

HUANGMEN (U.B.51) 肓门 (ENERGY GATE)

"Huang" (肓) refers to the energy produced by the kidney. "Men" (门) means gate. The point is at the level of Sanjiaoshu (U.B.22). The vital energy of the kidney and the defensive qi of the Sanjiao meet with each other at this point, hence the name Huangmen (Energy Gate).

Location:

Three cun lateral to the lower border of the spinous process of the 1st lumbar vertebra (Fig.II-124).

Indications:

Abdominal pain, constipation and mastitis.

Method:

Puncture perpendicularly about 0.5-0.8 cun deep.

ZHISHI (U.B.52) 志室 (WILL RESIDENCE)

"Zhi" (志) means the will. "Shi" (室) is a place for housing something. The kidney houses the will. The point is at the level of Shenshu (U.B.23), the kidney point, and it is indicated in kidney diseases. Hence the name Zhishi (Will Residence).

Location:

Three cun lateral to the lower border of the spinous process of the 2nd lumbar vertebra (Fig.II-124).

Indications:

Seminal emission, impotence, edema and lumbago.

Clinical Application:

Note: The point 3 cun lateral to the lower border of the spinous process of the 3rd lumbar vertebra is an extra point, called Yaoyan (Kidney Eye).

This point has the effect to tonify the kidney Yang, strengthen the kidney and remove damp-heat from the lower jiao.

Combinations:

With Shenshu (U.B.23) and Sanyinjiao (Sp.6) for impotence and seminal emission.

BAOHUANG (U.B.53) 胞肓 (BLADDER ENERGY)

"Bao" (胞) is another name for the urinary bladder. "Huang" (肓) means energy. The point is at the level of Pangguangshu (U.B.28), the urinary bladder point, and is mainly indicated in urinary bladder disorders. Needling the point can promote the function of urinary bladder, activate its qi circulation and remove obstruction so as to promote micturition. Hence the name Baohuang (Bladder Energy).

Location:

Three cun lateral to the lower border of the spinous process of the 2nd sacral vertebra (Fig.II-124).

Method:

Puncture perpendicularly about 1.5 cun deep.

*ZHIBIAN (U.B.54) 秩边 (ORDER EDGE)

"Zhi" (秩) is order, or being arranged in order. "Bian" (边) means the border or edge. The back points of the Urinary Bladder Meridian of foot-Taiyang are located in a very precise order, according to the positions of their corresponding internal zangfu organs. This point is at the lowest place on the back, hence its name Zhibian (Order Edge).

Locations:

Three cun lateral to the lower border of the spinous process of the 4th sacral vertebra (Fig.II-124).

Indications:

Pain in the lumbosacral region, muscular atrophy, motor impairment and pain of the lower extremities, dysuria, scrotum swelling, hemorrhoids, prolapse of the rectum and constipation.

Clinical Application:

This point has the effect to activate the meridians and collaterals, relax the tendons and remove damp-heat from the lower jiao.

Combinations:

With Dachangshu (U.B.25) and Weizhong (U.B.40) for treating lumbosacral pain.

With Yanglingquan (G.B.34) and Xuanzhong (G.B.39) for muscular atrophy and motor impairment of the lower extremities.

With Yinlingquan (Sp.9) and Pangguangshu (U.B.28) for dysuria, urgency and frequency of micturition.

With Baihui (Du 20) and Changqiang (Du 1) for prolapse of the rectum and hemorrhoids.

Method:

Have the patient lie on one side, extending the healthy leg and flexing the affected

---

Note: The distance from the transverse crease of the popliteal fossa to the tip of the external malleolus is 16 cun. The following 6 points are all needled perpendicularly about 1-2 cun deep.

one for disorders of the lower extremities, puncture perpendicularly 2-3 cun deep so as to induce the needling sensation down to the heel or toes. For disorders of the external genitalia, puncture obliquely towards the genital region, directing the needling sensation to the diseased area. For anal disorders, insert the needle slightly towards the anus and direct the needling sensation towards the diseased area.

HEYANG (U.B.55) 合 阳 (CONFLUENT YANG)

"He" (合) means confluent. Weizhong (U.B.40) is the He-sea point of the Urinary Bladder Meridian. The point is below Weizhong (U.B.40), being the place where the qi of the meridian reconverges. Hence the name Heyang (Confluent Yang).

Location:

Two cun directly below Weizhong (U.B.40), between the medial and lateral heads of the m. gastrocnemius (Fig.II-128).

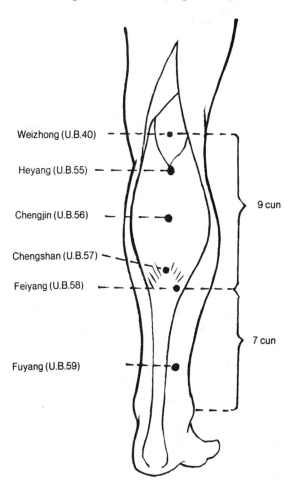

Weizhong (U.B.40)

Heyang (U.B.55)

Chengjin (U.B.56)

Chengshan (U.B.57)

Feiyang (U.B.58)

9 cun

7 cun

Fuyang (U.B.59)

Fig.II-128

Indications:

Back pain, profuse uterine bleeding as well as aching and soreness of the lower extremities.

CHENGJIN (U.B.56) 承筋 (SUPPORTING TENDON)

"Cheng" (承) here means to support or to hold. "Jin" (筋) means tendons. Needling the point can strengthen (support) the function of the leg so as to support the body, hence the name Chengjin (Supporting Tendon).

Location:

Midway between Heyang (U.B.55) and Chengshan (U.B.57).

Indications:

Spasm of the tendons of the leg, hemorrhoids, stiffness and motor impairment of the lower back.

*CHENGSHAN (U.B.57) 承山 (SUPPORTING HILL)

"Cheng" (承) means to hold or to support. "Shan" (山) means hill. The point is situated at the highest place at the muscles on the posterior aspect of the leg, likened here to a small hill. This small hill is an important factor in the maintenance of an upright stance, hence the name Chengshan (Supporting Hill).

Location:

In the upper end of the depression formed by the lambdoidal suture on the belly of the calf, the depression becomes clearer if the heel is raised with the toes still touching the ground. Alternatively, with the patient lying in a prone position, the point is located midway along the line connecting Weizhong (U.B.40) and the midpoint of the transverse line connecting the tips of the external and medial malleoli (Fig.II-129).

Indications:

Spasm of the gastrocnemius, pain in the lower back and the lower limbs, hemorrhoids, paralysis of the lower extremities, anal fissure and prolapse of the rectum.

Clinical Application:

This point has the effect to activate the meridians and collaterals, relax the tendons and regulate the functional activities of the zangfu organs.

Combinations:

Penetrate from Tiaokou (St.38) towards Chengshan (U.B.57) for spasm of the gastrocnemius.

With Shenshu (U.B.23), Weizhong (U.B.40) and Yanglingquan (G.B.34) for pain of the lower back and the lower limbs.

With Kunlun (U.B.60) for pain in the heel.

Method:

Puncture perpendicularly about 1-2 cun deep.

Needling Sensations:

Soreness or distention radiating down to the heel, or up to the popliteal fossa.

FEIYANG (U.B.58) 飞 扬 " ∧ " (FLYING-UP)

"Fei" (飞), meaning flying, refers to going fast here. "Yang" (扬) here means

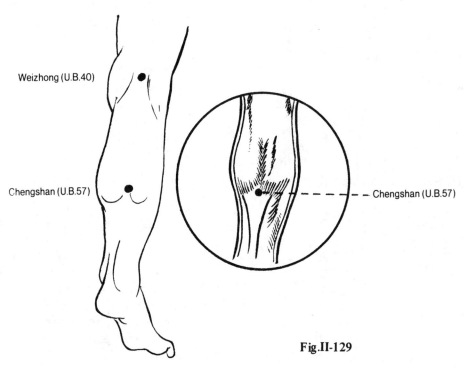

Weizhong (U.B.40)

Chengshan (U.B.57)

Chengshan (U.B.57)

Fig.II-129

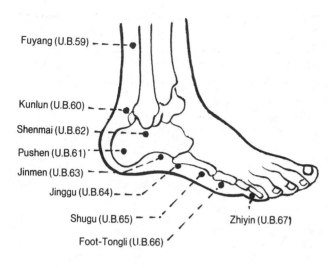

Fuyang (U.B.59)

Kunlun (U.B.60)

Shenmai (U.B.62)

Pushen (U.B.61)

Jinmen (U.B.63)

Jinggu (U.B.64)

Shugu (U.B.65)

Foot-Tongli (U.B.66)

Zhiyin (U.B.67)

Fig. II-130

to fly upward. This point is the Luo-connecting point of the meridian. The qi of the Urinary Bladder Meridian can pass quickly from this point to the Kidney Meridian of Foot-Shaoyin. For weakness of the lower extremities, this point can be needled; after which the patient can walk with a spring in his step. Hence the name Feiyang (Flying-up).

Location:

One cun inferior and lateral to Chengshan (U.B.57), on the lateral border to the m. gastrocnemius (Fig.II-128).

Indications:

Headache, blurring of vision, weakness and pain of the leg as well as lower back pain.

FUYANG (U.B.59) 跗阳 (YANG OF FOOT)

"Fu" (跗) means the dorsum of the foot. The point is from the Urinary Bladder Meridian of Foot-Taiyang and is located on the dorsum, the Yang aspect of the foot. Hence the name Fuyang (Yang of Foot).

Location:

Three cun directly above Kunlun (U.B.60) (Fig. II-130).

Indications:

Heaviness of the head, headache, lumbosacral pain, pain and swelling of the external malleolus, and paralysis.

Method:

Puncture perpendicularly about 1 cun deep.

*KUNLUN (U.B.60) 昆仑 "⊖" (BIG AND HIGH)

"Kunlun" (昆仑), which originally means the name of a famous mountain in the western part of China, here refers to something big and high. The location of the point is posteroinferior to the external malleolus, a prominent feature of the local anatomy of the lateral leg. Also, it is indicated in head problems, the head being the highest part of the body, hence the name Kunlun (Big and High).

Location:

In the depression between the external malleolus and the tendo calcaneus (Fig. II-130-131).

Indications:

Headache, stiffness of the neck, blurring of vision, epilepsy, shoulder, hip and lower back pain, swelling and pain of the heel, difficult labour, retention of the placenta and epistaxis.

Clinical Application:

This is the Jing-River point of the Urinary Bladder Meridian of Foot-Taiyang. It has the effect to activate blood circulation, alleviate swelling and pain, relax the tendons and strengthen the lower back and knees.

Combinations:

With Fengchi (G.B.20) and Tianzhu (U.B.10) for headache and neck rigidity;

With Shenshu (U.B.23) for lumbosacral pain; and

With Daling (P.7) for the pain in the heel.

Method:

Puncture perpendicularly about 0.5-1 cun deep.

Needling sensations:

Soreness and distention at the local area, radiating up or down along the course of the meridian.

PUSHEN (U.B.61) 仆参 (SERVANT'S WORSHIP)

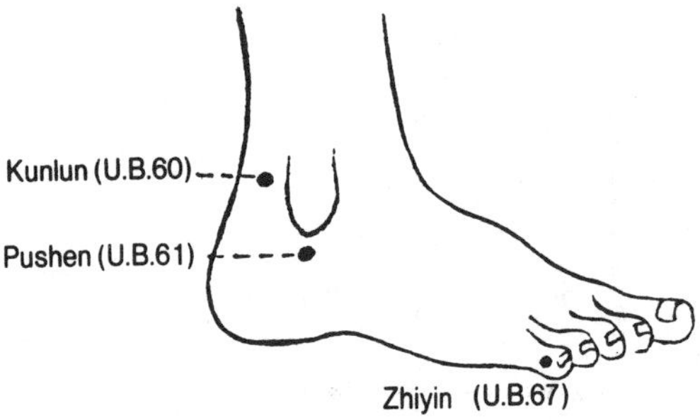

Kunlun (U.B.60)

Pushen (U.B.61)

Zhiyin (U.B.67)

Fig.II-131

"Pu" (仆) means servant. "Shen" (参) means to worship or salute. In the ancient times, when a servant met his master, he was obliged to salute by dropping on his knees. In this position, the point lies directly below the great trochanter and is pressed by it, hence the name Pushen (Servant's Worship).

Location:

Posteroinferior to the external malleolus, Two cun directly below Kunlun (U.B.60) at the junction of the red and white skin (Fig.II-130).

Indications:

Pain around the heel, contraction of the calf muscles and beriberi.

Method:

Puncture perpendicularly 0.3-0.5 cun deep.

*SHENMAI (U.B.62) 申脉 " ⊗ " (RELAXING MERIDIANS)

"Shen" (申) means to stretch or to relax. "Mai" (脉) refers to the blood vessels and the meridians. This point has the effect to relax the tendons, soothe the lumbar area and promote blood circulation. After needling, the meridians are regulated and the muscles relaxed. Hence the name Shenmai (Relaxing Meridians).

Location:

In the depression directly below the lower border of the external malleolus (Fig.-II-131).

Indications:

Soreness and pain of the lower extremities, occipital headache, dizziness with blurring of vision, epilepsy and malposition of fetus.

Clinical Application:

This is one of the Eight Confluent Points of the 8 extra meridians, being associated primarily with the Yangqiao Meridian and secondarily with the Du Meridian.

Combinations:

With Yamen (Du 15) and Dazhui (Du 14) for occipital headache, dizziness and vertigo; and

With Fengfu (Du 16), Baihui (Du 20) and Taodao (Du 13) for epilepsy.

Method:

Puncture perpendicularly 0.3-0.5 cun deep.

Needling Sensations:

Distention and pain at the local area.

JINMEN (U.B.63) 金门 "XI"   (GOLDEN GATE)

"Jin" (金) is gold, meaning great value. "Men" (门) means door or gate. It is one of the most important points of the meridian, as valuable as gold and jade, hence the name Jinmen (Golden Gate). It is anteroinferior to the anterior border of the external malleolus, in the depression below the cuboid bone, midway between Shenmai (U.B.62) and Jinggu (U.B.64) (Fig. II-130).

Indications:

Epilepsy, infantile convulsion, backache and pain in the external malleolus.

Method:

Puncture perpendicularly 0.3-0.5 cun deep.

JINGGU (U.B.64) 京骨 "O"   (BIG BONE)

"Jinggu" (京骨) is the name of the 5th metatarsal bone. The point is close to it, hence the name Jinggu (Big Bone).

Location:

In the depression below the tuberosity of the 5th metatarsal bone, at the junction of the red and white skin (Fig.II-130).

Indications:

Headache, neck rigidity, knee-joint pain and spasm of the foot.

Method:

Puncture perpendicularly 0.3-0.5 cun deep.

SHUGU (U.B.65) 束骨 " 尺 "   (BONE OF SHU)

"Shugu" (束骨) refers to the small head of the 5th metatarsal bone. The point is posteroinferior to the head of the 5th metatarsal bone at the junction of the red and white skin, hence the name Shugu (Bone of Shu) (Fig. II-130).

Indications:

Mental confusion, headache, neck rigidity and pain in the lower extremities.

Method:

Puncture perpendicularly about 0.3-0.5 cun deep.

FOOT-TONGGU (U.B.66) 足通谷 " ～ "   (PASSING VALLEY)

"Tong" (通) means to pass or go through. "Gu" (骨), meaning a valley, refers to a depression. It is the Ying-spring point of the Urinary Bladder Meridian of Foot-Taiyang, so the qi of the meridian passes quickly through it. Hence the name Foot-Tonggu

(Passing Valley).

Location:

In the depression anteroinferior to the 5th metatarsophalangeal joint, at the junction of the white and red skin (Fig.II-130).

Indications:

Headache, neck rigidity and blurring of vision.

Method:

Puncture perpendicularly about 0.2-0.3 cun deep.

*ZHIYIN (U.B.67) 至阴 " Θ "   (REACHING YIN)

"Zhi" (至) means to arrive or to reach. The flow of qi of the Urinary Bladder Meridian of Foot-Taiyang comes to an end at this point, after which it enters the Kidney Meridian of Foot-Shaoyang, the Yang qi coming to its end and the Yin qi starting to flow. Hence the name Zhiyin (Reaching Yin).

Location:

On the lateral side of the little toe, about 0.1 cun posterior to the corner of the nail (Fig.II-130).

Indications:

Headache, ophthalmalgia, dysuria, epistaxis, nasal obstruction, malposition of fetus, difficult labour and retention of placenta.

Clinical Application:

This point is the Jing-well point of the meridian, having the effect to remove the obstruction from the meridian, regulate the Yin and Yang, calm the mind, brighten the eye and deal with the malposition of fetus.

Combinations:

With Fengchi (G.B.20), Tianzhu (U.B.11) and Taiyang (Extra) for headache, and

With moxa stick to heat the point for about 20 minutes is very effective in treating malposition of the fetus.

Method:

Puncture obliquely about 0.1 cun deep.

Needling Sensation:

Slight pain in the local area.

III. Summary

The Urinary Bladder Meridian of Foot-Taiyang pertains to the urinary bladder and connects with the kidney. There are altogether 67 points from this meridian on either side of the body (Fig. II-132, 133, 134).

The Special Points from the Meridian

Weizhong	(U.B.40)	He Earth	Jinggu	(U.B.64)	O
Kunlun	(U.B.60)	O Fire	Feiyang	(U.B.58)	
Shugu	(U.B.65)	Wood	Jinmen	(U.B.63)	Xi
Foot-Tonggu	(U.B.66)	Water	Shenmai	(U.B.62)	
Zhiyin	(U.B.67)	O Metal			

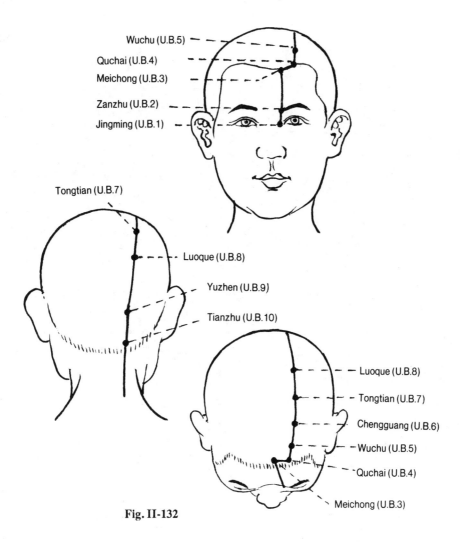

Fig. II-132

Point Indications of the U.B. Meridian According to Locations

Point Names	Locations	Indications	Regional Indications
Jingming U.B.1	0.1 cun superior to the inner canthus	Eye disease, visual hallucination	
Zanzhu U.B.2	On the medial extremity of the eye-brow	Headache, glaucoma	Diseases of the head and neck area
Meichong U.B.3	Directly above the eye-brow, 0.5 cun within the hairline	Headache, nasal obstruction, redness of the eye	
Quchai U.B.4	0.5 cun within the hairline, 1.5 cun lateral to the Du Meridian	Headache, nasal obstruction, epistaxis	

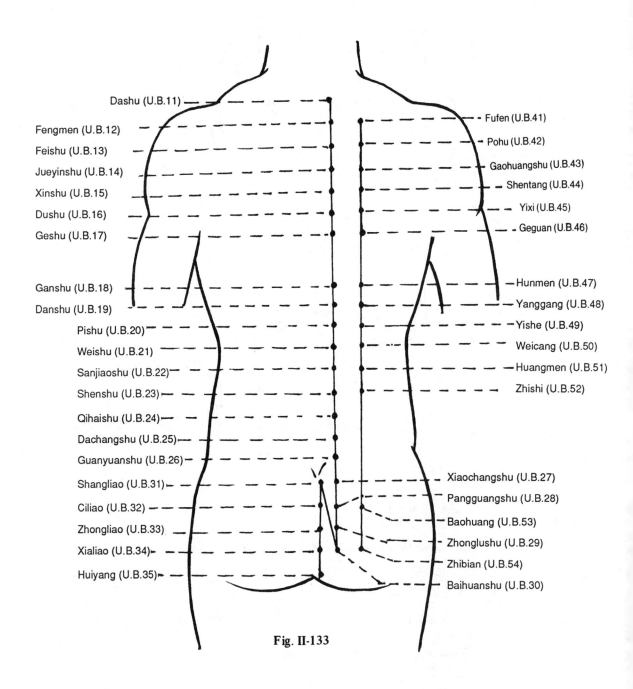

Fig. II-133

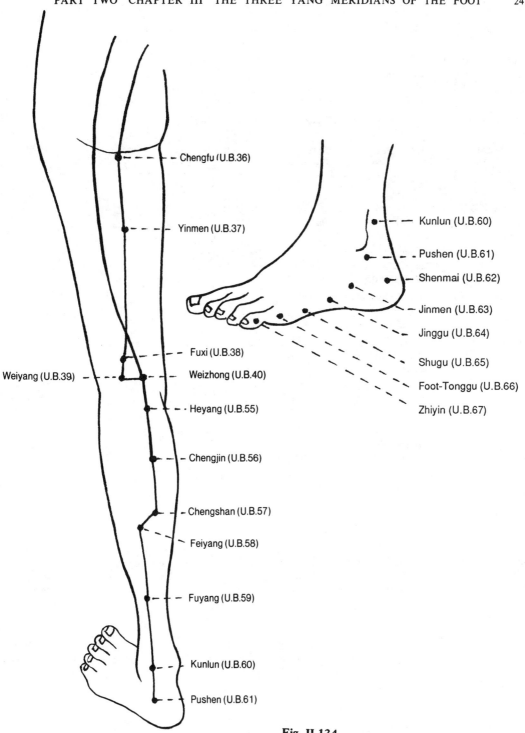

- Chengfu (U.B.36)
- Yinmen (U.B.37)
- Kunlun (U.B.60)
- Pushen (U.B.61)
- Shenmai (U.B.62)
- Jinmen (U.B.63)
- Jinggu (U.B.64)
- Shugu (U.B.65)
- Foot-Tonggu (U.B.66)
- Zhiyin (U.B.67)
- Fuxi (U.B.38)
- Weizhong (U.B.40)
- Weiyang (U.B.39)
- Heyang (U.B.55)
- Chengjin (U.B.56)
- Chengshan (U.B.57)
- Feiyang (U.B.58)
- Fuyang (U.B.59)
- Kunlun (U.B.60)
- Pushen (U.B.61)

Fig. II-134

Wuchu U.B.5	Directly above Quchai (U.B.4), 1 cun within the hairline	Headache, blurring of vision, epilepsy	
Chengguang U.B.6	1.5 cun posterior to Wuchu (U.B.5)	Nasal obstruction and running nose	
Tongtian U.B.7	1.5 cun posterior to Chengguang (U.B.6)	Headache, dizziness	
Luoque U.B.8	1.5 cun posterior to Tongtian (U.B.7)	Headache, dizziness	
Yuzhen U.B.9	On the lateral side of the superior border of the external occipital protuberance, above Tianzhu (U.B.10)	Headache, dizziness	Diseases of the head and neck area, etc.
Tianzhu U.B.10	At the level of Yamen (Du 15) on the lateral side of m. trapezius	Occipital headache, neck sprain	
Dashu U.B.11	1.5 cun lateral to the lower border of the spinous process of the 1st thoracic vertebra	Cough, asthma, common cold	
Fengmen U.B.12	1.5 cun lateral to the lower border of the spinous process of the 2nd thoracic vertebra	Cough, asthma, common cold	
Feishu U.B.13	1.5 cun lateral to the lower border of the spinous process of the 3rd thoracic vertebra	Cough, asthma, pneumonia	
Jueyinshu U.B.14	1.5 cun lateral to the lower border of the spinous process of the 4th thoracic vertebra	Angina pectoris, arrhythmia	
Xinshu U.B.15	1.5 cun lateral to the lower border of the spinous process of the 5th thoracic vertebra	Angina pectoris, arrhythmia	
Dushu U.B.16	1.5 cun lateral to the lower border of the spinous process of the 6th thoracic vertebra	Angina pectoris, cardiac pain, fever, aversion to cold	
Geshu U.B.17	1.5 cun lateral to the lower border of the spinous process of the 7th thoracic vertebra	Hemorrhagia, anemia	
Ganshu U.B.18	1.5 cun lateral to the lower border of the spinous process of the 9th thoracic vertebra	Diseases associated with the liver and gall bladder; hypochondriac pain	Disorders of the back or the lower back; diseases associated with the corresponding internal zangfu organs and their related sense organs and tissues
Danshu U.B.19	1.5 cun lateral to the lower border of the spinous process of the 10th thoracic vertebra	Diseases of the liver and gall bladder, hypochondriac pain	

Pishu U.B.20	1.5 cun lateral to the lower border of the spinous process of the 11th thoracic vertebra	Gastric disorders, indigestion	
Weishu U.B.21	1.5 cun lateral to the lower border of the spinous process of the 12th thoracic vertebra	Gastric disorders, indigestion	
Sanjiaoshu U.B.22	1.5 cun lateral to the lower border of the spinous process of the 1st lumbar vertebra	Diarrhea, enuresis	
Shenshu U.B.23	1.5 cun lateral to the lower border of the spinous process of the 2nd lumbar vertebra	Impotence, irregular menstruation, shortness of breath	
Qihaishu U.B.24	1.5 cun lateral to the lower border of the spinous process of the 3rd lumbar vertebra	Lumbago	
Dachangshu U.B.25	1.5 cun lateral to the lower border of the spinous process of the 4th lumbar vertebra	Acute or chronic pain in the abdominal area	
Guanyuanshu U.B.26	1.5 cun lateral to the lower border of the spinous process of the 5th lumbar vertebra	Motor impairment of the lumbar muscles, chronic pelvic inflammation	Diseases of the reproductive system, disorders of the posterior aspect of the lower extremities
Xiaochangshu U.B.27	1.5 cun lateral to the Du Meridian, at the level of the 1st posterior sacral foramen	Lower back pain, yellow and scanty urine	
Pangguangshu U.B.28	1.5 cun lateral to the Du Meridian, at the level of the 2nd posterior sacral foramen	Disorders related to the urinary bladder, pain in the lumbar or sacral region	
Zhonglüshu U.B.29	1.5 cun lateral to the Du Meridian, at the level of the 3rd posterior sacral foramen	Pain in the lumbosacral region	
Baihuanshu U.B.30	1.5 cun lateral to the Du Meridian, at the level of the 4th posterior sacral foramen	Chronic pelvic inflammation, prolapse of the rectum	
Shangliao U.B.31	In the centre of the 1st posterior sacral foramen	Pain of the lower back and knee, irregular menstruation, dysmenorrhea	
Ciliao U.B.32	In the centre of the 2nd posterior sacral foramen	Pain of the lower back and the lumbosacral region, leukorrhea, chronic pelvic inflammation	
Zhongliao U.B.33	In the centre of the 3rd posterior sacral foramen	Pain of the lower back and knee and the lumbosacral region; leukorrhea.	
Xialiao U.B.34	In the centre of the 4th posterior sacral foramen	Pain of the lumbosacral region; leukorrhea	
Huiyang U.B.35	0.5 cun lateral to the tip of the coccyx	Dampness or itching of the external genitalia	
Chengfu U.B.36	In the depression in the centre of the transverse gluteal fold	Sciatica	Diseases of the lower back and the posterior

			aspect of the lower extremities
Yinmen U.B.37	6 cun below Chengfu (U.B.36)	Acute disorders of the lower back, paralysis of the lower extremities	
Fuxi U.B.38	1 cun above Weiyang (U.B.39)	Spasm of the tendons of the legs	
Weiyang U.B.39	On the lateral end of the popliteal transverse crease. At the medial border of the tendon of m. biceps femoris	Rhinitis, urocystitis	
Weizhong U.B.40	Midpoint of the transverse crease of the popliteal fossa	Acute pain in the lower back and the lower extremities	
Fufen U.B.41	3 cun lateral to the lower border of the spinous process of the 2nd thoracic vertebra	Neck rigidity and pain	
Pohu U.B.42	3 cun lateral to the lower border of the spinous process of the 3rd thoracic vertebra	Pain in the shoulder and back, asthma	
Gaohuang U.B.43	3 cun lateral to the lower border of the spinous process of the 4th thoracic vertebra	Cough, asthma, afternoon fever	Disorders of the spleen, stomach, liver and the gall bladder; diseases of the lower back region
Shentang U.B.44	3 cun lateral to the lower border of the spinous process of the 5th thoracic vertebra	Pain of the shoulder or back; heavy chest	
Yixi U.B.45	3 cun lateral to the lower border of the spinous process of the 6th thoracic vertebra	Pain of the shoulder and back, asthma	
Geguan U.B.46	3 cun lateral to the lower border of the spinous process of the 7th thoracic vertebra	Pain of the back, hiccup	
Hunmen U.B.47	3 cun lateral to the lower border of the spinous process of the 9th thoracic vertebra	Pain of the lower back, dizziness	
Yanggang U.B.48	3 cun lateral to the lower border of the spinous process of the 10th thoracic vertebra	Diarrhea, borborygmus	
Yishe U.B.49	3 cun lateral to the lower border of the spinous process of the 11th thoracic vertebra	Pain of the back, diarrhea	
Weichang U.B.50	3 cun lateral to the lower border of the spinous process of the 12th thoracic vertebra	Pain of the lower back, abdominal distention due to spleen weakness	
Huangmen U.B.51	3 cun lateral to the lower border of the spinous process of the 1st lumbar vertebra	Cardiac pain, epigastric pain	Disorders of the urinary and reproductive systems, and of the lower back

Zhishi U.B.52	3 cun lateral to the lower border of the spinous process of the 2nd lumbar vertebra	Impotence, seminal emission, irregular menstruation	
Baohuang U.B.53	3 cun lateral to Du Meridian, at the level of the 2nd posterior sacral foramen	Diseases of the lumbar and sacral area	
Zhibian U.B.54	3 cun lateral to the hiatus of the sacrum, at the level of Yaoshu (Du.2)	Diseases of the lower back	
Heyang U.B.55	2 cun directly below Weizhong (U.B.40)	Pain in the back or the lower back, radiating to the abdominal region	Disorders of the back, lower back and posterior aspect of the lower extremities
Chengjin U.B.56	Midpoint of the line joining Heyang (U.B.55) and Chengshan (U.B.57)	Lumbago, pain in the heel	
Chengshan U.B.57	At the upper border of the lambdoidal suture formed by the belly of the m. gastrocnemius	Spasm of the gastrocnemius	
Feiyang U.B.58	7 cun above the external malleolus, lateral and inferior to Chengshan (U.B.57)	Pain of the lower back and the lower extremities, muscular atrophy of the lower limbs	
Fuyang U.B.59	3 cun directly above Kunlun (U.B.60)	Pain of the neck and headache	
Kunlun U.B.60	Midway between the external malleolus and the tendo calcaneus	Headache, pain in the neck	
Pushen U.B.61	Directly below Kunlun (U.B.60), in the depression of the calcaneum	Pain of the heel	
Shenmai U.B.62	In the depression directly below the tip of the external malleolus	Pain in the neck, headache, epilepsy	Mental disorders, disorders of the head and neck, local problems
Jinmen U.B.63	1 cun inferoanterior to Shenmai (U.B.62)	Epilepsy, mental disorders	
Jinggu U.B.64	In the depression anterior and inferior to the tuberosity of the 5th metatarsal bone	Headache, neck rigidity	
Shugu U.B.65	Posterior and inferior to the head of the 5th metatarsal bone	Severe pain in the lower back	
Foot-Tonggu U.B.66	In the depression anteroinferior to the 5th metatarsophalangeal joint	Headache, blurring of vision, epistaxis	
Zhiyin U.B.67	On the lateral side of the small toe, about 0.1 cun posterior to the corner of the nail	Malposition of the fetus, difficult labour	

Section 3   THE GALL BLADDER MERIDIAN OF FOOT-SHAOYANG

I. The Meridian

General Indications:

The points from this meridian are indicated in one-sided headache, deafness, tinnitus and diseases of the liver and gall bladder as well as diseases along the lateral aspects of the chest, hypochondriac region and the lateral aspect of the lower extremities.

Course of the Meridian:

(1) The Gall Bladder Meridian of Foot-Shaoyang originates from the outer canthus (Tongziliao, G.B.1), (2) ascends to the corner of the forehead (Hanyan, G.B.4), (3) then curves downwards to the retroauricular region (Fengchi, G.B.20) (4) and runs along the side of the neck in front of the Sanjiao Meridian of Hand-Shaoyang to the shoulder, entering Dazhui (Du 14). Turning back, it passes behind the Sanjiao Meridian of Hand-Shaoyang (5) and descends to the supraclavicular fossa.

The Retroauricular Branch:

(6) It arrives from the retroauricular region and enters the ear. (7) It emerges and passes the preauricular region, (8) going to the posterior aspect of the outer canthus.

The Outer Canthus Branch:

(9) It arises from the outer canthus, (10) descends to Daying (St.5), (11) and meets the Sanjiao Meridian of Hand-Shaoyang in the infraorbital region. (12) Then, passing through Jiache (St.6), (13) it descends to the neck and enters the supraclavicular fossa where it joins the main course of the meridian. (14) From there it descends into the chest, passes through the diaphragm, (15) connects with the liver, (16) and enters its pertaining organ, the Gall Bladder. (17) Then it runs inside the hypochondriac region, and (18) emerges from the lateral side of the lower abdomen, near the femoral artery at the inguinal region. (19) From there it runs superficially along the margin of pubic hair (20) and goes transversely to enter the hip-joint (Huantiao, G.B.30).

The Straight Portion of the Meridian from the Supraclavicular Fossa:

(21) It runs downwards from the supraclavicular fossa, (22) passes in front of the axilla, (23) along the lateral aspect of the chest (24) and through the free ends of the floating ribs (25) to the hip region, meeting the previous branch there. (26) Then it descends along the lateral aspect of the thigh (27) to the lateral aspect of the knee. (28) It continues to descend along the anterior aspect of the fibula, (29) to Xuanzhong (G.B.39), (30) reaches the anterior aspect of the external malleolus and follows the dorsum of the foot (31) to the lateral side of the tip of the 4th toe (Foot-Qiaoyin, G.B.44).

The Branch from the Dorsum of the Foot:

(32) From Foot-Lingqi (G.B.41) on the dorsum of the foot, it runs between the 1st and 2nd metatarsal bones to the distal portion of the great toe and terminates at Daduan (Liv.1), linking with the Liver Meridian of Foot-Jueyin (Fig. II-135).

Analytical Display of the Course of the Meridian

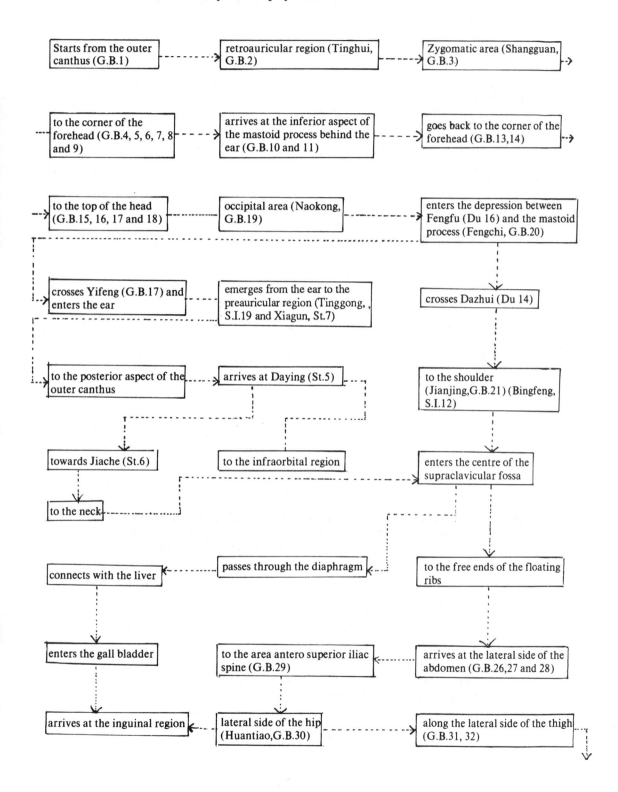

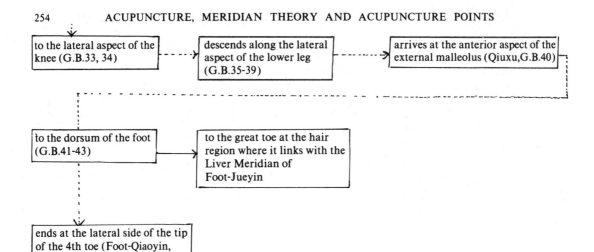

Related Zangfu Organs:

The Gall Bladder Meridian of Foot-Shaoyang pertains to the gall bladder and connects with the liver.

Coalescent Points of the Meridian:

Touwei (St.8), Xiaguan (St.7), Renying (St.9), Shangliao (U.B.31), Zhongliao (U.B.33), Xialiao (U.B.34), Tinggong (S.I.19), Bingfeng (S.I.12), Yifeng (S.J.17), Jiaosun (S.J.20), Ear-Heliao (S.J.22), Dazhui (Du 14), Zhangmen (Liv.13), Tianchi (P.1) and Tianrong (S.J.17).

II. The Points

There are 44 points from this meridian on either side of the body. Fifteen are located on the lateral aspect of the lower limb, the remaining 22 being located on the hip, the hypochondriac region or the lateral aspect of the head. The first point is Tongziliao (G.B.1) and the last one is Foot-Qiaoyin (G.B.44).

Point Names	Pinyin	Codes	Point Names	Pinyin	Codes
瞳子髎	Tongziliao	G.B.1	浮白	Fubai	G.B.10
听会	Tinghui	G.B.2	头窍阴	Head-Qiaoyin	G.B.11
上关	Shangguan	G.B.3	完骨	Head-Wangu	G.B.12
颌厌	Hanyan	G.B.4	本神	Benshen	G.B.13
悬颅	Xuanlu	G.B.5	阳白	Yangbai	G.B.14
悬厘	Xuanli	G.B.6	头临泣	Head-Linqi	G.B.15
曲鬓	Qubin	G.B.7	目窗	Muchuang	G.B.16
率谷	Shuaigu	G.B.8	正营	Zhengying	G.B.17
天冲	Tianchong	G.B.9	承灵	Chengling	G.B.18

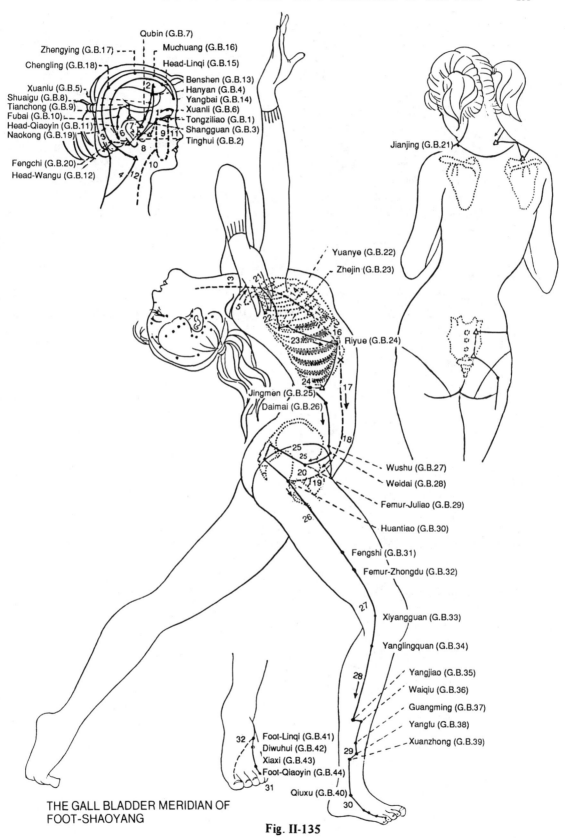

Qubin (G.B.7)
Zhengying (G.B.17)
Muchuang (G.B.16)
Chengling (G.B.18)
Head-Linqi (G.B.15)
Benshen (G.B.13)
Xuanlu (G.B.5)
Hanyan (G.B.4)
Shuaigu (G.B.8)
Yangbai (G.B.14)
Tianchong (G.B.9)
Xuanli (G.B.6)
Fubai (G.B.10)
Tongziliao (G.B.1)
Head-Qiaoyin (G.B.11)
Shangguan (G.B.3)
Naokong (G.B.19)
Tinghui (G.B.2)
Fengchi (G.B.20)
Head-Wangu (G.B.12)

Jianjing (G.B.21)

Yuanye (G.B.22)
Zhejin (G.B.23)
Riyue (G.B.24)
Jingmen (G.B.25)
Daimai (G.B.26)
Wushu (G.B.27)
Weidai (G.B.28)
Femur-Juliao (G.B.29)
Huantiao (G.B.30)
Fengshi (G.B.31)
Femur-Zhongdu (G.B.32)
Xiyangguan (G.B.33)
Yanglingquan (G.B.34)
Yangjiao (G.B.35)
Waiqiu (G.B.36)
Guangming (G.B.37)
Yangfu (G.B.38)
Xuanzhong (G.B.39)
Foot-Linqi (G.B.41)
Diwuhui (G.B.42)
Xiaxi (G.B.43)
Foot-Qiaoyin (G.B.44)
Qiuxu (G.B.40)

THE GALL BLADDER MERIDIAN OF
FOOT-SHAOYANG

Fig. II-135

脑空	Naokong	G.B.19		中渎	Zhongdu	G.B.32
风池	Fengchi	G.B.20		膝阳关	Xiyangguan	G.B.33
肩井	Jianjing	G.B.21		阳陵泉	Yanglingquan	G.B.34
渊液	Yuanye	G.B.22		阳交	Yangjiao	G.B.35
辄筋	Zhejin	G.B.23		外丘	Waiqiu	G.B.36
日月	Riyue	G.B.24		光明	Guangming	G.B.37
京门	Jingmen	G.B.25		阳辅	Yangfu	G.B.38
带脉	Daimai	G.B.26		悬钟	Xuanzhong	G.B.39
五枢	Wushu	G.B.27		丘墟	Qiuxu	G.B.40
维道	Weidao	G.B.28		足临泣	Foot-Linqi	G.B.41
居髎	Femur-Juliao	G.B.29		地五会	Diwuhui	G.B.42
环跳	Huantiao	G.B.30		侠溪	Xiaxi	G.B.43
风市	Fengshi	G.B.31		足窍阴	Foot-Qiaoyin	G.B.44

TONGZILIAO (G.B.1) 瞳子髎 (PUPIL CREVICE)

"Tongzi" (瞳子) means the pupil, but here refers to the eye in general. "Liao" (髎) means a bony cleft. The point is at the side of the eye, hence the name Tongziliao (Pupil Crevice).

Location:

0.5 cun lateral to the outer canthus (Fig. II-136).

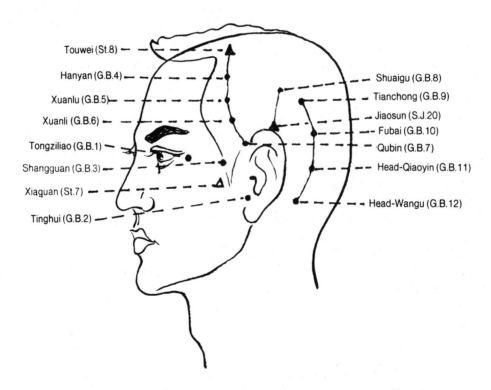

Fig. II-136

Indications:
Headache, eye diseases.
Method:
Puncture horizontally about 0.3-0.5 cun deep.

*TINGHUI (G.B.2) 听会 (HEARING CONFLUENCE)

"Ting" (听) means to hear, to listen to. "Hui" (会) means to gather together or convergence. The point is in front of the ear which dominates the hearing function. Needling the point can treat deafness, relieve obstructive sensations inside the ear and promote the auditory function, as though to converge sound. Hence the name, Tinghui (Hearing Convergence).

Location:

At the level of the intertragic notch, in the depression at the posterior border of the condyloid process of the mandible when the mouth is open. The point is sometimes also called "Houguan," the Posterior Hinge (后关) in contrast to Shangguan (G.B.3), Upper Hinge (上关) and Xiaguan (St.7), Lower Hinge (下关) (Fig. III-137).

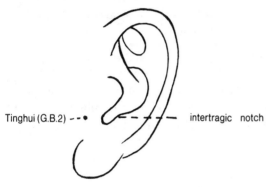

Tinghui (G.B.2) -- •   intertragic notch

Fig. II-137

Indications:
Tinnitus, otitis media, toothache, facial paralysis, parotitis.
Clinical Application:
The point has the effect to eliminate wind, remove obstructions from the ear and promote the auditory function.
Combinations:
With Waiguan (S.J.5), Hand-Zhongzhu (S.J.3) and Yifeng (S.J.17) for treating deafness, tinnitus, auditory hallucination;
With Xiaguan (St.7) and Shangguan (G.B.3) for arthritis of the mandibular joint.
Method:
Puncture perpendicularly about 1-1.5 cun deep with the mouth open.
Needling Sensations:
Distention and pain, radiating to the inside of the ear.

SHANGGUAN (G.B.3) 上关 (UPPER HINGE)

"Shang" (上) means upper. "Guan" (关), meaning hinge, refers to the mandibular joint. The point is above Xiaguan (St.7), Lower Hinge. Hence the name Shangguan (Upper Hinge).
Location:

Notes: The method to locate the points Hanyan (G.B.4), Xuanlu (G.B.5), Xuanli (G.B.6) and Qubin (G.B.7): Locate Jiaosun (S.J.20) first, then 1 finger-breadth anterior to it, find Qubin (G.B.7). Draw a line along the temporal hairline from Touwei (St.8) to Qubin (G.B.7), then divide the line into four equal parts. The points are located on the junctions of each part, from the tip down Hanyan (G.B.4), Xuanlu (G.B.5), Xuanli (G.B.6) and Qubin (G.B.7).

On the upper border of the zygomatic arch, directly above Xiaguan (St.7) (Fig. II-136).

Indications:
Headache, upper toothache, tinnitus and deviation of the mouth and eye.
Method:
Puncture perpendicularly about 0.5-1 cun deep.
Indications:
Headache, especially one-sided headache, toothache and dizziness.
Method:
Puncture perpendicularly about 0.5-1 cun deep.

HANYAN (G.B.4) 頷厭 (UNPLEASANT NODDING; JAW STRETCHING)

"Han" (頷) refers to the jaw. "Yan" (厭) means to stretch. The point is located below Touwei (St.8) and above the musculus temporalis. When the mandibular joint moves, the muscle is stretched, hence the name Hanyan (Jaw Stretching). "Han" (頷) can sometimes also mean to be nodding. "Yan" (厭) can mean unpleasant. The point has the effect to treat neck rigidity, pain, sprain of the neck and those problems creating difficulty in moving the head. Hence the alternative of the explanation of the name of the point Hanyan (Unpleasant Nodding).

Location:
See above note (Fig. II-136).
Indications & Method:
See above note.

XUANLU (G.B.5) 懸顱 (SKULL SUSPENSION)

"Xuan" (懸) means to suspend. "Lu" (顱) means the skull. The point is at the curving portion of the temporal hairline, below Hanyan (G.B.4) as though suspended on each side of the skull. Hence the name Xuanlu (Skull Suspension)

Location:
See above note (Fig. II-136).
Indications & Method:
See above note.

XUANLI (G.B.6) 懸厘 (CORRECT SUSPENSION)

"Xuan" (懸) means suspending. "Li" (厘) means correct or straight. The point is at the lateral side of the head and is indicated in headache, dizziness, blurring of vision, i.e. to restore the normal functions of the head and its organs. Hence the name Xuanli (Correct Suspension).

Location:
See above note (Fig. II-136).
Indications & Method:
See above note.

QUBIN (G.B.7) 曲鬢 (TURNING ON THE TEMPLE)

"Qu" (曲) means crooked or turning. "Bin" (鬢) refers to the temporal hairline.

The meridian turns upwards at this point towards Shuaigu (G.B.8), making a crooked line, hence the name Qubin (Turning On the Temple).

Location:

See above note (Fig.II-136).

Indications & Method:

See above note.

*SHUAIGU (G.B.8) 率谷 **(FOLLOWING VALLEY)**

"Shuai" (率) means to follow something. "Gu" (谷), meaning valley, refers to a depression. When locating the point, the operater should find the ear apex first, then slide a finger directly upwards to the depression 1.5 cun within the hairline. Hence the name Shuaigu (Following Valley).

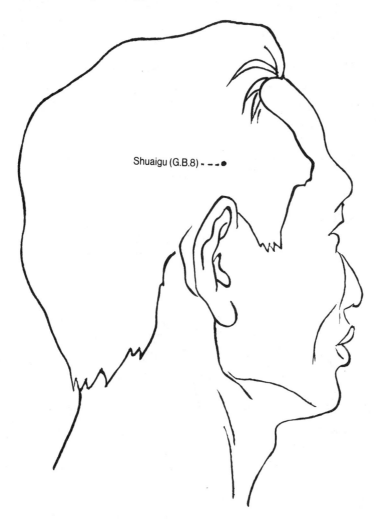

Shuaigu (G.B.8) - - - ●

Fig. II-138

Location:

Superior to the apex of the auricle, in the depression 1.5 cun within the hairline (Fig. II-138).

Indications:

One-sided headache, redness and pain of the eye, infantile convulsion.

Clinical Application:

The point has the effect to eliminate wind and remove obstructions, restore the consciousness, ease pain and dispel heat.

Combinations:

With Touwei (St.8) and Lieque (Lu.7) for treating one-sided headache and otogenic dizziness.

Method:

Puncture 0.5-0.8 cun deep horizontally along the skin.

Needling Sensations:

Distention and heaviness in the local area.

TIANCHONG (G.B.9) 天 冲 (CELESTIAL PASSAGE)

"Tian" (天) means the heaven, referring to Baihui (Du 20), which is on the vertex closest to the heaven. "Chong" (冲) means a passage. The point acts as a passage to Baihui (Du 20), hence the name Tianchong (Celestial Passage).

Location:

0.5 cun superoposterior to Shuaigu (G.B.8) on an extended vertical line drawn from the posterior border of the root of the auricle (Fig. II-139).

Indications:

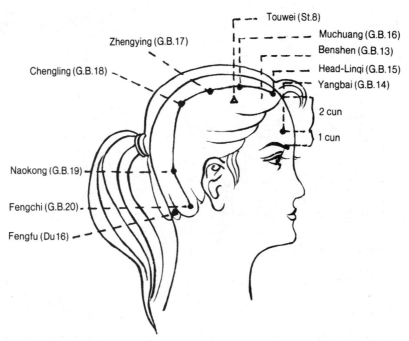

Fig. II-139

Headache, palpitation, blurring of vision and dizziness.

Clinical Application:

It is a coalescent point of the Gall Bladder Meridian of Foot-Shaoyang and the Urinary Bladder Meridian of Foot-Taiyang. It has the effect to treat the disorders of the two meridians on the head.

Combinations:

With Hegu (L.I.4) for headache,

With Waiguan (S.J.5) and Yifeng (S.J.17) for one-sided headache and insomnia.

Method:

Puncture about 0.5-0.8 cun deep along the skin.

Needling Sensations:

Pain and distention around the local area.

FUBAI (G.B.10) 浮白 (FLOATING WHITE)

"Fu" (浮) means floating, referring to the upward direction of the qi of the meridian. "Bai" (白), meaning white, refers to both the point Baihui (Du 20) and the floating of qi. The qi of the meridian comes from Tianchong (G.B.9) and floats upwards to Baihui (Du 20) on the vertex, hence the name (Floating White).

Location:

Posterior to the ear, 1 cun within the hair line at the level of the upper end of the auricle (Fig. II-139).

Indications:

Headache, tinnitus, and deafness.

Clinical Application:

It is the coalescent point of the Gall Bladder Meridian of the Foot-Shaoyang and the Urinary Bladder Meridian of Foot-Taiyang, and it has the effect to treat both Shaoyang headache and Taiyang headache.

Method:

Puncture horizontally 0.5-0.8 cun deep.

HEAD-QIAOYIN (G.B.11) 头窍阴 (HEAD-YIN-ORIFICE)

"Qiao" (窍) means an orifice. "Yin" (阴) refers to the Yin aspect. "Head" is added to the name of this point in order to differentiate it from Foot-Qiaoyin (G.B.44). It is posterior to the auricular orifice, on the Yin aspect of the head, hence the name Head-Qiaoyin (Head-Yin-Orifice).

Location:

In the depression on the root of the mastoid process (Fig. II-139).

Indications:

Headache, deafness, dizziness.

Method:

Puncture horizontally 0.5-0.8 cun deep.

HEAD-WANGU (G.B.12) 完骨 (INTACT BONE)

"Wangu" (完骨) means the mastoid process. In ancient times the mastoid process was called the intact bone. The point is located just below it. "Head" here is added to the name of this point in order to differentiate it from Hand-Wangu (S.I.4). Hence the name Head-Wangu (Intact Bone).

Location:

In the depression posterior and inferior to the mastoid process. (Fig. II-139).

Indications:

Headache, mastoid pain, swelling of the cheek and facial paralysis.

Method:

Puncture horizontally 0.5-0.8 cun deep.

BENSHEN (G.B.13) 本 神 (ORIGIN OF THE SPIRIT)

"Ben" (本) means the origin. "Shen" (神) means spirit or mind. The brain is considered to be the origin of a man, and the house of the spirit. The point is on the forehead, 3 cun lateral to Shenting (Du 24), above the brain, hence the name Benshen (Origin of the Spirit).

Location:

0.5 cun within the anterior hairline and 3 cun lateral to the anteroposterior midline of the head (Fig. II-139).

Indications:

Headache, blurring of vision, stiffness and pain of the neck.

Method:

Puncture horizontally 0.3-0.5 cun.

*YANGBAI (G.B.14) 阳 白 (YANG WHITE)

"Yang" (阳) means the Yang aspect, opposite to the Yin one. "Bai" (白) means white or brightening. The point is from the Gall Bladder Meridian of Foot-Shaoyang and one of the coalescent points with Yangwei Meridian. It has the effect to brighten the eye and is located on the forehead, where it is exposed to the sunlight. Hence the name Yangbai (Yang White).

Location:

On the forehead, 1 cun above the midpoint of the eyebrow (Fig. II-139).

Indications:

Headache, pain of the eye, blurring of vision, twitching of the eyelids.

Clinical Application:

The point has the effect to eliminate wind, brighten the eye, ease pain and relieve spasm.

Combinations:

With Jiache (St.6), Dicang (St.4) and Hegu (L.I.4) for facial paralysis,

With Taiyang (Extra) for headache.

Method:

Puncture horizontally about 0.3-0.5 cun deep along the skin with the needle directed downwards. The needle can be inserted as far as 2 cun down when treating facial paralysis.

Needling Sensations:

The needling reaction may spread down to the eyelids.

HEAD-LINQI (G.B.15) 头临泣 (TEAR-CONTROLLING)

"Lin" (临) means to control. "Qi" (泣) means tears. The point is on the forehead directly above the pupil, 0.5 cun within the hairline. It is particularly effective for treating and controlling excessive lacrimation and eye disorders, hence the name Head-Linqi (Tear-Controlling).

Location:

0.5 cun with the anterior hairline, midway between the anteroposterior midline of the head and Touwei (St.8) (Fig. II-139).

Indications:

Headache, scleritis, corneal opacity, excessive lacrimation and nasal obstruction.

Method:

Puncture horizontally 0.3-0.5 cun deep.

MUCHUANG (G.B.16) 目 窗 (EYE WINDOW)

"Mu" (目) means the eye. "Chuang" (窗) means window. The qi of the meridian from this point connects with the eye. It is indicated in eye problems, and brightens the eye, as though by opening the window of a house and letting in the light. Hence the name Muchuang (Eye Window).

Location:

1.5 cun posterior to Head-Linqi (G.B.15) and 2.2 cun lateral to the anteroposterior midline of the head (Fig. II-139).

Indications:

Headache, glaucoma, blindness, redness and pain of the eye.

Method:

Puncture horizontally about 0.3-0.5 cun deep.

ZHENGYING (G.B.17) 正 营 (RIGHT MEETING)

"Zheng" (正) means right or correct. "Ying" (营) here means to meet together. The point is a crossing point of the Gall Bladder Meridian of Foot-Shaoyang and Yangwei Meridian, hence the name Zhengying (Right Meeting).

Location:

1.5 cun posterior to Muchuang (G.B.16) and 2.2 cun lateral to the anterior and posterior midline of the head (Fig. II-139).

Indications:

One-sided headache, redness and pain of the eye, toothache.

Method:

Puncture horizontally 0.3-0.5 cun deep.

CHENGLING (G.B.18) 承 灵 (SPIRIT SUPPORT)

"Cheng" (承) means to hold or support. "Ling" (灵) means spirit. The point is on the top of the head, lateral to Tongtian (U.B.7). The head is the house of the spirit, hence the name Chengling (Spirit Support).

Location:

Note: The distance between each of the above 3 points, Muchuang (G.B.16), Zhengying (G.B.17) and Chengling (G.B.18) is about 1.5 cun. They are all indicated in head diseases and disorders of the eye.

1.5 cun posterior to Zhengying (G.B.17) and 2.2 cun lateral to the anterior and posterior midline (Fig. II-139).

Indications:

Headache, redness and pain of the eye, nasal obstruction.

Method:

Puncture horizontally 0.3-0.5 cun deep.

NAOKONG (G.B.19) 脑 空 (BRAIN DEPRESSION)

"Nao" (脑) means brain or head. "Kong" (空), meaning a hole, refers to a depression. The point is located lateral to Naohu (Du 17) in a depression on the occiput, hence the name Naokong (Brain Depression).

Location:

1.5 cun directly above Fengchi (G.B.20), midway between the upper border of the mastoid process and the external occipital protuberance (Fig. II-139).

Indications:

Headache, blurring of vision and stiffness of the neck.

Method:

Puncture 0.3-0.5 cun deep horizontally.

*FENGCHI (G.B.20) 风 池 (WIND POND)

"Feng" (风) means wind. "Chi" (池) means a pond, but here refers to a depression. It is the coalescent point of this meridian and Yangwei Meridian, is considered to be a place where pathogenic wind can lodge and is indicated in wind problems, such as invasion of wind cold, hemiplegia and wind stroke. Hence the name Fengchi (Wind Pond).

Location:

In the depression at the level of Fengfu (Du 16), between the upper portion of m. sternocleidomastoideus and m. trepzius (Fig. II-140).

Indications:

Pain and stiffness of the neck, headache, redness and pain of the eye, myopia, blurring of vision, common cold, nasal obstruction and hypertension.

Clinical Application:

It is the coalescent point of the Gall Bladder Meridian of Foot-Shaoyang and the Yangwei Meridian. It has the effect to remove obstruction from the meridian, promote the collaterals, regulate qi, activate blood, eliminate the wind and heat, restore consciousness, brighten the eye and promote the hearing function.

Combinations:

With Dazhui (Du 14), Hegu (L.I.4), Waiguan (S.J.5) and Taiyang (Extra) for treating common cold with fever and headache,

With Quchi (L.I.11), Zusanli (St.36), Taichong (Liv.3) and Neiguan (P.6) for hypertension.

Method:

Puncture obliquely with the needle directed towards the top of the nose, inserting about 0.8-1.2 cun deep, or puncture horizontally towards Fengfu (Du 16).

Needling Sensations:

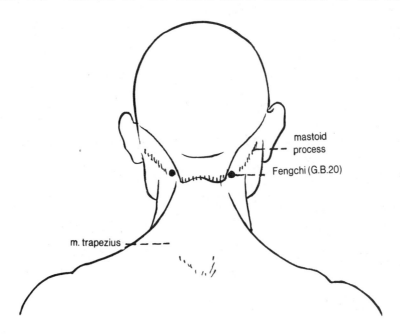

Fig. II-140

Needling reactions may radiate all over the head.

*JIANJING (G.B.21) 肩 井   (SHOULDER WELL)

"Jian" (肩) means the shoulder or shoulder area. "Jing" (井) means a well, referring to a deep depression. The point is located on the shoulder; underneath it is the chest cavity, which is hollow and deep, like a well, hence the name Jianjing (Shoulder Well).

Location:

Midway along a line joining the 7th cervical vertebra and the acromion (Fig. II-141-143). Alternatively the operator may stand behind the seated patient, placing his hand on the shoulder, with the transverse crease of the wrist pressing on the lower border of the scapular spine. The thumb is placed on the lower border of the spinous process of the 7th cervical vertebra, while the four fingers closed together, rest on the upper portion of the shoulder with the middle finger slightly curved, the point being located where the finger tip touches.

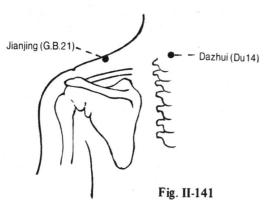

Fig. II-141

Indications:

Hypertension, pain of the shoulder and back, apoplexy, neck sprain, headache, pain of the neck, mastitis, uterine bleeding and thyroidism.

Clinical Application:

It is the coalescent point of the Gall Bladder Meridian of Foot-Shaoyang, the Stomach Meridian of Foot-Yangming and Yangwei Meridian. It has the effect to remove obstructions from the meridians, activate the collaterals, resolve sputum, restore consciousness, eliminate heat and ease pain.

Combinations:

With Jianyu (L.I.15), Jianliao (S.J.14) and Quchi (L.I.11) for pain of the shoulder and the upper arm,

With Dazhui (Du 14), Quchi (L.I.11) and Hegu (L.I.4) for fever.

Method:

Puncture 0.5-0.8 cun perpendicularly. Deep insertion is contraindicated. For safety, stretch the skin around the point and puncture either posteriorly or anteriorly about 1 cun deep.

Needling Sensations:

Soreness and distention, radiating around the shoulder and back.

YUANYE (G.B.22) 渊 液 (ARMPIT DEPRESSION)

"Yuan" (渊) refers to a depression. "Ye" (液) is the same as (腋) meaning armpit. It is located in the depression under the armpit, hence the name Yuanye (Armpit

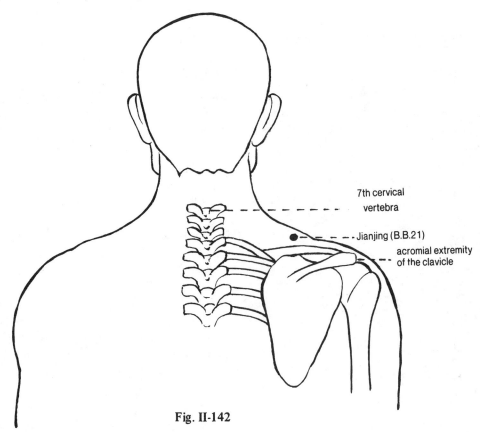

Fig. II-142

Depression).

Location:

On the midaxillary line, 3 cun below the axilla at the level of the 4th intercostal space (Fig.II-144).

Indications:

Fullness of the chest, pain of the arms with difficulty in lifting the arm, and hypochondriac pain.

Method:

Puncture obliquely about 0.5-0.8 cun deep.

ZHEJIN (G.B.23) 辄筋 (HOLDING TENDONS)

"Zhe" (辄) means the sides or border of a cart. "Jin" (筋) means tendons. The point is located at the hypochondriac region and needling it may help to strengthen the tendons, hence the name Zhejin (Holding Tendons).

Location:

One cun anterior to Yuanye (G.B.22), in the 4th intercostal space (Fig. II-144).

Indications:

Fullness of the chest, hypochondriac pain.

Method:

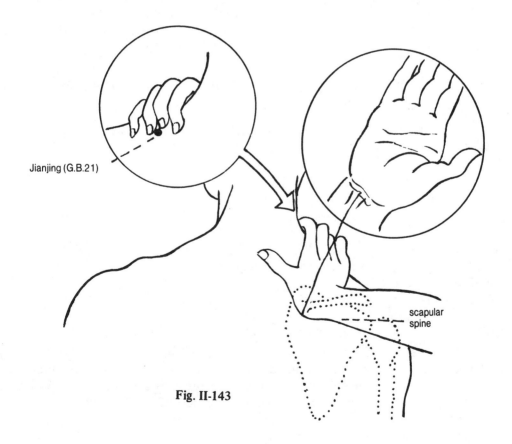

Jianjing (G.B.21)

scapular spine

Fig. II-143

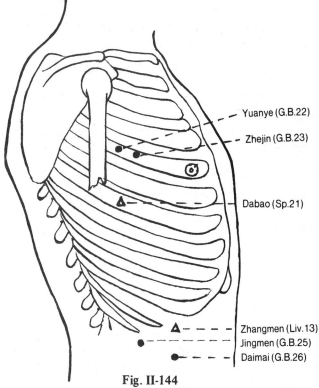

Yuanye (G.B.22)

Zhejin (G.B.23)

Dabao (Sp.21)

Zhangmen (Liv.13)
Jingmen (G.B.25)
Daimai (G.B.26)

Fig. II-144

Puncture horizontally about 0.5-0.8 cun deep.

*RIYUE (G.B.24) 日 月 "MU" (SUN AND MOON)

"Ri" (日) means the sun. "Yue" (月) means the moon. It is the Front-Mu point of the Gall Bladder and is indicated in disorders related to the gall bladder. The gall bladder is the organ dominating decision, and in making a decision one should be clear and distinct. The Chinese character for "clear" and "distinct" is written as (明) "ming," a combination of the characters for sun and moon, hence the name Riyue (Sun & Moon).

Location:

Inferior to the nipple in the 7th intercostal space, and one rib below Qimen (Liv.14) (Fig. II-145).

Indications:

Nausea and vomiting, acid regurgitation, pain in the hypochondriac region, hiccup and jaundice.

Clinical Application:

It is the Front-Mu point of the gall bladder, and a coalescent point of the Gall Bladder Meridian of Foot-Shaoyang, Urinary Bladder Meridian of Foot-Taiyang and Yangwei Meridian. It has the effect to soothe the liver, pacify the gall bladder, relieve heaviness sensation in the chest and regulate qi circulation.

Combinations:

With Danshu (U.B.19), Waiguan (S.J.5) and Yanglingquan (G.B.34) for treating hypochondriac pain.

Method:

Puncture obliquely about 0.5-0.8 cun deep.

Needling Sensations:

Distention and soreness radiating around the local area.

JINGMEN (G.B.25) 京 門 (CAPITAL GATE)

"Jing" (京) means the capital, referring to something important. "Men" (門) means the door through which qi and blood may come and go. The point is the Front-Mu point of the kidney, lying close to the organ and being indicated in kidney disorders. Because of its important indications, it is named Jingmen (Capital Gate).

Location:

On the lower border of the free end of the 12th rib (Fig. II-144).

Indications:

Chest distention, borborygmus, diarrhea, pain in the hypochondriac region and the lower back.

Method:

Puncture perpendicularly about 0.5-0.8 cun deep.

DAIMAI (G.B.26) 带 脉 (BELT POINT)

"Dai" (带) means belt. "Mai" (脉) means meridian, but here refers to a point. The point is located at the area on abdomen where the belt is worn, hence the name Daimai (Belt Point).

Location:

Directly below the free end of the 11th rib, at the level of the umbilicus. (Fig. II-144).

Indications:

Amenorrhea, pain in the abdominal area, irregular menstruation, leukorrhea, pain in the lower back and hypochondriac region.

Method:

Puncture perpendicularly about 1-1.5 cun deep.

WUSHU (G.B.27) 五 枢 (PIVOT OF THE FIVE)

"Wu" (五) means five, here referring to five zang organs. "Shu" (枢) means a pivot, but here referring to something important. The point is level with Guanyuan (Ren 4) alongside of Dantian (Elixir Field), where the qi of five zang organs converges, hence the name Wushu (Pivot of the Five).

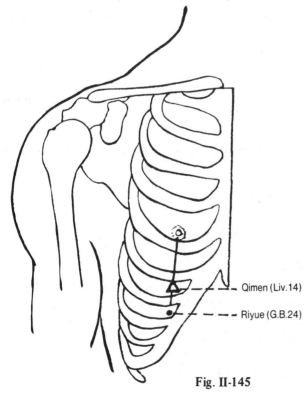

Qimen (Liv.14)

Riyue (G.B.24)

Fig. II-145

Location:

0.5 cun anterior to the antero-superior iliac spine, approximately at the level of the point Guanyuan (Ren 4) and Shuidao (St. 28) (Fig. II-146).

Indications:

Lower abdominal pain, uterine bleeding, leukorrhea and constipation.

Method:

Puncture perpendicularly about 1-1.5 cun deep.

WEIDAO 维 道 (G.B.28) (LINKING PATH)

"Wei" (维) means to connect with or to link. "Dao" (道) means a passage or a path. The point is the coalescent point of the Gall Bladder Meridian of the Foot-Shaoyang and the Dai Meridian, as well as being on the route via which the Dai Meridian connects with the front of the body. Hence the name Weidao (Linking Path).

Location:

0.5 cun anterior and inferior to Wushu (G.B.27) (Fig. II-146).

Indications:

Pain in the lower abdominal area, leukorrhea, and prolapse of the uterus.

Method:

Puncture 1-1.5 cun deep perpendicularly.

*FEMUR-JULIAO (G.B.29) 居 髎 (SQUATTING CREVICE)

"Ju" (居) means to bend, squat or flex. "Liao" (髎) means a depression. When a person squats down, a depression is formed in the muscle at the point area. Hence the name Juliao (Squatting Crevice).

Location:

Midway between the anterosuperior iliac spine and the greater trochanter (Fig.-II-146).

Indications:

Bi syndrome, pain in the back and lower limbs, paralysis.

Clinical Application:

It is the coalescent point of the Gall Bladder Meridian of Foot-Shaoyang and Yangqiao Meridian. It has the effect to eliminate the wind, promote circulation of qi and activate the collaterals.

Combinations:

With Fengshi (G.B.31) and Yanglingquan (G.B.34) for treating paralysis of the lower extremities.

Method:

Puncture perpendicularly 1-1.5 cun or 2 cun deep.

Needling Sensations:

Needling reaction goes into the deep part of the point.

*HUANTIAO (G.B.30) 環 跳 (CIRCLING JUMP)

"Huan" (環) means a circle. "Tiao" (跳) means to leap or jump. When a person squats in preparation for a jump, the lower limbs make a circle and the heels touch the point on the hip. Also, when needling the point on a patient suffering from wind Bi syndrome, the leg may jump. Hence the name Huantiao (Circling Jump).

Location:

At the junction of the middle and lateral third, of the distance along a line connecting the anterosuperior border of the greater trochanter with the hiatus of the sacrum. When the point is being located, have the patient assume a lateral recumbent position, with the leg extended and the thigh flexed about 90°. Place the transverse crease of the interphalangeal joint of the thumb on the highest point of the greater trochanter, with the tip of the thumb directed towards the spinal column. The point is where the tip of the thumb touches. If the patient is fat and the highest spot on the greater trochanter is difficult to locate, the operator may place the interphalangeal joint of the thumb against the tip of the coccyx by flexing the thumb into a 90° angle, with the index finger

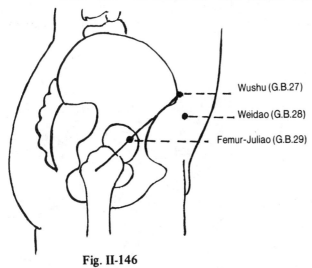

Fig. II-146

directed towards the area of the greater trochanter. The point is located where the tip of the index finger touches (Fig. II-147-149).

Indications:

Sciatica, hemiplegia, pain in the lower back and hip region, pain of the knee and shin.

Clinical Application:

It is the coalescent point of the Gall Bladder Meridian of Foot-Shaoyang and the Urinary Bladder Meridian of Foot-Taiyang. It has the effect to remove obstructions from the meridian, invigorate qi circulation in the collaterals, eliminate both cold and wind, strengthen the lower back and lower extremities.

Combinations:

With Zhibian (U.B.54), Yingmen (U.B.37) and Chengshan (U.B.57) for treating

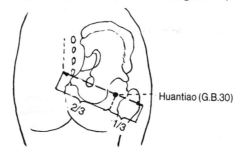

Fig. II-147

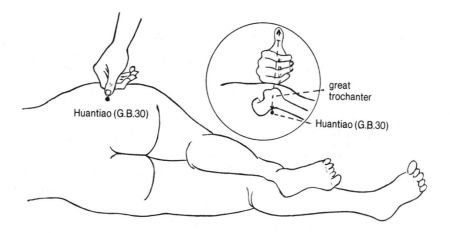

Fig. II-148

sciatica and pain of the lower leg,

With Yanglingquan (G.B.34), Lianqiu (St.34) and Xuanzhong (G.B.39) for arthritis of the knee and the ankle joints.

Method:

Puncture 2-3.5 cun deep perpendicularly.

Needling Sensations:

Soreness and numbness radiating down to the heel.

*FENGSHI 风市 (G.B.31) (WIND MARKET)

"Feng" (风) means wind. "Shi" (市) means market or a place where things converge. The point is mainly indicated in numbness and motor impairment due to

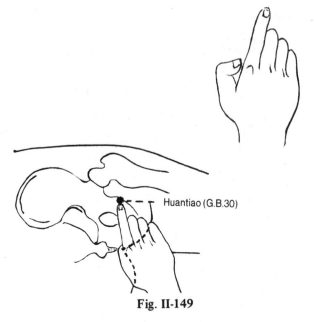

Fig. II-149

the wind attack, wandering pain, hemiplegia, pain of the foot, etc. It is considered to be the most important point for eliminating wind from the lower extremities, hence the name Fengshi (Wind Market).

Location:

Midway along the lateral aspect of the thigh, 7 cun above the transverse popliteal crease. When the patient is standing with the palms close to the sides of the legs, the point is where the tip of the middle finger touches (Fig.II-150,151).

Indications:

Hemiplegia, muscular atrophy, motor impairment and numbness of the lower extremities, general pruritus, and urticaria.

Clinical Application:

The point has the effect to eliminate wind and remove obstructions from the collaterals.

Combinations:

With Xuehai (Sp.10), Quchi (LI.11) and Dazhui (Du 14) for general pruritus and urticaria,

With Yanglingquan (G.B.34) and Huantiao (G.B.30) for paralysis of the lower

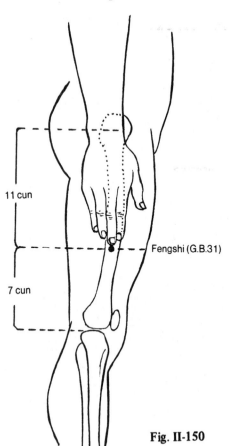

11 cun

7 cun

Fengshi (G.B.31)

Fig. II-150

limbs.
Method:
Puncture perpendicularly about 1-2 cun deep.
Needling Sensations:
Soreness, distention radiating down to the knee and leg.

ZHONGDU (G.B.32) 中凟 (MID STREAM)

"Zhong" (中) means middle. "Du" (凟) means a small river. The point is located midway between Fengshi (G.B.31) and Xiyangguan (G.B.33). The qi of the meridian arrives here like water flowing in the centre of a small river, hence the name Zhongdu (Mid Stream).

Location:
Two cun below Fengshi (Fig. II-151).
Indications:
Soreness and pain of the knees and the lower extremities, muscular atrophy, motor impairment of the lower limbs, and beriberi.
Method:
Puncture perpendicularly about 1-2 cun deep.

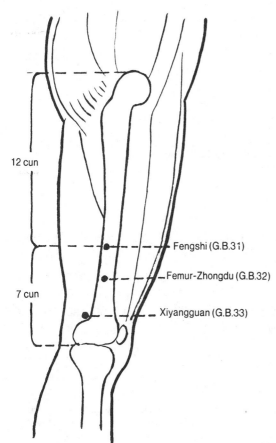

12 cun

7 cun

Fengshi (G.B.31)

Femur-Zhongdu (G.B.32)

Xiyangguan (G.B.33)

Fig. II-151

XIYANGGUAN (G.B.33) 膝阳关 (LATERAL TO KNEE JOINT)

"Xi" (膝) means knee joint. "Yang" (阳) here refers to the lateral aspect of the knee. "Guan" (关) means joint. The point is in the depression between the upper border of the external epicondyle of the femur and the tendon of m. biceps, hence the name Xiyangguan (Lateral to Knee Joint).

Location:
In the depression 3 cun above Yanglingquan (G.B.34) (Fig.II-151, 152).
Indications:
Pain and swelling of the knee joints, nausea, vomiting and numbness of the leg.
Method:
Puncture perpendicularly about 1-2 cun deep.

*YANGLINGQUAN (G.B.34) 阳陵泉 (OUTER MOUND SPRING)

"Yang" (阳) here refers to the lateral aspect of the leg. "Ling" (陵) means a mound and refers to a high place. In this case, it refers to the head of the fibula. "Quan" (泉) means a spring, but here refers to the depression anteroinferior to the head of the fibula. Hence the name Yanglingquan (Outer Mound Spring).

Location:

At the lateral aspect of the knee-joint, in the depression anterior and inferior to the head of the fibula (Fig. II-152-154).

Indications:

Diseases of the liver and gall bladder, pain in the hypochondriac region, bitter taste, sciatica, numbness at the lateral side of the lower extremities, pain of the lower limbs, shoulder pain, stomachache and neck sprain.

Clinical Application:

It is the He-Sea point of the Gall Bladder Meridian of Foot-Shaoyang, and one of the Eight Influential Points, relating to the tendons. It has the effect to smooth the liver, promote the function of the gall bladder, eliminate heat and damp, strengthen the lower back and the lower extremities. Clinical reports show that needling Yanglingquan (G.B.34) can invigorate the contraction and evacuation function of the gall bladder.

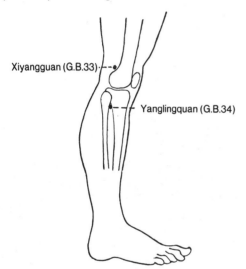

Xiyangguan (G.B.33)

Yanglingquan (G.B.34)

Fig. II-152

Combinations:

With Dubi (St.35), Yinlingquan (Sp.9) and Zusanli (St.36) for treating knee-joint pain,

With Taichong (Liv.33) for shoulder pain,

With Neiguan (P.6) for treating the pain around the liver and the gall bladder areas.

Method:

Puncture perpendicularly about 1-2 cun deep.

Needling Sensations:

Soreness, numbness and distention, radiating down to the knee and the dorsum of the foot.

YANGJIAO   (G.B.35) 阳交 **(YANG CROSSROAD)**

"Yang" (阳) refers to the lateral aspect of the leg. "Jiao" (交) means crossing. This point is the coalescent point of the Gall Bladder Meridian of Foot-Shaoyang, Yangwei Meridian, the Stomach Meridian of the Foot-Yangming and the Urinary Bladder Meridian of the Foot-Taiyang. Hence the name Yangjiao (Yang Crossroad).

Location:

See note below (Fig. II-154).

Indications:

Note: Yangjiao (G.B.35) and Waiqiu (G.B.36) are both 7 cun above the tip of the external malleolus, Waiqiu (G.B.36) being located on the anterior border of the fibula, while Yangjiao (G.B.35) is on the posterior border of the fibula. Yangfu (G.B.38) is 4 cun above the tip of the external malleolus, on the anterior border of the fibula.

Distention in the chest and hypochondriac region, knee-joint pain, muscular atrophy and weakness of the foot.

Method:

Puncture perpendicularly about 1-1.5 cun deep.

WAIQIU (G.B.36) 外 丘 (OUTER MOUND)

"Wai" (外) means outside, here referring to the lateral aspect of the leg. "Qiu" (丘) meaning a mound, here refers to a process, or a prominence. The point is on the lateral aspect of the leg and when one walks, the muscle around the point area forms a prominence. Hence the name Waiqiu (Outer Mound).

Location:

See above note (Fig. II-154).

Indications:

Neck pain, distention and pain in the hypochondriac region.

Method:

Puncture perpendicularly 1-1.5 cun deep.

*GUANGMING (G.B.37) 光明 "人"   (BRIGHT LIGHT)

"Guang" (光) means light. "Ming" (明) means bright. This point is the Luo-Connecting point of the Gall Bladder Meridian of Foot-Shaoyang which ascends to connect a branch arising from the point to link with the Liver Meridian of Foot-Jueyin, the liver opening into the eye. It is mainly indicated in eye diseases and it has the effect to invigorate circulation in the collaterals and brighten the eye. Hence the name Guangming (Bright Light).

Location:

Five cun directly above the tip of the external malleolus, on the anterior border of the fibula (Fig. II-154-155).

Indications:

Ophthalmalgia, night blindness, myopia, optic neuritis, one-sided headache, distend-

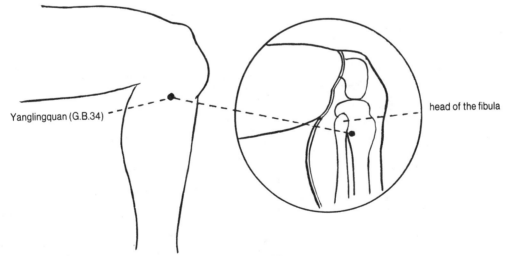

Yanglingquan (G.B.34)

head of the fibula

Fig. II-153

ing pain of the breast, especially during lactation, inadequate lactifuge, knee-joint pain and paralysis of the lower extremities.

Clinical Application:

It is the Luo-connecting point of the Gall Bladder Meridian of Foot-Shaoyang, linking with the Liver Meridian of Foot-Jueyin. It has the effect to remove obstruction from the two meridians, promote the circulation of qi in the collaterals, benefit the liver and brighten the eye.

Combinations:

With Fengchi (G.B.20) and Zanzhu (U.B.2) for treating ophthalmalgia and night blindness;

With Foot-Linqi (G.B.41) for distending pain of the breast and promotion of lactifuge.

Method:

Puncture perpendicularly about 1-1.5 cun deep.

Needling Sensations:

Soreness and numbness radiating upwards to the knee along the lateral aspect of the leg down to the dorsum of the foot.

YANGFU (G.B.38) 阳 辅 (LATERAL SUPPORT)

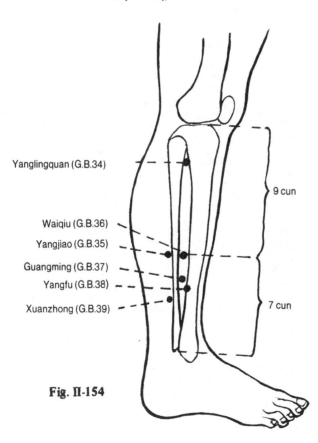

Yanglingquan (G.B.34)

Waiqiu (G.B.36)
Yangjiao (G.B.35)
Guangming (G.B.37)
Yangfu (G.B.38)
Xuanzhong (G.B.39)

9 cun

7 cun

Fig. II-154

"Yang" (阳) means lateral side or lateral aspect. "Fu" (辅) refers to the fibula. The point is at the lateral aspect of the fibula, known as the supporting bone (辅 骨 , Fugu) in Chinese. Hence the name Yangfu (Lateral Support).

Location:

See note above (Fig. II-154).

Indications:

One-sided headache, pain in the outer canthus and supraclavicular fossa, pain and distention in the chest and hypochondriac region.

Method:

Puncture perpendicularly 1-1.5 cun deep.

*XUANZHONG (G.B.39) 悬钟
"O" (SUSPENDED BELL)

"Xuan" (悬) means to suspend. "Zhong" (钟) means a small bell. In ancient times, children and dancers used to wear a

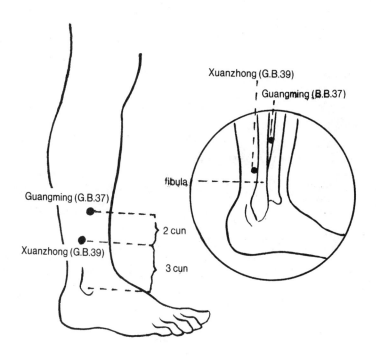

Fig. II-155

ring bell around the ankle at the level of the point, hence the name Xuanzhong (Suspended Bell). The point is sometimes also called Juegu. "Jue" (绝) means end. "Gu" (骨) means bone. The point is in the depression formed by the posterior border of the fibula and the tendons of m. peronaeus longus and brevis. If a finger is slid upwards along the bone from the external malleolus, the point is located in the depression when the bone "disappears" into the soft tissues, hence the name Juegu (End of Bone).

Location:

Three cun directly above the tip of the external malleolus on the posterior border of the fibula (Fig. II-155-156).

Indications:

Pain and rigidity of the neck, paralysis of the lower limbs, pain in the hypochondriac region, distention and fullness of the chest and abdominal area, neck sprain, one-sided headache, chest pain, hypochondriac distention, beriberi and indigestion.

Clinical Application:

It is one of the Eight Influential Points associated with the marrow. It has the effect to eliminate wind, remove obstruction from the collaterals, invigorate the circulation of blood and ease pain.

Combinations:

With Tianshu (U.B.10) and Houxi (S.I.3) for neck sprain,

With Quchi (L.I.11) and Zusanli (St.36) for hypertension,

With Yanglingquan (G.B.34) and Taichong (Liv.3) for hypochondriac distention.

Method:

Puncture perpendicularly about 1-1.5 cun deep.

Needling Sensations:

Soreness and numbness radiating down to the sole.

QIUXU (G.B.40) 丘 墟 "O"   (HILLOCK)

"Qiu" (丘) refers to a high place. "Xu" (墟) means hill. The point is in the depression anterior and inferior to the external malleolus, the latter being likened here to a hillock. Hence the name Qiuxu (Hillock).

Location:

Anterior and inferior to the external malleolus, in the depression on the lateral side of the tendon of m. extensor digitorum longus (Fig. II-158).

Indications:

Distending pain of the chest and hypochondriac region, muscular atrophy and motor impairment of the lower limbs.

Method:

Puncture perpendicularly about 0.3-0.5 cun deep.

*FOOT-LINQI (G.B.41) 足临泣 " 只 " (FOOT TEAR-CONTROL)

There are two Linqi points, namely Foot-Linqi (G.B.41) and Head-Linqi (G.B.15). The Urinary Bladder Meridian of Foot-Taiyang and the Gall Bladder Meridian of Foot-Shaoyang both start respectively from the inner canthus and the outer canthus, where tears appear when a person cries. Needling the two points can control excessive lacrimation, hence the name of this point Foot-Linqi (Foot Tear-Control).

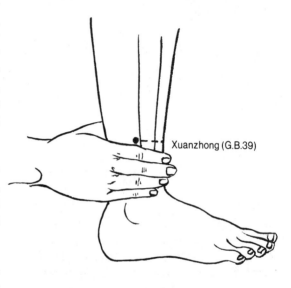

Xuanzhong (G.B.39)

Location:

In the depression distal to the junction of the 4th and 5th metatarsal bones, 1.5 cun above Xiaxi (G.B.43), lateral to the tendon of m. extensor distorum (Fig. II-157).

Indications:

Eye disorders, one-sided headache, mastitis, pain in the hypochondriac region, swollen and painful toes.

Fig. II-156

Clinical Application:

The point is the Shu-Stream point of the meridian and one of the Eight Confluent Points, connecting with Dai Meridian. It has the effect to reduce fire and stop pain.

Combinations:

With Fengchi (G.B.20), Baihui (Du 20) and Hegu (L.I.4) for treating headache and blurring of vision.

Method:

Puncture perpendicularly about 0.5 cun deep.

Needling Sensations:

Soreness and distention travelling down along the 4th metatarsal bone.

DIWUHUI (G.B.42) 地五会 (EARTH FIVE MEETING)

"Di" (地) means earth and refers to the foot. "Wu" (五) means the 5 toes of the foot. "Hui" (会) means to meet together. Needling the point can treat swelling and redness of the foot and painful toes, conditions which make it difficult to place the foot firmly on the ground, so that the five toes, "meet" the earth. Hence the name Diwuhui

(Earth Five Meeting).

Location:

Between the 4th and the 5th metatarsal bones, posterior to the metatarsodigital joints and 1 cun above Xiaxi (G.B.43) (Fig. II-158).

Indications:

Pain and swelling of the dorsum of the foot, bloody vomiting due to internal injury, itching of the eyes, ophthalmalgia, tinnitus and swelling of the breasts.

Method:

Puncture perpendicularly 0.3-0.5 cun deep.

XIAXI (G.B.43) 侠溪 " " (NARROW STREAM)

"Xia" (侠) means a small and narrow place. "Xi" (溪) means stream, also referring to a narrow place. The point is in the depression between the 4th and 5th toes on the dorsum of the foot, proximal to the margin of the web, hence the name Xiaxi (Narrow Stream).

Location:

See item below (Fig. II-158).

Indications:

Dizziness, blurring of vision, tinnitus, deafness, distention and fullness of the chest and hypochondriac region, swelling and pain of the breast, and amenorrhea.

Method:

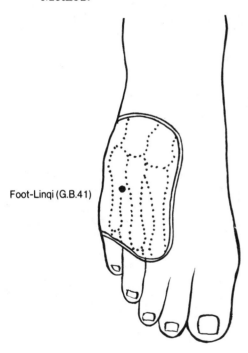

Foot-Linqi (G.B.41)

Fig. II-157

Puncture perpendicularly about 0.3-0.5 cun deep.

FOOT-QIAOYIN (G.B.44) 足窍阴 "O" (FOOT YIN ORIFICE)

"Qiao" (窍) means an orifice or cavity, referring here to the 5 sense organs on the face. The ancient physicians said "The liver opens into the orifice of the eye, the kidney opens into the ear, the heart opens into the tongue, the lung opens into the nose, and the spleen opens into the mouth." These five zang organs are Yin in nature and their openings are considered to be the Yin orifices. The point is mainly indicated in eye diseases, deafness, tongue rigidity, nasal obstruction, hiccup, cough, bitter taste, etc. Because of its location on the foot, it is named Foot-Qiaoyin (Foot Yin Orifice).

Location:

On the lateral side of the 4th toe, about 0.1 cun posterior to the corner of the nail (Fig. II-158).

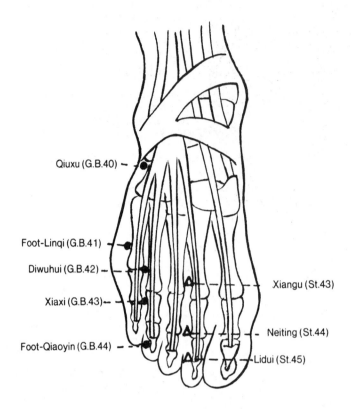

Qiuxu (G.B.40)

Foot-Linqi (G.B.41)

Diwuhui (G.B.42)

Xiangu (St.43)

Xiaxi (G.B.43)

Neiting (St.44)

Foot-Qiaoyin (G.B.44)

Lidui (St.45)

Fig. II-158

Indications:
See above item.
Method:
Prick to cause bleeding.

III. Summary

The Gall Bladder Meridian of Foot-Shaoyang pertains to the gall bladder, connects with the liver and links with the Liver Meridian of Foot-Jueyin on the foot. There are altogether 44 points on either side of the body (Fig. II-159).

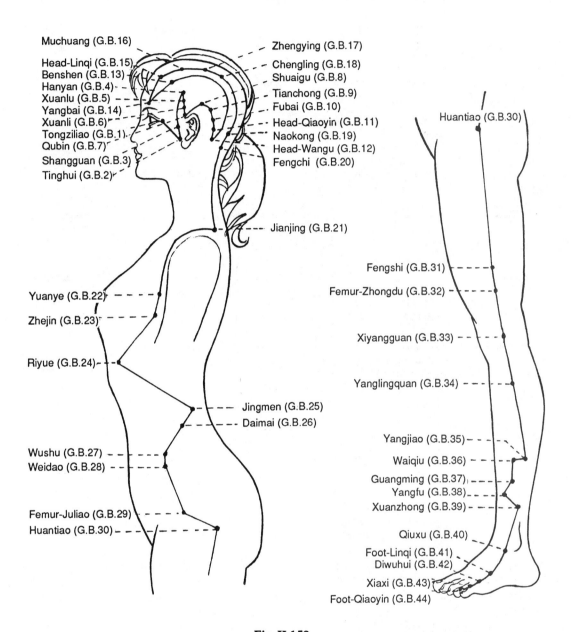

Muchuang (G.B.16)
Head-Linqi (G.B.15)
Benshen (G.B.13)
Hanyan (G.B.4)
Xuanlu (G.B.5)
Yangbai (G.B.14)
Xuanli (G.B.6)
Tongziliao (G.B.1)
Qubin (G.B.7)
Shangguan (G.B.3)
Tinghui (G.B.2)

Zhengying (G.B.17)
Chengling (G.B.18)
Shuaigu (G.B.8)
Tianchong (G.B.9)
Fubai (G.B.10)
Head-Qiaoyin (G.B.11)
Naokong (G.B.19)
Head-Wangu (G.B.12)
Fengchi (G.B.20)

Jianjing (G.B.21)

Yuanye (G.B.22)
Zhejin (G.B.23)
Riyue (G.B.24)

Jingmen (G.B.25)
Daimai (G.B.26)

Wushu (G.B.27)
Weidao (G.B.28)

Femur-Juliao (G.B.29)
Huantiao (G.B.30)

Huantiao (G.B.30)

Fengshi (G.B.31)
Femur-Zhongdu (G.B.32)
Xiyangguan (G.B.33)
Yanglingquan (G.B.34)
Yangjiao (G.B.35)
Waiqiu (G.B.36)
Guangming (G.B.37)
Yangfu (G.B.38)
Xuanzhong (G.B.39)
Qiuxu (G.B.40)
Foot-Linqi (G.B.41)
Diwuhui (G.B.42)
Xiaxi (G.B.43)
Foot-Qiaoyin (G.B.44)

Fig. II-159

The Specific Points of the Gall Bladder Meridian of Foot-Shaoyang

Yanglingquan	G.B.34	He O Earth	Qiuxu	G.B.40	O
Yangfu	G.B.38	♨Fire	Guangming	G.B.37	∧
Foot-Linqi	G.B.41	ℛ Wood	Waiqiu	G.B.36	Xi
Xiaxi	G.B.43	∼ Water	Xuanzhong	G.B.39	O
Foot-Qiaoyin	G.B.44	O Metal			

Point Indications of this Meridian According to Locations

Point Names	Locations	Indications	Regional Indications
Tongziliao G.B.1	Lateral to the outer canthus, on the lateral side of the orbit	One-sided headache, eye diseases	
Tinghui G.B.2	In the depression posterior to the mandibular joint, at the level of the lower border of the intertragic notch	Deafness, tinnitus	Diseases of the head, occurring along the temporal hairline
Shangguan G.B.3	Directly above Xiaguan (St.7) on the upper border of the zygomatic arch	Headache, toothache	
Hanyan G.B.4	On the temporal hair-line midway between Touwei (St.8) and Xuanlu (G.B.5)	One-sided headache, tinnitus	
Xuanlu G.B.5	On the temporal hair-line midway between Touwei (St.8) and Qubin (G.B.7)	One-sided headache, toothache	
Xuanli G.B.6	On the temporal hair-line midway between Xuanlu (G.B.5) and Qubin (G.B.7)	One-sided headache, redness of the eye	
Qubin G.B.7	Anterosuperior to the auricle, about 1 finger-breadth anterior to Jiaosun (S.J.20)	One-sided headache, eye diseases	
Shuaigu G.B.8	2 finger-breadths within the hairline, directly above Jiaosun (S.J.20)	One-sided headache, eye disorders	
Tianchong G.B.9	About 0.5 cun posterior to Shuaigu (G.B.8)	One-sided headache, epilepsy	Diseases of the head and neck
Fubai G.B.10	1 cun posterior and inferior to Tianchong (G.B.9)	Difficulty in lifting the arm and in walking	
Head-Qiaoyin G.B.11	1 cun below Fubai (G.B.10), posterosuperior to the mastoid process	Headache, eye diseases, tinnitus	
Head-Wangu G.B.12	In the depression posteroinferior to the mastoid process at the level of Fengfu (Du 16)	Headache, pain in the lateral aspect of the neck	

Benshen G.B.13	0.5 cun within the hairline of the forehead, at the junction of the lateral third of the distance from Shenting (Du 24) and Touwei (St.8)	Blurring of vision, salivation	
Yangbai G.B.14	1 cun above the midpoint of the eyebrow	Facial paralysis, trigeminal neuralgia	
Head-Linqi G.B.15	0.5 cun within the forehead hairline, directly above Yangbai (G.B.14)	Headache, blurring of vision	
Muchuang G.B.16	1.5 cun posterior to Head-Linqi (G.B.15)	Headache, dizziness and vertigo, blurring of vision, cataract	
Zhengying G.B.17	1.5 cun posterior to Muchuang (G.B.16)	Pain of the head and neck, toothache, dizziness and vertigo	
Chengling G.B.18	1.5 cun posterior to Zhengying (G.B.17)	Headache, nasal obstruction	
Naokong G.B.19	Directly above Fengchi (G.B.20), level with the external occipital protuberance	Severe headache, dizziness and vertigo	
Fengchi G.B.20	On the posterior aspect of the neck, in the depression at the lateral side of the upper portion of m. trapezius	Headache, dizziness and vertigo, hypertension, eye disorders	
Jianjing G.B.21	Midway between the acromion and Dazhui (Du 14)	Diseases of the shoulder or the back, mastitis	Diseases of the shoulder, lateral aspect of the chest and the hypochondriac region
Yuanye G.B.22	On the midaxillary line at the level of the 4th intercostal space	Pain in the hypochondriac region, difficulty in raising the arm	
Zhejin G.B.23	1 cun anterior to Yuanye (G.B.22), in the 4th intercostal space	Intercostal neuralgia	
Riyue G.B.24	Directly below the nipple, in the 7th intercostal space	Intercostal neuralgia distention, lower back pain	
Jingmen G.B. 25	On the lower border of the free end of the 12th rib	Abdominal distention, lower back pain	
Daimai G.B. 26	Directly below the midpoint of the line joining the free ends of the 11th and 12th ribs, at the level of the umbilicus	Irregular menstruation, pelvic inflammation	
Wushu G.B. 27	0.5 cun in front of the anterior superior iliac spine	Pain in the back, lower back; leukorrhea	Gynecological disorders
Weidao G.B. 28	0.5 cun anteroinferior to Wushu (G.B.27)	Pelvic inflammation, adnexitis	
Femur-Juliao G.B.29	Midway between the anterosuperior iliac spine and the greater trochanter	Pain and diseases of the back and lower extremities	
Huantiao G.B.30	In the depression posterosuperior to the greater trochanter	Sciatica, diseases of the lower extremities	

Fengshi G.B.31	At the place where the middle finger touches when standing with the hands held close to the sides of the thigh	Disease of the lower limbs	
Zhongdu G.B.32	2 cun directly below Fengshi (G.B.31)	Hemiplegia	Disease on the lateral aspect of the lower limbs
Xiyangguan G.B. 33	3 cun above Yanglingquan (G.B.34), in the depression superior to the external epicondyle of the femur	Knee-joint disorders	
Yanglingquan G.B.34	In the depression anteroinferior to the head of the fibula	Diseases of the liver and the gall bladder, hypochondriac pain	
Yangjiao G.B.35	7 cun above the tip of the external malleolus on the posterior border of the fibula	Pain in the chest and knee	
Waiqiu G.B.36	7 cun above the tip of the external malleolus on the anterior border of the fibula	Distending pain of the chest and hypochondriac region	
Guangming G.B.37	5 cun above the tip of the external malleolus on the posterior border of the fibula	Eye disorders, one-sided headache	
Yangfu G.B. 38	4 cun above the external malleolus on the anterior border of the fibula	Neck pain, pain of the ankle joint	
Xuanzhong G.B.39	3 cun directly above the tip of the external mallolus on the posterior border of the fibula	Neck pain, paralysis of lower limbs, distention, pain and fullness of chest and abdomen, one-sided headache, hypochondriac distention, beriberi and indigestion	
Qiuxu G.B.40	In the depression anteroinferior to the tip of the external malleolus	Gall bladder disorders, pain in the hypochondriac region	
Foot-Linqi G.B.41	In the depression distal to the junction of the 4th and 5th metatarsal bones, lateral to the tendon	One-sided headache, mastitis	Disease on the foot and toes
Diwuhui G.B.42	In the depression posterior to the 4th and 5th metatarso-digital joints	Pain and swelling of the dorsum of the foot, pain of the breasts	
Xiazi G.B.43	0.5 cun proximal to the margin of the web between the 4th and 5th toes	One-sided headache, deafness, tinnitus	
Foot-Qiaoyin G.B.44	On the lateral side of the 4th toe, about 0.1 cun posterior to the corner of the nail	Headache, excessive dreams, intercostal neuralgia	

Section 4 SUMMARY OF THE LOCATIONS OF SOME POINTS OF THE THREE YANG MERIDIANS OF THE FOOT

I. Toe area: The points at the roots of the toe nails Lidui (St.45), Foot-Qiaoyin (G.B.44) and Zhiyin (U.B.67) are all located on the lateral side of the toes and posterior to the corner of the nails (Fig. II-160).

II. Metatarsal phalangeal joint area: The points are either proximal or distal to the joints (Fig. II-161).

Neiting (St.44) and Xiangu (St.43) from the Stomach Meridian of Foot-Yangming;

Xiabai (G.B.43) and Diwuhui (G.B.42) from the Gall Bladder Meridian of Foot-Shaoyang;

Foot-Tonggu (U.B.66) and Shugu (U.B.65) from the Urinary Bladder Meridian of Foot-Taiyang.

These points are respectively distal and proximal to the metatarsal phalangeal joints.

III. Ankle area: The points are superior, inferior, anterior or posterior to the tip of the external malleolus (Fig. II-162).

Xuanzhong (G.B.39), 3 cun directly above the tip of the external malleolus.

Shenmai (U.B.62), directly below the tip of the external malleolus, 0.5 cun below the lower border.

Kunlun (U.B.60), posterior to the tip of the external malleolus.

Xiaxi (G.B.41), anterior to the external malleolus.

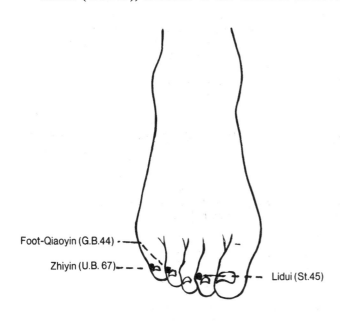

Foot-Qiaoyin (G.B.44)

Zhiyin (U.B. 67)

Lidui (St.45)

Fig. II-160

All these points are located by using the tip of the external malleolus as a landmark.

IV. Leg:

A. The Stomach Meridian of Foot-Yangming: The points are on the top, middle and lateral side of musculus tibialis anterior (Fig. II-163).

Zusanli (St.36) is at the tip; Shangjuxu (St.37), in the middle;

Xiajuxu (St.39) is at the end and Fenglong (St.40) at the lateral side of the muscle.

B. The Urinary Bladder Meridian of Foot-Taiyang: The points are on the junction of the muscles (Fig. II-164):

Heyang (U.B.55) is on the

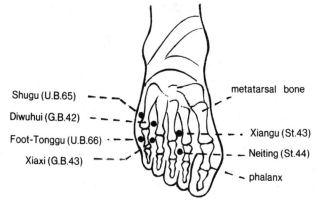

Shugu (U.B.65)
Diwuhui (G.B.42)
Foot-Tonggu (U.B.66)
Xiaxi (G.B.43)
metatarsal bone
Xiangu (St.43)
Neiting (St.44)
phalanx

Fig. II-161

upper junction between the medial and lateral heads of the m. gastrocnemius;

Chengjin (U.B.56) is 1 cun lateral and inferior to Chengshan (U.B.57), at the lateral border of m. gastrocnemius.

C. The Gall Bladder Meridian of Foot-Shaoyang: The points are either on the anterior or posterior border of the fibula.

Yanglingquan (G.B.34), Waiqui (G.B.36) and Yangfu (G.B.38) are on the anterior border of the fibula (Fig. II-165).

Yangjiao (G.B.35), Guangming (G.B.37) and Xuanzhong (G.B.39) are on the posterior border of the fibula.

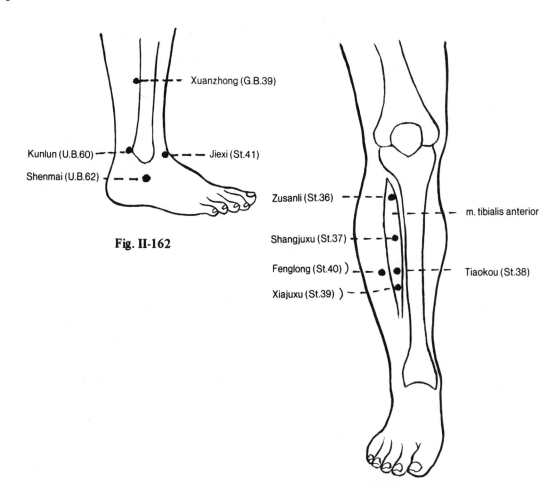

Xuanzhong (G.B.39)
Kunlun (U.B.60)
Shenmai (U.B.62)
Jiexi (St.41)

Fig. II-162

Zusanli (St.36)
m. tibialis anterior
Shangjuxu (St.37)
Fenglong (St.40)
Tiaokou (St.38)
Xiajuxu (St.39)

Fig. II-163

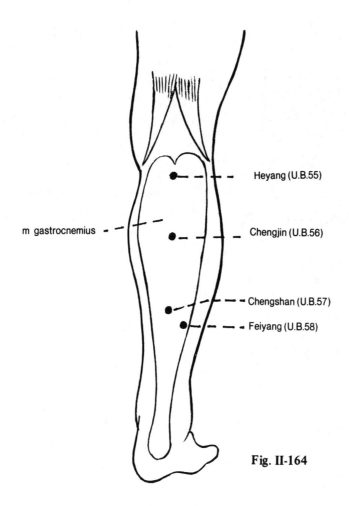

Fig. II-164

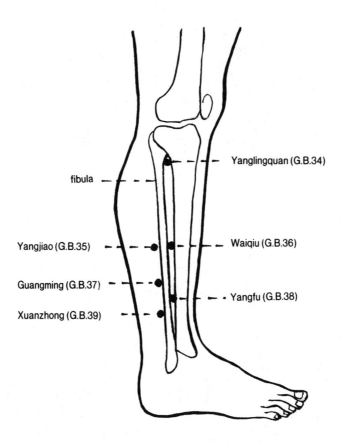

Fig. II-165

Chapter IV

THE THREE YIN MERIDIANS OF THE FOOT

Section I   THE SPLEEN MERIDIAN OF FOOT-TAIYIN

I. The Meridian

General Indications:

The points from this meridian are mainly indicated in epigastric pain, abdominal distention, weakness of both the spleen and stomach, diarrhea due to deficiency of the spleen, irregular menstruation, retention of urine, impotence, seminal emission, jaundice, heaviness sensation all over the body with general lassitude, etc, as well as in disorders such as swelling, distention or cold pain along the distribution of the meridian.

Course of the Meridian:

(1) The Spleen Meridian of Foot-Taiyin starts from the tip of the big toe (Yinbai, Sp.1). (2) It runs along the medial aspect of the foot at the junction of the red and white skin (3) and goes upward in front of the medial malleolus (4) to the leg. (5) It follows the posterior aspect of the tibia, (6) crosses and goes in front of the Liver Meridian of Foot-Jueyin. (7) Passing through the anterior medial aspect of the knee and thigh, (8) it enters the abdomen, then the spleen, its pertaining organ, (9) and connects with the stomach. (10) From there it ascends through the diaphragm, (11) and runs alongside the esophagus. (12) When it reaches the root of the tongue it spreads over its lower surface.

The Branch from the Stomach:

(13) This branch goes upwards through the diaphragm, (14) and flows into the heart (15) to link with the Heart Meridian of Hand-Shaoyin. (Fig. II-166)

Related Zangfu Organs:

The Spleen Meridian of Foot-Taiyin pertains to the spleen, connects with the stomach, and links with the heart.

Coalescent Points of the Meridian:

Zhongji (Ren 3), Guanyuan (Ren 4), Xiawan (Ren 10), Riyue (G.B.24), Qimen (Liv.14) and Zhongfu (Lu.1)

II. The Points

There are 21 points from this meridian on either side. Eleven of them are distributed on the anterior aspect of the medial side of the lower extremities, the remaining 10 being located on the abdomen and the chest.

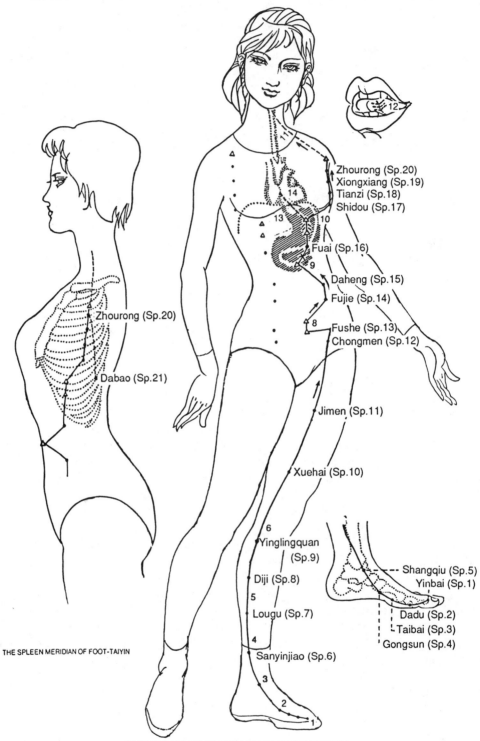

THE SPLEEN MERIDIAN OF FOOT-TAIYIN

THE SPLEEN MERIDIAN OF FOOT-TAIYIN

Fig. II-166

Analytical Display of the Course of the Meridian

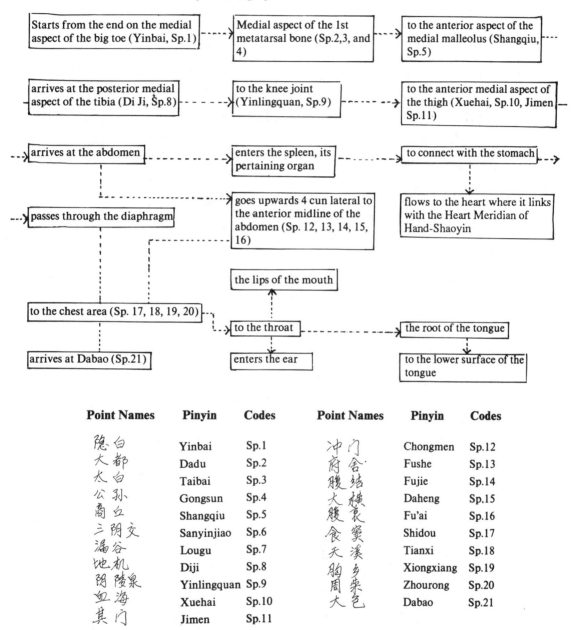

Point Names		Pinyin	Codes	Point Names		Pinyin	Codes
隐 白		Yinbai	Sp.1	冲 门		Chongmen	Sp.12
大 都		Dadu	Sp.2	府 舍		Fushe	Sp.13
太 白		Taibai	Sp.3	腹 结		Fujie	Sp.14
公 孙		Gongsun	Sp.4	大 横		Daheng	Sp.15
商 丘		Shangqiu	Sp.5	腹 哀		Fu'ai	Sp.16
三 阴 交		Sanyinjiao	Sp.6	食 窦		Shidou	Sp.17
漏 谷		Lougu	Sp.7	天 溪		Tianxi	Sp.18
地 机		Diji	Sp.8	胸 乡		Xiongxiang	Sp.19
阴 陵 泉		Yinlingquan	Sp.9	周 荣		Zhourong	Sp.20
血 海		Xuehai	Sp.10	大 包		Dabao	Sp.21
箕 门		Jimen	Sp.11				

*YINBAI (Sp.1) 隐白 "O"   (HIDDEN WHITE)

"Yin" (隐) means to hide, or a hidden place, but here refers to the foot. "Bai" (白) means white. Here it refers to the junction of the red and white skin, the white part being below the foot, hence the name Yinbai (Hidden White).

Location:

On the medial side of the big toe, about 0.1 cun posterior to the corner of the nail

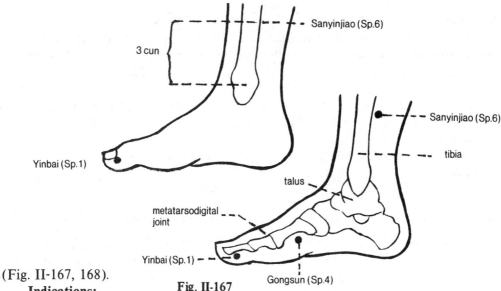

Fig. II-167

(Fig. II-167, 168).

Indications:

Abdominal distention, menorrhagia, profuse leukorrhea, uterine bleeding, infantile convulsion, dream-disturbed sleep, nightmare.

Clinical Application:

It is the Jing-Well point of the Spleen Meridian of Foot-Taiyin, having the effect to regulate the circulation of both qi and blood, and promote the functional activities of the spleen and stomach.

Combinations:

With Sanyinjiao (Sp.6), Xuehai (Sp.10), Guanyuan (Ren 4) and Tianshu (St.25) for treating functional bleeding of the uterus and irregular menstruation, with Pishu (U.B.20), Weishu (U.B.21), Zusanli (St.36) and Tianshu (St.25) for abdominal pain and distention.

Method:

Puncture about 0.1 cun deep to cause bleeding.

Needling Sensations:

Slight pain at the local area.

DADU (Sp.2) 大都 " ⌒ "   (BIG PROMINENCE)

"Da" (大) means big. "Du" (都) means toes or prominence. The point is located at the base of the great toe, where the muscles are comparatively thick, forming a prominence. Hence the name Dadu (Big Prominence).

Location:

It is on the medial side of the big toe, distal and inferior to the 1st metatarsal digital joint, at the junction of the red and white skin (Fig. II-168).

Indications:

Abdominal distention, gastric pain, indigestion, nausea and regurgitation.

Method:

Puncture perpendicularly about 0.5-0.8 cun deep.

TAIBAI (Sp.3) 太白 "O" " 尺 " (GRAND WHITE)

"Tai" (太) means grand or palpable. "Bai" (白) means white. The point is on the medial side of the great toe, at the junction of the red and white skin, but closer to the white part, hence the name Taibai (Grand White).

Location:

At the posterior border of the medial aspect of the 1st metatarsal distal joint, at the junction of the red and white skin (Fig. II-168).

Indications:

Gastric pain, abdominal distention, borborygmus, diarrhea, beriberi.

Method:

Puncture perpendicularly about 0.5-0.8 cun deep.

*GONGSUN (Sp.4) 公孙 " 八 " "⊗" (GRANDSON OF A PRINCE)

"Gong" (公) was originally a respectful form of address for high officials. "Sun" (孙) means a grandson. In ancient times, the sons of feudal princes and dukes were called "Gongzi" (公子), while their sons were called "Gongsun". The point is the Luo-Connecting point of the meridian, from which a branch emerges, hence the name Gongsun (Grandson of A Prince).

Location:

On the medial side of the great toe, in the depression distal and inferior to the base of the 1st metatarsal bone, at the junction of the red and white skin (Fig. II-168).

Indications:

Abdominal pain, gastric pain, weakness of the spleen and stomach, borborygmus, diarrhea, and dysentery.

Clinical Application:

It is the Luo-Connecting point of the Spleen Meridian of Foot-Taiyin, and one of the Eight Confluent Points, connecting with the Chong Meridian, having the effect to regulate the functional activities of the spleen and stomach.

With Neiguan (P.6) for treating diseases of the heart, chest and stomach; and

With Neiguan (P.6) and Liangqiu (St.34) for gastroxia.

Method:

Puncture perpendicularly 0.6-1.2 cun deep.

Needling Sensations:

Pain and distention may radiate towards the sole.

SHANGQIU (Sp.5) 商丘 "⊖" (METAL HILL)

"Qiu" (丘) means hill and here refers to the medial malleolus. The point is the Jing-River point, represented by metal according to the theory of the five elements. "Shang" (商) is one of the five notes of the ancient five-tone scale, also represented by metal and here indicating that this is the metal point. It is in the depression anterior and inferior to the medial malleolus, which looks like a hill. Hence the name Shangqiu (Metal Hill).

Location:

See above item (Fig. II-168).

Indications:

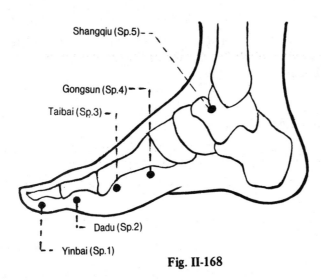

Shangqiu (Sp.5)- -

Gongsun (Sp.4)- -

Taibai (Sp.3) -

Dadu (Sp.2)

Yinbai (Sp.1)

Fig. II-168

Abdominal distention, constipation, diarrhea, retention of the food, jaundice and pain in the ankle area.

Method:

Puncture perpendicularly about 0.5-0.8 cun deep.

*SANYINJIAO (Sp.6)三阴交 (CROSSROAD OF THREE YIN)

"Jiao" (交) means the junction, or crossroad. "San-yin" (三阴) means the three Yin meridians of the foot. The point is on the junction of the three Yin merdians of the foot,

hence the name Sanyinjiao (Crossroad of Three Yin).

Location:

Three cun directly above the tip of the medial malleolus, on the posterior border of the tibia (Fig. II-167-169).

Indications:

Indigestion, borborygmus, diarrhea, abdominal distention and pain, uterine bleeding, leukorrhea, difficult labour, impotence, seminal emission, distending pain of the testis, enuresis, retention of urine, edema and insomnia. The point has a very wide range of indications, covering disorders of the digestive, reproductive and urinary systems.

Clinical Application:

This is the crossing point of the three yin meridians of the foot. It has the effect to tonify the spleen and kidney, promote the function of the spleen in transformation and transportation, remove obstruction from the meridians, invigorate the functional activities of the collaterals and regulate the circulation of qi and blood.

Combinations:

With Zhongji (Ren 3) and Guanyuan (Ren 4) for treating seminal emission, enuresis, impotence and prospermia,

With Qihai (Ren 6) and Zhongwan (Ren 12) for irregular menstruation,

With Zusanli (St.36) and Neiguan (P.6) for gastrointestinal disorders, and

With Shenmen (H.7) and Head-Wangu (G.B.12) for insomnia.

LOUGU (Sp.7)漏谷 (LEAKING VALLEY)

"Lou" (漏) means leaking or seeping. "Gu" (谷) means a valley, here referring to a depression. The point is mainly indicated in dysuria, a disease involving leakage, and lies in a depression at the posterior border of the tibia. Hence the name Lougu (Leaking Valley).

Location:

See note below (Fig. II-170).
Indications:
Abdominal distention, borborygmus, seminal emission, cold legs and knees.
Method:
Puncture perpendicularly about 1-1.5 cun deep.

DIJI (Sp.8) "XI" 地机 (EARTH CHANGE)

"Di" (地) means earth. "Ji" (机) means change. Needling the point can strengthen and nourish the qi and blood of the body, promoting vigorous change, and life on earth depends on the qi of the heavens (Vital Energy), hence the name Diji (Earth Change).

Location:
See above note (Fig. II-170).
Indications:
Abdominal distention, diarrhea, dysuria, seminal emission, irregular menstruation and edema.

Method:
Puncture perpendicularly about 1-1.5 cun.

*YINLINGQUAN (Sp.9) 阴陵泉 HE" (MOUND YIN SPRING)

"Ling" (陵) means a prominence or a mound. "Yin" (阴) indicates the nature of the meridian, as well as that of the spleen, which is the Yin organ of the Yin. "Quan" (泉) means spring. The point is the He-Sea point of the spleen meridian, being located on the medial aspect of the leg, inferior to the knee which is high and prominent, like a mound. The He-Sea point is a water point, water below a

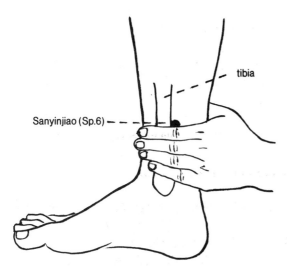

Fig. II-169

Note: Fig. II-170 shows the methods for locating the points Lougu (Sp.7), Diji (Sp.8) and Yinlingquan (Sp.9): The distance between the tip of the medial malleolus and the lower border of the medial condyle of the tibia is 13 cun.
Lougu (Sp.7) is 6 cun directly above the tip of the medial malleolus and one finger-breadth over the posterior border of the tibia.
Diji (Sp.8) is 4 cun above Lougu (Sp.7), and one finger-breadth over the posterior border of the tibia.
Yinlingquan (Sp.9) is in the depression on the lower border of the medial condyle of the tibia and one finger-breadth over the posterior border of the tibia.

mound signifying a spring. Hence the name Yinlingquan (Mound Yin Spring).

Location:

In the depression on the lower border of the medial condyle of the tibia (Fig. II-171).

Indications:

Edema, diarrhea, indigestion, jaundice, retention of urine, incontinence of urine, pain of the external genitalia, seminal emission, pain around the knee and irregular menstruation.

Clinical Application:

The point is the He-Sea point of the Spleen Meridian of Foot-Taiyin. It has the effect to eliminate heat, resolve damp and regulate the water passages, the Sanjiao.

Combinations:

With Shuifen (Ren 9), Zhongji (Ren 3), Zusanli (St.36) and Sanyinjiao (Sp.9) for treating dysuria and hydroperitoneum,

With Yanglingquan (G.B.34), Liangqiu (St.34) and Dubi (St.35) for knee-joint pain.

Method:

Puncture perpendicularly about 1-2 cun deep.

Needling Sensations:

The needling reaction goes down to the sole.

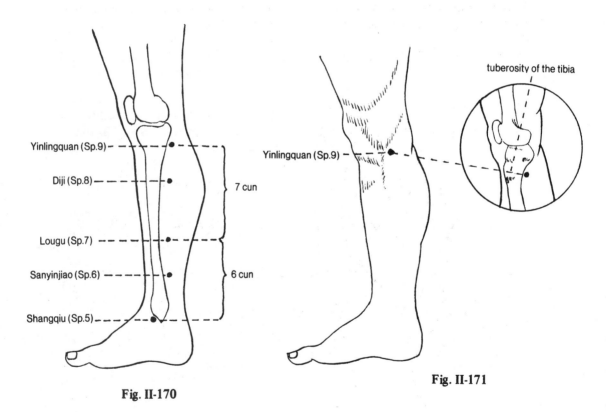

Fig. II-170

Fig. II-171

*XUEHAI (Sp.10) 血海 " "   **(SEA OF BLOOD)**

"Xue" (血) means blood. "Hai" (海) means the sea, where all waters merge. The point acts on the blood and promotes the spleen's function in controlling circulation, as though acting to guide the waters of various streams, springs and rivers on their courses to the sea. Hence the name Xuehai (Sea of Blood).

Location:

Two cun above the medio-superior border of the patella (Fig. II-172).

There is a simple method to locate the point: have the patient flex the knee, then the operator cups his left palm over the patient's right patella, the thumb forming an angle of about 45° on the medial side while the fingers are all directed upwards along the leg. The point is where the tip of the thumb touches.

Indications:

Irregular menstruation, amenorrhea, dysmenorrhea, uterine bleeding, eczema, urticaria, testitis and arthritis of the knee joints.

Clinical Application:

The point has the effect to eliminate wind, dispel heat and regulate the circulation of qi and blood.

Combinations:

With Dazhui (Du 14) and Quchi (L.I.11) and moxibustion for treating urticaria,
With Sanyinjiao (Sp.6), Hegu (L.I.4) and Zhongji (Ren 3) for amenorrhea.

Method:

Puncture perpendicularly about 1-1.5 cun deep.

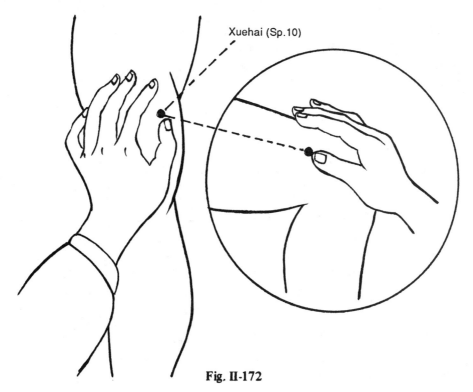

Xuehai (Sp.10)

Fig. II-172

Needling Sensations:

Soreness and distention radiating to the hip joint as well as to the knee.

JIMEN (Sp.11) 箕 門 (BASKET GATE)

"Ji" (箕) means a basket, referring to the abducted position of the legs and feet when this point is being located or used. Before it is located, the patient is asked to bend the knee and abduct the feet, as though holding a basket between the knees. "Men" (門) means a door or gate, hence the name Jimen (Basket Gate).

Location:

Six cun directly above Xuehai (Sp.10) (Fig. II-173).

Indications:

Dysuria, enuresis, pain and swelling in the inguinal region.

Method:

Puncture perpendicularly about 0.5-1 cun deep, avoid touching the artery.

CHONGMEN (Sp.12) 冲 門 (PULSATING DOOR)

"Chong" (冲) means rushing or pulsating. "Men" (門) door. The point is close to the femoral artery where the pulse is palpable. Also, the Spleen Meridian of Foot-Taiyin enters the abdominal cavity from this point as though through a door. Hence the name Chongmen (Pulsating Door).

Location:

At the level of the upper border of symphysis pubis, 3.5 cun lateral to the anterior midline (Fig. II-174).

Indications:

Abdominal pain, diarrhea, leukorrhea and uterine bleeding.

Method:

Puncture 0.5-1 cun perpendicularly and avoid touching the artery.

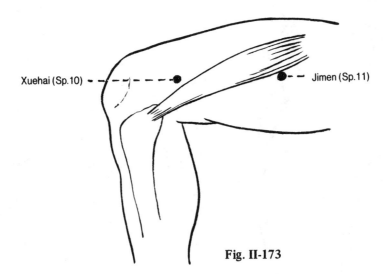

Xuehai (Sp.10)   Jimen (Sp.11)

Fig. II-173

FUSHE (Sp.13) 府舍 **(CONVERGING HOUSE)**

"Fu" (府) means a place where things converge. "She" (舍) means a dwelling place. The point is the place through which the Yinwei Meridian, the Spleen Meridian of Foot-Taiyin and the Liver Meridian of Foot-Jueyin converge and enter the abdomen, further connecting with the spleen, heart and lung. Hence the name Fushe (Converging House).

Location:

0.7 cun lateral and superior to Chongmen (Sp.12) and 4 cun lateral to the anterior midline (Fig. II-174).

Indications:

Abdominal pain and abdominal masses.

Method:

Puncture perpendicularly about 1-1.5 cun deep.

FUJIE (Sp.14) 腹 结 **(ABDOMINAL STASIS)**

"Fu" (腹) here only refers to the abdomen. "Jie" (结) means stasis or stagnation. The point is mainly indicated in stasis of qi in the abdomen and chest, i.e. stagnation of the qi attacking the heart area, pain around the umbilicus, cough and diarrhea. Hence the name Fujie (Abdominal Stasis).

Location:

1.3 cun below Daheng (Sp.15) (Fig. II-174).

Indications:

Dysentery, constipation, pain in the lower abdomen.

Method:

Puncture perpendicularly 1-2 cun deep.

DAHENG (Sp.15) 大 横 **(GREAT TRANSVERSE LINE)**

"Da" (大) means big or great. "Heng" (横) means a transverse or horizontal line, here referring to the transverse colon, which runs parallel to the line formed by the two points of each side. The points lie directly over the ascending and descending sections of the colon, and are indicated in various disorders of the large intestine, hence the name Daheng (Great Transverse Line).

Location:

Four cun lateral to the centre of the umbilicus (Fig. II-174).

Indications:

Constipation, diarrhea, dysentery, abdominal distention and pain.

Clinical Application:

It is the coalescent point of the Yinwei Meridian and the Spleen Meridian of Foot-Taiyin. It has the effect to regulate the functional activities of the stomach and intestines.

Combinations:

With Tianshu (St.25), Qihai (Ren 6) and Zhongwan (Ren 12) for treating abdominal distention and pain,

With Zhigou (S.J.6) for constipation.

Method:

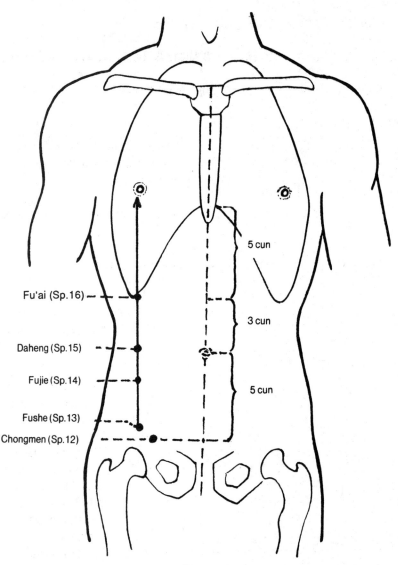

Fig. II-174

Puncture perpendicularly 1-2 cun deep.
Needling Sensations:
Soreness, distention and heaviness radiating to the inguinal area.

FU'AI (Sp.16) 腹哀　(ABDOMINAL CRY)

"Fu" (腹) means abdomen. "Ai" (哀) means to cry out, here referring to the sounds of hyperactive peristalsis. Hence the name Fu'ai (Abdominal Cry).
Location:

Note: The following five points are all punctured obliquely, with the tip of the needle being directed either laterally or medially, about 0.5-0.8 cun deep. The lung lies underneath these points, so deep insertion is dangerous and should be avoided (Fig. II-175).

Three cun directly above Daheng (Sp.15) (Fig. II-174).
Indications:
Abdominal pain and borborygmus, indigestion, constipation and dysentery.
Method:
Puncture perpendicularly about 1-2 cun deep.

SHIDOU (Sp.17) 食 窬 (FOOD CAVITY)

"Shi" (食) means food. "Dou" (窬) means a space. The point can be used to promote digestion and assist in the distribution of essential substances from the food to all parts of the body. Hence the name Shidou (Food Cavity).
Location:
Six cun lateral to the anterior midline, at the level of the 5th intercostal space (Fig. II-175).
Indications:
Fullness and pain in the chest and hyperchondriac region.
Method:
See above note.

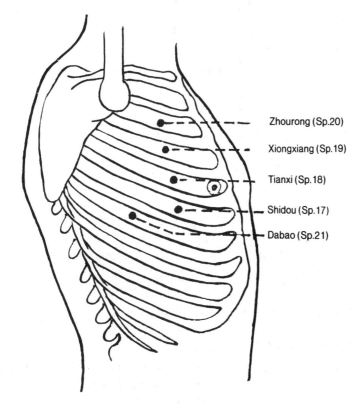

Zhourong (Sp.20)
Xiongxiang (Sp.19)
Tianxi (Sp.18)
Shidou (Sp.17)
Dabao (Sp.21)

Fig. II-175

TIANXI (Sp.18) 天 溪 (CELESTIAL STREAM)

"Tian" (天) refers to the upper part of the body, the celestial part. "Xi" (溪) means stream. The point is 1 cun lateral to Tianchi (P.1), and needling it promotes lactation, the flow of milk being likened here to the flow of a stream. Hence the name Tianxi (Celestial Stream).
Location:
Two cun lateral to the nipple, in the 4th intercostal space (Fig. II-175).
Indications:
Fullness and pain in the chest, cough, mastitis, lactation deficiency.
Method:
See above note.

XIONGXIANG (Sp.19) 胸乡 (CHEST HOME)

"Xiong" (胸) means

the chest. "Xiang" (乡) means a living place. The point is on the lateral side of the chest and is indicated in fullness of the chest and flank region, pain of the back and chest, difficulty in turning over after lying down, etc. Hence the name Xiongxiang (Chest Home).

Location:

Six cun lateral to the anterior midline, at the level of the 3rd intercostal space (Fig.II-175).

Indications:

Fullness and pain in the chest and hypochondriac region.

Method:

See above note.

ZHOURONG (Sp.20) 周荣 (WHOLE NOURISHMENT)

"Zhou" (周) here refers to the whole body. "Rong" (荣) means to nourish or nourishment. The point is from the Spleen Meridian of Foot-Taiyin, the spleen dominating the muscles and having the function to control blood circulation and distribute essential substances. Also, the qi of the meridians of the whole body arrives here before being further distributed to nourish the entire body. Hence the name Zhourong (Whole Nourishment).

Location:

Six cun lateral to the anterior midline in the 2nd intercostal space (Fig. II-175)

Indications:

Fullness of the chest and hypochondriac region, poor appetite and cough due to the derangement of qi circulation.

Method:

See above note.

DABAO (Sp.21) 大包 " ∧ "   (GENERAL CONTROL)

"Da" (大) means general or big. "Bao" (包) means to control something totally or to take care of something. The point is the general Luo-Connecting point of the Major Collateral of the Spleen Meridian, governing all the Yin and Yang meridians. Also the spleen is considered to irrigate all the zangfu organs and the four limbs, all the tissues of the body obtaining nourishment from the spleen. Hence the name Dabao (General Control).

Location:

Six cun below the axilla, on the mid-axillary line at the level of the 6th intercostal space (Fig. II-175).

Indications:

Pain in the chest and flank region, pain all over the body, asthma and general weakness.

Method:

See above note.

III. Summary

This meridian pertains to the spleen, connects with the stomach, links with the heart, passes through the tongue and esophagus, and there are 21 points on either side (Fig. II-176).

The Specific Points of This Meridian

Yinlingquan	(Sp.9)	He Water
Shangqiu	(Sp.5)	⊖ Metal
Taibai	(Sp.3)	O ⅄ Earth
Dadu	(Sp.2)	∼ Fire
Yingbai	(Sp.1)	⊙ Wood
Gongsun	(Sp.4)	⊗ ∧
Diji	(Sp.8)	Xi

Point Indications of the Spleen Meridian of Foot-Taiyin According to Regional Locations

Point Names	Locations	Indications	Regional Indications
Yinbai	On the medial side of the big toe, about 0.1 cun posterior to the corner of the nail	Menorrhagia, hysteria	Diseases of the stomach and the intestine
Dadu Sp.2	On the medial side of the big toe, distal and inferior to the 1st metatarsal digital joint	Febrile disease, abdominal distention	
Taibai Sp.3	Proximal and inferior to the head of the 1st metatarsal bone	Abdominal distention, borborygmus, dream-disturbed sleep	
Gongsun Sp.4	In the depression anterior and inferior to the base of the 1st metatarsal bone	Abdominal pain and distention	
Shangqiu Sp.5	In the depression anterior and inferior to the medial malleolus	abdominal distention, borborygmus, dream-disturbed sleep	
Sanyinjiao Sp.6	3 cun directly above the tip of the medial malleolus, on the posterior border of the tibia.	Irregular menstruation, dysmenorrhea, seminal emission	
Lougu Sp.7	6 cun directly above the tip of the medial malleolus, on the posterior border of the tibia	Abdominal pain and distention, emaciation	Disorders of reproductive and urinary systems.
Diji Sp.8	3 cun below Yinlingquan (Sp.9)	Irregular menstruation, dysmenorrhea	
Yinlingquan Sp.9	In the depression on the lower border of the medial condyle of the tibia	Infections of the urinary tract, retention of urine	

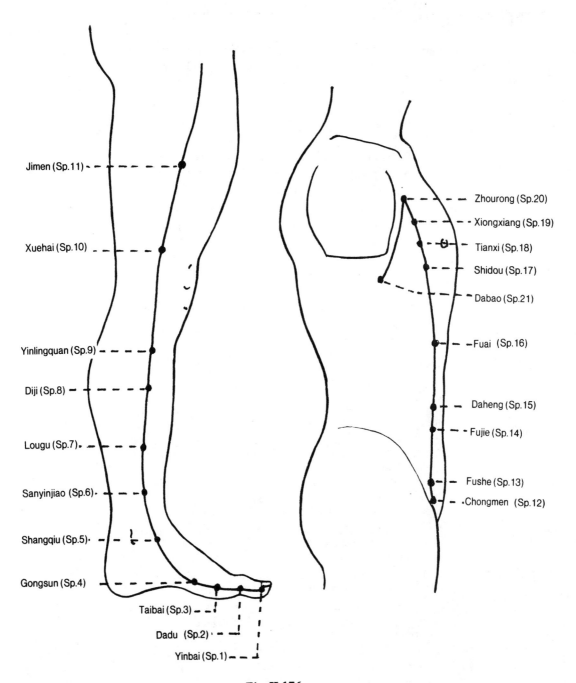

Jimen (Sp.11)

Xuehai (Sp.10)

Yinlingquan (Sp.9)

Diji (Sp.8)

Lougu (Sp.7)

Sanyinjiao (Sp.6)

Shangqiu (Sp.5)

Gongsun (Sp.4)

Taibai (Sp.3)

Dadu (Sp.2)

Yinbai (Sp.1)

Zhourong (Sp.20)

Xiongxiang (Sp.19)

Tianxi (Sp.18)

Shidou (Sp.17)

Dabao (Sp.21)

Fuai (Sp.16)

Daheng (Sp.15)

Fujie (Sp.14)

Fushe (Sp.13)

Chongmen (Sp.12)

Fig. II-176

Xuehai Sp.10	2 cun above the medio-superior border of the patella	Irregular menstruation, urticaria	
Jimen Sp.11	On the medial side of the thigh, 6 cun above Xuehai (Sp.100)	Wetting and itching of the external genitalia	Retention of urine and enuresis
Chongmen Sp.12	3.5 cun lateral to the Ren Meridian, at the level of the upper border of the symphysis pubis	Abdominal pain due to masses	
Fushe Sp.13	0.7 cun above Chongmen (Sp.12)	Fullness of the abdominal region, pain of the chest and abdomen	
Fujie Sp.14	1.3 cun below Daheng (Sp.15)	Pain around the umbilicus	Intestinal disorders
Daheng Sp.15	4 cun lateral to the centre of the umbilicus	Diarrhea, constipation	
Fu'ai Sp.16	3 cun above Daheng (Sp.15)	Cold pain in the gastric region, abdominal pain	
Shidou Sp.17	In the 5th intercostal space, 6 cun lateral to the anterior midline	Fullness and pain in the chest and flank area, nausea	
Tianxi Sp.18	In the 4th intercostal space, 6 cun lateral to the anterior midline	Pain in the chest, breast pain, mastitis, swelling or ulcer of the breast	
Xiongxiang Sp.19	In the 3rd intercostal space, 6 cun lateral to the anterior midline	Pain in the chest, difficulty in turning the body	Disorders on the lateral aspect of the chest
Zhourong Sp.20	In the 2nd intercostal space 6 cun lateral to the anterior midline	Fullness in the chest and flank area, poor appetite	
Dabao Sp.21	On the mid-axillary line, at the level of the 6th intercostal space	General aching, weakness	

Section 2   THE KIDNEY MERIDIAN OF FOOT-SHAOYIN

I. The Meridian

General Indications:

Diseases of the reproductive and urinary systems, chronic lumbago, sore throat, toothache, insomnia, dizziness and vertigo, tinnitus and hypoplasia.

Courses of the Meridian:

(1) The Kidney Meridian of Foot-Shaoyin starts from the inferior aspect of the small toe and runs obliquely towards the sole (Yongquan, K.1). (2) Emerging from the lower border of the tuberosity of the navicular bone (3) and running behind the medial malleolus, (4) it enters the heel. (5) It ascends along the medial aspect of the leg, (6) to the medial aspect of the popliteal fossa, (7) and goes further upward along the postero-medial aspect of the thigh (8) towards the vertebral column (Changqiang, Du 1), where it enters the kidney, its pertaining organ, (9) and connects with the urinary bladder.

The Straight Portion of the Meridian:

(10) It re-emerges and ascends from the kidney, (11) passes through the liver and diaphragm, (12) enters the lung, (13) runs along the throat (14) and terminates at the root of the tongue.

Branch of the Lung:

(15) A branch springs from the lung, connects with the heart and links with the Pericardium Meridian of Hand-Jueyin (Fig. II-177).

Analytical Display of the Course of the Meridian:

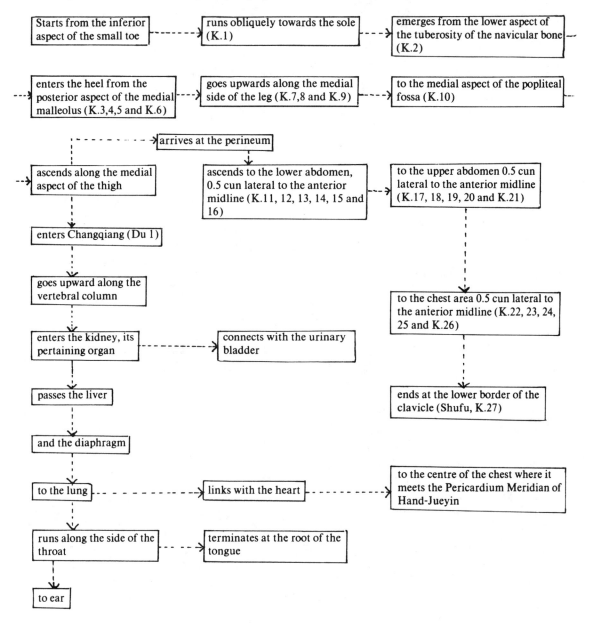

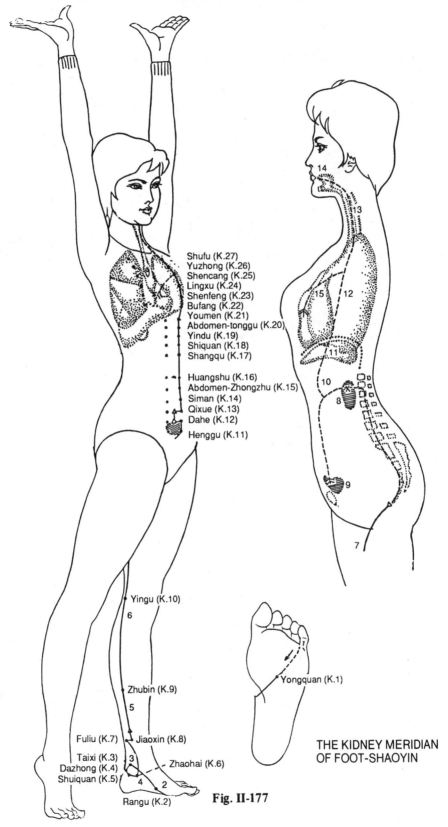

Shufu (K.27)
Yuzhong (K.26)
Shencang (K.25)
Lingxu (K.24)
Shenfeng (K.23)
Bufang (K.22)
Youmen (K.21)
Abdomen-tonggu (K.20)
Yindu (K.19)
Shiquan (K.18)
Shangqu (K.17)

Huangshu (K.16)
Abdomen-Zhongzhu (K.15)
Siman (K.14)
Qixue (K.13)
Dahe (K.12)

Henggu (K.11)

Yingu (K.10)
6

Zhubin (K.9)
5

Fuliu (K.7)   Jiaoxin (K.8)
Taixi (K.3)   3
Dazhong (K.4)   Zhaohai (K.6)
Shuiquan (K.5)   4   2
Rangu (K.2)

Yongquan (K.1)

THE KIDNEY MERIDIAN
OF FOOT-SHAOYIN

Fig. II-177

Related Zangfu Organs:

The Kidney Meridian of Foot-Shaoyin pertains to the kidney, connects with the urinary bladder, links with the liver, lung and heart, passes through the tongue and throat, and is associated with the marrow.

Coalescent Points of the Meridian:

Sanyinjiao (Sp.6), Changqiang (Du 1), Zhongji (Ren 3), Guanyuan (Ren 4) and Shangzhong (Ren 17).

II. The Points

There are 27 points on either side of the body. Among them, 10 are distributed on the posterior aspect of the medial side of the lower limb. The rest are located on the chest and abdominal region, bilateral to the anterior middle line. The starting point is Yongquan (K.1) and the last one is Shufu (K.27).

Point Names	Pinyin	Codes	Point Names	Pinyin	Codes
涌泉	Yongquan	K.1	注俞	Abdomen-Zhongzhu	K.15
然谷	Rangu	K.2	肓俞	Huangshu	K.16
太溪	Taixi	K.3	商曲	Shangqu	K.17
大钟	Dazhong	K.4	石关	Shiguan	K.18
水泉	Shuiquan	K.5	阴都	Yindu	K.19
照海	Zhaohai	K.6	腹通谷	Abdomen-Tonggu	K.20
复溜	Fuliu	K.7	幽门	Youmen	K.21
交信	Jiaoxin	K.8	步廊	Bulang	K.22
筑宾	Zhubin	K.9	神封	Shenfeng	K.23
阴谷	Yingu	K.10	灵墟	Lingxu	K.24
横骨	Henggu	K.11	神藏	Shencang	K.25
大赫	Dahe	K.12	彧中	Yuzhong	K.26
气穴	Qixue	K.13	俞府	Shufu	K.27
四满	Siman	K.14			

*YONGQUAN (K.1) 涌泉 **"Θ"**   (GUSHING SPRING)

"Yong" (涌) means pouring or gushing. "Quan" (泉) means underground water or a spring and refers to the location of the point on the sole of the foot, at the bottom of the body, like a spring under the ground. The point is the Jing-Well point of the meridian and it is in the depression of the lambdoidal suture in the sole where the qi of the Kidney Meridian of Foot-Shaoyin starts to flow, hence the name Yongquan (Gushing Spring).

Location:

In the depression of the sole, approximately at the junction of the anterior and middle third of its length, between the 2nd and the 3rd metatarsal bones   (Fig. II-178, 179).

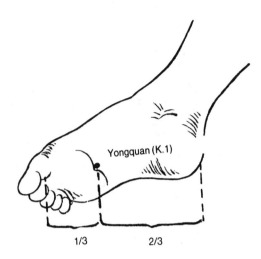

Fig. II-178

Indications:

Dizziness, blurring of vision, pain in the vertex, sore throat, hypertension, infantile convulsion, schizophrenia and toothache due to deficiency of the kidney.

Clinical Application:

It is the Jing-Well point of the Kidney Meridian of Foot-Shaoyin, having the effect to remove the obstruction of the meridian, clear the collaterals and restore consciousness.

Combinations:

With Renzhong(Du 26), Shixuan (Extra) and Zusanli (St.36) for treating loss of consciousness, shock and spasm.

Method:

Puncture perpendicularly about 0.5-1 cun deep or penetrate through to the point from Taichong (Liv.3).

Needling Sensations:

Soreness, distention and slight pain in the local area.

RANGU (K.2) 然谷 " ∼ "   (NAVICULAR BONE)

"Rangu" (然谷) is the ancient name for the navicular bone. The point is located at the lower border of this bone, hence the name Rangu (Navicular Bone).

Location:

In the depression anterior and inferior to the lower border of the tuberosity of the navicular bone (Fig.II-180).

Indications:

Pruritus vulvae, prolapse of the uterus, irregular menstruation, seminal emission, swelling and pain of the dorsum of the foot.

Method:

Puncture perpendicularly about 0.5-1 cun deep.

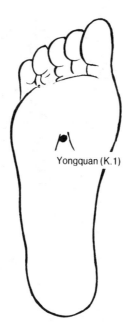

Yongquan (K.1)

Fig. II-179

*TAIXI (K.3) 太 渓 " 乑 ", "O"   (BIG STREAM)

"Tai" (太) means big, or great. "Xi" (渓) means stream. The flow of the qi of the kidney meridian pours out of Yongquan, passes through Rangu (K.2), converging and strengthening at this point, hence the name Taixi (Big Stream).

Location:

In the depression midway along the line connecting the tip of the medial malleolus with the tendo calcaneus (Fig.II-181).

Indications:

Sore throat, toothache, insomnia, tinnitus, deafness, mastitis, impotence, asthma, hemoptysis, enuresis and seminal emission.

Clinical Application:

It is the Shu-Stream and Yuan-Source point of the Kidney Meridian of Foot-Shaoyin, having the effect to regulate and tonify the qi of the kidney, promote and regulate the function of Sanjiao, as well as to strengthen the lower back and knees.

Combinations:

With Guanyuan (Ren 4) for impotence,

With Shenmen (H.7) and Sanyinjiao (Sp.6) for insomnia,

With Hegu (L.I.4) for sore throat

With Feishu (U.B.13) and Shenshu (U.B.23) for cough and asthma due to the insufficiency of kidney qi.

Method:

Puncture perpendicularly about 0.5-1 cun deep.

Needling Sensations:

Soreness and numbness, radiating down to the sole.

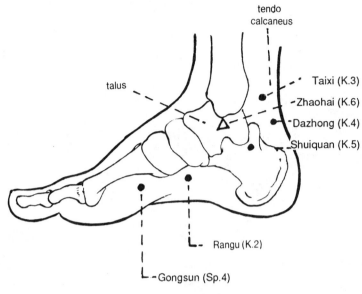

Fig. II-180

DAZHONG (K.4) 大钟 "∧" (GREAT BELL)

"Da" (大) means big or great. "Zhong" (钟) means a bell, but here referring to a convergent place of the qi of the meridian. The point is the Luo-Connecting point of the Kidney Meridian of Foot-Shaoyin, at which qi is abundant and flourishing. "Zhong" (钟) also can refer to the heel, which supports the whole weight of the body and on which the point is located, hence the name Dazhong (Great Bell).

Location:

0.5 cun posterior and inferior to Taixi (K.3), on the medial border of the tendo calcaneus (Fig. II-180).

Indications:

Hemoptysis, asthma, stiffness and pain of the lumbosacral region, somnolence and pain in the heel.

Method:

Puncture perpendicularly about 0.3-0.5 cun deep.

SHUIQUAN (K.5) 水泉 "XI" (SPRING WATER)

"Shui" (水) means water. "Quan" (泉) means spring. Shuiquan refers to the flow of water. The point is the Xi-Cleft and the water point of the meridian. The qi arriving here becomes stronger and pours out like water out of a big spring, hence the name Shuiquan (Spring Water).

Location:

One cun directly below Taixi (K.3) (Fig. II-180).

Indications:

Amenorrhea, irregular menstruation, dysmenorrhea and dysuria.

Method:

Puncture perpendicularly about 0.3-0.5 cun deep.

ZHAOHAI (K.6) 照海 "O" (SHINING SEA)

"Zhao" (照) means sunshine or brightness. "Hai" (海) means the sea, referring to a large depression. If a person sits on a flat surface, with the soles together, a large depression appears below the medial malleolus, in which the point is located. Also, it is effective in the treatment of eye disorders, hence the name Zhaohai (Shining Sea).

Location:

Directly below the tip of the medial malleolus and 0.4 cun inferior to its lower border. If the foot is abducted slightly, a depression may appear at the side of the point

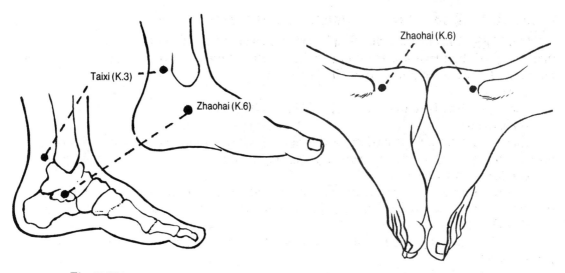

Fig. II-181

Fig. II-182

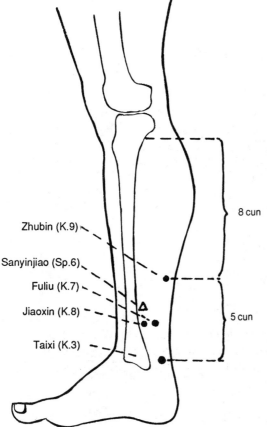

Fig. II-183

(Fig. II-182).

Indications:

Sore throat, irregular menstruation, insomnia, blurring of vision, pruritus vulvae, cough and prolapse of the uterus.

Clinical Application:

This is one of the Eight Confluent Points, connected with Yinqiao Meridian. It has the effect to invigorate qi and blood circulation in the meridian and the collaterals, dispel heat, reduce fire, ease the throat and calm the mind.

Combinations:

With Tianrong (S.I.17) for treating sore or swollen throat,

With Zhongji (Ren 3) for irregular menstruation and prolapse of the uterus,

With Lieque (Lu.7) for cough and asthma,

With Zhigou (S.J.6) for constipation,

With Fengchi (G.B.20) for blurring of vision.

Method:

Puncture perpendicularly about 0.5-1 cun deep.

Needling Sensations:

Soreness and distention radiating upward.

FULIU (K.7) 腹溜 " O "   (HIDE AND STAY)

"Fu" (腹) means to hide. "Liu" (溜) means to stay. The two characters indicate that the qi of the meridian accumulates here before flowing into the deeper part of the meridian. Hence the name Fuliu (Hide and Stay).

Location:
Two cun directly above Taixi (K.3) (Fig. II-183).

Indications:
Edema, abdominal distention, borborygmus, diarrhea, impotence, seminal emission, fever, anhidrosis, spontaneous sweating and night sweating.

Clinical Application:
It is the Jing-River point of the Kidney Meridian of Foot-Shaoyin, having the effect to relieve damp, calm the mind, strengthen and consolidate the yang of the body.

Combinations:
With Yinlingquan (Sp.9) and Zusanli (St.36) for treating borborygmus, night sweating and swelling,
With Zhongji (Ren 3) for impotence and prospermia;
With Neiguan (P.6) for insomnia.

Method:
Puncture 0.5-1.3 cun deep perpendicularly.

Needling Sensation:
Numbness sensation going downward to the sole.

JIAOXIN (K.8) 交信 (COMING IN TIME)

"Jiao" (交) means coming, connecting or passing over, the meridian crossing Sanyinjiao (Sp.6) from this point. "Xin" (佼) here means to be sure and arriving in time. The menstrual period is also known as "Xin" (信) because it comes regularly at a certain time. The point has the effect to regulate menstruation and restore the cycle to normal, hence the name Jiaoxin (Coming in Time).

Location:
Two cun above Taixi (K.3) (Fig. II-183).

Indications:
Irregular menstruation and uterine bleeding.

Method:
Puncture perpendicularly about 1 cun deep.

ZHUBIN (K.9) 筑宾 (STRONG HOUSE)

"Zhu" (筑) means strong or hard. "Bin" (宾) here means a dwelling place or a house. The point is located on the medial aspect of the lower border of m. gastrocnemius. When the leg is raised, the contraction of the muscle makes it seem stronger and harder, hence the name Zhubin (Strong House).

Location:
Five cun above Taixi (K.3), on the anterior border of the tendo calcaneus (Fig. II-183).

Indications:
Pain in the medial aspect of the leg, hernial pain, mental illness and vomiting with

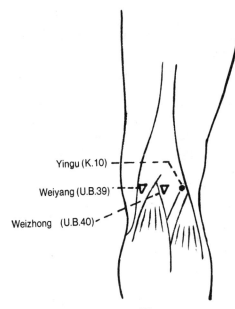

Yingu (K.10)

Weiyang (U.B.39)

Weizhong (U.B.40)

Fig. II-184

profuse saliva.
Method:
Puncture perpendicularly about 1 cun deep.

YINGU (K.10) 阴谷 "HE" (YIN VALLEY)

"Gu" (谷) means a depression. "Yin" (阴) refers to the medial aspect of the leg. The point is from the kidney meridian which is also a Yin meridian, and is located in the depression on the medial side of the popliteal fossa, hence the name Yingu (Yin Valley).

Location:
In the depression on the medial side of the popliteal fossa, between the tendons of m. semitendinous and semimembranous (Fig. II-184).

Indications:
Impotence, uterine bleeding, dysuria, soreness and pain of the knees or the popliteal fossa.

Clinical Application:
It is the He-Sea point of the Kidney Meridian of Foot-Shaoyin, having the effect to strengthen the kidney, dispel heat, regulate qi circulation and ease pain.

Combinations:
With Shenshu (U.B.23) and Mingmen (Du 4) for treating impotence, prospermia, irregular menstruation and uterine bleeding,

With Zhibian (U.B.54) and Yingmen (U.B.37) for weakness and muscular atrophy of the lower extremities,

With Pangguangshu (U.B.28) and Sanyinjiao (Sp.6) for dysuria.

Method:
Puncture perpendicularly about 1-1.5 cun deep.

Needling Sensations:
Soreness and distention at the local area.

HENGGU (K.11) 横谷 (TRANSVERSE BONE)

The pubic bone was called "Henggu" (横谷), the transverse bone, in ancient times. The point is at the side of the symphysis pubis, hence the name Henggu (Transverse Bone).

Note: There are altogether 11 points in Fig. II-185, 6 located on the upper abdomen and 5 on the lower abdomen. The points are 1 cun apart, except Shangqu (K.17) and Huangshu (K.16), which are 2 cun apart. All the points are 0.5 cun lateral to the anterior middle line. They are all punctured perpendicularly .5-1 cun deep, except Youmen (K.21), which is needled perpendicularly about 0.7-1 cun deep. Deep insertion is contraindicated at all these points, in order to avoid causing damage to the viscera.

Note: Points on the upper abdomen are mainly indicated in disorders or the disease of the digestive system.

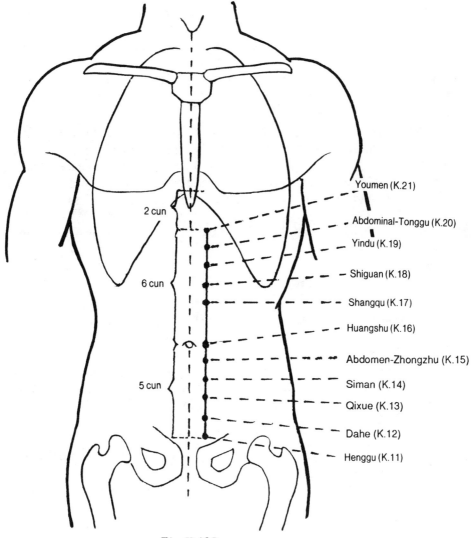

Fig. II-185

Location:

Five cun below the umbilicus, 0.5 cun lateral to the Ren Meridian, at the level of Qugu (Ren 2) (Fig. II-185).

Indications:

Pain in the external genitalia, seminal emission, impotence and retention of urine.

Method:

Puncture perpendicularly about 0.8-1 cun deep.

DAHE (K.12) 大赫 (GREAT PROMINENCE)

"Da" (大) means something great or big, or tremendous. "He" (赫) means clear or clarity. The uterus lies underneath the point and in pregnancy, the abdomen becomes bigger and more obvious. Hence the name Dahe (Great Prominence)

Location:

Four cun below the umbilicus and 0.5 cun lateral to Zhongji (Ren 3) (Fig. II-185).
Indications:
Pain in the external genitalia, seminal emission, leukorrhea.
Method:
Puncture perpendicularly about 1 cun deep.

QIXUE (K.13) 气 穴 (QI SOURCE POINT)

"Qi" (气) here refers to the source of qi. "Xue" (穴) means point. This is the coalescent point of the Kidney Meridian of the Foot-Shaoyin with the Chong Meridian. In Qigong (Breathing Exercises), the area around the point is the place where the qi is directed to be stored. The kidney receives the natural qi from the lung, which becomes the source of the general qi of the body, hence the name Qixue (Qi Source Point).

Location:
Three cun below the umbilicus and 0.5 cun lateral to Guanyuan (Ren 4) (Fig. II-185).

Indications:
Irregular menstruation, diarrhea and abdominal pain.

Method:
Puncture perpendicularly about 0.5-1 cun deep.

SIMAN (K.14) 四 满 (FOUR FULL)

"Si" (四) means four or the fourth. "Man" (满) means full or fullness. This is the fourth point of the Kidney Meridian located on the abdomen and needling it can relieve fullness, retention, obstruction and distention sensations of the abdomen. Hence the name Siman (Four Full).

Location:
Two cun below the umbilicus and 0.5 cun lateral to Shimen (Ren 5) (Fig. II-185).

Indications:
Uterine bleeding, irregular menstruation, postpartum abdominal pain, diarrhea.

Method:
Puncture perpendicularly 0.5-1 cun deep.

ABDOMEN-ZHONGZHU (K.15) 中 注 (CENTRAL FLOWING)

"Zhong" (中) means middle or central. "Zhu" (注) means to infuse or flow. The point, lateral to Abdomen-Yinjiao (Ren 7), is the place where the kidney qi converges before reaching the Dantian—the centre of the abdomen. Hence the name Abdomen-Zhongzhu (Central Flowing).

Location:
One cun below the umbilicus, 0.5 cun lateral to Abdomen-Yinjiao (Ren 7) (Fig.-II-185).

Indications:
Irregular menstruation, lower abdominal pain, constipation.

Method:
Puncture perpendicularly about 0.5-0.8 cun deep.

HUANGSHU (K.16) 肓 俞   (PERITONEUM POINT)

"Huang" (肓) here refers to the membrane or the tissues connecting the internal organs together. The qi of the kidney meridian infuses into the abdomen through this point, hence the name Huangshu (Peritoneum Point).

Location:

0.5 cun lateral to Shenque (Ren 8), the umbilicus (Fig. II-185).

Indications:

Abdominal pain, vomiting, abdominal distension, constipation.

Method:

Puncture perpendicularly about 0.5-0.8 cun deep.

SHANGQU (K.17) 商 曲   (SHANG CROOK)

"Shang" (商) here refers to the large intestine, which is represented by metal according to the theory of the five elements, and metal being associated with Shang (商) in the five-tone scale. "Qu" (曲) means crooked. This point can be used in disorders of the colon, which takes several crooked turns along its course. Hence the name Shangqu (Shang Crook).

Location:

Two cun above the umbilicus, 0.5 cun lateral to Xiawan (Ren 10) (Fig. II-185).

Indications:

Abdominal pain, abdominal distension, nausea, vomiting and constipation.

Method:

Puncture perpendicularly about 0.8-1 cun deep.

SHIGUAN (K.18) 石 关   (STONE PASS)

Obstructions and stagnation are described as "Shi" (石, Stone) disorders. "Guan" (关) means to pass. The point is mainly indicated in constipation, fullness and distention of the abdomen with qi stagnation, infertility, etc. hence the name Shiguan (Stone Pass).

Location:

Three cun above the umbilicus, 0.5 cun lateral to Jianli (Ren.11) (Fig. II-185).

Indications:

Besides the above-mentioned, it also can be used to treat nausea and vomiting, and abdominal pain.

Method:

Puncture perpendicularly about 0.8-1 cun deep.

YINDU (K.19) 阴 都   (YIN CAPITAL)

"Du" (都) means a capital city, referring to a convergent place of the qi of the meridian. The point is from a Yin meridian and the kidney dominates water and pertains to Yin. It is the coalescent point connecting with the Chong Meridian, known as the sea of the blood (Yin) and located in the abdomen, the yin aspect of the body, hence the name Yindu (Yin Capital).

The point is sometimes also called Shigong (Food Palace) because it is located 0.5 cun lateral to Zhongwan (Ren 12), the Front-Mu point of the stomach.

Location:

Four cun above the umbilicus, 0.5 cun lateral to Ren Meridian (Fig. II-185).

Indications:

Abdominal pain, borborygmus, distention and fullness of the upper abdomen and constipation.

Method:

Puncture perpendicularly 0.8-1 cun deep.

ABDOMEN-TONGGU (K.20) 腹通谷 (PASSING VALLEY)

"Tong" (通) means reaching or passing by. "Gu" (谷) means valley. The kidney and Chong Meridians pass here on their way to the chest, hence the name Abdomen-Tonggu (Passing Valley).

Location:

Five cun above the umbilicus and 0.5 cun lateral to Shangwan (Ren 13) (Fig. II-185).

Indications:

Abdominal distention, abdominal pain, nausea, vomiting, weakness and dysfunction of the spleen and stomach.

Method:

Puncture perpendicularly 0.8-1 cun deep.

YOUMEN (K.21) 幽门 (SE-CLUDED DOOR)

"You" (幽) means secluded or hidden. "Men" (门) means door or gate. The point is close to the upper orifice of the stomach, which is inside, as though secluded, hence the name Youmen (Secluded Door). It is sometimes also called Shangmen (上门), Upper Door.

Location:

Six cun above the umbilicus, 0.5 cun lateral to Juque (Ren 14) (Fig. II-185).

Indications:

Note: The 6 points on the chest are all located in the intercostal spaces, 2 cun lateral to the anterior midline. Points from Bulang (K.22) to Yuzhong (K.26) are located respectively in the 5th, 4th, 3rd, 2nd and 1st intercostal spaces. They are all punctured obliquely or transversely about 0.3-0.5 cun deep.

Caution: Deep and perpendicular insertion are contraindicated since the heart and lung lie underneath these points.

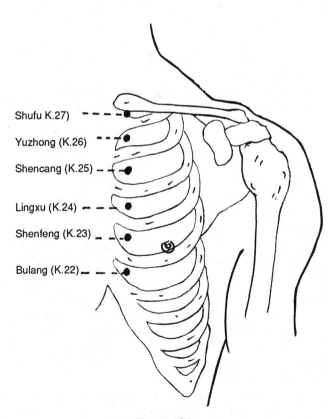

Shufu K.27)
Yuzhong (K.26)
Shencang (K.25)
Lingxu (K.24)
Shenfeng (K.23)
Bulang (K.22)

Fig. II-186

Pain in the chest and hypochondriac region, irritability, restlessness, localized pain due to stagnation.

Method:
Puncture perpendicularly 0.8-1 cun deep. Deep insertion is especially contraindicated at this point.

BULANG (K.22) 步廊 (WALKING CORRIDOR)

The central part of the chest is called "Ting" (厅), the hall, and both sides of the hall are the corridors "Lang" (廊). "Bu" (步) here means to walk slowly, referring to the qi of the meridian making its way upwards along either side of the chest from the point. Hence the name Bulang (Walking Corridor).

Location:
In the 5th intercostal space, at the level of Zhongting (Ren 16) (Fig. II-186).

Indications:
Cough, asthma, nausea and vomiting, fullness of the chest.

Method:
See the above note.

SHENFENG (K.23) 神封 (MIND'S FEOFF)

The point is close to the heart, which houses the mind "Shen" (神). "Feng" (封) means the feoff, referring to the area where the heart is located, hence the name Shenfeng (Mind's Feoff).

Location:
In the 4th intercostal space, at the level of the point Shangzhong (Ren 17) (Fig. II-186).

Indications:
Cough, asthma, fullness in the chest and hypochondriac region, mastitis and poor appetite.

Method:
See the above note.

LINGXU (K.24) 灵墟 (SOUL'S PLACE)

"Ling" (灵) refers to the soul or the spirit. "Xu" (墟) here means a place or area. The point is closely associated with the heart, hence the name Lingxu (Soul's Place).

Location:
In the 3rd intercostal space, at the level of Yutang (Ren 18) (Fig. II-186).

Indications:
Cough, asthma, sensation of fullness in the chest and hypochondriac region, poor appetite and mastitis.

Method:
See the above note.

SHENCANG (K.25) 神藏 (MIND STORAGE)

"Shen" (神) refers to the spirit, or the mind housed by the heart. "Cang" (藏) means to store. Underneath the point the branch of the kidney meridian from the diaphragm merges into the heart. Kidney qi is essential to enable the heart to store the mind. Hence the name Shencang (Mind Storage).

Location:

In the 2nd intercostal space, at the level of Chest-Zigong (Ren 19) (Fig. II-186).

Indications:

Chest pain, cough and asthma.

Method:

See the above note.

YUZHONG (K.26) 彧 中 (COMFORTABLE CHEST)

"Yu" (彧) means nice or glorious. "Zhong" (中) means centre, referring to the chest. The point has the effect to relieve stuffiness and distention of the chest, regulate qi circulation, thereby making the chest comfortable. It is mainly indicated in cough, asthma, etc. Hence the name Yuzhong (Comfortable Chest).

Location:

In the 1st intercostal space, at the level of Huagai (Ren 20) (Fig. II-186).

Indications:

Asthma, cough, fullness sensation and distention of the chest and hypochondriac regions, chest pain.

Method:

See above note.

SHUFU (K.27) 俞 府 (POINT RESIDENCE)

"Shu" (俞) means point. "Fu" (府) means the resident place or convergent place of the qi. The qi of the kidney meridian ascends from the foot, merging into the chest at this point, the last point on the meridian, hence the name Shufu (Point Residence).

Location:

In the depression on the lower border of the clavicle, and 2 cun lateral to the Ren Meridian (Fig. II-186).

Indications:

Cough, asthma and chest pain.

Method:

See the above note.

III. Summary

The Kidney Meridian of Foot-Shaoyin pertains to the kidney, connects with the urinary bladder and is associated with the liver, lung, heart, spinal cord, throat and tongue. There are 27 points on either side of the body, distributed on the sole, the heel, the posterior border of the medial aspect of the lower limbs and on the first and lateral lines of the abdomen and the chest. There are 6 points on the foot, 4 on the leg and 11 on the abdomen, the rest being located on the chest (Figs. II-187A and B).

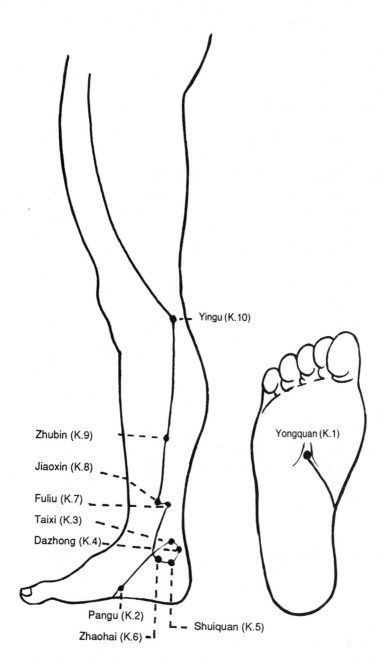

Fig. II-187A

The Specific Points from This Meridian

Yingu	K.10	He Wood	Yongquan	K.1	☉ Water	
Fuliu	K.7	⊖Fire	Zhaohai	K.6	⊗	
Taixi	K.3	O Earth ꝗ	Shuiquan	K.5	Xi	
Rangu	K.2	∼ Metal	Dazhong	K.4	∧	

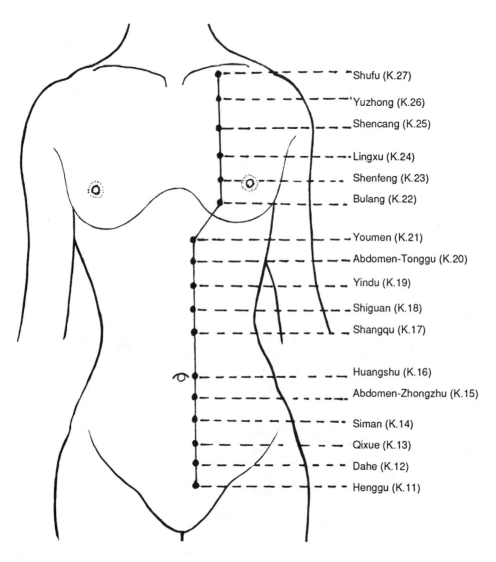

Shufu (K.27)
Yuzhong (K.26)
Shencang (K.25)
Lingxu (K.24)
Shenfeng (K.23)
Bulang (K.22)
Youmen (K.21)
Abdomen-Tonggu (K.20)
Yindu (K.19)
Shiguan (K.18)
Shangqu (K.17)
Huangshu (K.16)
Abdomen-Zhongzhu (K.15)
Siman (K.14)
Qixue (K.13)
Dahe (K.12)
Henggu (K.11)

Fig. II-187B

Point Indications of This Meridian According to Regional Locations

Point Names	Indications	Locations	Regional Indications
Yongquan K.1	In the depression appearing on the sole when the foot is in plantar flexion	Loss of the consciousness, infantile convulsion, pain of the heal, pain of the knee	
Rangu K.2	In the depression on the lower border of the tuberosity of the navicular bone	Infantile convulsion, pruritus vulvae	Diseases of the reproductive and urinary systems
Taixi K.3	In the depression between the medial malleolus and the tendo calcaneus, at the level of the tip of the medial malleolus	Dizziness, tinnitus, toothache, chronic laryngitis and for general tonification	
Dazhong K.4	Posterior and inferior to the medial malleolus, in the depression medial to the attachment of the tendo calcaneus	Swelling and pain of the heel, retention of the urine	
Shuiquan K.5	1 cun directly below Taixi (K.3)	Amenorrhea, dysmenorrhea, dysuria	
Zhaohai K.6	In the depression 1 cun below the medial malleolus	Chronic sore throat, acute infections of the urethra	
Fuliu K.7	2 cun directly above Taixi (K.3) on the anterior border of the tendo calcaneus	Acute inflammation of the urethra, night sweating, spontaneous sweating	
Jiaoxin K.8	2 cun above Taixi (K.3) between Fuliu (K.7) and the tibia	Irregular menstruation	
Zhubin K.9	5 cun directly above Taixi (K.3)	Menorrhagia, pain of the leg	
Yingu K.10	On the medial side of the popliteal fossa	Impotence, seminal emission	
Henggu K.11	On the superior border of the symphysis pubis, 0.5 cun lateral to Qugu (Ren2)	Retention of the urine, pain in the external genitalia	
Dahe K.12	1 cun above Henggu (K.11) and 0.5 cun lateral to Zhongji (Ren 3)	Seminal emission, pain in the external genitalia	
Qixue K.13	1 cun above Dahe (K. 12) and 0.5 cun lateral to Guanyuan (Ren 4)	Pain in the lower abdominal region with cold sensation, colicky pain of the intestines	
Siman K.14	1 cun above Qixue (K.13), and 0.5 cun lateral to Shimen (Ren 5)	Pain around the umbilicus, uterine bleeding	
Zhongzhu K.15	1 cun above Siman (K.14) and 0.5 cun lateral to Yinjiao (Ren 7)	Hot pain in the lower abdomen, pain in the lumbar region	

Huangshu K.16	0.5 cun lateral to Shenque (Ren 8), the umbilicus	Pain and distention of the abdomen	
Shangqu K.17	2 cun above Huangshu (K.16), and 0.5 cun lateral to Xiawan (Ren 10)	Abdominal pain	Disorders of the stomach and the intestines
Shiguan K.18	3 cun above Huangshu (K.16) and 0.5 cun lateral to Jianli (Ren 11)	Weakness and cold of the spleen and stomach, infertility and dysmenorrhea	
Yindu K.19	1 cun above Shiguan (K.18), and 0.5 cun lateral to Zhongwan (Ren 12)	Pain and distention of the abdomen	
Tonggu K.20	1 cun above Yindu (K.19) and 0.5 cun lateral to Shangwan (Ren 13)	Hypochondriac pain, gastrectasia, epigastric pain	
Youmen K.21	1 cun above Tonggu (K.20) and 0.5 cun lateral to Juque (Ren 14)	Stomach ache, lactation deficiency and mastitis	
Bulang K.22	In the 5th intercostal space, 2 cun lateral to Ren Meridian	Pain and fullness sensation in the chest and hypochondriac region, pleuritis	
Shenfeng K.23	In the 4th intercostal space, and 2 cun lateral to Ren Meridian	Intercostal neuralgia, cough	
Lingxu K.24	In the 3rd intercostal space, 2 cun lateral to Ren Meridian	Fullness sensation of the chest, intercostal neuralgia	Diseases of the chest and the lung
Shencang K.25	In the 2nd intercostal space and 2 cun lateral to Ren Meridian	Fullness sensation in the chest and hypochondriac region, cough, asthma	
Yuzhong K.26	In the 1st intercostal space, 2 cun lateral to Ren Meridian	Cough, asthma, mastitis	
Shufu K.27	In the depression on the lower border of the clavicle, 2 cun lateral to Ren Meridian	Cough, asthma, pain in the chest	

Section 3   THE LIVER MERIDIAN OF FOOT-JUEYIN

1. The Meridian

General Indications

The points from this meridian are mainly indicated in headache, dizziness and vertigo, distention, fullness sensation and pain in the chest and the hypochondriac region, dysuria, pain and itching of the external genitalia, twitching of the facial muscles, mental disorders, epilepsy, infantile convulsion, eye disorders, inguinal hernia, jaundice, etc.

Course of the Meridian:

(1) The Liver Meridian of Foot-Jueyin starts from the dorsal hairy region of the great toe (Dadun, Liv.1), (2) runs upwards along the dorsum of the foot, (3) passes through the area 1 cun anterior to the medial malleolus (Zhongfeng, Liv.4), (4) then

ascends to an area 8 cun above the medial malleolus, where it runs across and behind the Spleen Meridian of Foot-Taiyin. (5) It ascends further to the medial side of the knee, (6) along the medial aspect of the thigh (7) to the pubic region (8) where it curves around the external genitalia, (9) and goes up to the lower abdomen. (10) It continues upwards, curves around the stomach, enters the liver, its pertaining organ, and connects with the gall bladder. (11) It continues to ascend, passing through the diaphragm, (12) and branches out in the costal and hypochondriac region. (13) It ascends along the posterior aspect of the throat (14) to the nasopharynx (15) and connects with the "Eye System." (16) Running further upwards, it emerges from the forehead (17) and meets the Du Meridian at the vertex.

The Branch of the "Eye System":

(18) It arises from the "eye system", runs downwards into the neck, (19) and curves around the inner surface of the lips.

The Liver Branch:

(20) It arises from the liver (21), passes through the diaphragm (22), flows into the lung and links with the Lung Meridian of Hand-Taiyin (Fig. II-188).

Analytical Display of the Course of the Meridian:

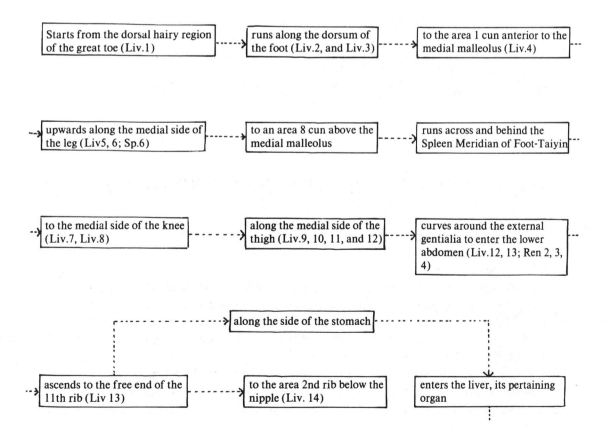

connects with the gall bladder	→ passes through the diaphragm	→ enters the lung to link with the Lung Meridian of Hand-Taiyin

branches out into the hypochondriac region	to the forehead	reaches the vertex where it meets the Du Meridian

passes the throat	→ reaches the pharynx	→ connects with the eye system	→ enters the brain

downwards to the cheek	→ curves around the inner surface of the lips

Related Zangfu Organs:

The Liver Meridian of Foot-Jueyin pertains to the liver, connects with the gall bladder, links with the stomach and the lung.

Coalescent Points of the Meridian:

Tianchi (P.1), Sanyinjiao (Sp.6), Chongmen (Sp. 12), Fushe (Sp. 13), Qugu (Ren 2), Zhongji (Ren 3) and Guanyuan (Ren 4).

II. The Points:

There are 14 points on this meridian on either side of the body. Twelve are distributed along the medial aspect of the lower extremities, the rest being on the abdomen and chest. The first point is Dadun (Liv.1), and the last one is Qimen (Liv.14).

Point Names	Pinyin	Codes	Point Names	Pinyin	Codes
大敦	Dadun	Liv.1	曲泉	Ququan	Liv.8
行间	Xingjian	Liv.2	阴包	Yinbao	Liv.9
太冲	Taichong	Liv.3	五里	Femur-Wuli	Liv.10
中封	Zhongfeng	Liv.4	阴廉	Yinlian	Liv.11
蠡沟	Ligou	Liv.5	急脉	Jimai	Liv.12
中都	Zhongdu	Liv.6	章门	Zhangmen	Liv.13
膝关	Xiguan	Liv.7	期门	Qimen	Liv:14

*DADUN (LIV.1) 大敦 **"o"**   (BIG MOUND)

"Da" (大) means big. "Dun" (敦) means a mound, here it refers to something thick. The front part of the great toe where the point is located is big and thick, hence the name Dadun (Big Mound).

Location:

On the lateral side of the great toe, 0.1 cun posterior to the corner of the nail. Draw

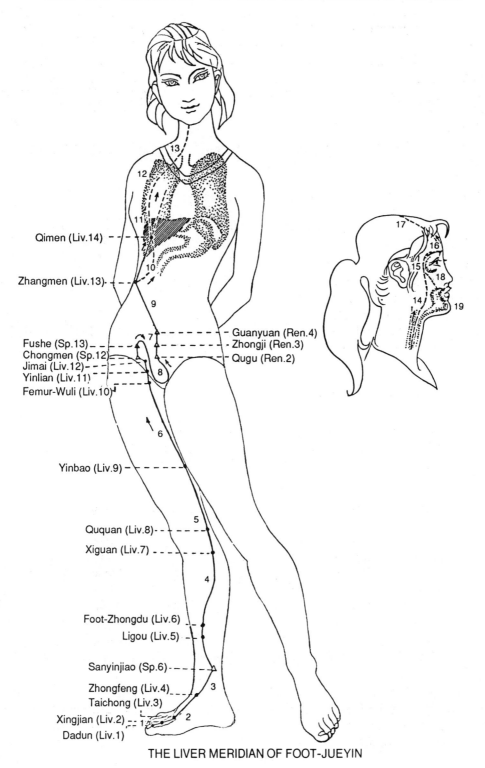

Qimen (Liv.14)

Zhangmen (Liv.13)

Fushe (Sp.13)
Chongmen (Sp.12)
Jimai (Liv.12)
Yinlian (Liv.11)
Femur-Wuli (Liv.10)

Guanyuan (Ren.4)
Zhongji (Ren.3)
Qugu (Ren.2)

Yinbao (Liv.9)

Ququan (Liv.8)

Xiguan (Liv.7)

Foot-Zhongdu (Liv.6)

Ligou (Liv.5)

Sanyinjiao (Sp.6)

Zhongfeng (Liv.4)
Taichong (Liv.3)

Xingjian (Liv.2)
Dadun (Liv.1)

THE LIVER MERIDIAN OF FOOT-JUEYIN

Fig. II-188

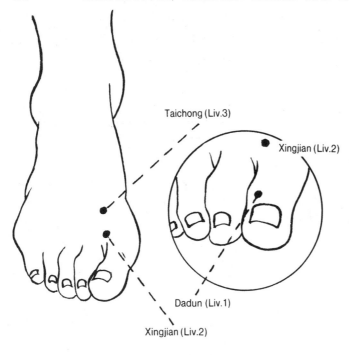

Fig. II-189

a " 田 " figure from the mid-point of the root of the nail to the dorsum of the terminal phalanx of the great toe, the point will lie in the middle of the " 田 " (Fig. II-189).

Indications:

Menorrhagia, prolapse of the uterus, pain in the external genitalia, enuresis and hernia.

Clinical Application:

It is the Jing-Well point of the Liver Meridian of Foot-Jueyin, having the effect to remove obstructions from the meridian and the collaterals and restore consciousness.

Combinations:

With Neiting (St.44), Xiaxi (G.B.43) and Xingjian (Liv.2) for treating the numbness sensation of the toe,

With Lidui (St.45), Yongquan (K.1) and Foot-Qiaoyin (G.B.44) for syncope.

Method:

Puncture about 0.1-0.2 cun deep, or prick to cause bleeding.

Needling Sensations:

Slight pain at the local area.

*XINGJIAN (LIV.2) 行间   " ～ "   (PASSING BETWEEN)

"Xing" (行) means to walk or pass by. It also means "Hang" (行), road or passage. "Jian" (间) means between. The point is located between the first and second toes, the meridian passing between the two. Hence the name Xingjian (Passing Between).

Location:

Between the 1st and 2nd toes, 0.5 cun proximal to the margin of the web and anterior to the metatarsal phalangeal joint (Fig. II-189).

Indications:

Redness, swelling and pain of the eye, glaucoma, menorrhagia, pain in the urethra, enuresis, hypochondriac pain, convulsion, headache and insomnia.

Clinical Application:

It is the Ying-Spring point of the Liver Meridian of the Foot-Jueyin and has the effect to soothe the liver and regulate qi circulation.

Combinations:

With Fengchi (G.B.20), Baihui (Du 20), Hegu (L.I.4) and Taiyang (Extra) for treating headache and redness of the eye,

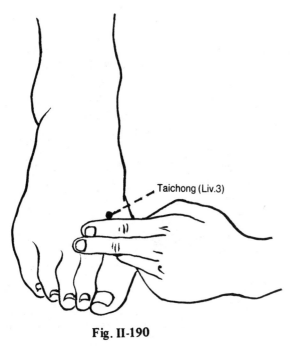

Taichong (Liv.3)

Fig. II-190

With Fengchi (G.B.20), Yingtang (Extra), Yamen (Du 15) and Zusanli (St.36) for dizziness and vertigo.

Method:

Puncture perpendicularly about 0.5-0.8 cun deep.

Needling Sensations:

Distention and pain in the local area, or radiating down to the toes.

*TAICHONG (LIV.3) 太冲 "兑" "O" (GREATER POURING)

"Tai" (太) means great, and is also a symbol of the Yuan-Source points of the Yin Meridians of the foot. "Chong" (冲) means to pour, but here it refers to an important place. The qi of the Liver Meridian of Foot-Jueyin infuses here, qi and blood are abundant. This point is also indicated in menstrual problems and can restore the menstrual flow to normal. Hence the name Taichong (Greater Pouring).

Location:

In the depression distal to the junction of the 1st and 2nd metatarsal bones, 1.5 cun above Xingjian (Liv.2), and posterior to the metatarso-phalangeal joints (Fig. II-190).

Indications:

Headache, hypertension, dizziness and vertigo, insomnia, pain in the hypochondriac region, biliary colic, uterine bleeding, retention of urine, dysentery, dream-disturbed sleep, convulsion, schizophrenia.

Clinical Application:

It is the Shu-Stream and Yuan-Source point of the meridian having the effect to soothe the liver, promote the qi and blood circulation of the body, and regulate the menstrual flow.

Combinations:

With Fengchi (G.B.20), Zusanli (St. 36) and Sanyinjiao (Sp.6) for treating hypertension, dizziness and vertigo,

With Shenmen (H.7), Hegu (L.I.4) and Sanyinjiao (Sp.6) for insomnia.

Method:

Puncture perpendicularly about 0.5-1 cun deep.

Needling Sensations:

Distention and soreness, radiating upwards along the course of the meridian.

ZHONGFENG (LIV.4) 中封 "O" (MIDDLE BORDER)

"Zhong" (中) means middle. "Feng" (封) here means the border or the edge.

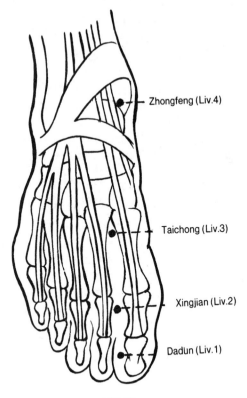

Zhongfeng (Liv.4)

Taichong (Liv.3)

Xingjian (Liv.2)

Dadun (Liv.1)

Fig. II-191

Location:

The point is located 1 cun anterior to the tip of the medial malleolus, in the depression between the tendons of m. tibialis anterior and m. extensor hallucis longus. It lies between the borders of the above two tendons, hence the name Zhongfeng (Middle Border).

See (Fig. II-191).

Indications:

Hernia, pain, seminal emission, dysuria, pain in the abdominal region or around the umbilicus.

Method:

Puncture perpendicularly about 0.5-0.8 cun deep.

LIGOU (LIV.5) 蠡沟 " ∧ " (IN-SECTS GNAWING)

"Li" (蠡) refers to the small holes gnawed in a piece of wood by insects. "Gou" (沟) refers to a small, narrow depression. When the foot is flexed upwards, there may appear a small narrow depression at the point area. The point is indicated in profuse leukorrhea, uterine bleeding and puritus vulvae. A patient with the above symptoms, especially with the last one, may feel a severe itching sensation, as though something were moving in the affected area. Hence the name Ligou (Insects Gnawing).

Location:

Five cun above the tip of the medial malleolus, on the medial aspect of the tibia (Fig. II-192).

Indications:

See the above item.

Method:

Puncture transversely about 0.5-0.8 cun deep.

ZHONGDU (LIV.6) 中都 "Xi" (CENTRAL CAPITAL)

"Zhong" (中) means the centre or the middle. "Du" (都) means a capital city, but here it refers to a convergent place. It is the Xi-Cleft point, where the qi and blood converge, besides which it is located 7 cun above the tip of the medial malleolus, approximately half way along the leg on the medial aspect of the tibia. Hence the name Zhongdu (Central Capital).

Location:

See the above item (Fig. II-192).

Indications:

Abdominal pain, diarrhea, profuse leukorrhea.

Method:

Puncture transversely about 0.5-0.8 cun deep.

XIGUAN (Liv.7) 膝关 (KNEE JOINT)

"Xi" (膝) means knee, "Guan" (关) means joint. The point is located close to the knee, hence the name Xiguan (Knee Joint).

Location:

One cun posterior to Yinlingquan (Sp.9) (Fig. II-192, 194).

Indications:

Sore throat and knee-joint pain.

Method:

Puncture perpendicularly about 1-1.5 cun deep.

*QUQUAN (LIV.8) 曲泉 "HE"   (CROOKED SPRING)

"Qu" (曲) means something curved or crooked. "Quan" (泉) means spring, here referring to a depression. When locating the point, have the patient flex the leg. The point lies in the depression which appears at the medial aspect of the knee, hence the name Ququan (Crooked Spring).

Location:

On the medial side of the knee joint. When the knee is flexed, the point lies in the depression posterior and superior to the medial end of the transverse popliteal crease, on the anterior border of the m. semimembranosus and posterior to the medial condyle of the tibia (Fig. II-193-194).

Indications:

Prolapse of the uterus, lower abdominal pain, dysuria, pain and swelling of the knee, puritus vulvae, impotence and seminal emission.

Clinical Application:

It is the He-Sea point of this meridian, having the effect to relax the tendons, promote the function of the collaterals and eliminate damp and heat from the lower jiao.

Combinations:

With Yanglingquan (G.B.34), Xiyangguan (G.B.33) and Dubi

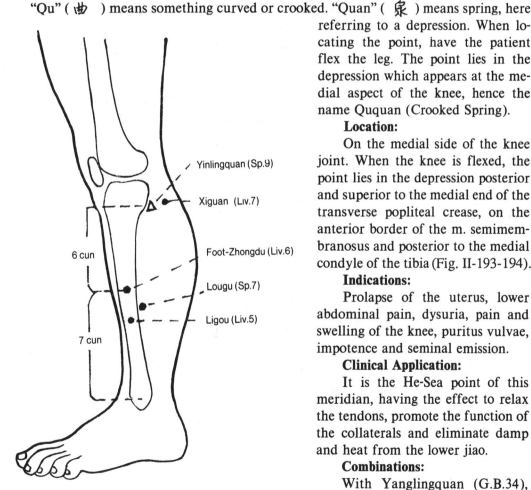

Yinlingquan (Sp.9)

Xiguan (Liv.7)

Foot-Zhongdu (Liv.6)

Lougu (Sp.7)

Ligou (Liv.5)

6 cun

7 cun

Fig. II-192

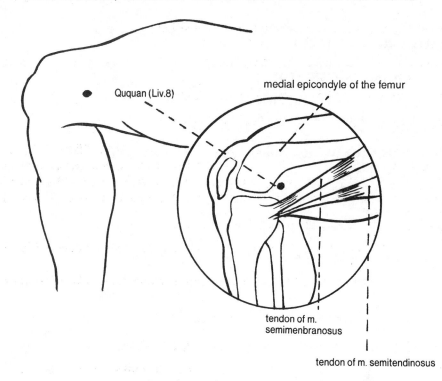

Ququan (Liv.8)

medial epicondyle of the femur

tendon of m. semimenbranosus

tendon of m. semitendinosus

Fig. II-193

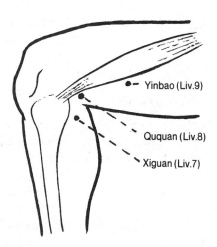

Yinbao (Liv.9)

Ququan (Liv.8)

Xiguan (Liv.7)

Fig. II-194

(St.35) for treating pain and swelling of the knee joint.
Method:
Puncture 1-1.5 cun deep perpendicularly.
Needling Sensations:
Soreness and distention around the local area.

YINBAO (LIV 9) 阴 包   (YIN'S CONTAINER)

The medial aspect of the thigh is the "Yin" (阴) side. "Bao" (包) means a container or being contained. The point lies between the spleen and kidney meridians, both of which are Yin. "Bao" (包) also refers to the uterus, the qi of the Liver Meridian of Foot-Jueyin communicating with the uterus through this point. Hence the name Yinbao (Yin's Container).
Location:
Four cun above Ququan (liv.8), on the border of m. vastus medialis (Fig. II-194).
Indications:
Pain in the lumbosacral region, abdominal pain, enuresis and irregular menstruation.
Method:
Puncture perpendicularly about 1-2 cun deep.

FEMUR-WULI (LIV.10) 五里   (FEMUR 5 MEASURES)

"Wu" (五) means 5. "Li" (里) means measure. This point is located 2 cun lateral and 3 cun directly below Qugu (Ren 2) and 5 cun above Jimen. Hence the name Femur-Wuli (Femur 5 Measures).
Location:
See the above item (Fig. II-195).
Indications:
Fullness of the lower abdominal region, retention of urine, general lassitude, and somnolence.
Method:
Puncture perpendicularly about 1-2 cun deep.

YINLIAN (LIV.11) 阴廉   (YIN EDGE)

The medial aspect is "Yin" (阴); "lian" (廉) refers to the edge or the margin, here referring to the site of the external genitalia. The point is 2 cun lateral to and 2 cun below Qugu (Ren 2), hence the name Yinlian (Yin Edge).
Location:
See the above item (Fig. II-195).
Indications:
Irregular menstruation, profuse leukorrhea, lower abdominal pain, pain of the thigh and leg.
Method:
Puncture 1-2 cun deep perpendicularly.

JIMAI (LIV.12) 急脉   (RAPID PULSE)

"Ji" (急) means quick or rapid. "Mai" (脉) here refers to the pulse. The point is located 2.5 cun lateral to the mid-point of the lower border of the symphysis pubis, at the inguinal groove. The pulse of the arteria femoralis passes the point, and can be palpated, hence the name Jimai (Rapid Pulse).

Location:

See the above item (Fig. II-195).

Indications:

Lower abdominal pain, hernia and prolapse of the uterus.

Method:

Puncture 0.5-0.8 cun deep perpendicularly. Avoid the artery.

*ZHANGMEN (LIV.13) 章门   "MU" "⊖"   (BRIGHT DOOR)

"Zhang" (章) here means bright. "Men" (门) means door. The point is from the Liver Meridian of Foot-Jueyin, represented by the colour green and the season of spring denoting the bright. The hypochondriac region is likened to a door, hence the name Zhangmen (Bright Door).

Location:

On the lateral side of the abdomen, below the free end of the 11th floating rib. When the elbow is flexed and the arm abducted, the point is located at where the tip of the elbow touches (Figs. II-196, 197).

Indications:

Vomiting, diarrhea, splenomegaly, distention and fullness sensation in the chest and hypochondriac region, weakness of the spleen and stomach, hepatitis.

Clinical Application:

This is the Front-Mu point of the spleen, and one of the Eight Influential Points being associated with the viscera (zang organs). It has the effect to soothe the liver, regulate the circulation of qi, invigorate blood circulation and resolve the coagulation of blood.

Combinations:

With Zusanli (St.36) for treating diarrhea;

With Neiguan (P.6) for vomiting, chest and hypochondriac distention or fullness;

With Sanyinjiao (Sp.6) and Taichong (Liv.3) for splenomegaly and hepatomegaly.

Method:

Puncture perpendicularly about 0.8-1 cun deep.

Needling Sensations:

Distention and heaviness at the local area, or radiating down to the abdomen.

QIMEN (LIV.14) 期门   "MU"   (CYCLIC DOOR)

"Qi" (期) means a cycle. "Men" (门) means door, referring to the point on the side of the trunk, and also a place where qi comes and goes. The qi and the blood circulation of the meridians starts from Yunmen (Lu.1), passes through the meridians of the lung, large intestine, stomach, spleen, heart, small intestine, urinary bladder, kidney, pericardium, Sanjiao, gall bladder and the liver, finally ending at Qimen (Liv.14). It is the last of the points from the 12 regular meridians, at the end of the qi cycle. Hence the name Qimen (Cyclic Door).

Location:

Two ribs directly below the nipple, in the depression of the 6th intercostal space

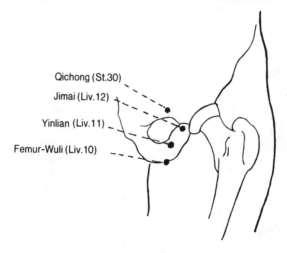

Qichong (St.30)
Jimai (Liv.12)
Yinlian (Liv.11)
Femur-Wuli (Liv.10)

Fig. II-195

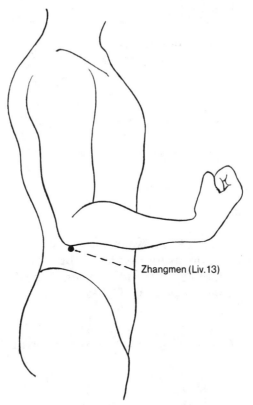

Zhangmen (Liv.13)

Fig. II-196

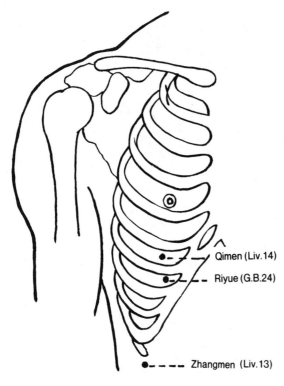

Qimen (Liv.14)

Riyue (G.B.24)

Zhangmen (Liv.13)

Fig. II-197

(Fig. II-197).

Indications:

Distention and fullness sensation in the chest, pain of the chest and hypochondriac region, vomiting, acid regurgitation and cholecystitis.

Clinical Application:

This is the Front-Mu point of the liver, and the coalescent point of the Liver Meridian of Foot-Jueyin with the Spleen Meridian of Foot-Taiyin and Yinwei Meridian. It has the effect to soothe the liver, regulate qi circulation and resolve coagulation of blood.

Combinations:

With Neiguan (P.6) and Shanzhong (Ren 17) for distention and fullness of the chest and the hypochondriac region, biliary colic pain;

With Danshu (U.B.19) and Ganshu (U.B.18) for cholecystitis;

With Zusanli (St.36) for indigestion.

Method:

Puncture transversely or obliquely about 0.5-0.8 cun deep.

Note: Perpendicular or deep insertion at this point is contraindicated.

Needling Sensations:

Distention and heaviness around the local area.

III. Summary

There are altogether 14 points on this meridian. They are located on the great toe, the dorsum of the foot, the medial aspect of the lower limb, the chest and the hypochondriac area. Four are located on the foot region, 4 on the leg, 4 on the thigh and the last 2 on the hypochondriac region (Fig. II-198).

Specific Points of This Meridian

Ququan	Liv.8	He-Water	Ligou	Liv.5	∧
Zhongfeng	Liv.4	⌒ Metal	Zhongdu	Liv.6	Xi
Taichong	Liv.3	Earth ⋔ O	Zhangmen	Liv.13	Mu O
Xingjian	Liv.2	Fire ⌢	Qimen	Liv.14	Mu
Dadun	Liv.1	Wood ⊙			

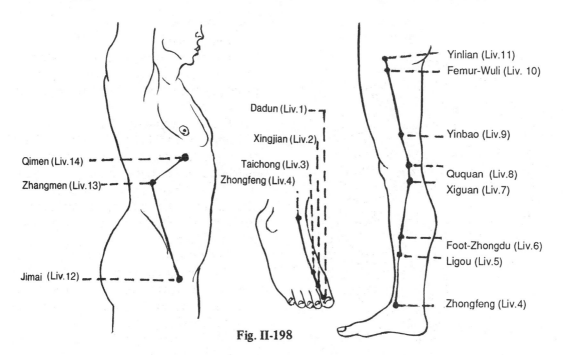

Fig. II-198

Point Indications of the Liver Meridian of Foot-Jueyin
According to Regional Locations

Point Names	Locations	Indications	Regional Indications
Dadun Liv.1	On the lateral side of the great toe, 0.1 cun posterior to the lateral corner of the nail	Inguinal hernia, testitis	
Xingjian Liv.2	0.5 cun proximal to the margin of the web of the 1st and 2nd toes	Headache, dizziness, vertigo, eye diseases	Diseases of the reproductive and urinary systems
Taichong Liv. 3	In the depression distal to the junctions of the 1st and 2nd metatarsal bones	Headache, dizziness, and vertigo, convulsion	
Zhongfeng Liv.4	Anterior to the medial malleolus, midway between Shangqiu (Sp.14) and Jiexi (St.41)	Distention and pain around the umbilicus	
Ligou Liv.5	5 cun above the tip of the medial malleolus on the medial aspect of the tibia	Irregular menstruation, pelvic inflammation, constant erection of the penis	
Zhongdu Liv.6	7 cun above the tip of the medial malleolus and 2 cun above Ligou (Liv.5)	Irregular menstruation	
Xiguan Liv.7	1 cun posterior and superior to Yinlingquan (Sp.9)	Bi syndrome of wind, knee-joint pain	

Ququan Liv.8	Superior to the medial transverse popliteal crease	Dysmenorrhea, infections of the urinary tract	
Yinbao Liv.9	4 cun above the medial epicondyle of the femur	Lumbosacral pain, enuresis	
Femur-Wuli Liv.10	3 cun below Qichong (St.30), on the medial side of the arteria femoralis	Enuresis, somnolence, retention of urine	
Yinlian Liv.11	2 cun directly below Qichong (St.30) on the medial aspect of the arteria femoralis	Irregular menstruation	
Jimai Liv.12	Inferior and lateral to the pubic spine, 2.5 cun lateral to the Ren Meridian	Pain in the external genitalia	
Zhangmen Liv.13	Below the free end of the 11th floating rib	Splenomegaly, jaundice	Diseases of the stomach and intestines, pain in the chest
Qimen Liv.14	Directly below the nipple in the 6th intercostal space	Jaundice, pain in the hypochondriac region, pain of the breast	

Section 4 SUMMARY OF THE LOCATIONS OF SOME POINTS OF THE THREE YIN MERIDIANS OF THE FOOT

I. Foot Area: Locations of points are at the centre of the sole, or at the posterior corner of the nail of the big toe (Figs. II-199,200).

Yongquan (K.1): In the depression on the sole.

Yinbai (Sp.1): 0.1 cun posterior to the medial corner of the nail of the big toe.

Dadun (Liv.1): At the junction of lateral one fourth to the posterior corner of the nail of the big toe.

II. Metatarsal Phalangeal Joint Area: Locations of points are either proximal or distal to the joints (Fig.II-201,202).

Dadu (Sp.2) and Taibai (Sp.3) from the Spleen Meridian,

Xingjian (Liv.2) and Taichong (Liv.3) from the Liver Meridian.

These points are respectively distal and proximal to the metatarsal phalangeal joints.

III. Ankle Area: Locations of points are superior, inferior, anterior or posterior to the tip of the medial malleolus (Figs. II-203,204).

Sanyinjiao (Sp.6): 3 cun directly above the tip of the medial malleolus, on the posterior border of the tibia.

Zhaohai (K.6): Directly below the tip of the medial malleolus, 0.4 cun inferior to the lower border of the medial malleolus.

Zhongfeng (Liv.4): Anterior to the tip of the medial malleolus.

Taixi (K.3): Posterior to the tip of the medial malleolus.

All these points are located by using the tip of the medial malleolus as a landmark.

IV. Leg: Locations of points are beside the bone, on the bone or beside the tendons (Figs. II-203,204).

Sanyinjiao (Sp.6) and Yinlingquan (Sp.9) are on the posterior border of the tibia.

Fuliu (K.7) and Zhubin (K.9) are on the anterior border of the tendo calcaneus.

Ligou (Liv.5) and Foot-Zhongdu (Liv.6) are on the medial aspect of the tibia.

V. Knee-Joint Area: Locations of points are superior, inferior, or posterior to the medial condyle of the tibia (Fig. II-205).

Yinlingquan (Sp.9): Directly below the lower border of the medial condyle of the tibia.

Xiguan (Liv.7): 1 cun posterior and superior to the lower border of the medial condyle of the tibia.

Yingu (K.10): Posterior to the medial condyle of the tibia, between the tendons of m. semitendinosus and semimembranosus.

Ququan (Liv.8): On the superior medial border of the medial condyle of the tibia.

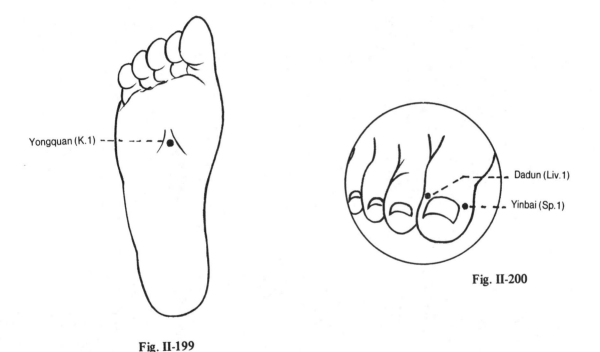

Fig. II-199

Fig. II-200

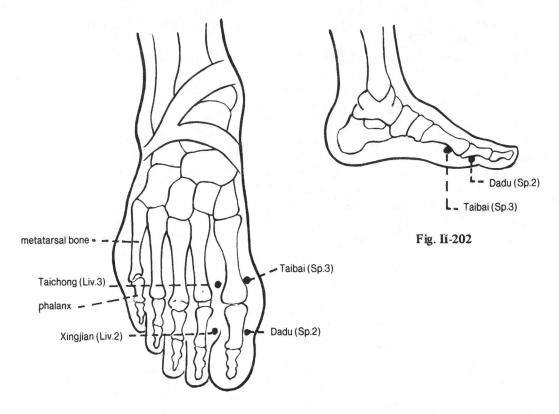

metatarsal bone

Taichong (Liv.3)

phalanx

Xingjian (Liv.2)

Taibai (Sp.3)

Dadu (Sp.2)

Dadu (Sp.2)

Taibai (Sp.3)

Fig. II-202

Fig. II-201

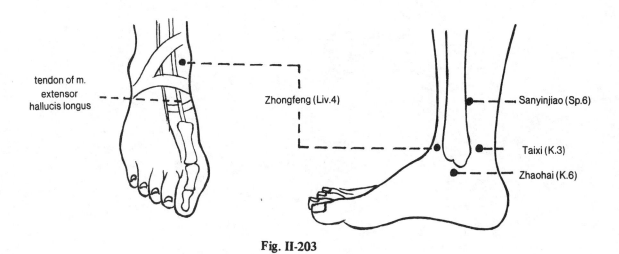

tendon of m.
extensor
hallucis longus

Zhongfeng (Liv.4)

Sanyinjiao (Sp.6)

Taixi (K.3)

Zhaohai (K.6)

Fig. II-203

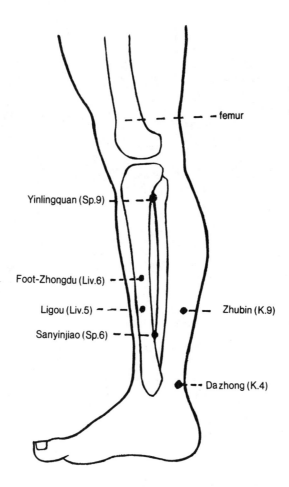

femur

Yinlingquan (Sp.9)

Foot-Zhongdu (Liv.6)

Ligou (Liv.5)

Zhubin (K.9)

Sanyinjiao (Sp.6)

Da zhong (K.4)

Fig. II-204

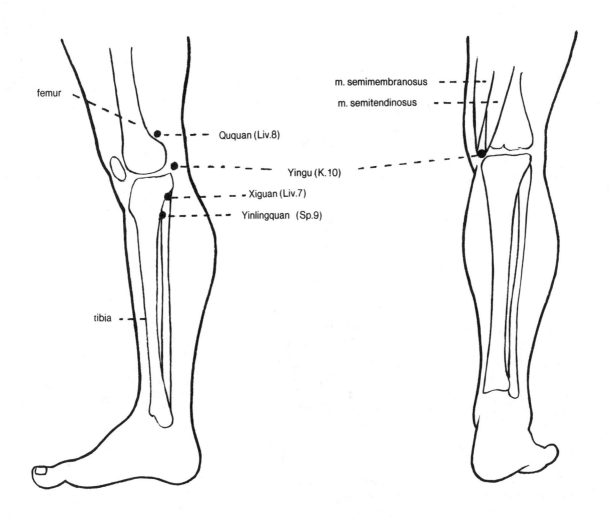

Fig. II-205

Chapter V

DU AND REN MERIDIANS

Section *I* THE DU MERIDIAN

I. The Meridian

General Indications:

Points from this meridian are mainly indicated in loss of consciousness, fever, infantile convulsion, malaria, psychosis, urogenital disorders, rigidity of the spinal column, neurasthenia, epilepsy, headache, impotence, leukorrhea, enuresis, diarrhea and internal disorders due to deficiency of Yang qi.

Course of the Meridian:

(1) The Du Meridian originates from the uterus in the lower abdomen (The Chong, Ren and Du meridians are all of the same origin). Descending, it emerges at the perineum, (2) then ascends along the interior of the spinal column (3) to Fengfu (Du 16) at the nape of the neck, where it enters the brain. (4) Reemerging, it ascends to the vertex (5) and winds along the forehead to the inferior aspect of the nasal columella.

The first branch emerges from the perineum and converges with the qi from the major part of Kidney Meridian of Foot-Shaoyin at the tip of the coccyx (Changqiang, Du 1). (6) It then runs into the spinal column and reemerges to enter the kidney.

(7) The second branch rises inside the lower abdomen, goes to the umbilicus (8) and ascends to the heart. (9) Running up to the throat region, it merges with both the Ren and Chong meridians, (10) then goes up to the mandibular region and curves around the lips (11) to connect with the infraorbital ridges of both eyes.

(12) Concurrently with the Urinary Bladder Meridian of Foot-Taiyang, the third branch of the Du Meridian emerges from the inner canthus and goes up into the forehead. (13) The two branches cross each other at the vertex (Baihui, Du 20), enter the brain and then reemerge. (14) Descending from the medial aspect of the scapula, (15) it runs down to the lumbar region along both sides of the spinal column to connect with the kidney (15) (Fig.II-206).

Related Zangfu Organs:

Brain, marrow, kidney, uterus, nose, eyes, mouth and lips.

Coalescent Points of the Meridian:

Note: The branches of Du Meridian are actually parts of the Urinary Bladder Meridian of Foot-Taiyang, the Kidney Meridian of Foot-Shaoyin, and the Chong and Ren meridians, which explains the close relationship between these meridians.

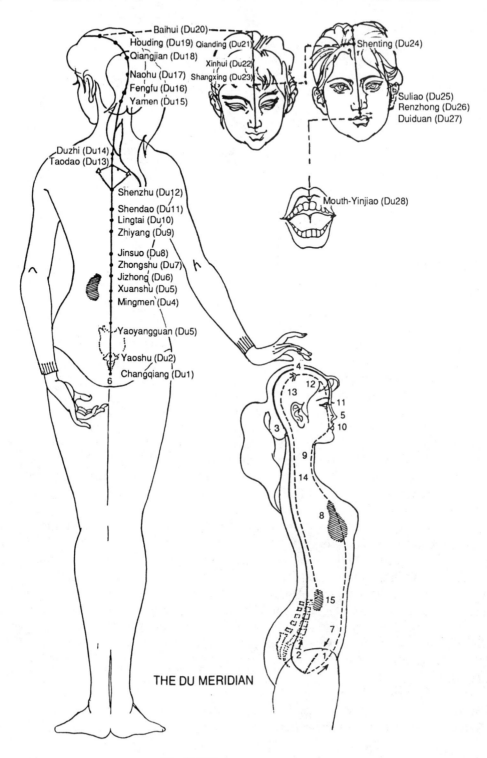

Baihui (Du20)
Houding (Du19) Qianding (Du21)
Qiangjian (Du18)
Xinhui (Du22)
Naohu (Du17) Shangxing (Du23)
Fengfu (Du16)
Yamen (Du15)
Shenting (Du24)
Suliao (Du25)
Renzhong (Du26)
Duiduan (Du27)

Duzhi (Du14)
Taodao (Du13)

Shenzhu (Du12)
Shendao (Du11)
Lingtai (Du10)
Zhiyang (Du9)
Jinsuo (Du8)
Zhongshu (Du7)
Jizhong (Du6)
Xuanshu (Du5)
Mingmen (Du4)
Yaoyangguan (Du5)
Yaoshu (Du2)
Changqiang (Du1)

Mouth-Yinjiao (Du28)

THE DU MERIDIAN

Fig. II-206

Huiyin (Ren 1) and Chengjiang (Ren 24). According to medical literature of the Ming Dynasty, the Du Meridian also communicates with Houxi (S.I.3).

Analytical Display of the Course of the Meridian

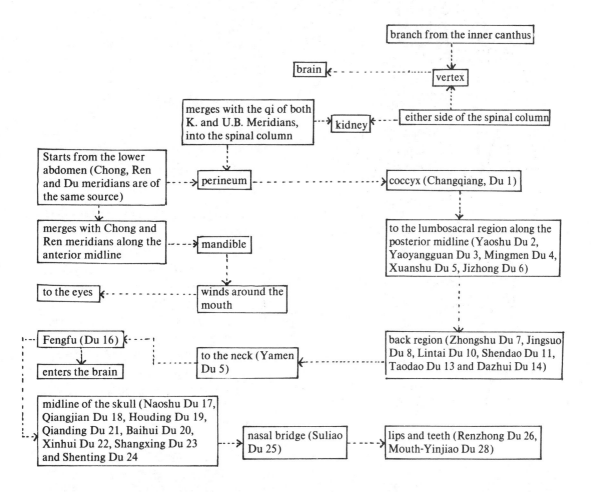

II. The Points

There are 28 single points from this meridian, distributed along the head, face, neck, back and lumbosacral region. The starting point is Changqiang (Du 1) and the terminating point is mouth-Yinjiao (Du 28). (See next page)

Note: Functionally, the Du Meridian is referred to as the "governor of Yang", as it communicates with the Yang Qi of the whole body through Dazhui (Du 14), Fengfu (Du 16), Yamen (Du 15) and Mingmen (Du 4). Another reason for the name Du Meridian (Governor Vessel Meridian) is that the meridian has its distribution in the brain. The brain governs the mentality and is known as the palace of mental activities, hence the name Du Meridian.

Point Names	Pinyin	Codes	Point Names	Pinyin	Codes
長強	Changqiang	Du 1	啞門	Yamen	Du 15
腰俞	Yaoshu	Du 2	風府	Fengfu	Du 16
腰陽關	Yaoyangguan	Du 3	腦戶	Naohu	Du 17
命門	Mingmen	Du 4	強間	Qiangjian	Du 18
懸樞	Xuanshu	Du 5	後頂	Houding	Du 19
脊中	Jizhong	Du 6	百會	Baihui	Du 20
中樞	Zhongshu	Du 7	前頂	Qianding	Du 21
筋縮	Jinsuo	Du 8	囟會	Xinhui	Du 22
至陽	Zhiyang	Du 9	上星	Shangxing	Du 23
靈台	Lingtai	Du 10	神庭	Shenting	Du 24
神道	Shendao	Du 11	素髎	Suliao	Du 25
身柱	Shenzhu	Du 12	人中	Renzhong	Du 26
陶道	Taodao	Du 13	兌端	Duiduan	Du 27
大椎	Dazhui	Du 14	齦交	Mouth-Yinjiao	Du 28

*CHANGQIANG (DU1) 長強 (LONG STRONG)

"Chang" (長) means something long, here referring to the length of the Du Meridian which starts from the perineum, ascends along the spinal column to the neck, the vertex and down to the face.

"Qiang" (強), meaning strong, refers to the fact that this point has a strong therapeutic effect, hence the name Changqiang (Long Strong). Another reason for the nomenclature of the point is its location near the coccyx. The whole spinal column from neck to sacrum is long and strong enough to bear the weight of the body and take the strain of the numerous activities of life.

Location:

Midway between the coccyx and the anus when the body is in a prone position (Fig. II-207).

Indications:

Prolapse of the rectum, hemorrhoids, constipation, hematochezia, tenesmus, lumbosacral pain and epilepsy.

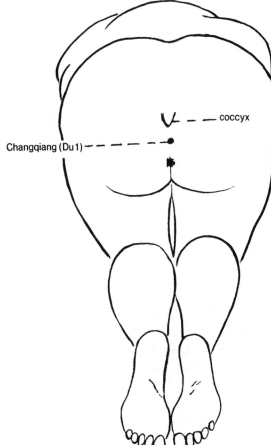

coccyx

Changqiang (Du1)

Fig. II-207

Clinical Application:

Changqiang (Du 1), the intersection of the Du Meridian with the Kidney Meridian of Foot-Shaoyin and the Gall Bladder Meridian of Foot-Shaoyang, has the effect to eliminate heat, stop bleeding and raise the rectum.

Combinations:

With Baihui (Du 20), Dachangshu (U.B.25) and Chengshan (U.B.57) for prolapse of the rectum and hematochezia;

With Shugu (U.B.65) for stabbing pain of the anus;

With Dazhui (Du 14) for epilepsy.

Method:

Puncture obliquely 1-2 cun deep. Perpendicular insertion may injure the rectum and is therefore considered not applicable.

Needling Sensations:

Soreness, distention and heaviness with contraction of the anus.

YAOSHU (DU 2)腰俞 (LUMBAR POINT)

"Yao" (腰) refers to the lumbosacral region. "Shu" (俞) means a point. The point is in the sacral hiatus, hence the name Yaoshu (Lumbar Point).

Location:

Have the patient assume a prone position and raise the sacrococcygeal region slightly. The point is in the hiatus of the sacrum when the lower extremities are in internal rotation, with the legs close together. This point and the two posterior superior iliac spines, together form an equilateral triangle in females. In recent years, another point Yaoqi (extra), 2 cun above the coccyx, has been added. Both points are roughly the same in location (Fig. II-210).

Indications:

Irregular menstruation and hemorrhoids.

Method:

Puncture obliquely upwards about 1 cun deep.

*YAOYANGGUAN (DU 3)腰阳关 (LUMBAR YANG PASS)

This point used to be called Yangguan (Yang Pass). Now the Chinese character "yao" (腰) has been added in order to differentiate it from Xiyangguan (G.B.33). Yaoyangguan (Du 3) is immediately below Mingmen (Du 4) where kidney Yang flourishes and is a gate through which the Yang qi passes, hence the name Yaoyangguan (Lumbar Yang Pass).

Location:

Midway along the line linking the two iliac crests, between the spinous process of the 4th and 5th lumbar vertebra (Fig. II-208).

Clinical Application:

This point has the effect to reinforce kidney qi, strengthen the lumbus, strengthen the knees and eliminate pathogenic wind and dampness.

Combinations:

With Shenshu (U.B.23), Huantiao (G.B.30), Yinmen (U.B.37), Zusanli (St.36) and Weizhong (U.B.40) for sciatica.

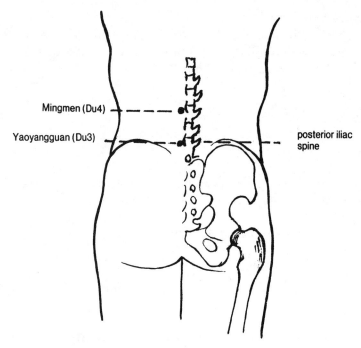

Fig. II-208

Method:
Puncture obliquely upwards 1-2 cun deep.
Needling Sensations:
Distention and heaviness in the local area.
Indications:
Lumbosacral pain, seminal emission, impotence, irregular menstruation, leukorrhea and Wei syndrome of the lower extremities.

*MINGMEN (DU 4) 命 门   (LIFE GATE)

"Ming" (命) means vital and living. "Men" (门) again means gate. The name implies that this point is the gate of life. Mingmen (Du 4), located between the two Shenshu (U.B.23) points, is an important point for the treatment of disorders related to the kidney, being the basic foundation of the body constitution. Hence the name Mingmen (Life Gate).
Location:
Below the spinous process of L2, at the crossing point of the spinal column and the line linking the inferior borders of the rib arches on either side of the body. This point is at the level of the centre of the umbilicus (Fig. II-208, 209).
Indications:
Lumbar pain, seminal emission, impotence, enuresis, irregular menstruation, leukorrhea and abdominal pain.
Clinical Application:

Note: There is a point below the spinous process of each vertebra, except T2, T4, T8, T12 and L3.

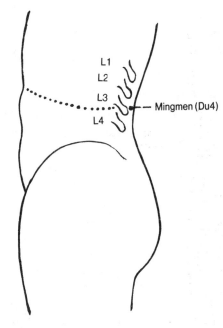

Fig. II-209

Mingmen (Du 4) is one of the important points for replenishing kidney Yin, consolidating kidney essence, reinforcing kidney Yang and strengthening the lower back and knees. It is also used for general tonification. It is effective in the treatment of lumbar pain, impotence, seminal emission, loose stool and diarrhea due to deficiency of the kidney.

Combinations:

With Shenshu (U.B.23), Shangliao (U.B.31), Ciliao (U.B.32), Zhongliao (U.B.3), Xialiao (U.B.34), Guanyuan (Ren 4) and Sanyinjiao (Sp. 6) for treating the above-mentioned diseases.

Method:

Puncture obliquely upwards 1-2 cun deep.

Needling Sensations:

Local heaviness and distention, radiating laterally.

XUANSHU (DU 5) 悬枢 (SUSPENDING PIVOT)

"Xuan" (悬) means suspending. "Shu" (枢) means a pivot, linking both the upper and lower portion of the spinal column. This point, below the point Jizhong (Du 6), meaning middle of the spine, is the fulcrum for transmission of the water and qi of the Sanjiao, hence the name Xuanshu (Suspending Pivot).

Location:

Below the spinous process of L1 (Fig. II-210).

Indications:

Deficiency of the spleen and stomach, loose stool, diarrhea and spinal rigidity in the lumbar region.

JIZHONG (DU 6) 脊中 (MIDDLE OF THE SPINE)

"Ji" (脊) refers to the spinal column. "Zhong" (中) means centre.

The point is located in the middle part of the spinal column between T1 and L5, hence the name Jizhong (Middle of the Spine).

Location:

At the level of Pishu (U.B.20), below the spinous process of T11 (Fig. II-210).

Indications:

Diarrhea.

Method:

Puncture perpendicularly about 1-1.5 cun deep.

ZHONGSHU (DU 7) 中枢 (CENTRAL PIVOT)

"Zhong" (中) means centre. "Shu" (枢) means pivot. This point, one spinous process above Jizhong (Du 6), is considered to be the central link in the transport of the

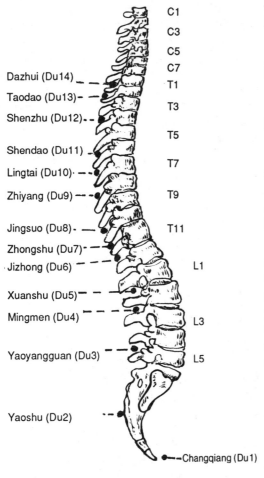

C1
C3
C5
C7
T1

Dazhui (Du14)

Taodao (Du13)

T3

Shenzhu (Du12)

T5

Shendao (Du11)

T7

Lingtai (Du10)

Zhiyang (Du9)

T9

Jingsuo (Du8)

T11

Zhongshu (Du7)

Jizhong (Du6)

L1

Xuanshu (Du5)

Mingmen (Du4)

L3

Yaoyangguan (Du3)

L5

Yaoshu (Du2)

Changqiang (Du1)

Fig. II-210

qi of this meridian, hence the name Zhongshu (Central Pivot).

Location:

Below the spinous process of T10 (Fig. II-210).

Indications:

Abdominal distention and lumbar pain.

Method:

Puncture perpendicularly about 1-1.5 cun deep.

JINSUO (DU 8) 筋 縮 (TENDON SPASM)

"Jin" (筋) means tendons or muscles. "Suo" (縮) means spasm or contraction. This point is at the level of Ganshu (U.B.18), the liver point. The liver pertains to wood and dominates the tendons. Also, the point can deal with spasm and convulsions, hence the name Jinsuo (Tendon Spasm).

Location:

Below the spinous process of T9 (Fig. II-210).

Indications:

Epilepsy, epigastric pain and spinal rigidity.

Method:

Puncture perpendicularly about 1-1.5 cun deep.

*ZHIYANG (DU 9) 至 阳 (REACHING YANG)

"Zhi" (至) means to reach or arrive. "Yang" (阳) refers to the back which is the Yang aspect of the body. The upper back is the Yang part of the Yang aspect, the meridian reaching the Yang part of the Yang aspect at this point, hence the name Zhiyang (Reaching Yang).

Location:

Below the spinous process of T7, midway between the line connecting the inferior angle of both scapulae when the patient looks forward (Fig. II-210).

Indications:

Cholecystitis, icterus, hypochondriac pain, epigastric pain, and pain in the back.

Clinical Application:

This point has the effect to relieve suffocating sensation in the chest.

Combinations:

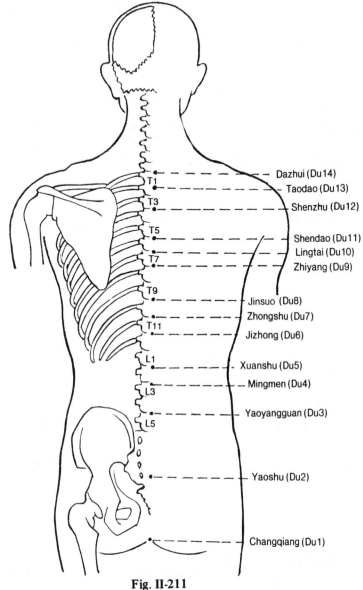

Dazhui (Du14)
Taodao (Du13)
Shenzhu (Du12)
Shendao (Du11)
Lingtai (Du10)
Zhiyang (Du9)
Jinsuo (Du8)
Zhongshu (Du7)
Jizhong (Du6)
Xuanshu (Du5)
Mingmen (Du4)
Yaoyangguan (Du3)
Yaoshu (Du2)
Changqiang (Du1)

Fig. II-211

With Xinshu (U.B.15) and Neiguan (P.6) for arrythmia,
With Yanglingquan (G.B.34) and Danshu (U.B.19) for cholecystitis.
Method:
Puncture obliquely upwards 1-2 cun deep.
Needling Sensations:
Local distention, radiating laterally.

LINGTAI (DU 10) 灵台 (SPIRITUAL PLACE)

"Ling" (灵) here refers to the heart or spirit. "Tai" (台) means a high, smooth place. This point is located posterior to the heart and is indicated in heart disorders, hence the name Lingtai (Spiritual Place).

Location:

Below the spinous process of T6 (Fig. II-210).

Indications:

Cough, asthma, pain in the back, neck rigidity and cardiac disorders.

Method:

Puncture obliquely upwards about 1-2 cun deep.

SHENDAO (DU 11) 神道 (SPIRITUAL PASSAGE)

"Shen" (神) refers to spiritual activities. "Dao" (道) means passage. This point is at the level of Xinshu (U.B.15) and communicates with its qi. It is indicated in mental illness, such as mental restlessness, poor memory, excessive worry and sorrow, palpitation, mental depression and irregular emotional disturbance. Hence the name Shendao (Spiritual Passage).

Location:

Below the spinous process of T5 (Fig. II-210).

Indications:

See the above item.

Method:

Puncture obliquely upwards about 1-2 cun deep.

*SHENZHU (DU 12) 身柱 (BODY PILLAR)

"Shen" (身) refers to the trunk of the body. "Zhu" (柱) means supporting pillar, implying that the spinal column is the pillar supporting the whole body. This point is at the level of Feishu (U.B.13, lung point), the lung communicating with the qi of the whole body, hence the name Shenzhu (Body Pillar).

Location:

Below the spinous process of T3, approximately at the level of the medial end of the scapular spine (Fig. II-211).

Indications:

Shortness of breath, cough, infantile convulsion, rigidity of the spinal column, onset of furuncle and carbuncles, psychosis and restlessness.

Clinical Application:

This point has the effect to regulate circulation of qi, stop the irregular ascending of qi, stop cough, relieve asthma and calm the mind.

Combinations:

With Dazhui (Du 14), Feishu (U.B.13) and Shangzhong (Ren 17) for fullness sensation in the chest, chest pain, cough and asthma.

Method:

Puncture obliquely 1-2 cun deep upwards.

Needling Sensations:

Local distention, radiating towards either side of the back or downwards.

TAODAO (DU 13) 陶道 (HAPPY ROAD)

"Tao" (陶) means to enjoy or be happy. "Dao" (道) means road This point is indicated in mental restlessness, mental depression, headache and neck pain. The Du Meridian governs the Yang of the body, fire and qi ascending through the meridian like smoke through a brick-kiln chimney, hence the name Taodao (Happy Road).

Location:

Below the spinous process of T1 (Fig. II-210).

Indications:

Headache, neck rigidity, febrile diseases and mental depression.

Method:

Puncture obliquely 1-2 cun deep upwards.

*DAZHUI (DU 14) 大椎 (BIG VERTEBRA)

"Da" (大) means tall and big. "Zhui" (椎) refers to the 7th cervical vertebra. This point is located below the large prominence of the spinous process of C7, anatomically, called the vertebra prominence. Hence the name Dazhui (Big Vertebra).

Location:

Below the spinous process of C7, approximately at the level of the shoulder, midway

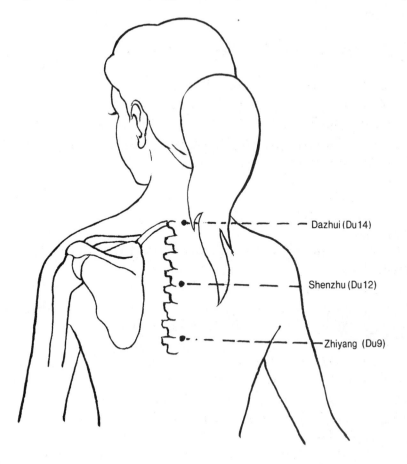

Fig. II-212

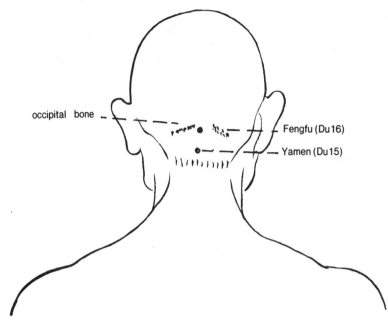

occipital bone

Fengfu (Du 16)

Yamen (Du 15)

Fig. II-213

between the two acromions (Fig. II-212).

Indications:

Febrile diseases, aversion to cold, cough and asthma, epilepsy, mental retardation, sequela of encephalitis, neck rigidity, distention, tightness and heaviness of the head, irritability and sweating due to weakness of the body.

Clinical Application:

Dazhui (Du 14) is the coalescent point of the Du Meridian and the three Yang meridians of the foot and hand. It has the effect to dispel wind and cold, eliminate superficial syndrome, remove obstruction from meridians, regulate qi circulation, cease irregular ascending of qi, calm the mind, restore consciousness and relieve spasm. It is also commonly used for general tonification.

Combinations:

With Quchi (L.I.11), Waiguan (S.J.5), Hegu (L.I.4) and Feishu (U.B.13) for common cold with fever;

With Pishu (U.B.20), Zusanli (St.36) and Sanyinjiao (Sp.6) for leukocytopenia.

Method:

Puncture obliquely upwards 1-2 cun deep.

Needling Sensations:

Soreness, numbness, distention and heaviness, radiating towards the back or shoulder.

*YAMEN (DU 15) 啞 門 (MUTE-SAVING GATE)

"Ya" (啞) means dumb. "Men" (門) means a gate. It was believed in the ancient times that mistaken use of moxa at this point could render a person unable to speak, but that needling it could treat the mute. Hence the name Yamen (Mute-saving Gate).

Location:

At the midpoint of the nape of the neck, in the deperession 0.5 cun within the posterior hairline (Fig. II-213).

Indications:

Headache, dizziness, deafness, mutism, windstroke, stiffness of the tongue, acute lumbar sprain, schizophrenia and craniocerebral accident.

Clinical Application:

The Du and Yinwei Meridians intersect at Yamen (Du 15). It has the effect to remove obstruction from the meridians and collaterals, restore consciousness and calm the mind. It is an important point for dealing with deafness and mutism and mental diseases.

Combinations:

With Lianquan (Du 23), Ermen (S.J.21), Tinggong (S.J.19), Tinghui (G.B.2), Hegu (L.I.4), Yifeng (S.J.17), Hand-Zhongzhu (S.J.3) and Waiguan (S.J.5) for deafness and mutism,

With Yongquan (K.1) for disabled speech due to windstroke,

With Renzhong (Du 26) for acute lumbar pain.

This point also has an excellent effect in treating hysterical aphasia.

Method:

Use extreme caution when needling this point. Puncture perpendicularly for no more than 1 cun so as to avoid the medulla oblongata, or puncture obliquely 1-1.5 cun towards the throat.

Needling Sensations:

Numbness and distention, radiating towards the head or shoulder.

*FENGFU (DU 16) 风府 (WIND MANSION)

"Fu" (府) means a mansion. "Feng" (风) refers to pathogenic wind. Wind is a Yang pathogenic factor characterized by upward-going and is the main pathogenic factor involved in diseases of the head and neck. The point is within the posterior hairline, in the depression between the trapezius muscles of either side. It is a coalescent point of the Urinary Bladder Meridian of Foot-Taiyang, the Yangwei Meridian and the Du Meridian. The point can be used to deal with any disorders caused by wind, hence the name Fengfu (Wind Mansion).

Location:

One cun within the posterior hairline, in the depression between the trapezius muscles (Fig. II-213).

Indications:

Headache, neck rigidity, dizziness and vertigo, epilepsy, sore throat, common cold with fever and disabled speech due to windstroke.

Clinical Application:

Fengfu (Du 16) is the coalescent point of the Du Meridian and the Yangwei Meridian and has the effect to dispel pathogenic wind from the head. It is commonly

---

Caution: Deep insertion at Yamen and Fengfu is contraindicated because of the risk to the medulla oblongata. The respiratory centre and other life centres are located in the rhombic depression of the 4th venticula. The maximum safe insertion is as far as the depth of the dura mater. Correct direction of needling is essential for safety.

used for treating disorders of the face and the five sense organs.

Combinations:

With Houxi (S.I.3) for occipital headache,

With Baihui (Du 20) and Taiyang (extra) for headache,

With Yanggu (S.I.5) for schizophrenia.

Pay attention to the direction and depth of insertion or the tip of the needle may enter the cranial cavity with dangerous consequences.

Method:

Use extreme caution when needling this point. Direction and restricted depth of insertion are essential for safety. Puncture perpendicularly 1 cun, or obliquely 1-1.5 cun towards the Adam's apple. Deep insertion is contraindicated because of the risk of puncturing the medulla oblongata.

Needling Sensations:

Local distention or heaviness, sometimes radiating towards the head.

NAOHU (DU 17) 腦户 (BRAIN GATE)

"Nao" (腦) means the brain. "Hu" (户) means a gate. This point is located above the foramen magnum considered to be the gate of the brain, hence the name Naohu (Brain Gate) (Fig. II-214).

Indications:

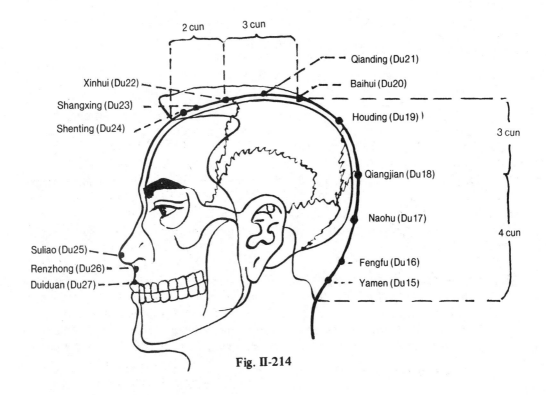

Fig. II-214

Dizziness and vertigo, neck rigidity, aphonia and epilepsy.
Method:
Puncture 0.3-0.5 cun horizontally along the skin.

QIANGJIAN (DU 18) 強闲 (ON STRENGTH)

"Qiang" (強) means strength. "Jian" (闲) means on or between. The name of this point refers to the fact that the skull is very hard. Hence the name Qiangjian (On Strength).
Location:
1.5 cun above the point Naohu (Du 17), midway between Fengfu (Du 16) and Baihui (Du 20) (Fig. II-214).
Indications:
Headache, neck rigidity.
Method:
Puncture 0.3-0.5 cun deep horizontally along the skin.

HOUDING (DU 19) 后顶 (POSTERIOR VERTEX)

"Hou" (后) means posterior. "Ding" (顶) means the vertex in this context. The point is located at the vertex, 1.5 cun posterior to Baihui (Du 20), hence the name Houding (Posterior Vertex) (Fig. II-214).
Indications:
Vertex pain, pain in the posterior aspect of the head and disorders of the neck.
Method:
Puncture 0.3-0.5 cun deep horizontally along the skin.

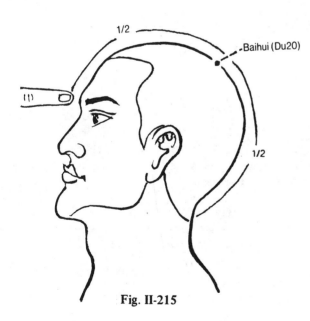

Fig. II-215

*BAIHUI   (DU 20)   百会 (HUNDRED MEETINGS)

"Bai" (百) means many in number. "Hui" (会) means to converge. All the Yang meridians merge into the head and intersect at this point which is in the centre of the vertex. The Urinary Bladder Meridian of Foot-Taiyang, the Gall Bladder Meridian of Foot-Shaoyang, the Sanjiao Meridian of Hand-Shaoyang, the Du Meridian and the Liver Meridian of Foot-Jueyin all directly converge here, hence the name Baihui (Hundred Meetings).
Location:
Five cun within the frontal hairline on the midsagittal line, or midway between the posterior hairline and the landmark one finger's width superior to Yintang (extra) (Fig. II-214, 215).

Indications:

Headache, dizziness and vertigo, heaviness in the head, prolapse of the rectum and shock.

Clinical Application:

Baihui (Du 20) is the coalescent point of the Du Meridian and the Yang meridians of both the foot and hand. It has the effect to restore consciousness, relieve heat, promote the brain functions, calm the mind, restore Yang qi from collapse, soothe the liver and dispel wind. Also, it can raise the sunken qi of the body organs.

Combinations:

With Fengchi (G.B.20), Jingming (U.B.1), Hegu (L.I.4) and Chuangming (G.B.37) for eye disorders,

With Fengchi (G.B.20), Yingxiang (L.I.20) and Hegu (L.I.4) for nasal disorders,

With Jianyu (L.I.15), Quchi (L.I.11), Hegu (L.I.4), Huantiao (G.B.30), Fengchi (G.B.20), Zusanli (St.36) and Xuanzhong (G.B.39) for hemiplegia,

With Renzhong (Du 26) and Neiguan (P.6) for shock,

With Changqiang (Du 1) and Chengshan (U.B.57) for prolapse of the rectum.

Method:

Puncture horizontally 0.5-0.8 cun deep, or prick to cause bleeding.

Needling Sensations:

Local distention and pain.

QIANDING (DU 21) 前頂 (ANTERIOR VERTEX)

"Ding" (前) refers to the vertex. The point is at the vertex, 1.5 cun anterior (qian 頂) to Baihui (Du 20), hence the name Qianding (Anterior Vertex) (Fig. II-214).

Indications:

Vertex pain and pain in the temporal region.

Method:

Puncture 0.3-0.5 cun deep horizontally along the skin.

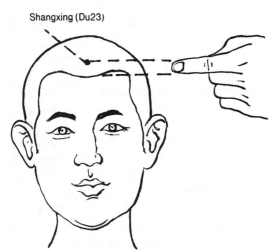

Shangxing (Du23)

Fig. II-216

XINHUI (DU 22) 囟会 (FONTANEL)

"Xin" (囟) refers to the fontanel. "Hui" (会) refers to the location of the fontanel in particular, hence the name Xinhui (Fontanel).

Location:

Three cun anterior to Baihui (Du 20) (Fig. II-215).

Indications:

Headache, blurring of vision, sinusitis and infantile convulsion.

Method:

Puncture 0.3-0.5 cun deep horizontally along the skin.

Caution: Acupuncture is contraindicated in the case of metopism.

*SHANGXING (DU 23) 上星 (SUPER STAR)

"Shang" (上) means a high place. "Xing" (星) means a star in the sky, but here refers to the point location. It was believed in the ancient times that the nose communicates with the celestial qi and the eyes were likened to the moon and stars in the sky. Hence the name Shangxing (Super Star) (Fig. II-216).

Location:
One cun within the anterior headline, 4 cun anterior to Baihui (Du 20).
Indications:
Headache, rhinitis, epistaxis, nasal obstruction and pain of the eyes.
Clinical Application:
Shangxing (Du 23) has the effect to sedate pain, dispel wind and help the lung perform its dispersing function.
Combinations:
With Hegu (L.I.4) and Lieque (Lu. 7) for headache,
With Zanzhu (U.B.2) and Sizhukong (S.J.23) for pain in the eye,
With Yingxiang (L.I.20) for nasal obstruction.
Method:
Puncture horizontally 0.5-0.8 cun, or prick to cause bleeding.

SHENTING (DU 24) 神庭 (SPIRITUAL COURTYARD)

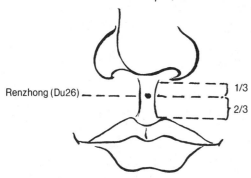

Renzhong (Du26)

1/3

2/3

Fig. II-217

"Shen" (神) means spirit. "Ting" (庭) means the yard in front of the house. This point is located on the forehead and the brain is considered to house the spirit. It has the effect to calm the mind and restore consciousness, hence the name Shenting (Spiritual Courtyard).

Location:
0.5 cun within the anterior hairline (Fig. II-214).
Indications:
Epilepsy, palpitation, restlessness and insomnia.
Method:
Puncture 0.3-0.5 cun deep horizontally along the skin with the needle directed upward.

SULIAO (DU 25) 素髎 (WHITE CREVICE)

"Su" (素) means the very beginning, but also refers to the colour white. "Liao" (髎) means a crevice, but here refers to an acupuncture point. In the ancient times, the nose was considered to be the beginning of life. The lung, represented by the colour white, has its opening into the nose, at the very tip of which is the point. Hence the name Suliao (White Crevice) (Fig. II-214).

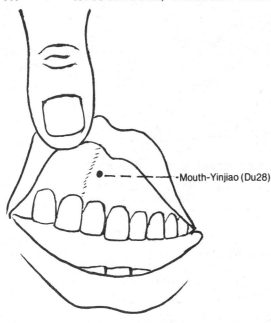

Fig. II-218

Indications:
Coma, nasal obstruction, epistaxis, profuse nasal discharge and rhinitis.
Method:
Puncture obliquely 0.3-0.5 cun deep, or prick to cause bleeding.
Needling Sensations:
Mild pain in the local area.

*RENZHONG (DU 26) 人中 (PERSON IN MIDDLE)

"Ren" (人) means a person. "Zhong" (中) means middle. The nose dominates celestial qi, breathing the air, while the mouth dominates the qi of the earth, eating grain produced on the earth. This point is located between the nose and the mouth, as though between heavens and earth. It is superior to the earth and inferior to the heavens, as is a standing man, hence the name Renzhong (Person in Middle). Another name for this point is Shuigou (ditch) because it is located in the nasalabial groove.

Location:
At the conjunction between the upper and middle third of the philtrum (Fig. II-217).
Indications:
Shock, collapse, sunstroke, coma, acute lumbar sprain, schizophrenia and infantile convulsion.
Clinical Application:
Renzhong (Du 26) is the coalescent point of the Du Meridian and the Yangming Meridians of both the hand and foot. It has the effect to restore consciousness, relieve heat, calm the mind, sedate pain and restore Yang qi from collapse. It is a commonly used point for emergency cases and acupuncture analgesia.
Combinations:
With Neiguan (P.6), Zusanli (St.36) and Yongquan (K.1) for shock,
With Hegu (L.I.4) and Shixuan (Extra) for hysteria and sunstroke,
With Yamen (Du 15) for acute lumbar sprain.
Method:
Puncture obliquely 0.3-0.5 cun deep.
Needling Sensations:
Pain in the local area.

DUIDUAN (DU 27) 兌端 (UPPER LIP PROMINENCE)

"Dui" (兌) in ancient Chinese, means mouth or lips. "Duan" (端) means the most prominent part. The point is located on the medial tubercle of the upper lip, hence the name Duiduan (Upper Lip Prominence) (Fig. II-214).

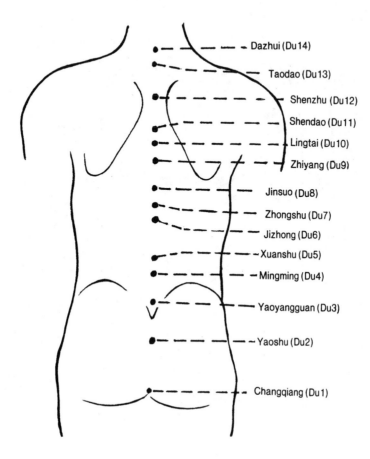

Dazhui (Du14)
Taodao (Du13)
Shenzhu (Du12)
Shendao (Du11)
Lingtai (Du10)
Zhiyang (Du9)
Jinsuo (Du8)
Zhongshu (Du7)
Jizhong (Du6)
Xuanshu (Du5)
Mingming (Du4)
Yaoyangguan (Du3)
Yaoshu (Du2)
Changqiang (Du1)

Fig. II-219

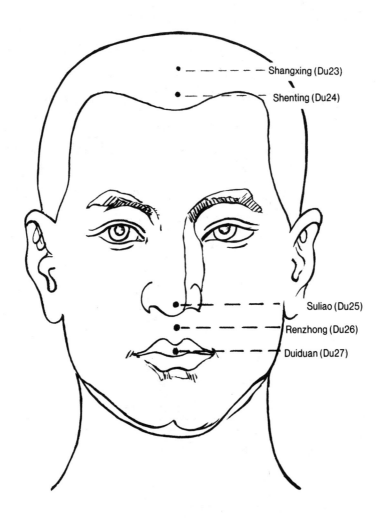

Shangxing (Du23)

Shenting (Du24)

Suliao (Du25)

Renzhong (Du26)

Duiduan (Du27)

Fig. II-220A

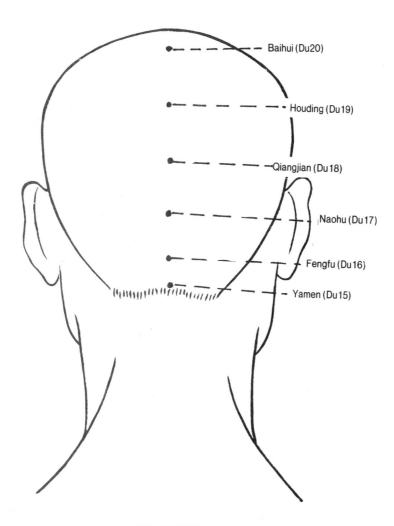

Fig. II-220B

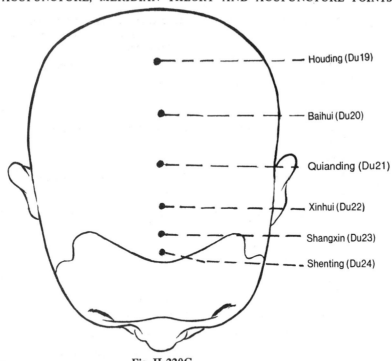

Houding (Du 19)

Baihui (Du 20)

Quianding (Du 21)

Xinhui (Du 22)

Shangxin (Du 23)

Shenting (Du 24)

Fig. II-220C

Indications:
Toothache, swollen gums, deviation of the mouth and trembling lips.
Method:
Puncture obliquely 0.2-0.3 cun deep.

MOUTH-YINJIAO (DU 28) 龈交 (GUM CROSSING)

"Yin" (龈) here refers to the upper gum. "Jiao" (交) means to intersect. The point is located between the upper gum and the upper labial gingiva, in the frenulum. It is the coalescent point of the Ren and Du Meridians, hence the name Yinjiao (Gum Crossing) (Fig. II-218).
Indications:
Acute lumbar pain, anal fissure, swollen gums, rhinitis and mental mania.
Method:
Prick to cause bleeding or puncture obliquely 0.2-0.3 cun deep (Fig. II-219, 220).

Point Indications of the Du Meridian According to Locations

Point Names	Locations	Indications	Regional Indications
Changqiang Du 1	Midpoint between coccyx and the anus	Hemorrhoids, bloody stool, prolapse of the rectum	
Yaoshu Du 2	At the lower border of the 4th sacral vertebra	Irregular menstruation, epilepsy	
Yaoyangguan Du 3	Below the spinous process of L4	Lumbosacral pain, paralysis of the lower extremities	Disorders of the urinary and reproductive systems

Mingmen Du 4	Below the spinous process of L2	Rigidity of the spinal column in the lumbar region, seminal emission, dysmenorrhea	
Xuanshu Du 5	Below the spinous process of L1	Loose stool, diarrhea, indigestion	
Jizhong Du 6	Below the spinous process of T11	Icterus, epilepsy	Mental diseases and epigastric disorders
Zhongshu Du 7	Below the spinous process of T10	Neck rigidity, epigastric pain	
Jinsuo Du 8	Below the spinous process of T9	Epigastric pain	
Zhiyang Du 9	Below the spinous process of T7	Icterus, gastric pain, cough, asthma	
Lingtai Du 10	Below the spinous process of T6	Back pain	
Shendao Du 11	Below the spinous process of T5	Palpitation, neurasthenia	Mental disorders, febrile diseases, cough, asthma, pulmonary disorders
Shenzhu Du 12	Below the spinous process of T3	Cough, back pain	
Taodao Du 13	Below the spinous process of T1	Malaria, fever, psychoses	
Dazhui Du 14	Below the spinous process of C7	Fever, common cold, cough	
Yamen Du 15	0.5 cun within the posterior hairline	Deafness, mutism, psychoses	Head, neck, tongue and mental illness
Fengfu Du 16	At the lower border of occipital bone, on the midsagittal line	Headache, neck rigidity, dizziness and vertigo, psychoses	
Naohu Du 17	1.5 cun above Fengfu (Du 16)	Painful eyes, myopia	
Qiangjian Du 18	1.5 cun above Naohu (Du 17)	Headache, dizziness and vertigo, neck rigidity	
Houding Du 19	1.5 cun above Qiangjian (Du 18)	Headache, dizziness and vertigo	
Baihui Du 20	5 cun within the anterior hairline	Rectal prolapse, uterine prolapse, shock	Mental illness and disorders involving head, eyes and nose
Qianding Du 21	1.5 cun anterior to Baihui (Du 20)	Rhinitis, headache, dizziness, vertigo, palpitation	
Xinhui Du 22	3 cun anterior to Baihui (Du 20)	Dizziness, vertigo, palpitation	
Shangxing Du 23	4 cun anterior to Baihui (Du 20)	Headache, psychoses, nasal disorders	
Shenting Du 24	0.5 cun within the anterior hairline	Headache, insomnia	
Suliao Du 25	on the tip of the nose	Shock, loss of consciousness, suffocation	
Renzhong Du 26	Between the upper and middle third of the philtrum	Shock, loss of consciousness, convulsion, lumbar pain	
Duiduan Du 27	On the medial tubercle of the upper lip	Swollen gums, syncope	Ear disorders, gum problems, mental illness
Mouth-Yinjiao Du 28	On the upper labial gingiva	Swollen gums, pain in the heart area	

Section 2 THE REN MERIDIAN

I. The Meridian

General Indications:

Points from this meridian are mainly indicated in diseases of the endocrineous and reproductive systems. In addition, they are commonly used in the treatment of abdominal distention, abdominal pain, vomiting, diarrhea, distention in the hypochondriac region, cough, asthma, sore throat and disorders in the areas supplied by the course of the meridian.

Course of the Meridian:

(1) The Ren Meridian rises from the uterus in the lower abdomen (the Chong, Ren and Du Meridians are all of the same origin) and emerges from the perineum. (2) It runs anteriorly to the pubic region (3) and ascends along the midline of the abdomen and thorax (4) to the throat. (5) Merging with the Chong Meridian, it runs further upward and curves around the lips (6), passes through the cheek and enters the middle of the infraorbital region (Chengqi St. 1). (7) A branch emerges concurrently with the Chong Meridian from the uterus, runs posteriorly and merges Du Meridian and Kidney Meridian of Foot-Shaoyin, connecting with their distribution in the interior of the spinal column (Fig. II-221).

Analytical Display of the Course of the Meridian

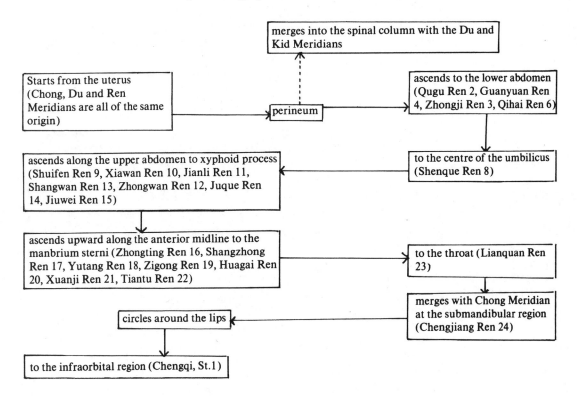

Chengjiang (Ren24)
Lianquan (Ren23)
Tiantu (Ren22)
Xuanji (Ren21)
Huagai (Ren20)
Chest-Zigong (Ren19)
Yutang (Ren18)
Shanzhong (Ren17)
Zhongting (Ren16)
Jiuwei (Ren15)
Juque (Ren14)
Shangwan (Ren13)
Zhongwan (Ren12)
Jianli (Ren11)
Xiawan (Ren10)
Shuifen (Ren9)
Shenque (Ren8)
Abdomen-Yinjiao (Ren7)
Qihai (Ren6)
Shimen (Ren5)
Guanyuan (Ren4)
Zhongji (Ren3)
Qugu (Ren2)

Huiyin (Ren1)

THE REN MERIDIAN

Fig. II-221

Related Zangfu Organs:

Uterus, lips and eyes.

Coalescent Points of the Meridian:

Chengqi (St.1) and Mouth-Yinjiao (Du 28). According to medical literature of the Yuan Dynasty, the Ren Meridian also communicates with Lieque (Lu. 7).

II. The Points

There are altogether 24 single points on this meridian. They are located on the facial region, the neck and the anterior midline of the chest and abdomen. The starting point is Huiyin (Ren 1) and the terminating point is Chengjiang (Ren 24).

Point Names	Pinyin	Codes	Point Names	Pinyin	Codes
会 阴	Huiyin	Ren 1	上 脘	Shangwan	Ren 13
曲 骨	Qugu	Ren 2	巨 阙	Juque	Ren 14
中 极	Zhongji	Ren 3	鸠 尾	Jiuwei	Ren 15
关 元	Guanyuan	Ren 4	中 庭	Zhongting	Ren 16
石 门	Shimen	Ren 5	膻 中	Shangzhong	Ren 17
气 海	Qihai	Ren 6	玉 堂	Yutang	Ren 18
阴 交	Abdomen-Yinjiao	Ren 7	紫 宫	Zigong	Ren 19
神 阙	Shenque	Ren 8	华 盖	Huagai	Ren 20
水 分	Shuifen	Ren 9	璇 玑	Xuanji	Ren 21
下 脘	Xiawan	Ren 10	天 突	Tiantu	Ren 22
建 里	Jianli	Ren 11	廉 泉	Lianquan	Ren 23
中 脘	Zhongwan	Ren 12	承 浆	Chengjiang	Ren 24

*HUIYIN (REN 1) 会阴 (MERGING PERINEUM)

"Hui" (会) means to converge. "Yin" (阴) here refers to both the genitalia and the anus between which the point is located. The perineum is considered a Yin part of the body in TCM and is the starting point for the superficial distribution of the Ren, Du and Chong Meridians. It was recorded in *Compendium of Acupuncture and Moxibustion* (*Zhenjiu Dacheng*) that "the Ren, Du and Chong Meridians emerge from the area between the anus and the external genitalia. Ren Meridian starts from the perineum and ascends along the abdomen. Du Meridian ascends from the perineum to the back. Chong Meridian also starts there to merge with the Kidney Meridian of Foot-Shaoyin." All of the three meridians converge at this point, hence the name Huiyin (Merging Perineum).

Note: "Ren" (任), in the name Ren Meridian, has the same meaning as (妊) which means to conceive or become pregnant. The Ren Meridian is closely related to the reproductive function and "dominates the growth of the fetus", hence the name Ren Meridian (Conceptional Vessel Meridian). "Ren" also means to receive, in the sense that the Ren Meridian communicates with all the Yin meridians of the body, through Zhongji (Ren 3), Guanyuan (Ren 4), Tiantu (Ren 22), Lianquan (Ren 23) and Sanyinjiao (Sp.6). Concurrently, the Ren Meridian is also known as the "sea of Yin". The branches of Ren Meridian are actually parts of the Kidney Meridian of Foot-Shaoyin, Du Meridian and Chong Meridian.

Location:
Between the anus and the scrotum in males, and between the anus and the posterior labial commissure in females (Fig. II-221).

Indications:
Respiratory failure, difficult bowel movement, dysuria, seminal emission, prostatitis, hemorrhoids, prolapse of the rectum and uterus.

Clinical Application:
This point has the effect to restore Yang qi, raise blood pressure and reinforce Kidney Yang.

Combinations:
With Renzhong (Du 26) for respiratory failure and shock;
With Zhongji (Ren 3) and Sanyinjiao (Sp.6) for seminal emission and prolapse of the rectum.

Method:
Puncture perpendicularly 0.5-1 cun deep.

Needling Sensations:
Distention and pain in the local area.

QUGU (REN 2) 曲 骨 (CROOKED BONE)

"Qu" (曲) means crooked. "Gu" (骨) means bone. The symphysis pubis is also known as "the transverse bone" and is crooked in shape like the crescent moon. The point is at the middle of the upper border of the symphysis pubis, hence the name Qugu (Crooked Bone) (Fig. II-222).

Indications:
Incontinence and dripping of urine, enuresis, seminal emission, impotence, leukorrhea and irregular menstruation.

*ZHONGJI (REN 3) 中 极 (MIDDLE POSITION)

"Zhong" (中) means middle. "Ji" (极) means position in this context. The point is approximately at the middle of the body from vertex to sole, hence the name Zhongji (Middle Position). It is the Front-mu point of the Urinary Bladder, which lies underneath the point. Other names for this point are: Yuquan (Pure Spring), referring to the urine stored in the bladder, or "Qiyuan" which implies that the point stores part of the Yuanqi (vital energy).

Location:
Four cun below the umbilicus, or 1 cun above the upper border of symphysis pubis on the anterior midline (Fig. II-222, 223).

Indications:
Impotence, seminal emission, enuresis, amenorrhea, uterine bleeding, retention of urine, irregular menstruation, leukorrhea and dysmenorrhea.

Clinical Application:
Zhongji (Ren 3) is the crossing point of the Ren Meridian and the three Yin

Note: The distance from the upper border of the symphysis pubis to the umbilicus is 5 cun. The distance between every two points on the anterior midline of the lower abdomen is one cun except for Qihai (Ren 6) which is 1.5 cun below the umbilicus. The depth of insertion for these points is 1-2 cun deep. Have the patient empty the bladder before receiving treatment.

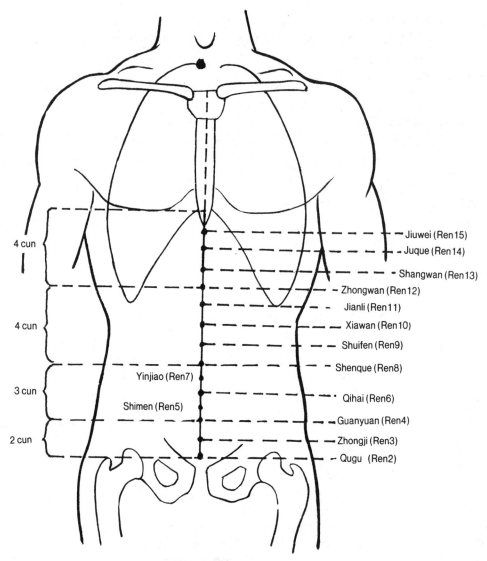

Fig. II-222

meridians of the foot as well as being the Front-mu point of the urinary bladder. It has the effect to reinforce Yuanqi (vital energy), promote the dispersion and distribution of qi, reinforce the kidney and regulate menstruation.

Combinations:

With Shenshu (U.B.23), Sanyinjiao (Sp.6) and Guanyuan (Ren 4) for enuresis, seminal emission, impotence, irregular menstruation and infertility.

Method:

Puncture perpendicularly 1-1.5 cun deep. Have the patient empty the bladder before receiving acupuncture treatment.

Needling Sensations:

Distention and numbness, radiating towards the pubic region.

GUANYUAN (REN 4) 关元 "MU"   (YUAN QI RESIDENCE)

"Guan" (关) means residence. "Yuan" (元) means Yuan qi (vital energy). This point is located below the umbilicus, where Yuan qi (vital energy) is stored, hence the name Guanyuan (Yuan Qi Residence).

Location:

Three cun below the umbilicus (Fig. II-222-223).

Indications:

Lower abdominal pain, loose stool and diarrhea, hematuria, enuresis, impotence, seminal emission, irregular menstruation, profuse leukorrhea, colic around the umbilicus, frequency and urgency of micturition and gastroptosis.

Clinical Application:

Guanyuan (Ren 4) is the crossing point of the Ren Meridian and the three Yin meridians of the foot, the place where the qi of the Sanjiao is produced, and the Front-mu point of the Small Intestine. It has the effect to generally tonify qi, reinforce vital energy,

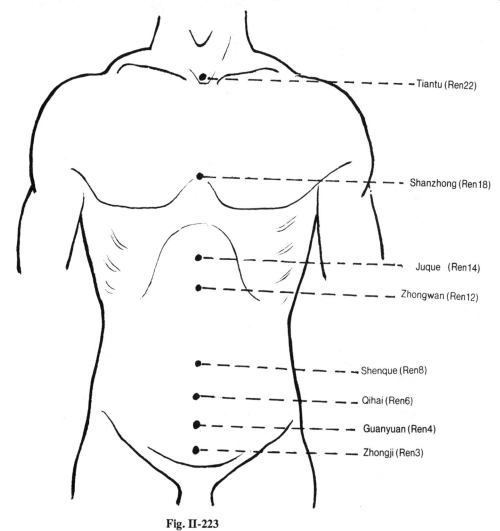

Fig. II-223

strengthen the kidney, restore Yang qi of the body and regulate menstruation.

Combinations:

With Shenshu (U.B.23), Sanyinjiao (Sp.6) and Zusanli (St.36) for diseases of the urinary system;

With Xiaochangshu (U.B.27), Tianshu (St.25) and Zusanli (St.36) for abdominal pain, diarrhea, leukorrhea and irregular menstruation;

With Sanyinjiao (Sp.6) for impotence, seminal emission and postpartum pain.

Method:

Puncture perpendicularly 1-2 cun deep.

Needling Sensations:

Distention and numbness, radiating towards the pubic region.

*SHIMEN (REN 5) 石 门   (STONY GATE)

"Shi" (石), meaning stone, refers to obstruction. "Men" (门) means a gate. Shimen (Ren 5) is the Front-mu point of the Sanjiao. It was recorded in medical classics of TCM that malpractice of acupuncture at this point could cause infertility, as though the reproductive gate were obstructed by a stone, hence the name Shimen (Stony Gate).*

Location: Two cun below the umbilicus (Fig. II-222).

Indications:

Abdominal pain, edema, difficult urination, irregular menstruation and profuse puerperal lochia.

QIHAI (REN 6) 气 海   (ENERGY SEA)

"Qi" (气), here refers to the congenital Yuan qi (vital energy).

"Hai" (海) meaning sea, refers to a convergent place. This point, 1.5 cun below the umbilicus, is the sea of congenital Yuan qi, qi here being in the most abundant and flourishing state. *Basic Readings of TCM (Yixue Rumen)* states that "Qihai (Ren 6) is indicated in disorders due to qi derangement of the whole body" such as asthma, ascending of a cold sensation from umbilicus, etc. It is also an important point for tonification, hence the name Qihai (Energy Sea).

Location:

1.5 cun below umbilicus. (Fig. II-222, 223).

Indications:

All syndromes due to deficiency of qi, lower abdominal pain, chronic diarrhea, seminal emission, impotence, enuresis, uterine bleeding, irregular menstruation, puerperal lochia, infertility, windstroke and collapse.

Clinical Application:

Qihai (Ren 6), a point for general tonification, has the effect to promote qi of the lower jiao, reinforce the deficiency of kidney, strengthen Yuan qi (vital energy), activate Yang qi and stop seminal emission.

Combinations:

With Zusanli (St. 36), Sanyinjiao (Sp. 6) and Shenshu (U.B.23) for diseases of the reproductive and urinary systems.

Method:

---

*Note: It is not true that malpractice of acupuncture at this point will lead to infertility.

Puncture perpendicularly 1-2 cun deep.
Needling Sensations:
Distention and numbness, radiating towards the pubic region.

ABDOMEN-YINJIAO (REN 7) 阴 交 (YIN CROSSING)

"Jiao" (交) means convergence or crossing. "Yin" (阴) refers to Yin meridians. The Ren Meridian is a Yin Meridian and the abdomen is a Yin aspect of the body. Yinjiao (Ren 7), below the umbilicus, is the place where the Ren Meridian, the Chong Meridian and the Kidney Meridian of Foot-Shaoyin converge, all of these being Yin meridians. Hence the name Yinjiao (Yin Crossing).

Location:
One cun below the umbilicus (Fig. II-222).

Indications:
Abdominal distention, amenorrhea, uterine bleeding, leukorrhea, itching of the pubic region and puerperal lochia.

SHENGQUE (REN 8) 神 阙 (SOUL PALACE)

"Shen" (神) here refers to the soul or something ever changing. "Que" (阙) means an important place, originally meaning the watchtowers on either side of a palace. The point is in the centre of the umbilicus and is also called Mingmen (命门), Life Base, because the fetus is supplied with nutrition by the mother through the umbilical cord. Also, the umbilicus was believed to be the gate of spiritual qi, hence the name Shenque (Soul Palace).

Location:
In the centre of the umbilicus (Fig. II-222, 223).

Indications:
Borborygmus, diarrhea, edema, chronic enteritis, prolapse of the rectum and various deficiency syndromes.

Clinical Application:
This is an important landmark for locating the other points. Needling is contraindicated, but indirect moxa therapy is often applied on ginger or salt. It can promote the

---

Note: Dantian
"Dan" (丹) refers to Yuan qi (vital energy); "Tian" (田) means a residence. Different opinions are still held regarding the location of the Dantian. Qigong masters place great emphasis on the importance of the qi in Dantian, but refer to its location in a broad sense. Acupuncturists seek greater precision, many locating it at Guanyuan (Ren 4), 3 cun below the umbilicus. This is considered to be the place where sperms are produced in males and where the uterus is located. It was recorded in *Nanjing* (*A Classics of Difficult Questions*) that "the active qi between the two kidneys underneath the umbilicus constitutes the primary source of qi of the twelve meridians and is the place where the Yuan qi (vital energy) is stored."
In a broader sense, the Dantian may be considered to occupy the area below the umbilicus from Qihai (Ren 6) to Shimen (Ren 5) to Guanyuan (Ren 4). Huan Fu-mi stated in *Zhenjiu Jiayi Jing* (*A Classic of Acupuncture and Moxibustion*) that "Shimen (Ren 5), the Front-mu point of Sanjiao, has two meanings, Dantian and Mingmen. This point, 2 cun below the umbilicus, is the place where the qi of the Ren Meridian flourishes." He regarded Shimen (Ren 5) as the Dantian. As well as this, Qihai (Ren 6) is considered to be the sea of Yuanqi (vital energy) in both males and females, being referred to as the Dantian.
Note: The distance between Shenque (Ren 8) and the junction between the xyphoid process and the sternum is 8 cun. There are 8 points on the upper abdomen along the anterior midline, the distance between every two points being 1 cun. The depth of insertion for these points is about 1 cun.

spleen and stomach, regulate the intestinal functions, stop diarrhea, warm up the Yang qi of the body, restore Yang qi from collapse and resuscitate the unconscious.

Combinations:

With Tianshu (St.25), Zhongwan (Ren 12), Neiguan (P.6) and Zusanli (St.36) for treating gastrointestinal disorders;

With strong moxa heating for collapse.

SHUIFEN (REN 9) 水分   (WATER SEPARATING)

"Shui" (水) means water. "Fen' (分) means to separate, referring to the function of small intestine in separating clear fluid from turbid. The waste water infuses into the bladder to become urine and the waste substance enters into the large intestine to become the stool. This point, 1 cun below the umbilicus, has the effect to promote the water metabolism, hence the name Shuifen (Water Separating).

Location:

One cun above the umbilicus, on the midline of the abdomen (Fig. II-222).

Indications:

Abdominal pain, borborygmus, edema, abdominal distention, dysuria, nausea and vomiting.

Clinical Application:

Moxa therapy at this point can produce good results in dealing with disorders due to poor water metabolism.

Method:

Puncture perpendicularly 1-2 cun deep.

XIAWAN (REN 10) 下脘   (INFERIOR EPIGASTRIUM)

"Xia" (下) means lower or inferior. "Wan" (脘) refers to the stomach. The point, 2 cun above the umbilicus, is at the level of the lower border of the epigastrium, on the anterior midline, hence the name Xiawan (Inferior Epigastrium).

Location:

See the above item (Fig. II-222).

Indications:

Poor digestion, vomiting, abdominal pain, borborygmus and deficiency of the spleen and stomach.

Method:

Puncture perpendicularly 1-2 cun deep.

JIANLI (REN 11) 建里 (BUILDING THE HOUSE)

"Jian" (建) means building up. "Li" (里) means a house, referring here to the stomach. This point, 3 cun above umbilicus or 1 cun below Zhongwan (Ren 12), has the effect to pacify stomach qi, hence the name Jianli (Building the House).

Location:

See above item (Fig. II-222).

Indications:

Gastric pain, vomiting, nausea, abdominal distention, borborygmus, edema and anorexia.

Method:
Puncture perpendicularly 1-2 cun deep.

ZHONGWAN (REN 12) 中脘 (MID EPIGASTRIUM)

"Zhong" (中) means middle or centre. "Wan" (脘) refers to the stomach. This is the Front-Mu point of the stomach, on the anterior midline, halfway between the junction of the sternum with the xyphoid process, and the umbilicus. It is in the centre of the epigastrium, hence the name Zhongwan (Mid Epigastrium).

Another name for this point is Taicang (太仓) (Big Barn), implying that the stomach receives and stores food like a grain barn.

Location:
Four cun above the umbilicus, on the anterior midline (Fig. II-222, 223).

Indications:
Gastric pain, abdominal pain, borborygmus, vomiting, diarrhea, dysentery, jaundice and deficiency of the spleen and stomach.

Clinical Application:
This is the Front-Mu point of the stomach, having the effect to promote the stomach and resolve dampness. It is the Influential Point associated with the fu organs and the coalescent point of the Lung Meridian of Hand-Taiyin, the Sanjiao Meridian of Hand-Shaoyang and the Stomach Meridian of Foot-Yangming.

Combinations:
With Neiguan (P.6), Zusanli (St.36), Gongsun (Sp.4) and Weishu (U.B.21) for treating epigastric distention, vomiting, diarrhea and dysentery.

Method:
Puncture perpendicularly 1-2 cun deep.

Needling Sensations:
Distention and heaviness, radiating to the surrounding area.

SHANGWAN (REN 13) 上脘 (SUPERIOR EPIGASTRIUM)

"Shang" (上) means superior. "Wan" (脘) refers to the stomach. Shangwan (Ren 13), 1 cun above Zhongwan (Ren 12), is in the upper epigastric region, hence the name Shangwan (Superior Epigastrium).

Location:
See the above item (Fig. II-222).

Indications:
Gastric pain, abdominal distention, vomiting and epilepsy.

Method:
Puncture perpendicularly 1-1.5 cun deep.

JUQUE (REN 14) 巨阙 (BIG GATEWAY)

"Ju" (巨) means big. "Que" (阙) means gateway, implying that qi may flow to the heart from this point. It is the Front-Mu point of the heart and was referred to in the *Zhenjiu Wendui* (*Acupuncture Questionnaire*) as "the palace of the heart," hence the name Juque (Big Gateway).

Location:
See (Fig. II-222).

Indications:

Cardiac pain, nausea, severe acid regurgitation, mania with emotional excitement, palpitation and hiccup.

Method:

Puncture perpendicularly 0.5-1 cun. Deep insertion of the needle at this point is contraindicated, because of the danger of puncturing the liver.

JIUWEI (REN 15) 鳩尾 (TURTLEDOVE TAIL)

"Wei" (尾) means tail. "Jiu" (鳩) means turtledove, the shape of the xyphoid process being likened to the tail of a turtledove. The point is at the xyphoid process, hence the name Jiuwei (Turtledove Tail).

Location:

See (Fig. II-222).

Indications:

Cardiac pain, nausea, epilepsy, mania with emotional excitement and insanity with emotional depression.

Clinical Application:

It is the Luo-Connecting point of the Ren Meridian.

Method:

Puncture subcutaneously either upward or downward. Deep insertion is contraindicated.

ZHONGTING (REN 16) 中庭 (CENTRAL COURT)

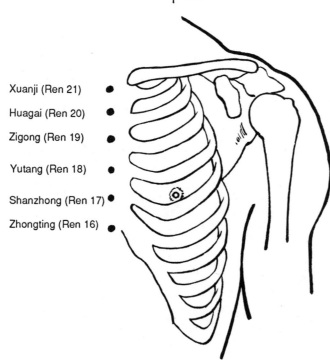

Xuanji (Ren 21)

Huagai (Ren 20)

Zigong (Ren 19)

Yutang (Ren 18)

Shanzhong (Ren 17)

Zhongting (Ren 16)

The Chinese term "Zhongting" (中庭) originally means the courtyard in front of a palace. The point is at the junction of the sternum and the xyphoid process, below Shangzhong (Ren 17). The heart (the monarch) is superior to the point, hence the name Zhongting (Central Court).

Location & Method:

See above note (Fig. II-224).

Indications:

Infantile vomiting, hypochondriac pain, poor appetite, nausea and vomiting.

Note: There are 6 points on the anterior midline of the chest. They are located respectively at each intercostal space. Subcutaneous insertion about 0.3-0.5 cun is applied at these points.

Fig. II-224

TANZHONG (SHANGZHONG) (REN 17) 膻中 (HEART PALACE)

"Tan" (膻) means the palace of the heart, referring to the outer tissues protecting the heart. "Zhong" (中) means internal-external corresponding, or inside the pleurae, hence the name Tanzhong (Heart Palace).

Location:

Below Yutang (Ren 18), between the two nipples at the level of the 4th intercostal space (Fig. II-224).

Indications:

Shortness of breath, cough, chest pain, difficulty in swallowing, and lactation deficiency.

Clinical Application:

It is one of the Eight Influential Points associated with qi. It can deal with the disorders of qi, such as cough and asthma. It is also the Front-Mu point of the pericardium and the coalescent point of the Ren Meridian, the Small Intestine Meridian of Hand-Taiyang, the Sanjiao Meridian of Hand-Shaoyang, the Spleen Meridian of Foot-Taiyin, and the Kidney Meridian of Foot-Shaoyin. It has the effect to suppress abnormal ascending of qi, relieve fullness sensation in the chest, calm the heart and promote lactation.

Combinations:

With Feishu (U.B.13) and Chize (Lu.5) for treating cough and asthma,

With Rugen (St.18) and Shaoze (S.J.1) for lactation deficiency.

Method:

Puncture horizontally 0.3-0.5 cun deep

Needling Sensations:

Distention and heaviness around the local area.

YUTANG (REN 18) 玉堂 (WHITE JADE HALL)

"Yu" (玉) means white jade. "Tang" (堂) means hall. "Yutang" together means a white hall made of white jade, a place of nobility where the heart resides. Another explanation for the name of this point is its relation to the lung, represented by white. It is mainly indicated in pulmonary disorders such as fullness sensation in the chest, cough and asthma aggravated after lying down, shortness of breath and restlessness, hence the name Yutang (White Jade Hall).

Location:

One cun above Tanzhong (Ren 17), on the anterior midline, at the level of the 3rd intercostal space (Fig. II-224).

Indications & Method:

See the above note.

CHEST-ZIGONG (REN 19) 紫宮 (PURPLE CENTRE)

"Zi" (紫) refers to purplish red. "Gong" (宮) means a central place. The Ren Meridian merges into the heart at this point, and the heart dominates the blood vessels which are purplish red in colour. Hence the name Zigong (Purple Centre).

Location:

Note: Chest-Zigong (Ren 19), Huagai (Ren 20) and Xuanji (Ren 21) have similar indications such as asthma, chest pain and sore throat.

At the level of the 2nd intercostal space, on the midline of the chest (Fig. II-224).
Indications & Method:
See above notes.

HUAGAI (REN 20) 华 蓋 (CANOPY)

The lung is considered to be the canopy of the five zang organs. "Huagai" (华 蓋) in the ancient times was the umbrella held above the carriage of the emperor when he was travelling. The heart, the emperor among the organs, is covered by the lung as though by an umbrella. The point is also indicated in lung disorders. Needling this point can help the lung disperse and relieve asthma, hence the name Huagai (Canopy).

Location, Indications & Method:
See above notes (Fig. II-224).

XUANJI (REN 21) 璇 玑 (BIG DIPPER)

"Xuanji" (璇玑) is the name for a certain segment of the constellation of the Plough, or the Big Dipper. It was believed in ancient times that "the Plough was the centre of the sky and the heart was the centre of the man." This is above Huagai (Ren 20), the canopy of the heart, hence the name Xuanji (Big Dipper).

Location, Indications & Method:
See above notes (Fig. II-224).

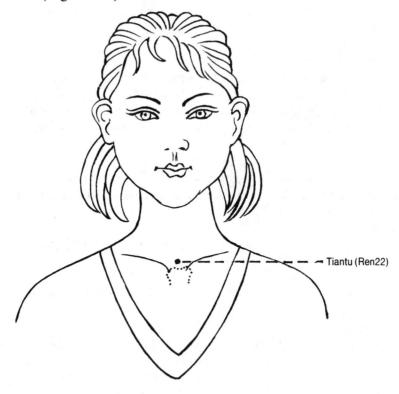

— Tiantu (Ren22)

Fig. II-225

TIANTU (REN 22) 天突 (HIGH PROMINENCE)

"Tian" (天) refers to a high place, implying the high portion of the body. "Tu" (突) means a process or prominence, referring to the Adam's apple. The point, 2 cun below the Adam's apple, is indicated in throat disorders. It can promote circulation of pulmonary qi and stop asthma, hence the name Tiantu (High Prominence).

Location:

In the depression at the upper border of manubrium sterni (Fig. II-225, 226).

Indications:

Asthma, cough, hoarseness of voice, sore throat, goiter, hiccup and whooping cough.

Clinical Application:

This is the coalescent point of Ren Meridian and Yinwei Meridian, having the effect to promote the lung in dispersing, resolve phlegm and clear the throat.

Combinations:

With Chize (Lu.5) for treating cough and asthma,

With Fenglong (St.40) for resolving phlegm,

With Tianrong (S.J.17) for the throat.

Method:

Puncture obliquely downwards at first for 0.3 cun, at an angle of 45°, then insert the needle a further 1-2 cun at an angle of 15°.

Needling Sensations:

Suffocating sensation in the throat.

LIANQUAN (REN 23) 廉泉 (PRISM SPRING)

"Lian" (廉) refers to the tongue, or the shape of a prism. "Quan" (泉) means spring, referring here to the saliva. The point is superior to the Adam's apple, which is likened to a prism. It is underneath the bottom of the tongue, and is indicated in tongue disorders. *Zhenjiu Jiayi Jin* (*A Classic of Acupuncture*) states that: "Swelling of the tongue creates difficulty in speaking, with saliva flowing out of the mouth," hence the name Lianquan (Prism Spring).

Location:

In the depression above the Adam's apple. Put the transverse crease of the thumb upon the middle of the chin when locating this point. The place where the tip of the thumb touches is Lianquan (Ren 23) (Fig. II-226, 227).

Indications:

Tongue rigidity, excessive salivation, difficulty in speaking, swollen tongue root, difficulty in swallowing and sudden hoarseness.

Clinical Application:

This is the coalescent point of Ren and Yinwei Meridians, having the effect to dispel hoarseness.

Combinations:

With Shaoshang (Lu.11) and Hegu (L.I.4) for treating acute and chronic laryngitis,

With Tongli (H. 5) for sudden hoarseness.

CHENGJIANG (REN 24) 承漿 (RECEIVING SALIVA)

"Cheng" (承) means to receive. "Jiang" (漿) refers to saliva. Saliva will accumulate here if it flows out of the mouth, hence the name Chengjiang (Receiving

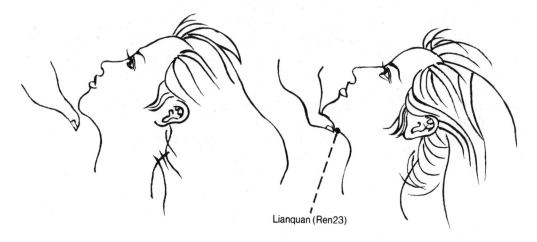

Fig. II-226

Saliva).

Location:

In the depression at the centre of sulcus mentolabialis (Fig. II-227, 228, 229).

Indications:

Facial paralysis, swollen gums, toothache, pain in umbilical region and excessive salivation.

Clinical Application:

Chengjiang (Ren 24), the coalescent point of Ren, Du and Yangming Meridians of both the foot and hand, has an excellent effect to sedate pain and calm the mind. It is commonly used for neurological and mental illnesses, as well as for acupuncture analgesia in surgical operations of the chest and neck.

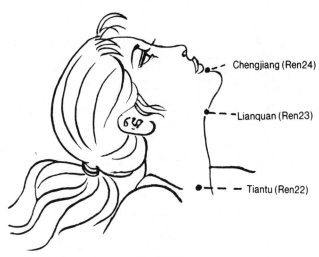

Fig. II-227

Combinations:

With Fengfu (Du 16) for treating neck rigidity,

With Lidui (St.45) and Dicang (St.4) for oral blisters.

Method:

Puncture obliquely 0.3-0.5 cun deep or horizontally 0.2-0.3 cun deep.

Needling Sensations:

Distension towards the root of the lower teeth.

Chengjiang (Ren24)

Fig. II-228

Point Indications of the Ren Meridian
According to Regional Locations

Point Names	Locations	Indications	Regional Indications
Huiyin Ren 1	Between the anus and scrotum	Disorders of the anus and genitalia, mania, suffocation, seminal emission, impotence	
Qugu Ren 2	Mid-point of the upper border of symphysis pubis	Seminal emission, impotence	Disorders of the urinary, reproductive and intestinal systems
Zhongji Ren 3	1 cun directly above Qugu (Ren 2)	Enuresis, dysmenorrhea	
Guanyuan Ren 4	1 cun above Zhongji (Ren 3) and 2 cun above Qugu (Ren 2)	Windstroke, collapse, general tonification	
Shimen Ren 5	1 cun above Guanyuan (Ren 4) or 3 cun above Qugu (Ren 2)	Menorrhagia, amenorrhea, hypertension	
Qihai Ren 6	0.5 cun above Shimen (Ren 5) or 1.5 cun below the umbilicus	Windstroke, collapse, diarrhea due to deficient cold for general tonification	
Yinjiao Ren 7	1 cun above Shimen (Ren 5) or 1 cun below the umbilicus	Colic around the umbilicus, leukorrhea	

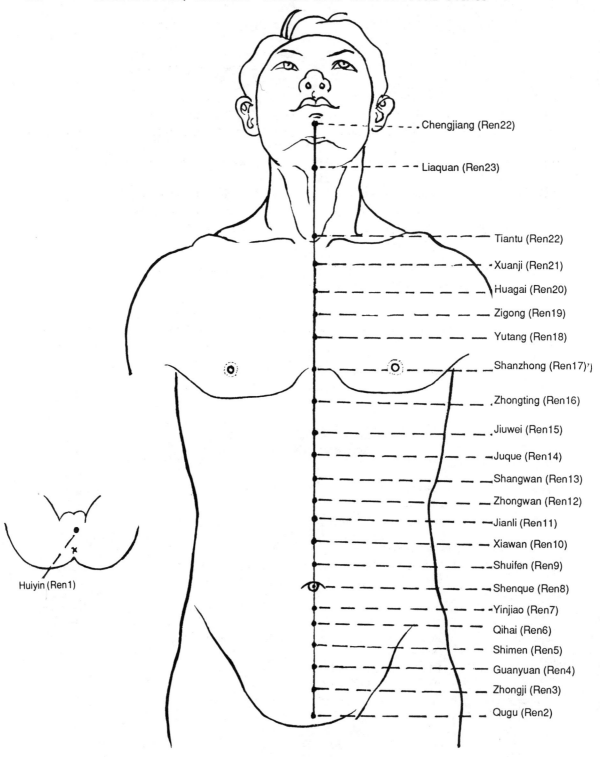

Chengjiang (Ren22)

Liaquan (Ren23)

Tiantu (Ren22)

Xuanji (Ren21)

Huagai (Ren20)

Zigong (Ren19)

Yutang (Ren18)

Shanzhong (Ren17)

Zhongting (Ren16)

Jiuwei (Ren15)

Juque (Ren14)

Shangwan (Ren13)

Zhongwan (Ren12)

Jianli (Ren11)

Xiawan (Ren10)

Shuifen (Ren9)

Shenque (Ren8)

Yinjiao (Ren7)

Qihai (Ren6)

Shimen (Ren5)

Guanyuan (Ren4)

Zhongji (Ren3)

Qugu (Ren2)

Huiyin (Ren1)

Fig. II-229

Shenque Ren 8	In the centre of the umbilicus	Windstroke with collapse, retention of urine	
Shuifen Ren 9	1 cun above the umbilicus	Edema, abdominal distention, pain around the umbilicus, gastric pain, indigestion	
Xiawan Ren 10	2 cun above the umbilicus	Gastric pain, indigestion	
Jianli Ren 11	3 cun above the umbilicus	General swelling, epigastric pain	
Zhongwan Ren 12	4 cun above the umbilicus	Gastric pain, abdominal distention, vomiting	Gastrointestinal disorders
Shangwan Ren 13	5 cun above the umbilicus	Vomiting, abdominal distention and pain	
Juque Ren 14	6 cun above the umbilicus	Gastric pain, hiccup, palpitation	
Jiuwei Ren 15	7 cun above the umbilicus	Angina pectoris, biliary ascariasis	
Zhongting Ren 16	On the junction of the sternum and the xyphoid process at the level of the 5th intercostal space	Globus hystericus, baby vomiting	
Tanzhong Ren 17	On the midline of the chest, at the level of the 4th intercostal space	Asthma, lactation deficiency, angina pectoris	
Yutang Ren 18	On the midline of the chest at the level of the 3rd intercostal space	Suffocating sensation in the chest with difficulty in breathing	Disorders of the tongue, throat, mouth and teeth
Zigong Ren 19	On the midline of the chest, at the level of the 2nd intercostal space	Cough, asthma, pain in both breasts	
Huagai Ren 20	On the midline of the chest, at the level of the 1st intercostal space, 1 cun below Xuanji (Ren 21)	Hypochondriac pain, asthma	
Xuanji Ren 21	1 cun below Tiantu (Ren 21)	Fullness in the hypochondriac region, asthma, cough	
Tiantu Ren 22	In the centre of the suprasternal fossa	Asthma, cough	
Lianquan Ren 23	Above the Adam's apple, in the depression at the upper border of the hyoid bone	Tongue rigidity, salivation	
Chengjiang Ren 24	In the centre of the sulcus mentolabialis	toothache, facial paralysis	

Appendix I EXTRA POINTS

The extra points are not regular points of the 14 meridians, although some of them are located on the courses of meridians. Many of them are commonly applied in the clinic, some being traditional and others having been recently discovered.

There exists, however, a great difference in the number of extra points mentioned in various sources over the last few decades. Some books record as few as 20 extra points, while others list up to 1,500. By and large, the number of extra points in common use varies from 30 to 60; this text lists and describes a total of 54 extra points.

The nomenclature of extra points is somewhat disordered and sometimes multiple names have been given to the same point. The names used in this text were ratified by the WHO Regional Office for the Western Pacific at its working conference on nomenclature of acupuncture points in Tokyo, May 1984; and at the 2nd working conference on nomenclature of acupuncture points sponsored by the same body in Hong Kong, July 1985.

The extra points here are listed in the order from head to neck, to body trunk, to upper extremities and to lower extremities.

I. HEAD AND NECK

SISHENCONG (EX-HN 1)四 神聰 (FOUR-SPIRIT BRIGHTENING)

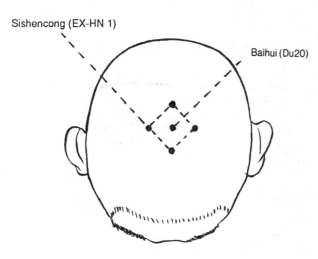

Sishencong (EX-HN 1)

Baihui (Du20)

Fig. III-1

"Si" (四) refers to the four localities, i.e. front, back, left and right. It also indicates that this is a group of four points. "Shen" (神) means mind or spirit; "cong" (聰) means to make one clever or to brighten the mind. The brain is the palace of spirit. This point has the effect to promote mental activities and sharpen the intelligence, hence the name Sishencong (Four-spirit Brightening).

Location:

This group of four points is located at the vertex, one cun respectively anterior, posterior and lateral to Baihui (Du 20) (Fig.III-1).

Indications:

Headache, dizziness and vertigo, insomnia, poor memory, epilepsy, hemiplegia and mental retardation.

Clinical Application:

This point has the effect to calm the mind, stop pain and relieve spasm.

Combinations:

With Baihui (Du 20) and Yamen (Du 15) for mental retardation and epilepsy,

With Shenmen (H.7) and Neiguan (P.6) for poor memory and insomnia,

With Taiyang (extra) and Yintang (extra) for headache, dizziness and vertigo.

Method:

Puncture horizontally 0.5-0.8 cun deep towards the anterior or posterior aspect of the head. Moxibustion is applicable.

Needling Sensations:

Mild pain and slight distention in the local area.

YINTANG (EX-HN 2) 印堂 (DECORATING HALL)

"Yin" (印) means to stain or dye. "Tang" (堂) means a place. In the ancient times, people used to dye the area between the two eyebrows with red ink for cosmetic purposes. This point is located in the same area, hence the name Yintang (Decorating Hall).

Location:

Midway between the eyebrows (Fig. III-2).

Indications:

Headache, dizziness and vertigo, sinusitis, epilepsy, pain and redness of the eye, nausea, vomiting, perpetual dizziness, insomnia, and acute or chronic infantile convulsion.

Clinical Application:

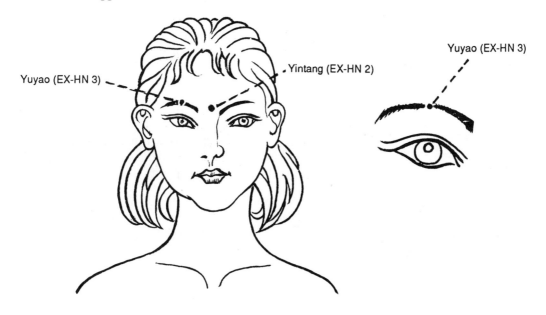

Fig. III-2

This point can dispel pathogenic wind, stop pain, eliminate heat and calm the mind.
Combinations:
With Zanzhu (U.B.2) for headache and heaviness sensation of the head,
With Taiyang (extra) for pain and redness of the eye,
With Yingxiang (L.I.20) and Shangxing (Du 23) for sinusitis and epistaxis,
With Neiguan (P.6) for nausea, vomiting, dizziness and vertigo,
With Renzhong (Du 26) for infantile convulsions.
Method:
Puncture horizontally 0.3-0.5 cun deep after pinching the skin up, or prick with a three-edged needle to cause bleeding. Moxibustion is applicable.
Needling Sensations:
Local soreness or distention, radiating towards the nose.

YUYAO (EX-HN 3) 魚腰　(FISH WAIST)

"Yu" (魚), meaning fish, refers to the eyebrow which looks like a small fish. "Yao", (腰), meaning waist, refers to the midpoint of the eyebrow where the point is located. Hence the name Yuyao (Fish Waist).
Location: At the midpoint of the eyebrow (Fig. III-2).
Indications: Pain and redness of the eye, flickering of the eyelid, ptosis, painful orbit and deviation of mouth and eye.
Clinical Application:
This point can eliminate liver heat, brighten the eyes, relieve spasm and stop pain.
Combinations:
With Taiyang (extra) and Taichong (Liv.3) for pain and redness of the eye;
With Sizhukong (S.J.23) and Zanzhu (U.B.2) for flickering eyelid, ptosis and painful orbit.
Method:
Puncture 0.3-0.5 cun laterally or inferiorly towards either side of the eyebrow along the skin. Moxibustion is contraindicated.

TAIYANG (EX-HN 4) 太陽　(THE GREAT YANG)

"Tai" (太) in ancient Chinese was the same as "da" (大), meaning great. "Yang" (陽) here refers to the head, as the convergence of the Yang meridians and where the Yang qi is the most abundant. In addition, the point deals with headache, caused by hyperactivity of Yang, hence the name Taiyang (the Great Yang).
Location:
In the depression about 1 cun posterior to the midpoint between the lateral end of the eyebrow and the outer canthus (Fig. III-3).
Indications:
One-sided headache, eye disorders and trigeminal neuralgia.
Clinical Application:
This point can expel pathogenic wind, relieve spasm, dispel heat and ease pain.
Combinations:
With Fengchi (G.B.20) and Ermen (S.J.21) for squint,
With Lieque (Lu.7) and Fengchi (G.B.20) for headache,

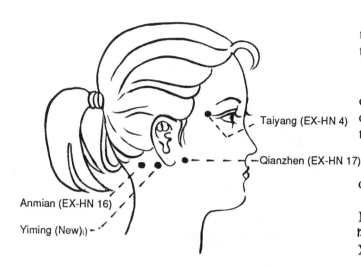

Taiyang (EX-HN 4)

Qianzhen (EX-HN 17)

Anmian (EX-HN 16)

Yiming (New)₁

Fig. III-3

With oblique insertion of the needle at this point for the treatment of upper toothache.

Method:

Puncture perpendicularly or obliquely 0.3-0.5 cun deep, or prick to cause bleeding with the three-edged needle.

Needling Sensations:

Local soreness, distention or heaviness.

NEIYINGXIANG (EX-HN 5) 内迎香 (MEDIAL YING-XIANG)

"Nei" (内) refers to the medial side of the nose. The point, inside the nose, has the similar indications to Yingxiang (L.I.20), hence the name Neiyingxiang (Medial Yingxiang).

Location:

Have the patient sit facing upwards. The point is inside the nasal cavity, opposite to Bitong (also known as Upper Yingxiang) (Fig. III-4).

Indications:

Pain and redness in the eye, nasal disorders, sore throat, sunstroke, dizziness and vertigo.

Method:

Prick with the three-edged needle to cause bleeding.

JINJIN (EX-HN 6)金 津 (GOLDEN FLUID) YUYE (EX-HN 7) 玉 液 (JADE FLUID)

"Jinjin" (金津) is derived from food essence and is one of the important components of blood. Puncturing these two points may increase the secretion of saliva (also part of the body fluid) which is important for moistening the mouth and assisting the digestion. It is considered as valuable as gold (Jin) or jade (Yu), hence the names Jinjin (Golden Fluid) and Yuye (Jade Fluid). They are located on the blood vessels, the left point being called Jinjin (Golden Fluid) and the right one Yuye (Jade Fluid).

Location:

Have the patient sit with the mouth open and the tip of the tongue placed on the hard palate. The two points are located on the large vein on either side of the glossodesmus (Fig.III-5).

Indications:

Oral ulcer, tongue rigidity, swollen tongue, diarrhea, nausea, vomiting and sore throat.

Clinical Application:

Caution: Contraindicated for those who have hemorrhagic diathesis.

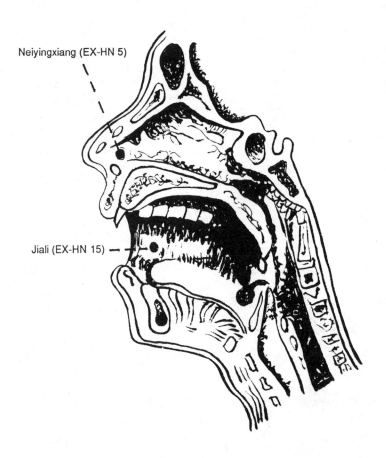

Fig. III-4

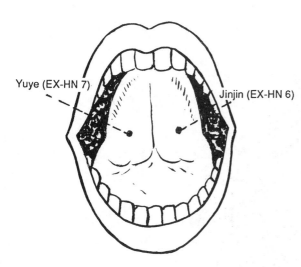

Yuye (EX-HN 7)

Jinjin (EX-HN 6)

Fig. III-5

These two points have the effect to dispel pathogenic wind, eliminate heat, relieve spasm, stop diarrhea and vomiting.

Combinations:

With Shaoshang (Lu.11) for mouth ulcer;

With Fengfu (Du 16), Yamen (Du 15) and Lianquan (Ren 23) for difficult speech due to tongue rigidity;

With Chengjiang (Ren 24) and Lianquan (Ren 23) for diabetic thirst.

Method:

Prick with the three-edged needle to cause bleeding.

Needling Sensations:

Mild pain in the local area.

JUQUAN (EX-HN 8)聚泉 (CONVERGENT SPRING)

"Ju" (聚) means to converge and "quan" (泉) means spring, referring to the saliva in this context. Hence the name Juquan (Convergent Spring).

Location:

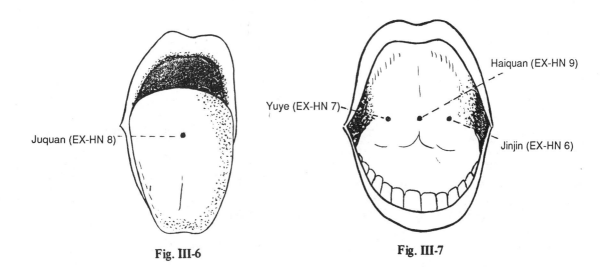

Juquan (EX-HN 8)

Yuye (EX-HN 7)

Haiquan (EX-HN 9)

Jinjin (EX-HN 6)

Fig. III-6

Fig. III-7

At the very centre of the tongue when the tongue is in full extension (Fig. III-6).

Indications:

Tongue rigidity, paralysis of the tongue, diabetic thirst, asthma, cough and loss of the sense of smell.

Method:

Puncture perpendicularly 0.2 cun deep, or prick with the three-edged needle to cause bleeding. Pull the tongue out with a piece of disinfected gauze before puncturing.

HAIQUAN (EX-HN 9) 海泉 (SPRING OF THE SEA)

"Hai" (海) means sea or merging of water. "Quan" (泉) means spring, referring to the saliva in this context, hence the name Haiquan (Spring of the Sea).

Location:

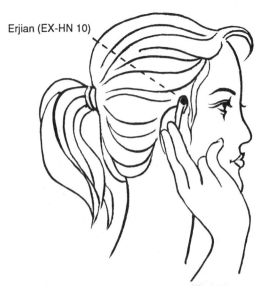

Erjian (EX-HN 10)

Fig. III-8

Midway between Jinjin (Ex-HN 6) and Yuye (Ex-HN 7) underneath the tongue (Fig. III-7).

Indications:

Nausea, vomiting, hiccup, diabetic thirst, oral ulcer and acute tonsillitis.

ERJIAN (EX-HN 10) 耳尖 (EAR APEX)

"Er" (耳) means ear. "Jian" (尖) here refers to the apex. The point was thus named because it is located immediately above the apex of the ear.

Location:

Fold the ear anteriorly. The point is at the very top of the auricle (Fig. III-8).

Indications:

Pain and redness of the eye, corneal opacity, one-sided headache, sore throat and stye.

Clinical Application:

This point can eliminate the liver heat, brighten the eye, dispel pathogenic wind and stop pain.

Combinations:

With Taiyang (Extra) and Yintang (Extra) for one-sided headache, redness and pain of the eye,

With Yamen (Du 15) for sore throat and aphonia.

Method:

Puncture perpendicularly 0.1-0.2 cun deep; or prick with the three-edged needle to cause bleeding. Moxibustion is applicable.

DANGYANG (EX-HN 11) 当阳 (ON YANG)

Caution: This point is contraindicated for those who have thrombocytopenia or hemophilia.

"Dang" (当) means being on or at; "yang" (阳) refers to the Gall Bladder Meridian of Foot-Shaoyang. The point is about 1 cun directly above Yangbai (G.B.14, a point of the Gall Bladder Meridian of Foot-Shaoyang). Hence the name Dangyang (On Yang).

Location:

Have the patient look straight forward. The point is directly above the centre of the pupil, 1 cun within the hairline (Fig. III-9).

Indications:

Headache, dizziness and vertigo, congestion in the eye and common cold with nasal obstruction.

Clinical Application:

This point has the effect to relieve pathogenic wind, dispel heat and stop pain.

Combinations:

With Shuaigu (G.B.8) for headache, dizziness and vertigo.

With Taichong (Liv.3) and Taiyang (Extra) for congestion in the eye;

With Hegu (L.I.4) and Yingxiang (L.I.20) for common cold with nasal obstruction.

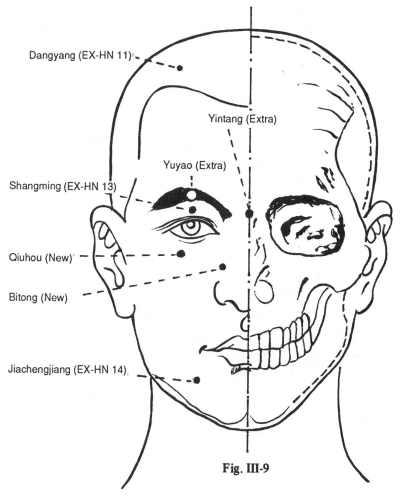

Fig. III-9

Method:
Puncture 0.2-0.3 cun deep. Moxibustion is applicable.
Needling Sensations:
Mild pain and distention in the local region.

JINGBAILAO (EX-HN 12) 頸百癆 (CERVICAL TB POINT)

"Jing" (頸) refers to the cervical area. "Bai" (百) here means something large in number. "Lao" (劳) was equal to "Lao" (癆) in ancient Chinese, meaning tuberculosis. The point was thus named because of its indications in a variety of forms of tuberculosis.
Location:
Have the patient sit with the head bent slightly forward, or lie in a prone position. The point is 1 cun lateral and 2 cun above Dazhui (Du 14) (Fig.III-10).
Indications:
Scrofula, cough, asthma, bone-steaming, tidal fever, spontaneous sweating, night sweating, neck rigidity, neck pain, sore throat and general pain after labour due to the invasion of exogenous pathogenic wind and dampness.
Clinical Application:
This point has the effect to soften nodules or scrofula, disperse the lung, stop cough, regulate qi circulation and remove obstruction from the channels and collaterals.
Combinations:
With Zhouliao (L.I.12) and Quchi (L.I.11) for scrofula,
With Feishu (U.B.13) for cough and asthma,
With Taixi (K.3) for night sweating due to Yin deficiency,
With Fengchi (G.B.20) for neck sprain.
Method:
Puncture perpendicularly 0.5-1 cun deep. Moxibustion is applicable. The sharp-hooked needle can also be used at this point to cause slight bleeding.

The depth of insertion of hot needle at the point is only about 0.3 cun deep, but press the point with a piece of disinfected gauze after withdrawing the needle.
Needling Sensations:
Filiform needle: local distention, numbness and heaviness;
Sharp-hooked needle: mild pain;
Hot needle: pain and feverish sensation.

Extra Points on the Head and Neck Commonly Used in China Only:

SHANGMING (EX-HN 13) 上明 (UPPER BRIGHTENING)

"Shang" (上) here refers to the superior aspect. "Ming" (明) means brightening. This point is located at the superior aspect of the eyeball. Puncturing Shangming (Ex-HN 13) can improve the eye sight, hence the name Shangming (Upper Brightening).
Location:
On the inferior aspect of the margo supraorbitalis, at the midpoint of the arcus supraciliaris (Fig. III-9).
Indications:
Ametropia, keratoleukoma, optic atrophy and redness of the eye, excessive lacrimation.

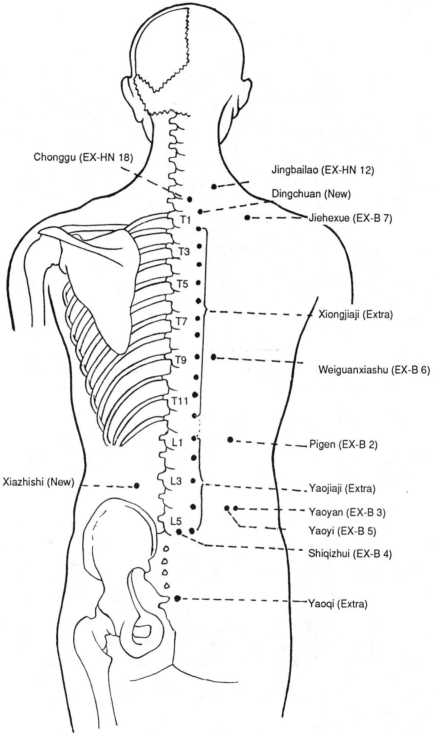

Chonggu (EX-HN 18)

Jingbailao (EX-HN 12)

Dingchuan (New)

Jiehexue (EX-B 7)

T1

T3

T5

Xiongjiaji (Extra)

T7

T9

Weiguanxiashu (EX-B 6)

T11

L1

Pigen (EX-B 2)

Xiazhishi (New)

L3

Yaojiaji (Extra)

Yaoyan (EX-B 3)

L5

Yaoyi (EX-B 5)

Shiqizhui (EX-B 4)

Yaoqi (Extra)

Fig. III-10

Method:

Insert the needle slowly about 0.5-1 cun while pushing the eyeball inferiorly. No manipulation should be done at this point other than scrapping the handle of the needle.

JIACHENGJIANG (EX-HN 14) 夹承漿 (LATERAL CHENGJIANG)

"Jia" (夹) means lateral to or beside. The point is located 1 cun lateral to Chengjiang (Ren 24), approximately at the mental foramen of the mandible, hence the name Jiachengjiang (Lateral Chengjiang) (Fig. III-9).

Indications:

Facial paralysis, facial spasm, gum ulceration and trigeminal neuralgia affecting the 3rd branch.

Method:

Puncture 0.5-1 cun horizontally or obliquely.

JIALI (EX-HN 15) 頰里 (MEDIAL CHEEK)

"Jia" (頰) means cheek. "Li" (里) refers to the medial aspect. The point is inside the mouth, about 1 cun posterior to the mouth corner, hence the name Jiali (Medial Cheek) (Fig. III-4).

Indications:

Ulcer of the gums, gastric heat with anorexia, and facial paralysis.

Method:

Puncture obliquely 0.3-0.5 cun towards the posterior aspect. Cutting the membrane with arrow-headed needle to cause bleeding will improve the therapeutic effect.

ANMIAN (EX-HN 16) 安眠 (SOUND SLEEP)

This point is indicated for insomnia and dream-disturbed sleep, hence the name Anmian (Sound Sleep).

Location:

Midway between Yifeng (S.J.17) and Fengchi (G.B.20) (Fig. III-3).

Indications:

Insomnia, headache, dizziness and vertigo, palpitation, restlessness, hypertension, deafness and hysteria.

Method:

Puncture perpendicularly 0.8-1 cun, or obliquely towards Yifeng (S.J.17) or Fengchi (G.B.20).

QIANZHENG (EX-HN 17) 牽正 (PULLING NORMAL)

This point is mainly indicated for deviation of the mouth and eye. Puncturing it can restore deviated mouth or eye to normal, hence the name Qianzheng (Pulling Normal).

Location:

0.5 cun anterior to the lobulus auriculae, where a sensitive spot or tubercle can often be felt (Fig. III-3).

Indications:

Deviation of the mouth and eye, mouth ulcer, foul breath and pain of the lower teeth.

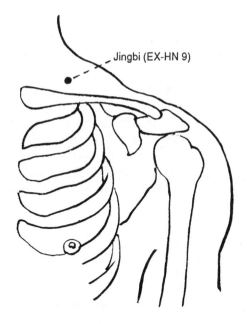

Jingbi (EX-HN 9)

Fig. III-11

Method:

Puncture anteriorly or horizontally 0.5-1 cun, or prick with the three-edged needle to cause bleeding.

CHONGGU (EX-HN 18) 崇骨 (RESPECTED BONE)

The spinous process of C7 used to be called Chonggu (respected bone). The point is located between the spinous process of C6 and C7, hence the name Chonggu (Respected Bone). It is also known as the Zhuiding (Prominence of C7) (Fig. III-10).

Indications: Cough, asthma, common cold, maniacal behaviour with emotional excitement, insanity with emotional depression, pulmonary tuberculosis, neck rigidity and sore throat with difficulty in swallowing.

Method:

Puncture obliquely upward 0.5-1 cun deep, or prick with the three-edged needle to cause bleeding, or prick with hot needle.

JINGBI (EX-HN 19) 颈臂 (UPPER ARM)

"Jing" (颈) means neck. "Bi" (臂) means upper arm. The point is located at the brachial plexus, hence the name Jingbi (Upper Arm).

Location:

Have the patient turn the head towards the opposite side when locating this point. It is 1 cun above the junction of the medial one third and the lateral two thirds of the length of the clavicle (Fig. III-11).

Indications:

Cervical spondylosis, numbness of fingers, painful fingers and paralysis of the upper limb.

Method:

Puncture perpendicularly 0.3-0.5 cun deep.

Needling Sensations:

Soreness, numbness and distention, radiating to the fingers.

II. CHEST AND ABDOMEN

ZIGONG (EX-CA 1) 子宫 (UTERUS)

This point is located close to the uterus and is indicated in prolapse of that organ, hence the name Zigong (Uterus).

Location:

Three cun lateral to Zhongji (Ren 3) (Fig. III-12).

Indications:

Prolapse of uterus, irregular menstruation, dysmenorrhea, uterine bleeding, infertil-

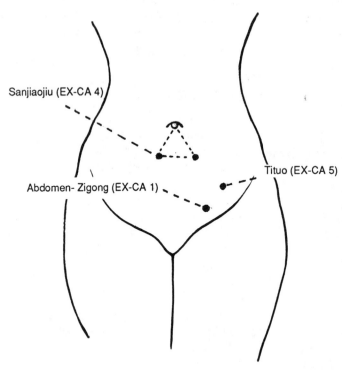

Fig. III-12

ity and lumbar pain.

Clinical Applications:

This point has the effect to restore Yang qi, regulate menstruation and ease pain.

Combinations:

With Baihui (Du 20) for prolapse of the uterus. Insert the needle towards the groin and manipulate to produce distention, heaviness and lifting sensations.

With Taichong (Liv.3) and Sanyinjiao (Sp.6) for dysmenorrhea, irregular menstruation and infertility.

This point can also be applied to treat lumbar pain in the corresponding area of the back.

Method:

Puncture perpendicularly 0.8-1.2 cun deep, or obliquely 2-3 cun, but only 0.5 cun deep with the hot needle. Moxibustion is applicable.

Needling Sensations:

Distention or heaviness radiating towards the groin.

Extra Points on the Chest and Abdomen Commonly Used in China Only:

WEISHANG (EX-CA 2) 胃上 (STOMACH LIFTING)

"Wei" (胃) means stomach. "Shang" (上) means to lift or go upwards. This point can treat gastroptosis. Puncturing it may help the stomach ascend to its normal position, hence the name Weishang (Stomach Lifting).

Location:

Have the patient lie supine when locating this point. It is 2 cun above the level of the umbilicus and 4 cun lateral (Fig. III-13).

Indications:

Gastric pain, abdominal distention and gastroptosis.

Method:

Puncture obliquely 2-3 cun towards the umbilicus or Tianshu (St.25).

QIZHONGSIBIAN (EX-CA 3) 脐中四边 (FOUR POINTS AROUND THE UMBILI-CUS)

"Qizhong" (脐中) means the centre of the umbilicus. "Sibian" (四边), meaning the four sides, refers to the locations of these four points, respectively 1 cun lateral, superior and inferior to the centre of the umbilicus. Hence the name Qizhongsibian (Four Points Around the Umbilicus) (Fig. III-13).

Indications:

Epigastric pain, borborygmus, diarrhea, indigestion and swelling.

Method:

Puncture perpendicularly 0.5-1 cun or prick to cause bleeding with the three-edged needle. Moxibustion is applicable.

SANJIAOJIU (EX-CA 4) 三角灸 (TRIANGLE MOXA)

"Sanjiao" (三角) means triangle. "Jiu" (灸) means moxa therapy. This pair of points is only prescribed for moxa therapy. The length of the patient's mouth is taken as

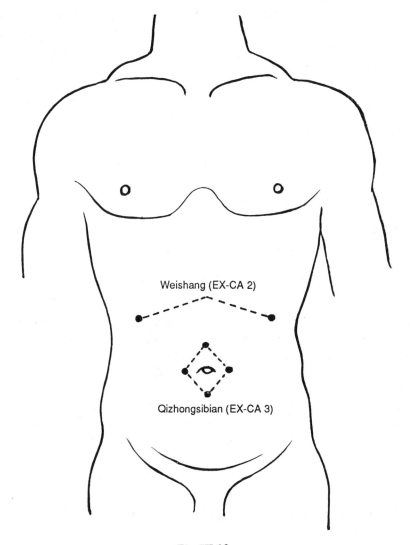

Weishang (EX-CA 2)

Qizhongsibian (EX-CA 3)

Fig. III-13

the side of the equilateral triangle, the vertex angle coinciding with the umbilical centre and the bottom side being horizontal. The points are located at the two bottom angles, hence the name Sanjiaojiu (Triangle Moxa) (Fig. III-12).

Indications:

Hernia, lower abdominal pain, pain around the umbilicus and infertility.

Method:

5-7 moxa cones are used on each point.

TITUO (EX-CA 5) 提托 (LIFTING)

Both "ti" (提) and "tuo" (托) mean to help ascend or lift. Puncturing this point can help ascend the proplapsed uterus, hence the name Tituo (Lifting).

Location:

Three cun lateral to Guanyuan (Ren 4), on the mammillary line, 3 cun below the umbilicus (Fig. III-12).

Indications:

Prolapse of the uterus, dysmenorrhea, abdominal pain, abdominal distention and hernia.

Method:

Puncture perpendicularly or obliquely 0.5-1 cun deep. Moxibustion is applicable.

III. BACK REGION

JIAJI (EX-B 1) 夹脊 (BESIDE THE VERTEBRAE)

"Jia" (夹) means lateral to or beside. "Ji" (脊) means spinal column. Jiaji (Ex-B 1) consists of a group of 17 points bilateral to the spinal column, hence the name Jiaji (Beside the Vertebrae). They are also referred to as Huatuojiaji Points, because Huatuo is believed to be the physician who discovered and first used them.

Location:

The 17 points in this group are located 0.5 cun lateral to the spinal column, at the level of the lower border of each spinous process from T 1 to L 5. The Jiaji points from T1 to T12 are known as thoracic Jiaji, and those from L 1 to L 5 are known as lumbar Jiaji (Fig. III-10).

Indications:

Jiaji points cover a wide range of indications as underneath them lie the dorsal rami of the spinal nerves, the corresponding intercostal arteries and the posterior branches of lumbar arteries. These nerves and arteries are closely related to the zangfu organs. Specifically, Jiaji points of the upper back are used for disorders of the heart, lung and upper limbs. Jiaji points of the lower back are used for gastrointestinal and lumbar disorders. Jiaji points of the lumbar region are used for disorders of the lumbar region and the lower limbs (see the table).

Clinical Application:

When a specific zang or fu organ becomes diseased, tenderness or a nodule can often be felt at the corresponding Jiaji points. Reinforcing or reducing with filiform needles can be used according to the patient's condition. Hot needles are applicable to Jiaji points of the upper back, in the case of chronic cough or asthma, neurasthenia, sore back or neck, and motor impairment. 8-12 bilateral Jiaji points are often used with hot needles in the case of rachitis, hemiplegia, syringomyelia, mental retardation, chronic gastroenteritis and rheumatic arthritis. Deep insertion is contraindicated.

Method:

Puncture perpendicularly 0.3-0.8 cun deep with filiform needles, 0.3-0.5 cun deep with hot needles, or tap with the plum blossom needle. Moxibustion is applicable.

Needling Sensations:

Distention and heaviness, radiating downwards or upwards.

PIGEN (EX-B 2) 痞 根 (DISTENTION-ELIMINATING)

"Pi" (痞), characterized by a feeling of distention and fullness, refers to a sort of uncomfortable sensation caused by abnormal qi circulation in the thoracic cavity. "Gen" (根) means thorough elimination. This point has the effect to eliminate the above-mentioned sensation, hence the name Pigen (Distention-eliminating).

Location:

Below the spinous process of L1, 3.5 cun lateral to the spinal column, or 0.5 cun lateral to Huangmen (U.B.51) (Fig. III-10).

Indications:

Abdominal masses, stuffiness and fullness in the chest and abdomen, splenomegaly, hepatomegaly, nephroptosis, hernial pain, lumbar pain and nausea.

Method:

Puncture obliquely 0.8-1 cun deep. Moxibustion is applicable.

Needling Sensations:

Local distention and heaviness, radiating towards the abdominal region.

YAOYAN (EX-B 3) 腰眼 (LUMBAR EYE)

"Yao" (腰) means lumbus. "Yan" (眼), meaning eye, refers to the two symmetrical depressions on either side of the lumbar region, likened here to eyes. When a person stands, or lies in a prone position, these two depressions will appear, hence the name Yaoyan (Lumbar Eye).

Location:

In the two depressions, below the spinous process of L 4, about 3.5 cun to 4 cun lateral to the spinal column (Fig. III-10).

Indications:

Lumbar pain, chronic pelvic inflammation, chronic adenic inflammation, frequent urination, diabetic thirst and general weakness.

Method:

Puncture perpendicularly 1-2 cun deep. Moxibustion is applicable.

Needling Sensations:

Distention and heaviness, radiating to the lower limbs.

SHIQIZHUI (EX-B 4) 十七 椎 (THE 17TH VERTEBRA)

This point was thus named because of its location in the depression below the spinous process of the 17th vertebra counting from T1.

Location:

Below the spinous process of L5, one vertebra inferior to Yaoyangguan (Du 3)

(Fig. III-10).

Indications:

Lumbosacral pain, leg pain, malposition of the fetus, dysmenorrhea, uterine bleeding, enuresis and seminal emission.

Method:

Puncture perpendicularly 0.5-1 cun deep. Moxibustion is applicable.

Needling Sensations:

Local distention and heaviness.

YAOQI (EX-B 5) 腰奇   (EXCELLENT LUMBAR POINT)

"Yao" (腰) refers to the lumbar region. "Qi" (奇) refers to something excellent or special. The point is located in the lumbar region and can produce excellent results in the treatment of mania with emotional excitement and insanity with emotional depression. Hence the name Yaoqi (Excellent Lumbar Point).

Location:

Two cun directly above the end of the coccyx (Fig. III-10).

Indications:

Mania with emotional excitement, insanity with emotional depression, headache, insomnia and constipation.

Method:

Puncture horizontally upwards 1-1.5 cun deep. Moxibustion is applicable.

Needling Sensations:

Local distention and heaviness.

WEIWANXIASHU (EX-B 6)胃脘下俞 (INFERIOR STOMACH POINT)

"Weiwan" (胃脘) means the epigastric region. "Xiashu" (下俞) means a lower point. This point is mainly indicated in stomach problems, hence the name Weiwanxiashu (Inferior Stomach Point).

Location:

At the level of the lower border of the T 8, 1.5 cun lateral to the posterior midline, approximately at the same level as pancreas. It is also called Weiguanxiashu, Bashu or Yushu (Fig. III-10).

Indications:

Stomach pain, pancreatitis, hypochondriac pain, diabetic thirst, dry throat and cough.

Method:

Puncture obliquely 0.3-0.5 cun deep.

Needling Sensations:

Distention, soreness and heaviness, radiating downwards.

Clinical Application:

This point has the effect to regulate the circulation of qi, remove obstruction from the meridians and ease pain.

Combinations:

With Weishu (U.B.21) and Weizhong (U.B.40) for acute gastric pain and diarrhea,
With Taixi (K.3) and Hegu (L.I.4) for hypochondriac pain and pancreatitis.

Extra Points on the Back Commonly Used in China Only:

JIEHEXUE (EX-B 7) 结核穴 (TB POINT)

This point was named Jiehexue (TB Point) because of its indication in pulmonary tuberculosis and other types of tuberculosis.

Location:
3.5 cun lateral to Dazhui (Du 14) (Fig. III-10).

Method:
Puncture perpendicularly 0.5-0.8 cun deep.

IV. UPPER EXTREMITIES

ZHOUJIAN (EX-UE 1) 肘 尖 (ELBOW TIP)

"Zhou" (肘) means elbow. "Jian" (尖) means tip or process. The point is at the tip of the olecranon, hence the name Zhoujian (Elbow Tip).

Location:
Flex the elbow approximately 90 degrees with arms akimbo. The point is at the tip of the olecranon (Fig. III-14).

Indications:
Scrofula, carbuncle, furuncle and boil.

Method:
Apply 7-15 moxa cones, or in the case of scrofula 30-45 small moxa cones.

ERBAI (EX-UE 2) 二 白 (DOUBLE UNDERSTANDINGS)

"Er" (二), meaning two, refers to two points on the medial aspect of the forearm. "Bai" (白), meaning white, implies that something should be clear or understood. On

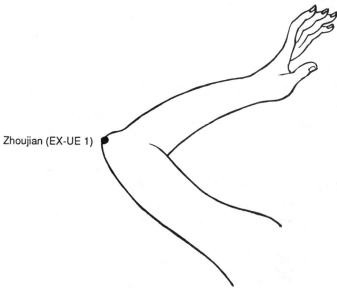

Fig. III-14

Zhoujian (EX-UE 1)

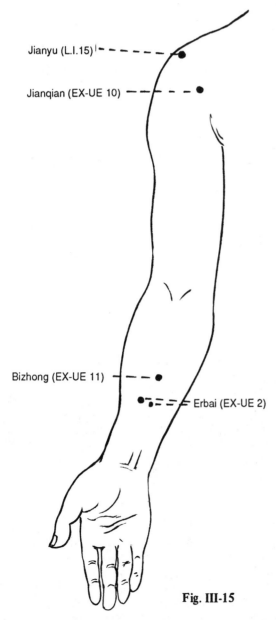

Jianyu (L.I.15)

Jianqian (EX-UE 10)

Bizhong (EX-UE 11)

Erbai (EX-UE 2)

Fig. III-15

each forearm, there are two Erbai points, which have special indications, thus requiring clear understanding. Hence the name Erbai (Double Understandings).

Location:

Four cun above the transverse crease of the wrist, on either side of the tendon of m. flexor carpi radialis. The two points are at the same level (Fig. III-15).

Indications:

Hemorrhoids, prolapse of the rectum, pain in the forearm and hypochondriac pain.

Method:

Puncture perpendicularly 0.5-0.8 cun deep. Moxibustion is applicable.

ZHONGQUAN (EX-UE 3) 中泉 (DORSAL SPRING)

"Zhong" (中) here refers to the dorsum of the hand. "Quan" (泉), meaning spring, refers to a depression, hence the name Zhongquan (Dorsal Spring).

Location:

Midway along the line between Yangxi (L.I.5) and Yangchi (S.J.4), in the depression on the radial side of the tendon of m. extensor digitorum communis (Fig. III-16).

Indications:

Fullness and distention in the hypochondriac region, cough, asthma, epigastric pain, feverish sensation in the palm, abdominal distention and pain.

Method:

Puncture perpendicularly 0.3-0.5 cun deep. Moxibustion is applicable.

ZHONGKUI (EX-UE 4) 中魁 (MIDDLE PROMINENCE)

"Zhong" (中) here refers to the middle finger. "Kui" (魁), meaning great, refers to a prominence, hence the name Zhongkui (Middle Prominence).

Location:

On the dorsal surface, at the midpoint of the transverse crease of the interphalangeal joint of the middle finger (Fig. III-17).

Indications:

Hiccup, belching, nausea, vomiting, toothache and epistaxis.

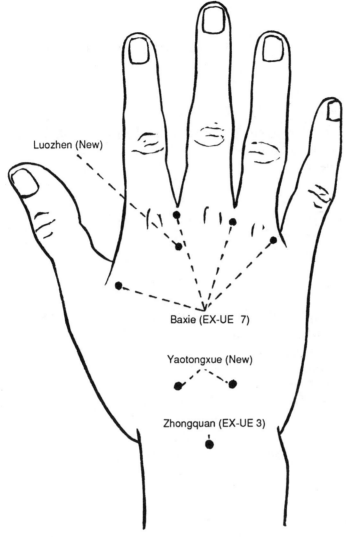

Fig. III-16

Method:

Apply 5-7 moxa cones, or prick with a hot needle.

DAGUKONG (EX-UE 5) 大骨空 (THUMB BONY SPACE)

"Da" (大) here refers to the digital joint of the thumb. "Gukong" (骨空) means a bony space. Also, the point is on the dorsum of the thumb, hence the name Dagukong (Thumb Bony Space).

Location:

On the dorsal surface, at the midpoint of the transverse crease of the digital joint of the thumb when a loose fist is made (Fig. III-17).

Indications:

Painful eyes, corneal opacity, lacrimation deficiency, cataract, vomiting, diarrhea and epistaxis.

Clinical Application:

Direct moxa using small moxa cones is applied to this point, especially for epistaxis. Apply moxa at the right Dagukong (Ex-UE 5) for epistaxis of the left nasal cavity, and vice versa. 5-7 small moxa cones are used at a time, or prick 3-5 times with a hot needle.

XIAOGUKONG (EX-UE 6) 小骨空 (LITTLE FINGER BONY SPACE)

"Xiao" (小) here refers to the interphalangeal joint of the little finger. "Gukong" (骨空) means a bony space. This point is on the little finger, hence the name Xiaogukong (Little Finger Bony Space).

Location:

On the dorsal surface, at the midpoint of the transverse crease of the proximal interphalangeal joint of the little finger when a loose fist is made (Fig. III-17).

Indications:

Pain and redness of the eyes, corneal opacity, sore throat and painful finger joint.

Method:

Apply moxa or prick 3-5 times with a hot needle.

BAXIE (EX-UE 7) 八邪 (PATHOGENIC-ELIMINATING POINT)

"Ba" (八) here refers to a group of eight points on both hands. "Xie" (邪) refers to the pathogenic factors leading to diseases. These eight points all have the effect to reinforce anti-pathogenic qi and eliminate pathogenic qi, hence the name Baxie (Pathogenic-eliminating Point). Since there are four on the webs between the fingers of each hand, 8 in all, Baxie (Ex-UE 7) is also called Baguan (the Eight Webs).

Location:

On the dorsal surface, at the junction of the red and white skin, in the webs between the five fingers when a loose fist is made (Fig. III-16).

Indications:

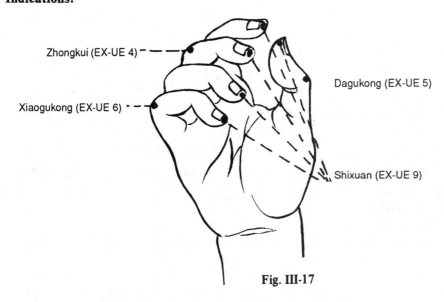

Fig. III-17

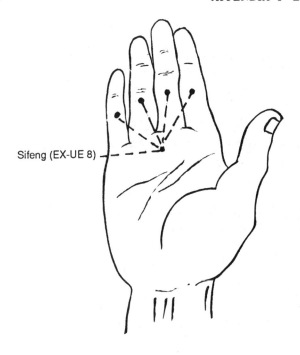

Sifeng (EX-UE 8)

Fig. III-18

Numbness of the fingers, dorsal swelling, neck rigidity, sore throat, toothache, painful eyes and fever with irascibility.

Method:

Puncture obliquely 0.5-0.8 cun upwards, or prick to cause bleeding. Moxibustion is applicable.

Needling Sensations:

Local distention, numbness and mild pain.

SIFENG (EX-UE 8) 四 缝 (FOUR CREASES)

"Si" (四), meaning four, refers to the index, middle, ring and little fingers. "Feng" (缝) refers to the transverse crease of the proximal interphalangeal joints of these fingers. There is one point on each of these creases, hence the name Sifeng (Four Creases).

Location:

On the proximal interphalangeal joints of the index, middle, ring and little fingers (Fig. III-18).

Indications:

Infantile malnutrition, whooping cough, infantile diarrhea, cough, asthma and indigestion.

Method:

Prick 0.1-0.2 cun, or prick to sequence out some yellow sticky fluid or blood.

SHIXUAN (EX-UE 9) 十 宣 (TEN-DISPERSING POINT)

"Shi" (十), meaning ten, refers to the tips of the ten fingers. "Xuan" (宣) means to disperse. These ten points have the effect to disperse pathogenic wind and heat, hence the name Shixuan (Ten-dispersing Point).

Location:

On the tips of the ten fingers, about 0.1 cun distal to the nails (Fig. III-17).

Indications:

High fever, coma, syncope, sunstroke, infantile convulsions, sore throat and numbness of the fingers.

Method:

Puncture shallowly 0.1-0.2 cun deep, or prick to cause bleeding.

Extra Points on the Upper Extremities Commonly Used in China Only:

JIANQIAN (EX-UE 10) 肩前 (ANTERIOR SHOULDER)

"Jian" (肩) means shoulder. "Qian" (前) means anterior. The point is at the midpoint of the line connecting the upper end of the anterior axillary crease and Jianyu (L.I.15). It is also called Jianneiling (Medial Mound of the Shoulder) because it is located on the prominence which appears when the arm is abducted (Fig. III-15).

Indications:

Pain in the shoulder and upper arm, motor impairment, frozen shoulder and paralysis of the upper limbs.

Method:

Puncture perpendicularly 1-1.5 cun deep. Moxibustion is applicable.

BIZHONG (EX-UE 11) 臂中   (ARM CENTRE)

"Bi" (臂) here refers to the forearm. "Zhong" (中) means centre. The point is midway between the transverse crease of the wrist and that of the elbow, between the radius and the ulna, hence the name Bizhong (Arm Centre) (Fig. III-15).

Indications:

Pain of the forearm, hypochondriac pain, paralysis of the upper limbs and hysteria.

Method:

Puncture perpendicularly 1-1.5 cun deep. Moxibustion is applicable.

V. LOWER EXTREMITIES

HEDING (EX-LE 1) 鹤顶 (CRANE HEAD)

This point is at the middle of the upper border of the patella, likened in this case to a crane's head, hence the name Heding (Crane Head). It is also known as Xiding (Knee Top).

Location:

In the depression at the midpoint of the upper border of the patella when the knee is flexed (Fig.-III-19).

Indications:

Knee-joint pain, heaviness sensation and weakness in the leg, beriberi.

Method:

Puncture perpendicularly 0.5-0.8 cun deep, or prick to cause bleeding with the three-edged needle. Moxibustion is applicable.

Needling Sensations:

Local pain and heaviness.

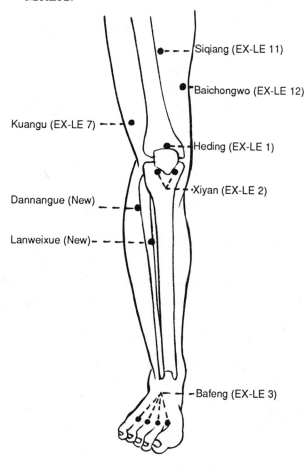

Siqiang (EX-LE 11)

Baichongwo (EX-LE 12)

Kuangu (EX-LE 7)

Heding (EX-LE 1)

Xiyan (EX-LE 2)

Dannangue (New)

Lanweixue (New)

Bafeng (EX-LE 3)

Fig. III-19

XIYAN (EX-LE 2) 膝 眼 (KNEE EYE)

"Xi" (膝) here refers to the knee joint. "Yan" (眼), meaning eye, refers to the two symmetrical depressions, like two eyes on the knee joint, hence the name Xiyan (Knee Eye). The medial one is called medial Xiyan whilst the lateral one is called lateral Xiyan or Dubi (St.35).

Location:
Have the patient flex the knee. The points are located in the two depressions on either side of the patellar ligament, for in all, two on each knee (Fig- III-19).

Indications:
Knee-joint pain, knee-joint arthritis, painful leg and beriberi.

Method:
Puncture obliquely 0.5-1 cun deep towards ligamentum cruciatum, or towards the opposite Xiyan. Moxibustion is applicable.

Needling Sensations:
Local soreness, numbness, distention and heaviness.

BAFENG (EX-LE 3) 八 风 (EIGHT-WIND POINT)

"Ba" (八), meaning eight, refers to the eight points between the ten toes. "Feng" (风) refers to the pathogenic wind. The eight points in this group are located on the junction of the red and white skin on the webs between the ten toes. They have the effect to eliminate pathogenic wind, ease pain, activate blood circulation and remove obstruction from the meridians, hence the name Bafeng (Eight-wind Point) (Figs. III-19, 20).

Indications:
Distention, and pain of the dorsal aspect of the foot, weakness of the feet, headache, toothache, irregular menstruation, cyanosis of the toes and snake bite.

Method:
Puncture obliquely 0.5-0.8 cun, or prick with a three-edged needle to cause bleeding. Xingjian (Liv.2), Neiting (St.44) and Xiabai (G.B.43) are included in the group Bafeng (Ex-LE 3).

WAIHUAIJIAN (EX-LE 4) 外踝 尖 (EXTERNAL MALLEOLUS)

"Waihuai" (外踝) refers to the external malleolus. "Jian" (尖) refers to the tip of the external malleolus. The point is at the tip of the external malleolus, hence the name Waihuaijian (External Malleolus) (Fig. III-20).

Indications:
Toothache and beriberi.

Method:
Puncture shallowly about 0.1 cun deep.

Needling Sensations:
Mild pain in the local area.

NEIHUAIJIAN (EX-LE 5) 内踝 尖 (MEDIAL MALLEOLUS)

"Neihuai" (内踝) refers to the medial malleolus. "Jian" (尖) means the tip of the malleolus. The point is on the top of the medial malleolus, hence the name Neihuaijian (Medial Malleolus) (Fig. III-20).

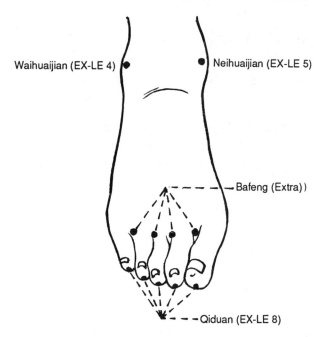

Waihuaijian (EX-LE 4)   Neihuaijian (EX-LE 5)

Bafeng (Extra))

Qiduan (EX-LE 8)

Fig. III-20

Indications:
Toothache, tonsillitis and spasm of m. gastrocnemius.
Method:
Puncture shallowly about 0.1 cun deep.
Needling Sensations:
Mild pain in the local area.

DUYIN (EX-LE 6) 独阴 (UNIQUE YIN)

"Du" (独) means something unique. "Yin" (阴) implies that the point is at the sole which is a Yin aspect, opposite to the dorsum of the foot. There is only one point on the sole of each foot, hence the name Duyin (Unique Yin).
Location:
On the transverse crease of the distal phalangeal joint of the 2nd toe (Fig. III-21).

Indications:
Sudden angina pectoris, hypochondriac pain, nausea, vomiting, bloody vomiting, dead-fetus, retained placenta, irregular menstruation and hernia.
Method:
Prick shallowly 0.2-0.3 cun deep, or apply 5-7 small moxa cones, or moxa sticks for about 20 minutes.

KUANGU (EX-LE 7) 髋骨 (HIPBONE)

"Kuangu" (髋骨) originally means the hipbone on either side of the hip joint, irregularly formed, but here is referred to the name of an acupuncture point. The point can be used to treat hip pain, hence the name Kuangu (Hipbone).
Location:
Two cun above the patella, 1 cun lateral to either side of the point Liangqiu (St.34) (Fig. III-19).
Indications:
Pain in the hip joint and thigh, knee-joint arthritis.
Clinical Application:
This point has the effect to soothe tendons and remove obstructions from channels and collaterals.
Combinations:
With Femur-Juliao (G.B.29) and Zhibian (U.B.54) for hip-joint pain and pain in the lower extremities,
With Dubi (St.35) and Yanglingquan (G.B.34) for knee-joint arthritis,
With Bafeng (Extra) for numbness and swelling in the foot.

Method:

Puncture perpendicularly 1-1.5 cun deep. Moxibustion is applicable.

Needling Sensations:

Local numbness and distention.

QIDUAN (EX-LE 8) 气端 (QI END)

"Qi" (气) in terms of function may refer to the original force leading to the normal functional activities of all body organs. "Duan" (端) means extremity, referring to the tip of the toe in this context. Also, this point is indicated in beriberi, hence the name Qiduan (Qi End).

Location:

At the very tips of the ten toes (Fig. III-20).

Indications:

Beriberi, sudden abdominal pain and syncope.

Clinical Application:

This point has the effect to promote the circulation of qi, resolve dampness and relieve acute pain.

Combinations:

With Yinlingquan (Sp.9) and Bafeng (Extra) for beriberi and swollen foot;

With Liangqiu (St.34) for acute abdominal pain, especially for functional gastrointestinal spasm.

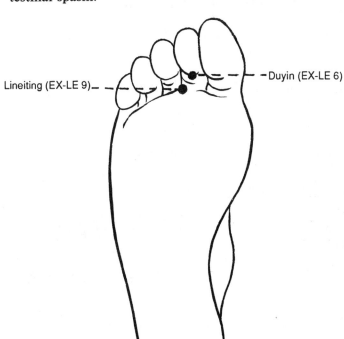

Lineiting (EX-LE 9)

Duyin (EX-LE 6)

Fig.III-21

Method:

Prick to cause bleeding, or hammer with the plumblossom needle.

Moxibustion is applicable.

Needling Sensations:

Slight pain in the local area.

LINEITING (EX-LE 9)里内庭 (MEDIAL INNER-ROOM)

This point, opposite to Neiting (St.44), is on the sole, between the 2nd and 3rd toes, hence the name Lineiting (Medial Inner-Room) (Fig. III-21).

Indications:

Acute gastric pain, painful toes, infantile convulsion, maniacal emotional excitement and insanity with emotional depression.

Method:

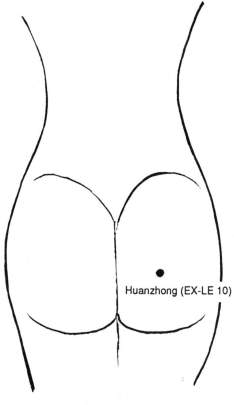

Fig. III-22

Puncture perpendicularly 0.3-0.5 cun deep.

HUANZHONG (EX-LE 10) 环中 (CIRCLE CENTRE)

"Huan" (环) here refers to Huantiao (G.B.30). "Zhong" (中) means centre. This point is midway between Huantiao (G.B.30) and Yaoshu (Du 2), hence the name Huanzhong (Circle Centre) (Fig. III-22).

Indications:

Lumbar pain, pain in the leg, sciatica, inflammation of the urinary system and hemorrhoids.

Method:

Puncture perpendicularly about 2.5 cun deep.

SIQIANG (EX-LE 11) 四强 (MUSCLE STRENGTHENING)

"Si" (四), meaning four, refers to musculus quadriceps femoris. "Qiang" (强) means strong and powerful. This point is at the musculus quatriceps femoris and has the effect to strengthen muscles, hence the name Siqiang (Muscle Strengthening).

Location:

4.5 cun above the midpoint of the upper border of the patella (Fig. III-19).

Indications:

Paralysis and muscular atrophy of the lower extremities.

Method:

Puncture perpendicularly 1-2 cun deep. Moxibustion is applicable.

BAICHONGWO (EX-LE 12) 百虫窝 (INSECTS' NEST)

"Baichong" (百虫) means many an insect. "Wo" (窝) means nest. This point is indicated in pruritis, urticaria and rashes as if many insects were crawling all over the body from their nests to cause itching, hence the name Baichongwo (Insects' Nest).

Location:

One cun above Xuehai (Sp.10), approximately 3 cun above the medial superior corner of the patella (Fig. III-19).

Indications:

Pruritis, urticaria and rashes.

Method:

Puncture perpendicularly 1-2 cun. Moxibustion is applicable.

Appendix II NEW POINTS

QIUHOU 球后 (BEHIND THE EYEBALL)

"Qiu" (球) means eyeball here. "Hou" (后) refers to the posteroinferior region of the eyeball. Also, the point is indicated in eye disorders, hence the name Qiuhou (Behind the Eyeball).

Location:
Have the patient look straight ahead, then close the eyes slightly. The point is at the junction of the lateral one fourth and medial three fourths of the margo supraorbitalis (Fig. III-9).

Method:
Puncture the needle slowly 0.5-1 cun towards the foramen, optimally with no rotation of the needle except for slight scraping of the needle. Press the point with a cotton ball for a while after the withdrawal of the needle.

SHANGYINGXIANG 上迎香 (UPPER YINGXIANG)

This point bears similar indications as the point Yingxiang (L.I.20) and is located superior to Yingxiang (L.I.20), hence the name Shangyingxiang (Upper Yingxiang), also called Bitong (Fig. III-9).

Location:
At the upper end of the nasolabial groove, at the junction of the nasal shell and the cartilage of ala nasi.

Indications:
Nasal obstruction, headache, nasal polyp and redness in the eye with lacrimation.

Method:
Puncture obliquely 0.3-0.5 cun deep towards the medial superior aspect of the nose.

YIMING 翳明 (EYE BRIGHTENING)

"Yi" (翳) refers to Yifeng (S.J.17). "Ming" (明) means brightening. This point is 1 cun posterior to Yifeng (S.J.17). It has the effect to improve eyesight so that the vision will be more brightening, hence the name Yiming (Eye Brightening) (Fig. III-3).

Indications:
Hyperopia, night blindness, early symptoms of glaucoma and cataract, headache, insomnia, dizziness and vertigo, tinnitus, hysteria and emotional excitement.

Method:
Puncture perpendicularly 0.5-1 cun deep.

DINGCHUAN 定喘 (ASTHMA RELIEVING)

"Ding" (定) means calming or relieving. "Chuan" (喘) means asthma. This point is used for treating difficult sleep due to asthmatic attacks, hence the name Dingchuan (Asthma Relieving).

Location:

Below the spinous process of the 7th cervical vertebra, 0.5 cun lateral to Dazhui (Du 14) (Fig. III-10).

Indications:

Asthma, cough, sprain, shoulder pain, back pain, pain of the upper extremities with motor impairment and urticaria.

Method:

Puncture perpendicularly or obliquely 0.5-1 cun towards the medial aspect. Moxibustion is applicable.

YAOYI 腰宜 (LUMBAR PAIN POINT)

"Yao" (腰) refers to the lumbar region. "Yi" (宜) means something fitful or appropriate, implying that the point is good for treating pain in the lumbar region, hence the name Yaoyi (Lumbar Pain Point).

Location:

Four fingers' width lateral to the spinal column, below the spinous process of L4.

Indications:

Lumbar pain, lumbar soreness, pelvic inflammation and profuse uterine bleeding.

Clinical Application:

This point has the effect to soothe tendons and activate blood circulation in the meridians.

Combinations:

With Dachangshu (U.B.25) for lumbar pain and soreness,

With Shenshu (U.B.23) for chronic pelvic inflammation,

With Xuehai (Sp.10) for profuse uterine bleeding.

XIAZHISHI 下志室 (LOWER ZHISHI)

This point is below the point Zhishi (U.B.52) which is basically applied for kidney problems. Kidney houses the will. The place to house something is often known as "Shi" (室) as seen in the nomenclature of Zhishi Point (U.B.52), hence the name Xiazhishi (Lower Zhishi).

Location:

Between the 3rd and 4th lumbar vertebrae, 3 cun lateral to the spinal column.

Indications:

Impotence, seminal emission and lumbar soreness.

Clinical Application:

This point has the effect to strengthen kidney Yang and stop seminal emission.

Combinations:

With Shenshu (U.B.23) and Mingmen (Du 4) for impotence, seminal emission and premature ejaculation,

With Dachangshu (U.B.25) for lumbar soreness,

With Zhibian (U.B.54) for bloody urine.

YAOTONGXUE 腰痛点 (LUMBAGO POINT)

"Yaotong" (腰痛) means lumbar pain. The point is indicated in acute lumbar pain and lumbar sprain, hence the name Yaotongxue (Lumbago Point).

Location:

On the dorsal aspect of the hand, on both sides of the tendon of m. digital communis, 1 cun distal to the transverse crease of the wrist, 2 points on each hand (Fig.III-16).

Method:

Puncture obliquely 0.5-0.8 cun deep towards the palmar centre from both sides of the tendon of m. digital communis. The therapeutic effect will be better if the patient does some lumbar exercises during the treatment.

LUOZHEN 落枕 (NECK SPRAIN)

"Luozhen" (落枕) means neck sprain. This point can treat neck sprain in particular, hence the name. It is also called Wailaogong.

Location:

Between the 2nd and 3rd metacarpal bones, 0.5 cun proximal to the metacarpophalangeal joint (Fig. III-16).

Indications:

In addition to neck sprain, the point is also indicated in acute gastric pain, painful shoulder and pain in the arm.

Method:

Puncture perpendicularly or obliquely 0.6-0.8 cun deep with lifting, thrusting and rotating when the needle is inserted into the point. Ask the patient to do some exercises during the treatment.

LANWEI 阑尾 (APPENDIX POINT)

This point has the drastic effect in dealing with acute and chronic appendicitis, especially at the very onset of acute appendicitis, hence the name Lanwei. Usually the point is in a variable location, at the most palpable tenderness between Zusanli (St.36) and Shangjuxu (St.37) along the course of the Stomach Meridian of Foot-Yangming, 1.5 cun below Zusanli. In addition, it is also indicated in epigastric pain, indigestion and early muscular atrophy. Puncture perpendicularly 1.5-2 cun deep. Moxibustion is applicable (Fig. III-19).

DANNANG 胆囊 (GALL BLADDER POINT)

This point is effective for acute and chronic cholecystitis, especially at the very onset of cholecystitis, hence the name Dannang (Gall Bladder Point). The location of the point is changeable, usually at the most palpable tender point, about 1-2 cun below Yanglingquan (G.B.34) along the course of the Gall Bladder Meridian of Foot-Shaoyang (Fig. III-19).

Indications:

Cholecystitis, biliary ascariasis and hypochondriac pain.

Method:

Puncture perpendicularly 0.5-1 cun deep. Moxibustion is applicable.